This book presents, concisely and readably yet with thoroughness and depth, a description and an original critique of the major radical ideologies of our time—Leninism and Leninisms, Fascism, National Socialism, Apartheid, and African Socialism. Drawing heavily on primary source material—the writings and public statements of the chief thinkers of each system—Professor Gregor reconstructs and analyzes the arguments employed by contemporary ideologists to justify their belief systems and vindicate their policies. The sections on Fascism and Apartheid are especially notable, for there are few adequate accounts in English of these systems as ideologies. Each chapter is fully documented, and a bibliography of primary and secondary source materials available in English enhances the book's value as a work of both interpretation and reference.

CONTEMPORARY RADICAL IDEOLOGIES

Totalitarian Thought in the Twentieth Century

Random House • New York

A. James Gregor

UNIVERSITY OF CALIFORNIA, BERKELEY

CONTEMPORARY RADICAL ● IDEOLOGIES

Totalitarian Thought in the

Twentieth Century

First Printing
© *Copyright, 1968 by Random House*
All rights reserved under International and Pan-American Copyright Con-
ventions. Published in New York by Random House, Inc. and simultaneously
in Toronto, Canada, by Random House of Canada Limited
Library of Congress Catalog Card Number: 68-13159
Manufactured in the United States of America
by The Haddon Craftsmen, Inc., Scranton, Pa.
Design by Leon Bolognese

This book is dedicated to my Mother
MARIA GIMIGLIANO
as a token payment against an inestimable debt

Preface

This volume is written in the conviction that reasoned discourse constitutes the only legitimate recourse in the effort to resolve social and
political disagreement. The central thesis of this book, therefore, is
that radical social and political ideologies can be generally (but not
always or necessarily) shown to rest on corrigible beliefs about the
constitution of man and society. Any social and political dispute that
is not trivial or beset by linguistic handicap logically involves factual
and theoretical considerations as relevant. When we, or our opponents,
have been made to recognize that an argument turns on faulty logic,
neglects relevant empirical facts, or is theoretically impaired, that
argument may no longer be considered a justification for social or
political prescription or proscription. What generally occurs is a
reformulation of justificatory argument, a reassessment of facts, and a
searching scrutiny of logic. Hopefully, significant changes in doctrine
and, ultimately, policy result. The most imposing considerations promoting doctrinal or policy change are, of course, tactical. Since we
recognize this to be the case, we tend to say that totalitarian political
leaders are "opportunistic." We, on the other hand, acting under the
same goad are "pragmatic." Nonetheless, change takes place both in our
own and in our opponents' case.

The fact is that Leninism, fascism, and apartheid have, as doctrines,
undergone substantive change in the course of time. That such systems
of thought are corrigible, in whatever sense, should be heartening to
those, like myself, who entertain the conviction that reasoned discourse
is pertinent to social and political argument. Any disagreement about
social or political judgments that is not a disagreement about the facts
of the particular case need not simply be an ultimate and irreducible
disagreement; rather it may be amenable to an indefinitely wide range
of empirical or theoretical considerations not immediately evident in
the judgment in apparent dispute. By representing social and political
judgments as ultimate and irreducibly distinct from ordinary empirical,
logical, or theoretical judgments, some political theorists have implicitly
or explicitly suggested that social or political judgments are simply
irrational and impervious to reason. One of the principal theses of
this work will be that even radical social and political ideologies are

in significant measure the products of reason, experience, and observation and are, consequently, to some degree corrigible. Actually, there is no real alternative to this thesis. Recourse to violence, the alternative to reasoned argument, is precluded by the "over-kill" potential of modern weaponry.

The second conviction around which this book is organized is the conviction that ideology is important in our own time. First of all, as totalitarian regimes undertake essentially pedagogical functions in the inculcation of collective belief systems, they become, at least in some measure, captive to those systems. The belief system fostered in youth groups, in schools, in labor organizations, and in fraternal associations becomes the conscience of the regime. The discrepancy between inculcated principles and Soviet practices under Stalin was at least partially responsible for the crisis of de-Stalinization that shook the Leninist system. Similar, if not as spectacular, crises beset the Fascist regime, particularly when Fascist Italy undertook its anti-Semitic campaign. In fact, a breach in the party itself developed when the alliance with National Socialist Germany forced the regime to abandon what had been prized as Fascist toleration and humanity on the race issue. The discrepancy between preachment and practice was too evident to obscure. What resulted was serious alienation among critically essential elements of the intellectual elite. Similar pressures seem to motivate the leaders of the National party of South Africa to attempt to provide at least the semblance of practice that fulfills ideological expectations. The precipitate establishment of "self-governing" Bantu areas in South Africa has become a necessity if apartheid is not to seem guilty of hypocrisy in the eyes of its adherents. The only case in which something similar cannot be said is that of National Socialist Germany. That National Socialist Germany should be an exception must be qualified by the realization that Hitler remained in power only twelve years. It is at least conceivable that the tensions between putative ideological commitment and political practice would have ultimately created the same internal crisis of conscience that the Stalin period ultimately created for the Soviet Union. None of this can, of course, be argued with much conviction, for there is much counterevidence. But it remains a consideration that contemporary circumstances recommend we consider.

In any event, a knowledgeable grasp of the ideology of our opponents permits us to argue with them intelligently. The contemporary discussion in the West, which turns on the values advanced in the writings of the young Marx, has forced contemporary Leninists to make a searching reappraisal of their own position. Certainly some changes have been forthcoming. How extensive and significant such changes are or will be is difficult to determine, but the dialogue has been joined. That such dialogue is at least potentially capable of effecting change is enough to warrant a full and objective understanding of radical ideologies. To have as authoritative a statement as possible of our opponents' arguments is to be prepared to meet them.

Finally, an objective and adequate grasp of radical ideologies permits a more adequate understanding of our time of troubles. To understand the ideologies entertained by contemporary totalitarians permits us to better understand their domestic and international postures. That some social and political values function in the major premises of the deliberations of totalitarians seems the case. That the values that so function should be those explicitly formulated in the ideological system need *not*, of course, be the case. But such explicitly formulated values provide (1) an initial point of departure for inquiry and (2) a measure against which totalitarian practice may be effectively gauged.

For at least these reasons I am convinced that an objective and historically accurate account of radical ideologies deserves a place in our deliberations. To serve this purpose, I shall attempt to provide an exposition of radical ideologies without polemics. This volume is intended as an exposition of justificatory arguments that have served, and are now serving, radical ideologies. I have permitted myself to advance immanent criticisms only when the ideological system under consideration made such criticism unavoidable. In general, I have not undertaken extrinsic criticism. Almost any book devoted to radical ideologies will provide such arguments. Significant and responsible criticism, however, must begin with what this book attempts to provide: an accurate account of the ideology in question. The essential function of this volume is the rational reconstruction of the justificatory arguments advanced to support radical ideologies. That, in itself, is a difficult enough task. Whenever possible I have used primary source material, and wherever possible I have used direct quotation. Long quotations encumber the text already encumbered by extensive notes and references, but I felt that both the quotations and references were essential to the requirements of faithful exposition.

For the opponents of radical ideologies I shall, no doubt, have conceded too much. For the protagonists of such ideologies I shall have failed in my effort to provide an accurate and objective rendering. Nonetheless, I should like to think that I have provided an account that has some saving graces. Among the elements this volume contains that I think are original is a brief account of fascist racism all but unknown to American readers both lay and professional, an exposition of apartheid social and political thought more comprehensive than any in the available English language literature, and a survey of African socialism that reveals, for what I believe to be the first time, its affinities with fascism. Having attempted so much in so brief a compass, I am certain that many shortcomings, if not rank errors, infect the text.

Whatever is of merit in this book is largely the result of conversations with many Soviet and East European philosophers at various international philosophical conferences, public officials and academicians in the Republic of South Africa, particularly J. D. Krige, the Director of Social Welfare Services in South West Africa, Sir Oswald Mosley, leader of the prewar British Union of Fascists and National Socialists; Dr. Werner Naumann, the former Assistant to Paul Joseph Goebbels; and former public officials of Fascist Italy and the Fascist Republic of Salò. Particular mention should be made of the insights provided by the late Professor Corrado Gini, who was extremely influential in Italian academic circles during the Fascist regime, and Ing. Giovanni Perona, whose knowledge of the Fascist period proved invaluable. In the United States contact with American Marxists such as Howard Selsam and Herbert Aptheker proved equally significant, and my activities as regional secretary of the Society for the Philosophical Study of Dialectical Materialism offered me many opportunities to discuss with colleagues some of the problems with which this volume is concerned. Naturally, whatever shortcomings afflict this account are my own responsibility.

Finally, I should like to express my gratitude to both Professors Martin M. White and John Kuiper of the University of Kentucky, without whose kindnesses the work necessary for this volume would have been much more difficult, and to Thomas Birch, whose comments and criticisms assisted me in avoiding some serious misinterpretations. Mrs. Michael McGrath worked indefatigably in preparing this manuscript for publication, and my wife, Dorothy, with saintly patience, labored long and hard to make intelligible English of my all-too-often tortured prose. I should like to thank all these people publicly.

Berkeley, California   *A.J.G.*

Contents

CONTEMPORARY RADICAL IDEOLOGIES

Totalitarian Thought in the Twentieth Century

I · *INTRODUCTION*

This book is primarily intended to provide descriptive and analytic insight into contemporary radical ideologies. A brief account of each of the major radical ideologies of our time will be combined with an analysis that focuses on the nature and structure of the arguments advanced in their support by their most responsible adherents. It is offered as a contribution to the literature devoted to historical and critical social and political philosophy and political theory.

Such descriptive and analytic efforts are not calculated to inspire verification studies or generate predictions. There is no pretense, for example, of relating personality, class, stratification, or institutional variables to manifest political behavior or to explaining how ideologies develop or why individuals, singly or collectively, make ideological commitments. There is no essential concern with experimentation or empirical explanation, although the material might ultimately be included in some explanatory account having experimental and predictive character. Whether a descriptive and analytic work lends itself to such incorporation is, in fact, one of the criteria for judging its merits. In and of themselves, however, descriptive and analytic treatments are essentially didactic and heuristic. If nothing else, a

competent description based on clear and defensible distinctions
is a mnemonic aid of significant importance. It constitutes a
conceptual and analytic framework for the convenient storage and
ready retrieval of otherwise unrelated pieces of information.
Furthermore, by indicating certain descriptive similarities between elements in the domain under scrutiny, such studies can
suggest empirical research.

This having been said, a still further distinction should be
made since the description and analysis contained in this work
concerns itself with normative issues. The purposes of the
present exposition preclude any attempt at adequate analysis of
the distinction between empirical and normative concerns, but
some indication should be given that the difference between them
is acknowledged.

The answers to scientific questions can be obtained through
the use of tolerably well understood techniques of verification
and/or validation. Observations, in some sense or another, furnish
the warrant for truth claims with respect to empirical questions.
The truth status of formal propositions is, in turn, determined
by calculation employing the machinery of contemporary logic.
In effect, it is possible to construct a science only where there
are generally accepted empirical or formal methods of procedure
for producing the warrant that supports truth ascriptions.

Normative questions, on the other hand, involve specifically
philosophical procedures. There are no generally accepted techniques for the resolution of philosophical puzzlement; there are
no universally recognized truth conditions to which decisive
appeal can be made. Yet some of the most obstinately philosophical questions are of perennial importance to the study of political
systems. Questions concerning freedom and authority and the
"good life" for man, questions that necessarily involve value
judgments, occur and recur not only in texts devoted to the
history of social and political philosophy, but in the ordering of
our daily lives.

Social and political philosophy is qualitatively distinct from
science in that it attempts to assess the intrinsic merits of normative arguments. It is concerned with the force and substance of
justificatory arguments irrespective of their origins or authors,
and it is therefore indifferent to the efforts made to explain
empirically the advent and prevalence of any specific ideology

or ideologies in general. Assessment of the validity of the various theories advanced to account for ideologies is not one of the obligations of critical social and political philosophy. Such a responsibility is methodological and substantive, and falls within the province of the philosophy of the social sciences and the empirical behavioral sciences per se.

Science is ideally concerned with the ordering of phenomena by means of a regularity analysis that, in conjunction with a specification of initial conditions, provides an explanatory account calculated to increase predictive and explanatory power. The formalized sciences have been remarkably successful in so ordering experience. The partially or negligibly formalized sciences of sociology, psychology, political science, and all their subsidiary disciplines have been notably less successful; nonetheless, they are in principle animated by the same purpose and techniques. Science, in effect, is concerned with nature (whether physical or human) as it is—not as it should be. Vilfredo Pareto succinctly characterized science as concerning itself "with nothing more than determining the relationships that obtain between things, phenomena, and to discover the uniformities these relationships provide."[1]

But the behavioral sciences are inevitably concerned with the values men harbor. Significant aspects of human behavior become meaningful only when we see the point of them, only when motives, intentions, and normative goals figure in our explanatory accounts. There are instances when we come to understand the conduct of individuals and groups of individuals only when we understand their reasons and their reasoning.

Such efforts at understanding are not essentially different from explanatory accounts provided in any science. An adequate explanation of the behavior of an individual or an aggregate of individuals includes a catalogue of cherished values and anticipated goals from which we can infer (with appropriate safeguards) motives and intentions and predict behaviors. Whether an individual or individuals harbor such values or aspire to such ends is certified by evidence, well-documented instances of spoken or written commitment, expressions of intention, and behavior compatible with them. While involving an enormously more complex and sensitive procedure, confirming or disconfirming ascriptions of values, motives, and intentions to individuals or groups of individuals and predicting their behavior does not differ essentially from the procedures employed in confirming or disconfirming any hypothesis in science. First evidence is collected to support the hypothesis under test. Other statements are inferred which describe directly observable phenomena that should be found to occur under appropriate circumstances if the hypothesis is true. Those inferred statements are tested directly by establishing that the specified phenomena do in fact, or did in fact, occur. In this sense values, motives, and intentions are simply the subject matter of scientific investigation. Cultural anthropology and political science regularly employ empirical techniques in describing the value systems, the motives, and the intentions of peoples in other cultures or political environments.

One can further ask why individuals or peoples should entertain such values, motives or intentions. Answers to these questions are, at least in substantial part, empirical. Relationships between ideological commitments, for example, and child-rearing practices, status variables, class membership, operant and respondent conditioning, system and institutional requirements, as well as historical circumstances, can be hypothesized and subsequently confirmed and disconfirmed. These are all serious and significant inquiries. An adequate appraisal of any political culture would at least consider these matters. A comprehensive account of any historical or extant political system would require reference to historical, personality, status, class, institutional, and system requisite variables. It would require that some determinate relationship be confirmed as obtaining between them and the political culture.

This volume does not make any pretense to comprehensiveness in this final sense and concerns itself with properly empirical matters only peripherally. Its purposes are relatively modest. It attempts to reconstruct the justificatory reasoning that subtends the radical social and political ideologies of the twentieth century. It attempts to outline, in as objective and as accurate a manner as possible, the rationale of contemporary totalitarianisms or potential totalitarianisms. Its references to totalitarianism concern only those systems whose ideological rationale provides the grounds for rejecting the distinction traditionally made in the West between private and public interests, grounds for conceiving the individual and his community as in some sense indistinguishable. The concern here, as a consequence, is not with totalitarian *practice* (however that is conceived), but with totalitarian *argument*. There will be included in our account political systems that could be characterized empirically as moderate or even benign. Their inclusion means only that the arguments offered in their support share common "totalitarian" traits. To suggest the distinction between those regimes that have taken up practices generally characterized as totalitarian and those that have not, but which employ essentially the same justificatory arguments, references will sometimes be made to "potential totalitarianism," "prototototalitarianism," or "quasi-totalitarianism." Obviously such a designation is not intended as a prediction about subsequent behavior or practice. Predictions turn on some adequate statement of attendant or initial conditions—an obligation this study cannot hope to discharge.

What is attempted here is a brief account of the normative reasoning advanced to legitimize what are characterized as "nondemocratic" political systems. It is a reconstruction of the justificatory arguments offered by the principal spokesmen of what is here identified as radical collectivism. It further attempts to illustrate, by example, how normative arguments proceed in a social and political context. It attempts, again by illustrative example, to indicate how factual and analytic propositions, conjoined with explicit or implicit values, generate normative conclusions and political vindications.

Each example is provided in descriptive outline. In being descriptive, the volume makes the same truth claims made by any such account. The evidence for its truth is contained in the relevant literature available. Finally, the present account is heuristic in the sense that it provides a classificatory or taxonomic schema that can be useful in a comparative study of ideologies.

The proposed taxonomy identifies contemporary radical ideologies as collectivist and organicist—their respective justificatory arguments sharing diagnostic species traits. Such a characterization is in the tradition of John Dewey who, among many others, emphasized just such a distinction:

Society is composed of individuals: this obvious and basic fact no philosophy, whatever its pretensions to novelty, can question or alter. Hence these three alternatives: Society must exist for the sake of individuals; or individuals must have their ends and ways of living set for them by society; or else society and individuals are correlative, organic to one another, society requiring the service and subordination of individuals and at the same time existing to serve them. Beyond these three views, none seem to be logically conceivable.[2]

This volume identifies radical ideologies with the third alternative and as such suggests criterial attributes which permit a broad categorization of certain argument forms. The presence of these specific argument forms in complex justificatory rationales identifies those social and political belief systems in which they appear as a unit series, as totalitarian. Any number of further distinctions can and should be made. This initial distinction is offered as a broad descriptive category suitable for essentially expository purposes.

The specific object of the present narrative, employing the techniques of critical social and political philosophy, is the assessment of *contemporary radical* social and political *ideologies.* "Contemporary" is taken to refer to those social and political ideologies developed during and immediately preceding the twentieth century. The designation "radical" is intended to direct attention to conceptions of the nature of man and the true ends of human existence that differ in a fundamental way from that which subtends the tradition of Western "liberalism." An "ideology" is understood to be an implicit or explicit value system accompanied by a relatively coherent system of doctrinal beliefs about nature, society, and man that a group offers in justification of the issuance of social and political directives, prescriptions, and proscriptions, as well as the directives, prescriptions, and proscriptions themselves.

This is a stipulative definition of ideology. Its use will be justified by its utility. The term has often been used with a meaning too restricted for present purposes. Karl Mannheim has used it to denote a "pattern of basic political symbols" whose function is to preserve the social structure. The distinction would then be between conservative and revolutionary doctrines, with "ideology" applying only to the former and "utopia" to the latter. Daniel Bell, in turn, has used the expression "ideology" to refer to a "special complex of ideas and passions that arose in the nineteenth century . . . as a way of translating ideas into action." Thus, only the left-wing Hegelians, Karl Marx and Friedrich Engels among them, produced an ideology.[3] Marx and Engels themselves seem to have employed the term ideology in a still more restricted sense. An ideology was understood to be a false consciousness, the application of abstract, logical, or metaphysical schemata to reality, the deduction of reality not from itself but from a concept.[4] Carl Friedrich and Z. K. Brzezinski use ideology to identify those explicit systems of thought that arise in connection with parties and movements in an age of mass communication.[5]

All these definitions restrict the denotation of ideology sufficiently to impair its use in the present exposition. Here the term ideology or the expression ideological system is understood to denote a unity of three interrelated elements: (1) A fairly systematic and coherent body of argued judgments concerning nature, society, and man; (2) a relatively loose collection of these ideas along with their application and expression in particular political situations; and finally, (3) formal or informal imperatives issued as codified law or supported by social sanctions. The first component is the *social and political philosophy* upon which an ideological system ultimately rests. This is usually the work of one man or a small group of men. The second component is *doctrine*, which differs from social and political philosophy because of its local and contingent character and the simplicity of its ideas. Doctrine involves only rudimentary internal coherence and a pretense of finality that possesses emotional overtones. Brzezinski characterizes doctrine as

. . . essentially an action program suitable for mass consumption, derived from certain . . . assumptions about the general nature of the dynamics of social reality, and combining some assertions about the inadequacies of the past and/or present with some explicit guides to action for improving the situation and some notions of the desired eventual state of affairs.[6]

Doctrines are, in short, essentially action-related systems of ideas. They characteristically contain a program and a strategy for its fulfillment, and their essential purpose is to provide a belief system for organizations that are built around them.

The final component of ideological systems is legislation, the institutions and social sentiments codified, instituted, or fostered by a regime committed to a given social and political philosophy and its doctrinal derivatives. Laws restricting the ownership of private property in the Soviet Union, for example, are warranted by appeals to doctrinal notions about the nature of capitalism, property ownership, and class antagonisms. The arguments that justify ascribing value to the entire enterprise appeal to a form of secular humanism. Only with the abolition of private property, classes, and of the "alienations" that they produce, it is argued, can man achieve his "true stature"—what contemporary Marxist theorists call "the creation of objective conditions for the full development of the personality."[7] In effect, Marxism serves Soviet rulers as a means of justification and rationalization of Soviet law.

In Fascist Italy not only were there regular appeals to ultimate values to legitimize legislation, but also the most important single pieces of legislation were preceded by a doctrinal rationale. The introductory clauses of the Labor Charter of 1927, for example, are clearly doctrinal and the Charter served to "concretize the development of practical applications of Fascist . . . doctrines. . . ."[8] The social and political values that gave normative force to doctrine were humanistic. Legislation was calculated to create the conditions that would foster a life in which the individual could realize, as Mussolini put it, his full "value as man."

Similarly, National Socialist legislation appealed to a body of doctrinal views concerning race, the nature of society, and the world for its rationale. The value component of such a rationale, which gave imperative force to legislative enactments, was again a form of secular humanism. The full development of human personality was possible only within the confines of the *Volksgemeinschaft*, of which the state was the coherent expression.

Such a stipulative explication of the term ideology (or ideological system) permits the isolation of primary value commitments and is conducive to a systematic scrutiny of the justificatory arguments mustered to their support. This is a specifically philosophical task. Doctrine can then be assessed as a derivative of more fundamental commitments. This tactic is designed to avoid using elaborate analytic machinery against doctrinal aspects of an ideology, since most doctrines stand or fall on a relatively restricted base of critical judgments—a speculative social and political philosophy.

Finally, such a conception of ideological systems permits the comparison, for example, of specific instances of codified law with the doctrinal or philosophical bases of the system. In some instances, practice—political, legislative, or organizational—may be found to violate doctrinal or philosophical antecedents. These violations may in turn lead to some essential changes in the principles of the system through a complex feedback effect.

Historically, the distinction here suggested between social and political philosophy, doctrine, and applications conforms to distinctions made in practice by at least one of the ideological systems that will be considered: Italian Fascism.

Antonio Canepa, one of the most competent of the Fascist theoreticians, drew a distinction between what he called "successive theoretical systematizations," Fascism's social and political philosophy, and the "collection of ideas, principles, sentiments, and suggestions which constitute the soul of action," the doctrine of Fascism.[9] Similarly, Sergio Panunzio distinguished the "theoretical" substance of Fascism from its "practical, active, more immediate, one might say more physical, mechanical side,"[10] and Luigi Volpicelli spoke of the "universal political values" of Fascism, which remained constant through the course of changing political practice.[11] Mussolini himself made the distinction between what we have identified as social and political philosophy and doctrine by characterizing the former as a "system" and as "a 'body of doctrine' . . . reviewed, corrected, amplified, corroborated . . . and elaborated," which he did not hesitate to call the philosophy of Fascism.[12] As early as 1908, as a young socialist theoretician, he identified what we have termed ideology as a "complete, harmonious and synthetic doctrine," composed of three types of elements: ideal, doctrinal, and practical.[13] A quarter of a century later, in the *Dottrina del fascismo*, he argued that Fascist practice could not be understood without an appreciation of its philosophical conception of life—and that its conception of life found expression in *doctrine* which was contingent and correlative to exigencies of time and place. In the *Dottrina* this reads:

Like every sound political conception, Fascism is practice as well as thought, action in which doctrine is immanent, doctrine which, arising out of a given system of historic forces, remains and operates within the context of those forces. It therefore has a form correlative to the contingencies of place and time, but it has an ideal content as well which elevates it to a formula of truth in the higher level of the history of thought.[14]

Mussolini seems to have maintained this distinction consistently. In a speech before the Assembly of the Council of Corporations, for example, he insisted that the Corporations, as the institutional manifestation of Fascist principles, were not ends in themselves. As he understood them, they served the "supreme ends of life" which only philosophy could illuminate. On many occasions he argued that philosophy alone could provide the normative guides to everyday activity. Doctrine, as he understood it, occupied a position between the two—a local and contingent application of normative principles. It was the local application of universal postulates that made fascism *Italian* fascism[15]—an application Canepa further characterized as being less rigorous than its political philosophy.[16]

That this preliminary distinction of ideological components can be argued does not necessarily mean that a discussion utilizing it will be significant as well as informative. It is an entrenched conviction among many American thinkers that any such discussion of radical ideologies is perverse in principle. There is a widespread conviction, even among professional political analysts, that the rationale proffered by radicals is not worthy of serious attention—that radical ideologues are little more than Machiavellians (in the most pejorative sense of the term) who systematically obscure real intentions beneath the cloak of philosophical profusions. There is, of course, some strength to such arguments. On the other hand, such arguments unavoidably beg the question. They presume what they are obliged to prove. Marxist ideologues of every stripe, for example, level similar arguments in their analysis of the "bourgeois liberal state." Lenin insisted that the bourgeois state, no matter what its apologists say of it, is the best political shell for class oppression.[17]

After having issued such a pronouncement, one is still required to prove it. This could only be accomplished by a careful and objective comparison of explicit philosophical or doctrinal intention and manifest practice. Such a comparison must be based on a responsible scrutiny of the philosophical and doctrinal bases of ideology. Furthermore, there is no conclusive reason to suppose that the principal ideologues of radical creeds were or are insincere in advancing their views. On the contrary, there is good evidence that many of them sacrificed personal interest and tactical advantage in the defense of what they believed to be the truth. Anyone who knows something of the life of Marx or Lenin realizes the single-mindedness with which each pursued his understanding of the truth. Marx literally condemned the First International to death in his effort to impose his theory—his own exclusive and *alleinseligmachende* dogma of salvation—on that body. Lenin all but destroyed the Unification Congress of the Russian Social Democratic Party of 1903 in his insistence upon the purity of his interpretation of Marxism. At several junctures in his life he found himself almost totally isolated as a consequence of his dedication to what he conceived to be correct theory.[18] Similarly, Allan Bullock has argued that Hitler revealed a considerable consistency in adhering to certain ideas and conceptions throughout twenty-five years of political activity.[19] Mussolini, at several critical points in his political life, placed his political future and physical liberty in jeopardy in the service of his political ideals. Even against the objections of the Germans who all but controlled the ephemeral Fascist Republic of Salò, Mussolini insisted on proceeding with his plans for a Fascist socialization of the economy. Regardless, the assertion that the ideologues of radicalism are merely opportunists (and their protestations of philosophical commitment merely propaganda) rests upon its proponent's ability to indicate that radical practices contradict putative radical philosophical commitments. The arguments must then rest on the knowledge of what those commitments, in fact, were or are.

The intention of this volume is to sketch those commitments in brief and present them in an objective outline. As a contribution to the history of social and political ideas, it will be "thought about thought." It will be left, by and large, to the political historian or the empirically orientated political scientist to compare the practice of radical regimes with radical political philosophy and social doctrine and to attempt to relate ideology to specific system variables.

Finally, to return once again to the term radicalism: The term is here intended to have philosophical relevance. It refers to those ideologies that rest upon a conception of man and society that departs in some significant sense from that of the liberal traditions of the West. It should not be understood to refer to the methods employed by one group or another to effect their purposes. Political activists who employ violence or civil disobedience to attain their ends might be referred to as extremists to satisfy the demands of the common distinction made in ordinary language. "Radical" is used in the present discussion to refer to a *philosophical* difference that distinguishes those ideologies that are the subjects of the present discussion from the broad and perhaps ill-defined tradition of Western European liberalism.

Admittedly, the concept of Western liberalism is open-textured: In general, it is identified with the tradition that developed as an adjunct of what has been called the "triumph of individualism." It is understood to include all those social and political philosophies in which the individual, the empirical or psychological self, is conceived as historically, morally, or logically prior to any collection of individuals. The unit of political or social analysis is the empirical individual, and society or the state is conceived as an aggregate of mutually exclusive selves. Society and the state are understood to arise out of a compromise, which in turn is understood as the consequence of a real or virtual contract between individuals.

The social and political philosophy of Thomas Hobbes illustrates the essential traits of generic liberalism as an ideological tradition. Hobbes' "resolutive-compositive" method conceives society and the state as being reducible to the individual wills that are their elements. The collective or social will results from an effective compromise between antagonistic and mutually exclusive individual wills.

It would thus seem that the characteristic contents of Hobbes' political philosophy—the absolute priority of the individual to the state, the conceptions of the individual as asocial, of the relation between the state of nature and the state as an absolute antithesis, and finally the state itself as Leviathan—is determined by and, as it were, implied in the method.[26]

The long tradition of Anglo-American political thought has never abandoned critical elements of this method. The method is essentially a reductive analysis. The ultimate unit of analysis is the empirical individual conceived in a moral, logical or historical sense as being possessed of certain natural or inalienable rights, which can never be fully abridged and which can only be compromised by voluntary contracts. Liberal theory assumes that society consists of an aggregate of individuals preoccupied with their own interests, and it regards the state as an emanation of individual wills calculated to mediate the conflicts arising between individuals. The conception of the body politic suggested by such a view would be one that understood society and the state to be the consequence of a system of agreements. To be a member of such a community would mean that the individual was party to that system of agreements. The paradigm of this relationship is voluntary contract. A society is understood to be composed of an aggregate of individuals who, in pursuit of a common purpose, agree to act in concert, placing themselves under a conditional common discipline, authority, and obligation.

Such a view is all but the analytic consequence of conceiving each individual as an autonomous entity possessed, *ab initio*, of an unspecified number of natural or inherent rights. Such a conception is axiomatic to Jeffersonian democracy and is the tacit premise necessary to the rational reconstruction of Madisonian political philosophy.[27] Thus the Declaration of Independence was written by a disciple of Locke who contended that men are each individually possessed of the natural right to "order their actions and dispose of their possessions and persons as they think fit, within the bounds of the law of nature, without asking leave, or depending upon the will of any other man."[22] The notion of "freedom" follows analytically, for freedom in such a context is understood as freedom from restraint. Any restraint imposed without the consent of the individual constitutes tyranny. Freedom means the absence of constraint in the exercise of natural right. T. V. Smith, in our own time, maintains that "liberty means no less than doing as one pleases."[23] This is in the tradition of Herbert Spencer, who maintained that "liberal changes . . . diminish the range of governmental authority, and increase the area within which each citizen may act unchecked," and whose conception of the ideal political polity was described as a "regime of contract."[24] Some of the corollaries of this conception are that "all restraint, *qua* restraint is an evil" and "that government is best which governs least." There is an initial presumption in favor of the unrestricted liberty of the individual that any efforts at governmental regulation must overcome. Even contemporary political theorists, such as Franz Neumann, argue that

> Freedom is first and foremost the absence of restraints. There is little doubt that this view underlies the liberal theory of freedom. . . . Its basic presupposition is philosophic individualism—the view that man is a reality quite independent of the political system within which he lives. . . . A political theory based upon an individualistic philosophy must necessarily operate with a negative juridical concept of freedom, freedom as absence of restraint. . . . Legally, civil liberties establish a presumption in favor of the rights of the individual and against the coercive power of the state. . . . From the simple proposition that there exists a presumption in favor of the individual's freedom there follows every element of the liberal legal system. . . . [Such conceptions are], moreover, equally decisive in the operation of the social system of a competitive-contractual society.[25]

Political liberalism rests upon an explicit form of philosophical individualism, which is advanced in a set of factual propositions describing the nature of man coupled with one or a number of value judgments. The value judgments are generally covert, disguised as simple descriptive statements. That they are, nonetheless, value judgments is indicated by their incorporation of words with high emotional salience and strong commendatory force. *Freedom* and *liberty* are two such words. Identifying the locus of freedom psychologically entails a recommendation to protect and foster it. When the individual is characterized as free in the state of nature, one in effect prescribes a presumption in favor of the individual's freedom to do as he wishes in society.

To picture individual man as an autonomous agent, as a reality quite independent of the community in which he lives, to argue that man is *not* a political animal by nature, is to tacitly recommend rules by which the very serious game of government is to be played. The rules are suggested by the definition of man. Alternative rule systems are suggested by redefining man. But the proposed redefinition of man is more profitably compared to a redefinition in science than to change in the rule system of a game. The physicist who recommends the redefinition of space with the suggestion that we henceforward speak of it in terms of spatiotemporal coordinates does so for specific and specifiable reasons. The redefinition permits physicists to describe the phenomena that fall within the range of their interests more adequately and economically. Such a redefinition must meet tests of admissibility: criteria of coherence involving compatibility with other elements in the propositional system of theoretical physics and perhaps criteria of elegance or simplicity, as well as empirical criteria, that is, the possibility of increasing control and prediction if the proposed redefinition is employed. Obviously, the criteria that warrant redefinition in science are more stringent than any criteria employed in social and political philosophy; yet any proposed redefinition in social and political philosophy must meet criteria of internal coherence, economy of thought, and correspondence with established empirical fact. But while the criteria for admissibility in social and political philosophy are not as rigorous as those governing redefinition in the mature sciences, they are certainly more demanding than, and intrinsically different from, the reasons advanced for a change in the rules of a game. Reasons will be advanced for proposed changes in the rules governing a sport, and in general, the proposals will rest upon factual considerations. But whatever changes are undertaken, they are undertaken with the intention of enhancing those values (whatever they are understood to be) that the sport delivers. Redefinitions in social and political philosophy, on the other hand, often, if not always, alter the focus of values. A redefinition of man and a subsequent redefinition of freedom, for example, generally entail a fundamental change in the individual or societal value hierarchy.

What is here suggested is that a social and political philosophy rests upon some conception of man, nature, and society that is generally expressed in essentially descriptive propositions. This conception is warranted, at least in part, by an appeal to evi-dence—facts about individual or collective psychology, biology, or history. Furthermore, a conception of man is advanced with the assumption that it will aid in the explication of normative concepts like freedom, authority, and obligation without courting paradox. Finally, implicit, and sometimes explicit, in the con-ception is a recommendation. The recommendation, resting on a value judgment, imparts normative character to the otherwise descriptive narrative. Words like "liberty" or "purpose" have a persuasive force, and their very use implies a recommendation to their protection and furtherance. One *ought* to protect liberty and fulfill purpose. If someone does opt for bondage and refuse fulfillment, rational discussion seems to have reached an impasse. Rather than justificatory argument, one would seek explanation in psychopathology. If our opponent is serious, then he has opted not for bondage and debasement; he is instead advancing a re-definition of man (and perhaps nature and society as well) in which what had hitherto been conceived as liberty has become bondage and in which what had been our purpose is construed as no purpose at all.

This is the contention upon which the subsequent discussion will be based. The Communist, Fascist, or National Socialist does not reject the value of freedom, fulfillment, or any number of other normative concepts. What he has done is redefine them. Such redefinitions are the analytic consequence of a redefinition of man himself and roughly follow the logic briefly outlined above. This is not to say that there are no Communists, Fascists, or National Socialists who are, in the strictest clinical sense, mad—any more than it commits us to the contention that all liberals are psychologically well adjusted. But arguments that seek to explain commitment to radical social and political philosophies in terms of psychopathology presume that no rational explanation can be forthcoming. Putative explanations in terms of psychological disease presume what they should, in anticipation, prove. To identify Marx or Hitler as a megalo-maniac does nothing to defeat his arguments.

The argument advanced here, to reiterate, will be that radical social and political ideologies rest upon a conception of man fundamentally different from that of traditional liberalism. As a consequence of this different conception, the cognitive content of political vocabulary undergoes correlative change. Different presumptions are favored and diverse political institutions are advanced as protecting and fostering treasured values.

The radical sociopolitical ideologies herein discussed are all cataloged under the generic rubrics "collectivist" and "organicist." This means, in effect, that radical sociopolitical philosophy shifts its focus from the individual to some collectivity with which he is conceived to be organically related. The individual is no longer understood to be the sole and ultimate source of value, but whatever is of value in the individual is seen to be a derivative product of his membership in some collectivity—a class, nation, state or race. Individuals are understood as elements in an interactive context rather than as atomic isolates. Opposed to the negative juridical conception of freedom central to Western liberalism, the conception of freedom in such contexts is positive. Freedom is construed as freedom *from*—freedom from ignorance, freedom from error, freedom from oppression, freedom from alienation.

Although the negative juridical conception of freedom implies restraint on public power insofar as it fosters a procedural rule favoring the actions of individuals in the pursuit of their own interests against public restrictions, the positive conception of freedom tends to morally oblige the public power to undertake measures calculated to free individuals from ignorance, error, exploitation, and so forth. Moreover, the positive conception of freedom tends to undermine the distinction between public and private interests. Individuals are conceived as "organically" related, and in some sense their individual interests and the public interest are substantially one and the same. Public power therefore tends to be understood to will, in some ultimate sense, only that which the individual himself would will if he were fully informed and possessed of objectivity. And freedom loses most of the descriptive meaning it has for Western liberalism. In Western parliamentary systems an individual can be compelled to attend school by law, but because such law is frankly characterized as "compulsory school attendance" it must be defended, since it is conceived as an initial violation of the individual's right (or his parents' right) to do as he pleases. In political systems that rest on a liberal social and political philosophy, public power must justify its infractions of the individual's initial freedom to do anything he chooses.

When, on the other hand, public power characterizes its action as promoting freedom from any number of putative disabilities, any compulsion it employs is construed as enhancing the individual's freedom. Any constraint imposed on the individual is justified as serving his "real" or "ultimate" freedom. The distinction between freedom and constraint, as between public and private, becomes increasingly diaphanous. Moreover, there is an initial presumption favoring the "liberating" acts of public power which individual resistance (now seen as "egoistic" or "eccentric") must overcome.

Only within such a context can radical ideologies characterize the political systems they legitimize as "true" democracies, devoted to the enhancement of the "true" or "real" freedom of individuals. The use of the qualifiers indicates that redefinitions have been effected and that the redefined terms no longer have the same cognitive meanings they have in the context of Western ideological systems. In collectivist and organicist political systems, for example, the banning of all political parties other than the unitary single party is understood to constitute, for the citizenry, freedom from error or dissident obstruction. Censorship constitutes, in such a system, freedom from moral and intellectual corruption. The roster of such freedoms would include restraints on the most intimate and most self-regarding of activities.

In effect, such arguments provide the legitimizing rationale for totalitarian or potentially totalitarian political systems. For the purposes of this exposition, a totalitarian political system is understood to be one minimally characterized by:

1. An official ideology that provides a belief system that is to animate an entire society. It is a revolutionary call to action, essentially chiliastic and messianic, making claims on every aspect of the individual's life.

2. A unitary party that acts as an organizational cadre for a movement of solidarity charged with fostering and maintaining the integralist system of beliefs. The party, under a charismatic or pseudocharismatic leader, is a political elite

hierarchically organized and charged with extensive and imposing enterprisory, tutelary, and pedagogical responsibilities.

3. A government police, communications, and weapons monopoly.

4. A highly centralized control of the economy.[26]

Obviously some of the features of totalitarianism are technologically conditioned. Only in the circumstances that have arisen as a consequence of the industrial revolution would it be possible for a public agency to obtain a police, communications, and weapons monopoly or effective bureaucratic control of the economy. Our concerns, however, will focus upon the ideological rationale for the system. And that rationale is not a modern product by any means. Collectivist and organicist conceptions of society and the state can be found in the thought of ancient Greece. Only when they become radical collectivisms and when their rationale is united with the technological achievements of the past century does totalitarianism become a real possibility.

We shall therefore restrict our discussion to the radical collectivisms that have developed within the past hundred years. Thus restricted, our reconstruction of the justificatory arguments advanced to support totalitarian or potentially totalitarian systems begins with Hegel and Marx. Out of their social and political philosophies one can isolate an argument form isomorphic with those advanced to vindicate the political practices of a variety of radical ideologies in our own time. Irrespective of compelling differences in social and historical circumstances, arguments appear in contemporary radical ideologies that, despite specific differences in content, display the same logical structure.

What this means for theory construction in political science or political sociology can only be drawn out when all the wealth of historical and sociocultural detail that makes each ideology unique is restored—a task outside the competence of this volume.

Notes

Throughout the volume, all translations from foreign-language publications are the author's unless otherwise identified in the particular footnote. Abbreviations for works frequently cited are given in brackets following the title in the first citation in each chapter.

1. V. Pareto, *I sistemi socialisti* (Turin: Unione Tipografico, 1954), p. 3.

2. J. Dewey, *Reconstruction in Philosophy*, enlarged edition (Boston: Beacon, 1957), p. 187.

3. D. Bell, *The End of Ideology*, rev. ed. (New York: Collier, 1962), pp. 17, 393f.

4. F. Engels, *Anti-Duehring: Herr Eugen Duehring's Revolution in Science* (Moscow: Foreign Languages, 1962), p. 134; see also F. Engels, *Dialectics of Nature* (Moscow: Foreign Languages, 1962), pp. 238f.

5. C. J. Friedrich and Z. K. Brzezinski, *Totalitarian Dictatorship and Autocracy* (New York: Praeger, 1962), p. 73.

6. Z. K. Brzezinski, *Ideology and Power in Soviet Politics* (New York: Praeger, 1962), pp. 4f.

7. *Die Grundlagen der kommunistischen Erziehung*, edited by the Academy of Social Sciences of the Central Committee of the Communist Party of the Soviet Union (Berlin: Volk und Wissen, 1964), pp. 46ff. See also O. V. Kuusinen, *Fundamentals of Marxism-Leninism*, trans. by C. Dutt (Moscow: Foreign Languages, 1963), pp. 613ff.

8. G. Bottai, *La Carta del Lavoro* (Rome: Diritto del Lavoro, 1928), p. 33. See also B. Mussolini, *The Corporate State* (Florence: Vallecchi, 1938), Appendix, pp. 109ff.

9. A. Canepa, *Sistema di dottrina del fascismo* (Rome: Formiggini, 1937), I, p. 7.

10. S. Panunzio, *Lo stato fascista* (Bologna: Cappelli, 1925), pp. 15f.

11. L. Volpicelli, *Motivi su Mussolini* (Rome: Istituto Nazionale Fascista di Cultura, 1935), p. 18.

12. B. Mussolini, "Per la Medaglia dei Benemeriti del Commune di Milano," *Opera Omnia [Opera]* (Florence: Fenice, 1951–1963), XXI, p. 424; letter to M. Bianchi, August 26, 1921, *Opera*, XVII, pp. 414–15.

13. "Socialismo e socialisti," *Opera*, I, p. 142; see also p. 139.

14. "Dottrina del fascismo," *Opera*, XXXIV, p. 117.

15. See, for example, his "Al congresso delle scienze prima del quarto attentato," *Opera*, XXII, p. 251; "Discorso di Bologna," *Opera*,

XVI, p. 242; "Al congresso dei filosofi," *Opera*, XXIV, p. 109.

16. Canepa, *op. cit.*, I, pp. 8–13.

17. V. I. Lenin, "The State and Revolution," *Collected Works* (Moscow: Foreign Languages, 1960–), XXV, p. 393.

18. See also N. K. Krupskaya, *Lenin* (Moscow: Foreign Languages, 1959), pp. 95, *passim*.

19. A. Bullock, "The Political Ideas of Adolf Hitler," in M. Baumont, J. Fried, and E. Vermeil (eds.), *The Third Reich* (New York: Praeger, 1955), p. 351.

20. L. Strauss, *The Political Philosophy of Hobbes* (Chicago: University of Chicago, 1963), p. 2.

21. R. A. Dahl, *A Preface to Democratic Theory* (Chicago: University of Chicago, 1956) pp. 6, 7, 11.

22. J. Locke, *Of Civil Government* (Chicago: Regnery, 1962), p. 4.

23. T. V. Smith, *The Democratic Way of Life* (New York: Mentor, 1960), p. 55; see also p. 53.

24. H. Spencer, *The Man versus the State* (Caldwell, Idaho: Caxton, 1940), pp. 5, 1.

25. F. Neumann, *The Democratic and the Authoritarian State* (New York: Free Press, 1964), pp. 162–65. ". . . the ability of people to do as they wish. . . . is defined as liberty or freedom." (A. de Grazia, *Political Behavior* [New York: Free Press, 1962], I, p. 342.)

26. These diagnostic traits are adapted from the list provided by Friedrich and Brzezinski (*op. cit.*, pp. 9f.). They are formulated here in descriptive terms to serve taxonomic purposes; as such, they do not contain evaluative terms.

II · *THE FOUNDATIONS*
IN HEGEL AND MARX

Much of the intellectual substance of contemporary radical ideologies finds its first full expression in the philosophy of Georg Wilhelm Friedrich Hegel. Forbidding in its complexity, obscure in its cryptic prose, Hegel's philosophy has been the well-spring for many of the philosophical and doctrinal ideas expressed in the ideologies that have revolutionized our time. In this sense Hegel is father to the series of revolutions that have characterized the twentieth century. An attempt will be made to trace his influence through classical Marxism to Leninism, fascism, and National Socialism and from these to the ideologies of the socialist, communitarian, and racist revolutions of the countries outside the complex of Western nations. In ideologies that have developed through protracted intellectual elaboration, specifically Leninism and fascism, the dependency is relatively clear. In ideologies that remained immature, such as National Socialism, or are still immature, such as the various forms of African socialism, the relationship to Hegelianism is more obscure. Historically, almost all contemporary radical ideologies are rooted in Hegelianism; philosophically, all have tacitly or explicitly accepted its view of man and society. This is not to suggest that Hegelianism was the first philosophical system to articulate such a view, for much the same conception was explicitly formulated as early as Plato. The contention here is simply that Hegelianism provides the immediate point of origin of contemporary radicalism.

The brief and inadequate outline of Hegel's social and political philosophy presented here is an illustration of the kinds of justificatory arguments that appear and reappear in the radical collectivisms with which we shall be concerned. Hegel offers what shall be referred to as a "normic conception of man," an account of man and society that permits emotive terms like freedom, self-development, right, and obligation to take on specific conceptual content. The dynamic quality of such expressions permits a licit transition from descriptive propositions to moral imperatives. The emotive force of expressions such as freedom remains constant while the conceptual meaning undergoes significant change. What results is a paradigm argument in social and political philosophy—and a social and political conception radically different from that of classical liberalism.

Hegel

• Hegel's prose, it is true, leaves much to be desired: His treatments are prolix, pedantic, and all too frequently mystifying, and the bulk of his writing is patently, in the most pejorative sense, metaphysical. But for all that, Hegel was intensely preoccupied with the political events of his time, a time of revolution. In 1819, in a letter to G. F. Creuzer, Hegel said that of his fifty years, thirty had been fraught with profound social disorder. He had lived through the French Revolution, the Napoleonic period, the Restoration, and the subsequent dislocations. In his essay on the English Reform Bill, written just before his death in 1831, he said that there were forces in operation which would one day precipitate not reform, but revolution. "We find ourselves," Hegel contended, "in a significant epoch, a turning point, in which the spirit is in movement, in which it has transcended its previous form and advances to another. All previous ideas, concepts, the ligaments of the world, have been dissolved and fall away as a dream. A new forward movement of the spirit prepares itself."[2] It was a period that began with the "glorious mental dawn" of the French Revolution, a dawn that augured the birth of the Idea of Freedom.[3] "All thinking beings [shared] in the jubilation of this epoch." It is the epoch in which we live: the age of secular ideology.

The central problem for political philosophy was posed by the French Revolution, in which the principle that animated an age made its appearance. That principle was freedom and the problem posed, but unresolved by that revolution, was: "How is the political realization of freedom to be achieved?"[4]

Hegel's entire political philosophy (if not his entire philosophical enterprise) was concerned with the realization of the individual's freedom and its relationship to community life. "*Recht*," inadequately rendered in English by "Right," or "Law" meant for Hegel not only codified law, but also morality, ethical life, and world history. In Hegelianism "the system of right is the realm of freedom made actual. . . ."[5] Political freedom was to find its expression in a "community of persons seen not as a reduction of the true freedom of the individual but as its amplification."[6] Even in his early theological writings, Hegel advanced the concept that the individual's freedom could not contradict the ultimate freedom of the whole but would be fulfilled only within and through the whole. This conception was advanced as an answer to Rousseau's search for a "method of associating" that would defend and protect the individual, but in which the individual would still obey only himself and remain as free as before.

All the elements of Hegel's mature political philosophy are found in these early works, written before he was thirty years of age. They contain a conception of the individual in which

. . . a human being is an individual life insofar as he is to be distinguished from all the elements and from the infinity of individual beings outside himself. But he is only an individual life insofar as he is at one with all the elements, with the infinity of lives outside himself. He exists only inasmuch as the totality of life is divided into parts, he himself being one part and all the rest the other part; and again he exists only inasmuch as he is no part at all and inasmuch as nothing is separated from him.[7]

It is this conception that animates Hegel's analysis of *knowledge* (truth "is the whole; the union of the particular and the universal"),[8] *love* ("In love the separate does still remain, but as something united and no longer as something separate. . . ."),[9] and the *true community* (where "personal individuality and its particular interests not only achieve their complete development and gain explicit recognition for their right . . . but, . . . they also pass over of their own accord into the interest of the universal. . . .").[10]

This central conviction, the unity of the individual and the collectivity, characterizes Hegel's entire conception of the individual and society. As early as the "Fragment of a System" (1800) he contended that living beings must be thought of as "organizations." "True independence consists alone in the unity and in the interpenetration of both the individuality and the universality with each other."[11] The true being of living individuals is determined not only by their real relations but is actually constituted by relations with other things and other persons. The individual becomes an entity by being brought into opposition with other things, and he becomes a conscious human being by entering into relationships with other human beings.[12]

To explicate Hegel's system adequately would involve an elaborate inquiry into his metaphysics, an inquiry not warranted for this discussion—nor possible in the space provided. For our purposes an adequate appreciation can be obtained by a consideration of those activities that exemplify "self-consciousness in its immediate actuality": *language* and *labor*. Language, for Hegel, is that element in which the "complete isolation of independent self-existent selves is at once fluent continuity and universally communicated unity of the many selves. . . ." It is "the perfect element in which the inwardness is as external as the externality is inward. . . ." It is the express unity of the individual with the universal. "Language is both subjective and objective. It is the objective medium in which subjective minds can meet."[13]

Perhaps it is possible to make Hegel's point in less Hegelian terms. In considering the nature of language, one realizes that speaking necessarily involves establishing criteria for correct usage. That is, in order to speak clearly and meaningfully to others, language must be intersubjective or "universal."[14] Speech must obey the rules of correct usage. It is only in terms of a given rule that one can attach a specific sense to words. Without such a regulative one remains confined by subjectivism, which "is private and not communicable . . . [in] abstraction from community."[15] The individual who uses language follows the rules, and to say that he follows a rule is to say that he undertakes an appropriate act on appropriate occasions. Rule-following language behavior entails the possibility of making a mistake, and it does not make sense to contend that an individual in complete isolation from other individuals can significantly charge himself with error. To say of someone that he is following a rule means that one can ask whether he is doing what he does correctly or not. Otherwise there is no place in his behavior in which the notion of a rule can find a foothold. There is, consequently, no sense in describing his behavior in such a fashion since anything he might do is as good as anything else, whereas the point of the concept rule is that it should permit us to evaluate what is being done.

For an individual in complete isolation, then, an evaluative procedure seems at least psychologically impossible. The isolated individual who claimed to be following a rule, that is, appropriately employing language, would have to specify for himself the conditions that could count as correct or incorrect usage. When a word is used referentially, for example, we learn the rules of its usage by having others indicate examples or by observing others employ it and then performing before their scrutiny. They confirm our use when it is correct and rebut it when it is incorrect. For the isolated individual this procedure seems impossible. His only appeal, it would seem, is to veridical memory states. But to say that we have correct memory states requires that we can say that what *seems* correct to us *is*, in fact, correct. That is, we have some technique for distinguishing right from wrong other than memory itself. If all we have is the impression that our memory *seems* right and we cannot certify that memory by some external criterion, it seems that the concepts right and wrong, correct and incorrect, cannot apply. The distinction between seeming to be correct and actually being so is lost for the isolated individual, and no standard for describing language behavior as rule-following can be forthcoming. A mistake is a contravention of what is established as correct, and as such it must be recognizable as a contravention. Others must be in a position to indicate the error. If this is not so, one can perform as one likes, and no external check obtains; that is, neither correct nor incorrect usage is established. Establishing a standard is not the sort of activity that it makes sense to ascribe to any individual in complete isolation from other individuals. It is contact with others that makes possible the intersubjective check on one's actions that is inseparable from an established standard.

Any conceivable external check on language usage would involve, for the *isolated* individual, antecedent knowledge of the meaning of concepts such as meaning, language, use, and words. The development of a *private* language would, in effect, require an antecedent, and established, language.

The analysis of referential terms undertaken by Hegel in *The Phenomenology of Mind* illustrates the social character of language as he conceived it. His analysis indicates that the uses of language necessarily entail the point of view and interests of other persons involved in the "language-game" and suggests that conscious life tends to move in the direction of rigorous intersubjective rules. To assign the name "Spirit" to this rule-governed association of thinking subjects is to do no more than call our attention to the fact that language is a highly developed and objective expression of symbolic communication within a social group. It is a complex symbol system that, when internalized, constitutes the thinking of the individual subject. Thinking, in this view, is implicit speech, the internalized employment of symbols standardized by the rules for correct usage. Since the employment of rules entails a social situation, sociality constitutes not only the ultimate necessary condition for, but the very development of self-conscious individual personality itself.

It is clear that Hegel intends an acknowledgment of the dependence of man's true humanity on his involvement with others. To acknowledge the role of interpersonal collaboration in establishing rules and accrediting the rule-following behavior that makes the self-centered animal creature that man is upon his entry into this world a truly human being is to recognize the necessary unity of men under law and in Spirit.

Only in an environment of other persons, who freely acknowledge us as we acknowledge them, can we be finally freed, not merely from outside pressures, but also from the restrictions of our particular personality. It is this acknowledgement, however dim and confused, which is for Hegel the foundation of Reason, Reason being a subjectivity which is *inter*subjective and therefore objective. Quite obviously the realms of meaning, of scientific verity, of well-conceived planning and execution, are all realms which have a public as well as a private status, which are inseparable from that use of language to which Hegel is to give so important a place. Phenomenology therefore passes over into Psychology, the study of the individual functioning in a way which presupposes a *social* setting and experience.[16]

Hegel's discussion of labor has essentially the same implications. Labor commences with an effort to satisfy individual needs. But it immediately becomes obvious that the satisfaction of human needs, which are distinct from animal needs in that they can multiply without limits, inevitably comes to involve others. In the effort to satisfy his needs the individual man is compelled to enter into a law-governed association with others. To this extent everything private becomes something social. Hegel describes such associations in the following fashion:

Particular spheres of action fall into groups, influence others, and are helped or hindered by others. The most remarkable thing here is this mutual interlocking of particulars, which is what one would least expect because at first sight everything seems to be given over to the arbitrariness of the individual, and it has a parallel in the solar system, which displays to the eye only irregular movements, though its laws may nonetheless be ascertained.[17]

The entire labor process is concerned with the self-development of man. In his activity, mediated through the instrument of labor, the individual defines himself against an objective world. He projects himself into the object and suffuses the object with himself. The object of his labor becomes in a significant sense an extension of himself. Yet even the most primitive labor is *shared* labor, labor that is inextricably bound to a community. Every commodity embodies a social relationship. Thus in every instance of concrete labor a general social principle finds expres-

sion. Evidence of the sociality of labor reveals itself in the immediate labor process, in the division of labor and its increasing
rationalization, in the rules governing the ownership of property
and in commodity exchange. The labor process involves the
intersubjective elements of appropriate techniques; the division
of labor is an embodiment of rational productivity; the ownership of property necessitates a reciprocity of rights and obligations; and commodity exchange requires an assessment of
exchange value governed by rule. If man is to proceed with
self-development, he must become increasingly involved in the
community of labor, in the real rule-governed relations established by a working society.[18]

To enter into such real relations in a concrete community,
to speak a language, and to engage in productive labor is not to
diminish "freedom." This entry is the first moment in the
dialectical development of real freedom. Only an entirely abstract
conception of man could conceive him as free outside the real
relations that constitute the determinations making him a person.
Such an abstract notion entails a notion of man in which every
relation is understood to constitute a constraint, every rule a
restriction.[19] Only in such an abstract system would the state
and society be conceived as antagonistic to the "self" or "true
individuality" of man. The theoreticians of these abstract systems
contend that every law is a constraint and every constraint a
moral infraction. At best, the result of such a conviction is a
speculative and pious anarchism. At worst, it is the fanatic and
destructive anarchism that brought terror to individuals and
destruction to institutions during the French Revolution.[20]

The idea which people most commonly have of freedom is that it
is arbitrariness—the mean, chosen by abstract reflection, between the
will wholly determined by natural impulses, and the will free absolutely. If we hear it said that the definition of freedom is ability to do
what we please, such an idea can only be taken to reveal an utter immaturity of thought, for it contains not even an inkling of the absolutely
free will, of right, ethical life, and so forth.[21]

But the caprice of the individual is not freedom. In fact, the
theoreticians of "negative freedom"—in particular Rousseau—
have always posited a minimum of social constraint, embodied in

the notion of the social contract, as the necessary condition of any significant or effective freedom. For the state of nature, which is conceived as the state of perfect freedom, is in fact "the state of injustice, violence, untamed natural impulses, of inhuman deeds and emotions" in which no effective freedom is found. The restraints that constitute the necessary preconditions for effective freedom are the laws of nature, which in effect means "reason." For only within the confines of reason could man make the transition that substitutes justice for instinct as the controlling factor in his behavior and transforms "a stupid and dull-witted animal [into] an intelligent being and a man."[22]

In order that reason may function in this critical fashion language is necessary, and language, in turn, necessitates the antecedent existence of a rule-governed association of men. Reason and law could not be the consequence of a contract, for the very possibility of a contract presupposes the possession of reason on the part of the contracting parties. The notion of a social contract is a pernicious fiction because the idea that individuals can collectively opt to enter into a society implies the antecedent exercises of reason, which is itself predicated upon the existence of society.[23] The very idea of reason, the only context in which freedom can be spoken of without manifest contradiction, implies virtual law and morality. Correct language usage implies rule-following behavior, and the concept of following rules implies a disposition to accept the judgment of others as our equals at least in principle. The procedural canons of rule-following behavior imply a readiness to prescind from caprice and willfulness and to accept the judgment of others unless *significant* reasons can be mustered against it. Significance cannot characterize subjective whimsy or arbitrary preference, or privilege. When the question at issue is correct usage, it is inappropriate to make determinations of correctness or incorrectness rest on personal preference. Judgment requires that one assume a rigorous neutrality, abjuring personal privilege which is not warranted by relevant and accredited superiority. One must be prepared to admit one's fallibility and to accede to one's opponent when relevant reasons so require. Conscious life tends to move in the direction of impersonal, intersubjective rules that entail a virtual morality. If these are "limitations," they are limitations that produce "the consciousness of and the desire for freedom in its true, that is, rational and ideal form. . . . Thus the limitation of impulse, desire, passion—pertaining merely to the particular individual as such—of caprice and willfulness, . . . is the very condition leading to liberation; and society and the state are the very conditions in which freedom is realized."[24]

The paradigm of association for Hegel is membership in a language group. Being a member of a body politic, or a language community, is not the result of a contract. Being politically related is like sharing common language rules. Both the body politic and language are logically prior to their component members. The unit of analysis is something general, collective. One does not understand society or language by studying the individual; the individual becomes comprehensible only within the context of a collectivity. Both language and society have a history that transcends the confines of empirical individuality. The individual who seeks to reconstitute language from his own perspective or to generate a private language of his own has missed the point of language. Language grows out of and exemplifies the historical experience of a given community. Only when the individual has come to a mature awareness of this and has made a historical language of his own can he begin to conceive of a change in its elements. Such change must respect the historic and objective conditions that determine both the form and content of language and make it the matrix within which effective thought takes place.

The state, in the comprehensive sense in which it is understood by Hegel, also has a determinate history. It is the concrete form

. . . under which everything that is, is subsumed—is that which constitutes the culture of a nation. . . . This spiritual content is something definite, firm, solid, completely exempt from caprice, the particularities, the whims of individuality, of chance. . . . This spiritual content then constitutes the essence of the individual as well as that of the people. It is the holy bond that ties the men, the spirits together. It is one life in all, a grand object, a great purpose and content on which depend all individual happiness and all private decisions.[25]

It is this content of the state that gives determinate being to the empirical individual—and this content is governed by rules either in the form of habit or codified law. Social institutions, originally extrinsic to the individual, appear as constraints only to the immature consciousness innocent of the knowledge that the communal will provides the substance of thinking and acting effectively[26] and that the web of rule-governed associations provides the essence of meaningful individuality. The necessary connections among persons, organized into morality and law, exemplify their fundamental spiritual freedom in "reason."

Recht, for Hegel, means an intersubjective order that is the necessary expansion of freedom. The collective reasonable will utilizes the contingencies of individual impulse and passion as the material for its own organizing activities. Organized will is reasonable since it must conform to the procedural requirements of intersubjective order. In other words, it must meet the minimal requirements of publicity and neutrality and be raised above what is merely personal and finite. The organized will is expressed in the categories and canons of science and logic, the rules of legal and moral conduct and esthetic taste. Only upon assimilating all that the state contains, by recognizing in the existing order the essential elements of himself as a person, is the individual in a position to operate as a rational human being in full and conscious freedom. "The rational, like the substantial, is necessary. We are free when we recognize it as law and follow it as the substance of our own being." Only the will that obeys the law is free, for it obeys reason, which is the very substance of man. All true laws are the embodiment of reason. Thus the collective will expressed in codified law in the state is a matter of trained intelligence. It is the absolutely rational element in the will. Existing law-governed states, of course, only approximate (and often most inadequately) the Idea of the State. Thus, the system of laws prevailing in pre-Revolutionary France presented a "confused mass of privileges altogether contravening thought and reason—an utterly irrational state of things, and one with which the greatest corruption of morals, of Spirit was associated. . . ."[27] Realization of this "shameless destitution of right" manifested itself in revolution. World historical individuals, those who serve the World Spirit, undertook to restore reason to the state. But these individuals were successful, could only be successful, insofar as they themselves embodied reason. Their will was not their subjective will but the substantial will of their historic community. They acted to bring to pass that which the times required. No act, no law can be imposed that violates that will, a will that is "still hidden beneath the surface but already knocking against the outer world as against a shell. . . ."[28]

The reason to which Hegel appeals is *historical.* Reason (as the creator of world history), in its self-articulation, traverses stages in its development. Thus, language, a manifestation of reason, was not the product of abstract reasoning. Language arose from historical need through a dialectical development. Similarly, society and the state are not the product of abstract reason. They develop dialectically. Community satisfies need. In satisfying those needs both language and the state conformed to the historic peculiarities of the constituent community—determinations of race,[29] geographic circumstances, and economic conditions. The well-spring of action is need; man makes himself in activity. But activity takes place only within a determinate situation. Every age has conditions of its own and is an individual situation; decisions must and can be made only within, and in accordance with, the age itself.[30]

Hegel's reasonings constitute a justificatory argument attempting to support a presumption in favor of a rule-governed collectivity over the empirical individual. His argument is that unless man is understood essentially as a unity in diversity, as a derivative of a prior collectivity, one is driven into paradox. Any alternative definition of man makes the use of words like freedom bizarre. The isolated man, the social atom of the contract theorists, has freedom—but in order to have freedom in society, the individual submits to restraint. This conception of freedom is self-contradictory, for freedom is acquired only by compromising the individual's freedom in the social contract. Furthermore, the atomistic conception of the individual and his freedom renders certain social phenomena incomprehensible. If the state is understood to be the consequence of a contract that an individual enters into to enhance his personal well-being, that is, in order to protect his life and property, then the state's demand for sacrifice, even to the extent of risking property and life in war, becomes incomprehensible. The security of life and property cannot reasonably be understood to be based on their own sacrifice.[31]

Hegel has therefore proposed a redefinition of the concept "man." Man is a "communal being" (a *"Gemeinwesen"*), a being that finds fulfillment only in a superindividual whole (*ein Allgemeines*), the totality of the historical life experiences of a people.[32] This *Allgemeines* is a complex interrelationship of custom, rules, and laws. It is the vehicle for the transmission of the spiritual patrimony of a people. It is the necessary ground of language, morality, art, and religion. The individual man becomes a person only within such a system. "All the value man has, all spiritual reality, he has only through the state," for the state is the ethical will of the national community, the form into which national culture is cast.[33]

All these arguments are mustered to support the proposed definition of man, which in turn entails an initial presumption in favor of the rule-governed community. This is manifest in Hegel's claim that "the actual world is as it ought to be" and that "rational insight . . . reconciles us to the actual. . . ." From this initial presumption we can derive a procedural maxim: "Nonconformity, *qua* nonconformity, is an evil," for Hegel's conception of man requires that nonconformity, the violation of established customs and rules, requires justification. It is *non*conformity, rather than conformity, that requires an explanation.

The redefinition of man proposed by Hegel is vindicated, like stipulative redefinitions in general, by arguments illustrating its utility, economy, and theoretical fruitfulness. The arguments that support the redefinition are not formal. They are attempts to vindicate the proposed use. Once the redefinition is vindicated, its use involves assuming a normative position: Man is essentially a social animal. Everything we value in man presupposes his membership in a rule-governed association of virtual equals. In this sense the model, even though couched in descriptive language, has a normative character. Deceptively descriptive, it *implicitly* recommends. The consequence of such a recommendation is the subversion of the liberal maxim: "Restraint, *qua* restraint, is an evil." Conformity to rule, for Hegel, is not conceived as restraint but as fulfillment. Association in the "tranquility of law" is not the loss of freedom; it is not only its necessary precondition, but its fulfillment as well. The model society was one in which the individual found in

. . . the idea of his country or of his state . . . the invisible and higher reality for which he strove, which impelled him to effort . . . the final end of his world or in his eyes the final end of the world, an end which he found manifested in the realities of his daily life or which he himself co-operated in manifesting and maintaining. Confronted by this idea, his own individuality vanished; it was only this idea's maintenance, life, and persistence that he asked for, and these things which he himself could make realities.[34]

A general theoretical bias follows from these conceptions. If the bias is formulated as a proposition about the essential sociality of man and conjoined with descriptive propositions, it will deliver the normative assessments that we have identified as peculiar to social and political philosophy. It permits Hegel to talk of a "living union" of individuals in association, "happy and beautiful associations" in which the individual realizes the "fulfillment of his nature."[35] The state, the confines within which all these associations are effected, can be spoken of as a living, organic unity, which "as the mind of a nation, is both the law permeating all relationships . . . and also at the same time the manners and consciousness of its citizens."[36] All these propositions are advanced with emphatic commendatory force.

This conception of man, in which the collectivity is understood to constitute the true essence of the individual, was conjoined by Hegel with the conviction that an elite minority, possibly a single "world historical individual," could intuit the course of history. They could anticipate the requirements of the immediate future and their will was the true and ultimate will of the community. Against the immediate interests of the men of their times, such men represented the real will of history—and history was their sole vindication.

If the individual was nothing more than the particular expression of his historical community, those individuals who could anticipate its progressive unfolding were authorized to speak in the name of each individual's most profound interest. The ordinary individual lives a life in conformity to rule and custom; the world historical individual, as the motor of history, stands outside the confines of common rule and law. He speaks in the name of what man, in the unfolding logic of history, must be.

Hegel had seen "the World Spirit on horseback" when Napoleon rode through Jena. Napoleon was but the first of the Hegelian world historical individuals that modern times would see. Since his time they have appeared with surprising regularity. To vindicate their role, they have often made appeal to arguments not unlike those made popular by Hegel at the beginning of the nineteenth century.

Marx

· Hegelianism exercised its most profound influence in Germany during the period of Karl Marx's sojourn at the University of Berlin. The social and political philosophy of classical Marxism bore the imprint of that influence, for whatever theoretical modifications Marx made in the Hegelianism he inherited, he never substantially altered Hegel's normic conception of man and society. Of course, Marx was never a Hegelian in the strict sense, but in the sense important for the present discussion he remained a Hegelian in orientation.

As early as 1837 Marx, then nineteen years of age, gave himself over to dialectical idealism; in 1839, he was still engaged in a passionate defense of Hegel.[37] More significant for our purposes is the evidence of the persistent influence of Hegelian normic concepts in Marx's work throughout the formative years immediately preceding the publication of the *Communist Manifesto* in 1848. Not that elements of Hegelianism ceased to influence the theoretical bias of Marx after that date, but Marx from that point on makes a conscious effort to avoid the language of the neo-Hegelianism of his formative period. Why such a change took place will be discussed later.

Marx's writings of 1841 to 1845 include all the elements of Hegel's conception of man, society, and the state. The central notion is that man is not to be conceived as an "atom," but rather as a "communal being" (a *"Gemeinwesen"*) who attains *true* humanity only insofar as he establishes real relations with other men in a community. "The individual *is* the *social being*. His life . . . is . . . an expression and confirmation of social life. Man's individual and species life (*Gattungsleben*) are not different. . . . Man, much as he may therefore be a *particular* individual . . . is just as much the *totality*. . . ."[38] These notions were common to all the left-wing Hegelians. Moses Hess, a left-wing Hegelian himself and a mentor of both Marx and Engels, identified these conceptions as the species traits of modern German philosophy. According to Hess, "The individual . . . according to contemporary German philosophy, is the species, the All. Every man . . . is the state, humanity. Every man is the species, the totality, humanity. . . ."[39] Social life, then, is the medium in which man establishes real relations with his equals and thereby realizes himself as a human being. "Only as a social being," Hess contended, "is the human being truly and really alive."[40]

This essentially Hegelian conception of man and society was all but universal among the young Hegelians who were the companions of the young Marx. Once Marx's conception of man is understood, the normative commitments that characterized all his subsequent work become comprehensible. For the young Marx it was the task of philosophy to foster the realization of "rational freedom." The state or society that failed to foster that rational freedom was understood to be a bad state or society. "Philosophy," Marx contended, "interprets the rights of humanity and demands that the state constitute itself a state of human nature." The state is to be the instrument of human freedom, human realization. Whatever force Marx's subsequent ethical injunctions possess is derived from this commitment, for Marx held that the accession to rational freedom could only be the consequence of a correct appraisal of the nature of man—and the conformity of the state and society to that appraisal. For Marx, human nature to which the good state must conform was not to be understood as a pervasive universal form or abstract essence in which particular human beings participate; nor was it to be understood as a mere aggregate composed of "monads" or the "irreducible ultimates" of metaphysics. The individual man is neither an abstract essence nor a particular thing; he is rather an existence that *is* social activity, a variable in an interactive context.

A good state would be one that rested on the full awareness that the nature of man is that of a social being, a "real species being." The true state would be the "essence of the community"[41] and, consequently, would fully reflect the essence of man. ". . . [C]ontemporary philosophy," Marx contended in 1842, "constructs the state out of the idea of the totality (*Idee des Ganzen*). It conceives the state as a great organism in which legal, moral and political freedom attain their realization and the individual citizen obeys in the laws of the state only his own reason, human reason."[42] This is simply a modest reformulation of Hegel's conception of society and the state. "Hegel's social ideal is the free state, the state whose citizens accede to the general will which finds expression in law because it is the 'spirit of their spirit,' because they rediscover in its laws their own rational (and general) will."[43]

This normic conception of man, the state, and society generated all the imperatives that characterized Marx's political and philosophical writing of the early period. The normative ideal that Marx entertained during this period was "human emancipation," and human emancipation meant that "at those times when the state is most aware of itself, political life seeks . . . to establish itself as the genuine and harmonious species-life of man." This is a transliteration of the Hegelian ideal in which through "reconciliation of the atom [that is, the ego] and its othernesses individuals are what we call happy, for happy is he who is in harmony with himself."[44]

Marx's normic conception was originally a very vague model of social man. The model provided a descriptive frame of reference, simpler than the being it was understood to model and calculated to resolve paradox and facilitate insight into the more complex and elusive real being. His contention was essentially that valued traits of individual members of the species man were not explicable and analyzable in meaningful terms if the proffered explanation and analysis restricted itself to the individual's personal traits and the individual's environment exclusive of other members of the species. The model Marx advanced was conceived as (1) intuitively more tenable than the atomistic model of liberal political theorists; (2) having specific empirical referents; and (3) being more useful in the articulation of systematic social theories.

Thus the liberal model of man and society leaves us with a conception in which the individual is withdrawn into his private interests and separated from the community. Society appears to act as a continual restraint on the individual, as a limit to his putative original independence. Moreover, the notion of man as a self-subsistent atom is incorrigibly abstract and inherently nonempirical.

The specific property of the atom is that it has no properties and is therefore not connected with being outside it. . . . The atom has no needs, it is self-sufficient; the world outside it is absolute vacuum, i.e., it is contentless, senseless, meaningless, just because the atom has all its fullness in itself. The egotistic individual in civil society may in his non-sensuous imagination and lifeless abstraction inflate himself to the size of an atom, i.e., to an unrelated, self-sufficient, wantless, absolutely full, blessed being. . . . [but] every activity and property of his being, every one of his vital urges becomes a need, a necessity, which his self-seeking transforms into seeking for other things and human beings outside him.[45]

On the basis of these objections Marx maintained that the real science of society could only be established by making "the social relationship 'of man to man' the basic principle of . . . theory."[46] Even though one recognizes the general vagueness of the young Marx's redefinition of man, it can still be considered a conceptual model and assimilated into the scientific enterprise. As such it would have nothing of the normative features that characterize social and political philosophies.

Positive social science tends to assimilate normative elements into the category of contributing conditions or to treat them as derived. Its task is the formulation and issuance of "if-then" or "theoretical" propositions, descriptive or explanatory accounts systematically relating recurrent phenomena for purposes of prediction and control. The issuance of imperatives, or the identification of ideals toward which men should aspire, are not among the legitimate obligations of social science. Marx's analysis, on the other hand, leads to the conclusion that "the doctrine that man is the supreme being for man . . . ends, therefore, with the categorical imperative to overthrow all those conditions in which man is an abased, enslaved, abandoned, contemptible being. . . ."[47]

Much of Marx's prose of this period is charged with imperative. "Man is the highest being for man," a value, is conjoined with the injunction, "One must rekindle in the hearts of . . . men their human self-consciousness, freedom. Only this sentiment . . . can make out of a society a community of men devoted to their supreme ends. . . ."[48] Marx's model of man supported normative propositions as well as purely descriptive ones.

The theoretical and normative bias of the young Marx offers

striking insight into the Hegelian genesis of Marx's thinking about society. Marx remains convinced that man is and should be what Hegel had argued he is and should be. Man, for Marx, is "the human world, the state, society." The human essence is "the *ensemble* of social relations."[49] The distinction between Hegelianism and Marxism was largely the consequence of Marx's attempt to eliminate Hegel's mysticism, which, Marx felt, was the result of Hegel's abuse of the language. Hegel had reified predicates and made them subjects. Man's consciousness was shorn of all determinations and elevated to the status of Consciousness—an immanent subject that somehow logically precedes individual consciousness. Consciousness, Spirit, the Idea become the true subjects of history; and individual, empirical men are only "moments" in a mystic self-generating life process. Marx identified this inversion of subjects and predicates as the secret of Hegelian mystification.

> For Hegel the essence of man—man—equals self-consciousness. . . . [It] is not real Man . . . who as such is made the subject, but only the abstraction of man—self-consciousness. . . . Real man and real nature become mere predicates—symbols of this esoteric, unreal man and of this unreal nature. Subject and predicate are, therefore, related to each other in an absolute inversion. . . .[50]

Marx's procedure here is not radically different from the conceptual analysis undertaken by empirical science. In their assessment of experimental concepts scientists use the measure of falsifiability of a concept as a rough standard of meaningfulness. In empirical science a concept is more informative when it is open to more occasions in which it might be falsified. That is, a concept which in principle is subject to more empirical tests is intrinsically more informative. Marx argued, in effect, that Hegel's mistake was to conceive of his conceptual model in terms of *essences*—to think that behind the world of testable things and processes there was a permanent essence which should itself be the object of inquiry but which was forever insulated from empirical test. Marx presented his conceptual model of man with its essentially Hegelian structure in descriptive or empirical terms. His position seems to have been quite nominalistic. He argued that "it would be a contradiction to say, on the one hand, that all ideas have their origin in the world of the senses and to maintain, on the other hand, that a word is more than a word, that besides the beings represented, which are always individual, there also exist general beings." Marx suggested that Hegelian essentialism argued "from real apples, pears, strawberries and almonds [to] the general idea 'Fruit,' [which is conceived as the] *true* essence of the pear, the apple, etc., . . . what is essential to these things is not their real being, perceptible to the senses, but the essence . . . extracted from them and then foisted on them. . . . Particular real fruits are no more than semblances whose true essence is the 'Substance'—'Fruit.' "[51] What results is an empty abstraction that pretends to account for *all* conceivable events but is subject to no known test of verification, is unfalsifiable in principle, and, consequently, could not be considered informative in any serious sense of the word.

Marx held that general terms like "consciousness," "reason," or "history" were names that covered a set of related things or processes; they were not something to be studied independently of the things to which they refer. He objected to the Hegelian and neo-Hegelian philosophy of his time because it reified general terms into substantive essences. History, Marx argued, has become for speculative philosophy "a metaphysical subject of which real human individuals are but the bearers." But, he continued, "history does nothing, it 'possesses no immense wealth,' it 'wages no battles.' It is man, real living man, that does all that, that possesses and fights; 'history' is not a person apart, using man as a means for its own particular aims; history is nothing but the activity of man pursuing his aims."[52] Unless this is understood, history remains a transcendent subject whose progress can only be pursued through logical categories—and categories, rather than offering explanations, must themselves be explained.

Marx offered a conceptual model of man that provided a set of descriptive sentences which could be taken as premises for the formulation of a comprehensive empirical theory. The premises that serve as underived postulates for the theoretical system are broad empirical generalizations that generate theorems of increasing specificity. The latter are subject to empirical confirmation or disconfirmation. Thus Marx maintained that the

... premises from which we begin are ... real premises ... which
... can be verified in a purely empirical way. ... The first premise
of all human history is, of course, the existence of living human beings. ... [who] must be in a position to live in order to be able to
"make history." ... The first historical act is thus the production of
the means to satisfy these needs, the production of material life
itself. ... The first necessity therefore in any theory of history is to
observe this fundamental fact in all its significance and all its implications and to accord it its due importance. ... The second fundamental
point is that as soon as a need is satisfied (which implies the action
of satisfying, and the acquisition of an instrument), new needs are
made. ...[53]

The third premise states that men must enter into a special
procreative relationship in order to reproduce their own kind.

All these premises presuppose that individuals interact with
one another and describe social activities. "Social" is defined as
"the cooperation of several individuals, no matter under what
conditions, in what manner and to what end." In satisfying their
needs individuals produce their means of subsistence, an activity
that distinguishes men from animals. (Marx equates production
with the acquisition of an instrument and consequently defines
man as a tool-making animal.)[54] "The way in which men produce their means of subsistence depends first of all on the nature
of the actual means they find in existence and have to reproduce. ... [It] is a definite form of activity of these individuals,
a definite form of expressing their life, a definite mode of life
on their part." Marx follows this contention with a proposition
of far-reaching theoretical implication: "As individuals express
their life, so they are"—by which he means, "What they are ...
coincides with their production, both with what they produce
and with how they produce. The nature of individuals thus depends on the material conditions determining their production."
Thus Marx "set out from real, active men, and on the basis of
their real life-process [demonstrated] the development of the
ideological reflexes and echoes of this life-process. The phantoms
formed in the human brain are ... necessarily sublimates of
their material life-process, which is empirically verifiable and
bound to material premises. Morality, religion, metaphysics, all
the rest of ideology and their corresponding forms of conscious-

ness, thus no longer retain the semblance of independence."[55]

In his maturity Marx formulated these propositions in the following order:

> (1) In the social production of their life, men enter into definite relations that are indispensable and independent of their will. . . . (2) [These] relations of production . . . correspond to a definite state of development of their material productive forces. (3) The sum total of these relations of production constitutes the economic structure of society. . . . (4) [This is] the real foundation, on which rises a legal and political superstructure and to which correspond definite forms of social consciousness. The mode of production of material life conditions the social, political and intellectual life process in general. It is not the consciousness of men that determines their being, but on the contrary, their social being that determines their consciousness.[56]

Marx gave these propositions greater specificity by formulating a set of theoretical statements that related variables in a specified or specifiable way. He contended that each new productive force brought about a development of the division of labor. The division of labor, in turn, determined the development of economic classes. Membership in a specific class conditioned and determined the personality of the individual. In the *Poverty of Philosophy*, written in 1847, this chain of propositions is expressed in this sequence:

> In acquiring new productive forces men change their mode of production; and in changing their mode of production, in changing the way of earning their living, they change all their social relations. The hand-mill gives you society with the feudal lord; the steam-mill, society with the industrial capitalist. The same men who establish their social relations in conformity with their material productivity, produce also principles, ideas and categories, in conformity with their social relations.[57]

Elsewhere the relationship between variables is telescoped into the following elliptical proposition: "The fundamental form of . . . activity is, of course, material, from which depend all other forms—mental, political, religious, etc."[58] The direction in which the several variates influence each other is obvious. The sequence makes the new productive force or instrument of production a cause or determinant, the division of labor is its proximate effect and the appearance of classes, which subsequently determine personality, is the ultimate effect.

The unit of analysis remains a collectivity, a structured totality of some sort. It is the dynamic constancy and structural properties of some collectivity that provide an account of the empirical properties of its components. Thus, for Marx, the observed behavioral traits of given individuals are accounted for by subsuming them under specific social classes.

> . . . [I]ndividuals are dealt with only insofar as they are the personifications of economic categories, embodiments of particular class relations and class interests. My standpoint, from which the evolution of the economic formation of society is viewed as a process of natural history, can less than any other make the individual responsible for relations whose creature he socially remains. . . . [T]he capitalist is merely capital personified. . . .[59]

The surface events of history are explained as a struggle between classes. Individuals represent, consciously or unconsciously, the interests of their respective classes. These interests—the "great driving forces" of history—are, in turn, simply the reflections of developments within the economic base of society.[60] Within the material substructure of society, when the productive forces find their development restricted by the confines of productive relations (property relations, developed to accommodate earlier productive forces), the entire social structure is subject to severe internal stress. A period of social revolution ensues with classes representing the now-divergent elements of the material base of society. Individuals represent the contending classes. They are the active agents of historical development, but in pursuing what they conceive to be their private interests, they serve what Hegel called the "cunning of history." Historical events are "always governed by inner, hidden laws and it is only a matter of discovering these laws."[61] Changes in the productive forces generate changes in the division of labor in society, and this change entails alterations in property or productive relations. (Marx contends that the "division of labor and private property are . . . identical expressions . . . ," and property relations are "but a legal expression for the same thing.")[62] Existing relations of production find their advocates in the members of the economic class that profits from them. As productive forces develop, they generate change in the division of labor that becomes incompatible with the existing order of production handed down by history and sanctified by law. The tensions produced are expressed in the restiveness of a revolutionary class which represents the new forces. When those who defend the established relations of production resist the changes necessitated by the developments in the productive forces, social revolution bursts the now confining fetters of the old order to permit the growth of the new. This whole sequence is sometimes telescoped by the founders of classical Marxism into locutions like "the productive forces are in rebellion against the mode of production which they have outgrown."[63] This elliptical rendering can only mean that changes in the productive forces (apparently technological changes) generate changes in the division of labor which, in turn, find expression in class differences that condition and determine the material life interests of individual agents. The sentimental, philosophical, religious, and political attachments of individuals are explained as dependent variables that are the consequences of a chain of complex interdependency relationships determined *ultimately* by ordered development of the productive forces.[64]

The structure of the analysis remains Hegelian. The individual is to be understood only as an element in a specific collectivity. The collectivity has determinate character at any time only because it functions as an element in some dynamic, dialectical "whole," in this case, history. The surface features of events, the whimsies, rational choices, and accidents in history, really have a "logic" and an upward progression, what Engels on at least one occasion called "the chain of mankind's universal progress."[65] The ultimate end of that progression is "universal human emancipation"—personal freedom—a value that both Marx and Engels harbored throughout their maturity and to which Marx referred in his last manuscript as the realm of freedom. In the four decades that separated the writing of the *German Ideology* and *Capital*, this value did not change for Marx. The ultimate end of the entire prehistory of man was the freedom to be found "only in community with others. . . . In the real community the individuals obtain their freedom in and through their association."[66]

The difference between the Hegelian and the Marxist analysis turns upon the nature of the relations that bind the individual to a collectivity and a particular collectivity to the whole. For Hegel, the ultimate unifying substance is ethical; the true community in which men find fulfillment is the "actuality of the ethical Idea."[67] For Marx, that which unites men in community is the historically developed material need and the economic relations that need fosters. Hegel's analysis refers to ethical significance and Marx's to empirical regularities. Hegel's avowed concerns are normative; Marx's concerns are essentially scientific. Hegel *analyzes* the ethical significance of the Oriental political form; Marx seeks to *explain* it. For Hegel, Oriental despotism meant that only the despot could be *ethically* free; his subjects were ruled by law and maxim, and social caste was imposed upon them. For Marx, Oriental despotism was explained by the fact that because of climatic and territorial conditions artificial irrigation by canals and waterworks were the necessary basis of Oriental agriculture. Because of the low population density and the vast territorial extent of the irrigation system a highly centralized despotism was necessary to maintain a viable productive system.[68]

This does not mean that Hegel could not give plausible explanations of historical development. He realized that men were motivated by need to form communities; he argued that the decline of the Greek communities of antiquity was to be explained by an increase in material wealth and an increasing divergence of class interest. He was equally aware of the fact that constitutional law was frequently nothing but private property exalted into statutes.[69] Hegel also knew that when man's real relations with his fellow man were obstructed, they often sought a fictive, compensatory fulfillment in religion; this offered them in dream that which they did not possess in fact. Thus in his youth he spoke of Christianity as the "realization of a moral ideal [that] could no longer be willed but only wished for . . . a fantasy . . . a consolation." Later he spoke of the followers of Jesus having sundered their living relationship with their community and having snapped "one important bond of association, . . . they . . . lost one part of freedom . . . a number of active relationships and living ties."[70] The result was that their nature could not be fulfilled and they sought restoration in the ideal world. Elsewhere he argued that where the community does not provide the individual with a sense of participation, of belonging to a higher and more inclusive reality, the church might.[71] A generation later Marx argued essentially the same thesis. Religion offered man the "fantastic realization" of the humanity that the degraded community in which he found himself denied him.[72] What Marx went on to argue was that Hegelian notions of fulfillment in the family, civil society, and the state were equally false. Marx and Engels claimed ultimate fulfillment can come only in a community of men

> . . . openly and directly taking possession of the productive forces which have outgrown all control execpt that of society as a whole. . . . The social anarchy of production gives place to a social regulation of production upon a definite plan, according to the needs of the community and of each individual. . . . Only from that time will man himself, with full consciousness make his own history. . . . It is the ascent of man from the kingdom of necessity to the kingdom of freedom. . . . [This act of] universal emancipation is the historical mission of the modern proletariat.[73]

To reiterate, because the "fundamental form of activity is . . . material, from which depend all other forms—mental, political, religious, etc.," man's fulfillment can only be forthcoming in a rationally organized productive community. For Marx, ethics was a by-product of the organization of the productive community. Again Marx is not concerned with the *significance* of historical codes of ethics; he is concerned with their *explanation*. "We maintain," Engels wrote, "that all moral theories have been hitherto the product, in the last analysis, of the economic conditions of society obtaining at the time."[74]

Marx's focus on explanation and Hegel's concern with significance should not obscure the fact that some of the essential conclusions reached by the two social and political philosophers remain the same. Man is essentially a denizen of a collectivity. To treat the individual as something apart from his group is to court paradox and error. The individual undertakes activity motivated by his own immediate interests but, in fact, is responding to objective forces that operate below the surface phenomena. Freedom is not in any sense understood to mean freedom from constraint; it means behavior in conformity to law. Engels recognizes his definition of freedom to be Hegelian. To be free means to obey the law—the laws that govern nature and social development. Behavior that does not conform to law is not freedom—it is caprice. Similarly, the "laws" of morality reflect the particular phase of historical development of a particular community. For both Hegel and Marx obedience to these laws constitutes morality. Slavery in antiquity was "moral" because it reflected a necessary moment in the historical development of mankind. Thus, for Hegel, although slavery was a perversion of the principle of freedom, philosophy could comprehend and so justify the circumstance, since it was not so much *from* slavery as *through* slavery that humanity was emancipated.[75] Engels could similarly argue that slavery was not in accord with contemporary moral sentiments; yet he maintained that

. . . without slavery, no Greek state, no Greek art and science; without slavery, no Roman Empire. But without the basis laid by Grecian culture, and the Roman Empire, also no modern Europe. We should never forget that our whole economic, political and intellectual development presupposes a state of things in which slavery was as necessary as it was universally recognized. In this sense we are entitled to say: Without the slavery of antiquity [there is] no modern socialism. . . .[76]

Hence, without slavery in antiquity, there could be no modern emancipation of man. At the end of his life Engels could thus contend, "There is no great historical evil without a compensating historical progress."[77]

Morality follows a historically determined course. At certain critical nodal points special individuals must stand outside the morals of their time in order to effect the higher purposes of history. When the community enters a period of crisis, these world historical individuals are driven to act in order to bring about that which the times require. Hegel maintained that these men were heroes, since they did not derive their sanction from the existing order but from a more profound source:

[A source] whose content is still hidden and has not yet broken through into existence. The source of their actions is the inner spirit, still hidden beneath the surface but already knocking against the outer world as against a shell, in order, finally, to burst forth and break it into pieces. . . . They see the very truth of their age and their world, the next genus, so to speak, which is already formed in the womb of time. . . . [In effecting their purpose] such men may treat other great and even sacred interests inconsiderately—a conduct which indeed subjects them to moral reprehension. But so mighty a figure must trample down many an innocent flower, crush to pieces many things in its path. . . . [The] so-called prosperity or misfortune of this or that isolated individual cannot be regarded as an essential element in the rational order of the universe. . . . For the history of the world occupies a higher ground than that on which morality has properly its position. . . . What the absolute aim of Spirit requires and accomplishes— what Providence does—transcends the obligations, and the liability to imputation and the ascription of good or bad motives, which attach to individuality in virtue of its social relations. . . . It is irrelevant and inappropriate from that point of view to raise moral claims against world-historical act and agents. They stand outside of morality.[78]

The interests they serve are the interests of the Spirit, whose aim is freedom.

The founders of classical Marxism articulated essentially the same argument. The underlying substructure of society, its mode of production, necessitates a supporting superstructure, the ethical components of which are morality and codified law. Forms of conduct are good or bad at different stages of historical development insofar as they support or impair the viability of a specific economic substructure. In ethics as well as law, a system of values provides the norms of conduct, and this system reflects the ideas and interests of the controlling economic class, which itself represents the needs of the economic system of which it is an embodiment. Communists, therefore, do not preach morality. The personal virtues of individuals correspond to positive norms of conduct established to satisfy demands leveled by the economic conditions prevailing in a specific historic context. As long as an economic system is viable, morality means conformity to established norms. When a new historical period commences, there is a "growing perception that existing social institutions are unreasonable and unjust, that reason has become unreason and right wrong. . . ."[79] As a consequence of this conception of morality, individual morality is treated as though it belonged to a subordinate order of real existence. It is sacrificed in the conflict of economic forces. G. D. H. Cole[80] recognizes that this disposition to so conceive individual morality is a consequence of Marx's (and Engels') commitment to a quasi-Hegelian conception of man as an *essentially* social being. The ultimate moral justification of behavior is its conformity to the "hidden laws" of social development, for, as Engels argues, in the course of that development "there has on the whole been progress in morality. . . . A really human morality that stands above class antagonisms and above any recollection of them becomes possible only at a stage of society which has not only overcome class antagonisms but has even forgotten them in practical life."[81] The really human morality is realized only in that society defined as the association of free producers in which man as man will be fulfilled. Marxian morality, like Hegelian morality, finds the ultimate standard of justification in history itself: in the final historic fulfillment of man as man, in a community of men, for community is the essence of man.

Thus, neither Marx nor Engels ever lost sight of the ultimate normative character of history. They never invoked moral sentiments because they understood such sentiments to be nothing but by-products of the forces governing the *essentially moral process of history itself*. Revolution was not inevitable because moral sentiments were aroused against the order of things—rather, moral sentiments were aroused because the order of things was involved in insoluble contradictions and made revolution inevitable. The historical action of the revolutionary proletariat was not the outcome of what this or that proletariat or the entire proletariat itself considered the good life—rather revolution would be the consequence of what the proletariat *was*. The proletariat represented the next, and final, stage of historical development. It represented productive forces in rebellion against outmoded economic conditions of the present. But that the revolution *was*, in some ultimate sense, moral was implicit in everything they wrote. Marx speaks of "advance" in the conception of equality and deplores the "defects" in application of equal rights that will be unavoidable even in the earlier phases of communism. Engels speaks of the "really human morality" that communism will bring, and the "realm of freedom" was always the normative ideal of classical Marxism.

The distinctions between Hegelianism and classical Marxism arise out of the endeavor on Marx's part to produce a science of society. Marx attempted to lay the foundations of an empirical study of men in association. The paradigmatic model that he sought to emulate was one which was eminently successful in the natural sciences. As early as 1843, when he was twenty-five years of age, he announced his intention of studying the relations that obtained between individuals and groups in society with the same techniques that produced the theoretical propositions of chemistry; in his maturity, in his preface to *Capital*, he again indicated his intention of studying society in the same manner as the physicist studies physical phenomena. The result was the postulational system briefly outlined above. Out of the wealth of phenomena select variables were identified as primary and having determinate causal priority. The specific scientific merits of the attempt are not the present concern. Instead we have focused on the fact that classical Marxism, although it shares some of the essentials of the Hegelian analysis, entertains a much more confining conception of morality and ethics than that of Hegelianism.

Furthermore, because of its attempt at rigor, classical Marxism tended to assimilate into its system the concepts of race, people, nation, and state as dependent rather than independent determinates. These concepts could have no explanatory function in historical analysis, but instead they required explanation in terms of the economy of any specific period. Thus, although race is spoken of as a "factor," and the Aryan and Semitic races are characterized as "superior," race is understood to be determined, in the last analysis, by economic causes. The superiority of the gifted Aryans and Semites is explicable on the grounds of their plentiful meat and milk diet, and their virtues are the consequence of their economic organization.[82] Such differences are induced and can be altered by historical, that is, economic, influences. The same analysis is pursued with respect to "dying" and "energetic" peoples. When Engels speaks of the Bohemian and South Slavonian people and the "mighty" Germans, he is not to be understood to be assigning causal efficacy to peoples as such.[83] When he deprecates a people as a "phthisical body of men," his judgment is based on their lack of economic viability. A "dying" or "retrograde" people is a people that does not possess the "very first conditions of national existence"; they are opposed to the "historical tendency" and can only be absorbed, subdued and assimilated by the "physical and intellectual power of the Germans."[84]

Thus, the analysis of nationality and nationalism follows a similar and equally remorseless logic. Classical Marxism was ardently reductivist, monocausal, and unilinear. A primitive communist community was impelled by a qualitative improvement in productive forces to develop a larger territorial confine and the city-state was the consequence. When the economy matured and commerce increased, the city-state no longer remained an adequate vehicle, and the drive for empire began. The modern nation-state was the consequence of the rise of the bourgeoisie. Given the developments in the forces of production and the processes of exchange, the bourgeoisie required a large geographic base of operations protected by a strong state that maintained specific constitutional guarantees protecting individual property and enforcing contracts.[85] The political structure of the productive community always provides an adequate vehicle for specific class interests. When society achieves that level of economic development required for the advent of socialism—the development of a world market, international trade, and the uniformity of the mode of production—national differences and antagonisms between peoples vanish. Knowing this, Communists have no national loyalties; they have no interests separate from those of the proletariat as a whole. They know no fatherland. Unlike other revolutionary socialists, the Marxists, as Marx understood them, bring to the front the common interests of the entire proletariat, independently of all nationality. National sentiment, as such, is a bourgeois snare, although national liberation movements may be progressive in the sense that they move with the tendency of history. National sentiment is retrograde and reactionary when it attempts to retard historical development. Historical development means rapid industrial exploitation and expanding trade. Thus Engels, in discussing the

Mexican War in North America, considers American nationalism serving "the interests of civilization" by wresting California "from the lazy Mexicans who did not know what to do with it." The "energetic Yankees have increased the medium of circulation, have concentrated in a few years a heavy population and an extensive trade on the most suitable part of the Pacific Coast, have built great cities, have opened up steamship lines, are laying railroads from New York to San Francisco. . . . Because of this the 'independence' of a few Spanish Californians and Texans may suffer, occasionally 'Justice' and other moralistic principles may be injured, but what do they count compared to such world historic events?"[86] He went on to argue, "When it is a question of the existence, of the free development of all the resources of great nations, then . . . sentimentalities . . . will decide nothing." It is a question of "trade, industry and profitable methods of agriculture, . . . [the] level of social development of the individual peoples, . . . [the] influence of the more highly developed nation on the undeveloped one." It is the destiny of advanced industrial nations to bind "tiny, crippled, powerless little nations together in a great Empire, and thereby [enable] them to take part in an historical development which, if left to themselves, would [remain] entirely foreign to them! To be sure such a thing is not carried through without forcibly crushing many a delicate little national flower. But without force and without an iron ruthlessness nothing is accomplished in history. . . ."[87]

Such national conquest is justified by history, since it promotes industrial development. The expansion of the productive forces strengthens the revolutionary proletariat, which, in turn, is destined to abolish classes and consequently nationalities and nationalism in universal emancipation.[88] Nationalisms are licensed only by serving the interests of the international proletariat. Those nationalisms that serve the proletarian interests are commended; those that do not are deplored. Nationalism, as such, has no value—its historic import is derived. The class-conscious proletariat recognize nationalism for what it is. They use it when it is in the international and historic interests of their class, but they themselves are immune to its contagion. In the *Communist Manifesto* nationalism among the proletariat of the advanced capitalist countries was declared already moribund, a residue of an earlier historic epoch that was about to dissipate itself forever.

Classical Marxism's pronouncements on the state were equally unequivocal. The state, as such, was not an independent historical determinant. The state was a machine for class oppression generated by the productive forces of society. Increased productivity had riven society into mutually opposed classes, and the state was the instrument of ensuring internal stability.

The state is . . . by no means a power forced on society from without; just as little is it "the reality of the ethical idea," "the image and reality of reason," as Hegel maintains. Rather, it is a product of society at a certain stage of development; it is the admission that this society has become entangled in an insoluble contradiction with itself, that it is cleft into irreconcilable antagonisms which it is powerless to dispel.[89]

The state represents the class interests of the oppressors in a a state divided into the oppressed and their oppressors. Should a state come to represent the interests of society as a whole, it would become superfluous. It would render itself unnecessary. It would proceed to "wither away of itself." When society organizes production on the basis of a free and equal association of producers the "whole machinery of state [will be put] where it will then belong: into the Museum of Antiquities, by the side of the spinning wheel and the bronze axe."[90]

Society thus far, based upon class antagonisms, had need of the state, that is, of an organization of the particular class, which was *pro tempore* the exploiting class, for the maintenance of its external conditions of production, and, therefore, especially, for the purpose of forcibly keeping the exploited classes in the condition of oppression corresponding with the given mode of production. . . . When at last it becomes the representative of the whole of society, it renders itself unnecessary. As soon as there is no longer any social class to be held in subjection; as soon as class rule, and the individual struggle for existence based upon our present anarchy in production, with the collisions and excesses arising from these, are removed, nothing more remains to be repressed, and a special repressive force, a state, is no longer necessary. The first act by virtue of which the state really consti-

tutes itself the representative of the whole of society—the taking possession of the means of production in the name of society—this is, at the
same time, its last independent act as a state. State interference in social
relations becomes, in one domain after another, superfluous, and then
withers away of itself. . . . The state is not "abolished." *It withers
away.*[91]

In a society in which the productive relations are compatible
with the fully matured productive forces, there is no material
base for the existence of classes. Where there are no classes,
there can be no state, for the state is a machine for oppression.
Where there is no state, there is a free association of producers,
a community of rational freedom, the fulfillment of man as man.

Classical Marxism constitutes perhaps the most ambitious
attempt in the history of social and political philosophy to provide a justificatory argument for a specific organization of society.
Its ultimate appeal is to a set of theoretical propositions supporting a special interpretation of history. That interpretation sees
history impelled upon a dialectical course which necessarily
culminates in an ideal society. That society is ideal because it is
in accord with the very essence of man—it is his fulfillment.
History is infused with moral purpose.

One final but critical difference distinguishes classical Marxism from Hegelianism. Both Marx and Engels were convinced
that capitalism itself would produce a *majority* of men aware of
the identity of their immediate interests with those of the collectivity that constituted their essence. Much of what Marx and
Engels wrote supports the thesis that they were radical democrats, that they were convinced that the forces in operation in
capitalist society would produce a majority of critically conscious human beings who would identify their person interests
with the interests of their productive community. This consciousness would arise spontaneously. It would be an "efflux," a
"reflex" of prevailing material conditions. The tensions that
transformed classical Marxism into Leninism center around this
notion of a spontaneous, majoritarian revolution.

Notes

1. G. Hegel, *Reason in History: A General Introduction to the Philosophy of History* [*RH*], trans. by R. S. Hartman (New York: Bobbs-Merrill, 1953), pp. 52, 55. Copyright © 1953, by The Liberal Arts Press, Inc. Reprinted by permission of The Liberal Arts Press Division of The Bobbs-Merrill Company, Inc.

2. G. Hegel, "Aus Jenenser Vorlesungen," *Dokumente zu Hegels Entwicklung*, ed. by J. Hoffmeister (Stuttgart: Frommanns, 1936), p. 352. See also G. Hegel *Encyklopädie der philosophischen Wissenschaften im Grundrisse*, Rosenkranz edition (Berlin: Heimann, 1870), pp. 2f.

3. G. Hegel, *The Philosophy of History* [*PH*], trans. by J. Sibree (New York: Dover, 1956), p. 447.

4. J. Ritter, *Hegel un die französiche Revolution* (Frankfurt am Main: Suhrkamp, 1965), pp. 24f.

5. G. Hegel, *The Philosophy of Right* [*PR*], ed. and trans. by T. M. Knox (New York: Oxford University Press, 1942), Para. 4.

6. G. Hegel, "Differenz des Fichteschen und Schellingschen Systems der Philosophie," *Werke* (Berlin: Duncker und Humblot, 1832), I, p. 237.

7. G. Hegel, "Fragment of a System," *Early Theological Writings* [*ETW*], trans. by T. M. Knox (Chicago: University of Chicago Press, 1948), p. 310.

8. G. Hegel, *The Phenomenology of Mind* [*PM*], ed. by Baille (New York: Macmillan, 1949), p. 81.

9. "Love," *ETW*, p. 305.

10. *PR*, Para. 260.

11. G. Hegel, *The Philosophy of Fine Arts* (London: George Bell, 1920), I, p. 243.

12. *PM*, Sec. II and p. 229; Hegel, *Encyklopädie*, Paras. 431ff.

13. *PM*, pp. 716f., 729. See also Hegel, *Encyklopädie*, Paras. 445–68; *PM*, pp. 340, 529f.

14. *PM*, p. 729.

15. See also G. Mueller's translation of the first edition of the *Encyclopedia* (New York: Philosophical Library, 1959), Para. 370.

16. J. N. Findlay, *Hegel: A Re-examination* (New York: Collier, 1962), p. 304.

17. *PR*, Para. 192, Addition, 120; see also Para. 190.

18. *PM*, pp. 229–40; *PH*, p. 241; *PR*, Para. 67. See also G. Lukacs, *Der junge Hegel: Über die Beziehungen von Dialektik und Ökonomie*

(Zurich: Europa Verlag, 1948), pp. 411f., 439; and G. Stiehler, *Die Dialektik in Hegels "Phänomenologie des Geistes"* (Berlin: Akademie Verlag, 1964), p. 201; see also *PR*, Para. 71.

19. See also *PR*, Para. 5 and Addition.

20. G. Hegel, *Kritik der Verfassung Deutschlands* (Kassel: Fisher, 1893), p. 118; *PR*, Para. 5.

21. *PR*, Para. 15.

22. J. Rousseau, *The Social Contract*, trans. by W. Kendall (Chicago: Regnery, 1954), Chap. vii.

23. *PR*, Para. 273.

24. *RH*, pp. 54f.

25. *Ibid.*, p. 52.

26. Hegel, *Encyklopädie*, Paras. 396, 409ff.

27. *PH*, p. 446.

28. *RH*, p. 40; see also Hegel, "Über die neuesten inneren Verhältnisse Württembergs," *Kritik*, p. 139.

29. Hegel, *Encyklopädie*, Para. 393. See also Hegel's discussion of race in *PH*, pp. 95, 96, 98, 288, 420f.

30. Stiehler, *op. cit.*, pp. 205f. See also *RH*, pp. 26ff., 49; *PR*, Paras. 189–98; and Lukacs, *op. cit.*, Chap. iii, Sec. 6.

31. *PR*, Para. 29; see also Paras. 273 and 324.

32. Hegel, *Kritik*, pp. 1–3; "Erster Entwurf zur 'Verfassung des Deutschen Reiches,'" *Dokumente*, pp. 284f. See also J. Barion, *Hegel und die marxistische Staatslehre* (Bonn: Bouvier, 1963), pp. 18, 24.

33. *RH*, p. 63.

34. "The Positivity of the Christian Religion," *ETW*, p. 154.

35. "The Spirit of Christianity," *ETW*, pp. 284–86.

36. *PR*, Para. 274; see also Paras. 267, 269, 272.

37. K. Marx in K. Marx and F. Engels, *Historisch-Kritische Gesamtausgabe* (Frankfurt am Main: Verlagsgesellschaft M.B.H., 1927), Part I, Vol. I, Sec. I, p. 63; see also T. I. Oiserman, *Die Entstehung der marxistischen Philosophie* (Berlin: Dietz, 1965), p. 27.

38. K. Marx, *Economic and Philosophic Manuscripts* [*EPM*] (Moscow: Foreign Languages, n.d.), pp. 104f. Italics supplied.

39. M. Hess, "Die letzten Philosophen," *Philosophische und sozialistische Schriften: 1837–1850* (Berlin: Akademie, 1961), p. 381.

40. Hess, "Über die Sozialistische Bewegung in Deutschland," *ibid.*, p. 284. See also *ibid.*, p. 285 and "Über das Geldwesen," *ibid.*, p. 330.

41. K. Marx, "On the Jewish Question" *Early Writings*, ed. by T. Bottomore (New York: McGraw-Hill, 1964), pp. 15, 20.

42. K. Marx, "Der leitende Artikel in Nr. 179 der 'Kölnischen Zeitung,'" in K. Marx and F. Engels, *Werke* [*MEW*] (Berlin: Dietz, 1957–), I, p. 104.

43. I. Fetscher, "Das Verhältnis des Marxismus zu Hegel," *Marxismusstudien* (Tübingen: Mohr, 1960), III, p. 85.

44. Compare Marx, "On the Jewish Question" *Early Writings*, pp. 8, 10, 15, 16 and *RH*, p. 33.

45. K. Marx and F. Engels, *The Holy Family or Critique of Critical Critiques* [*HF*] (Moscow: Foreign Languages, 1956), p. 162.

46. *EPM*, p. 145.

47. K. Marx, "Contribution to the Critique of Hegel's Philosophy of Right," *Early Writings*, p. 52.

48. *Ibid.*, p. 59; "Briefe aus den 'Deutsch-Französischen Jahrbüchern,'" *MEW*, I, pp. 338f.

49. K. Marx, "Contribution . . .," *Early Writings*, p. 43; "Theses on Feuerbach," in K. Marx and F. Engels, *The German Ideology* [*GI*], ed. and trans. by R. Pascal (New York: International, 1947), p. 198. Copyright © 1947, by International Publishers Co., Inc. Reprinted by permission of International Publishers Co., Inc.

50. *EPM*, pp. 176, 178, 180. This same thesis is developed in "Kritik des Hegelschen Staatsrechts," *MEW*, I, pp. 206, 209, 213, 224, 233.

51. *HF*, pp. 78f., 173. See also K. Marx, *The Poverty of Philosophy* [*PP*] (Moscow: Foreign Languages, n.d.), pp. 120f.

52. *HF*, pp. 107, 125. See also *ibid.*, pp. 59, 81f.; *GI*, pp. 5, 17, 28, 33f., 42f.; *PP*, p. 118.

53. *GI*, pp. 6f., 14, 16–18.

54. K. Marx, *Capital* (Moscow: Foreign Languages, 1954), I, p. 179.

55. *GI*, pp. 7, 14.

56. K. Marx, *A Contribution to the Critique of Political Economy* (Chicago: Charles Kerr, 1918), pp. 11f.

57. *PP*, p. 122.

58. *GI*, p. 71.

59. K. Marx, *Capital*, I, p. 10; III, p. 798. See also M. M. Bober, *Karl Marx's Interpretation of History* (New York: Norton, 1965), p. 81.

60. F. Engels, *Anti-Duehring: Herr Eugen Duehring's Revolution in Science* [*AD*] (Moscow: Foreign Languages, n.d.), p. 367.

61. F. Engels, *Ludwig Feuerbach and the End of Classical German Philosophy*; K. Marx and F. Engels, *Selected Works in Two Volumes* [*MESW*] (Moscow: Foreign Languages, 1955), II, p. 390.

62. *GI*, p. 22; Marx, *A Contribution*, p. 12.

63. *AD*, p. 378.

64. Engels to Starkenburg, January 25, 1894, in *MESW*, II, pp. 504f.

65. Engels, "Outlines of a Critique of Political Economy," *EPM*, p. 183.

66. *GI*, pp. 74f. See also Marx, "On the Jewish Question," *Early Writings*, pp. 8, 10f., 15; *Capital*, III, p. 799.

67. *PR*, Para. 257.

68. "Die britische Herrschaft in Indien," *New York Daily Tribune*, June 25, 1853, in *MEW*, IX, p. 129; see also K. Wittfogel, *Oriental Despotism* (New Haven: Yale, 1963), p. 374.

69. *PH*, pp. 308f.; Hegel, "Erster Entwurf zu 'Verfassung des Deutschen Reiches,'" *Dokumente*, p. 285.

70. "The Positivity of the Christian Religion," *ETW*, p. 158f.; "The Spirit of Christianity," *ETW*, p. 284.

71. Hegel, "Politische Studien," *Dokumente*, p. 281.

72. Marx, "Contribution . . . ," *Early Writings*, pp. 43f.

73. *AD*, pp. 382, 388f., 391. See also *GI*, pp. 71–75.

74. *AD*, pp. 131f.

75. *PH*, pp. 254, 378, 382f., 407.

76. Engels to N. F. Danielson, October 17, 1893, *MESW*, II, p. 503.

77. *Ibid.*

78. *RH*, pp. 39f., 42f., 82f.

79. *AD*, p. 365.

80. G. D. H. Cole, *The Meaning of Marxism* (Ann Arbor: University of Michigan, 1964), p. 60.

81. *AD*, p. 132.

82. Engels, "Origin of the Family, Private Property and the State," *MESW*, II, p. 189; *Zur Geschichte und Sprache der deutschen Frühzeit* (Berlin: Dietz, 1952), pp. 32f.

83. F. Engels, *Germany: Revolution and Counter-revolution* (New York: International, 1933), pp. 85f.

84. See F. Engels, "Hungary and Panslavism" and "Democratic Panslavism," in K. Marx and F. Engels, *The Russian Menace to Europe*, ed. by P. Blackstone and B. Hoselitz (New York: Free Press, 1952), pp. 56–67, 67–84.

85. *GI*, p. 59.

86. Engels, "Democratic Panslavism," *The Russian Menace to Europe*, p. 71.

87. *Ibid.*, pp. 71, 74, 75, 76.

88. *GI*, p. 69.

89. Engels, "Origin . . . ," *MESW*, II, pp. 317f.

90. *Ibid.*, p. 321. See also Engels' Introduction to Marx, "The Civil War in France," *MESW*, I, p. 485; *AD*, pp. 383–89.

91. *AD*, pp. 384f.

III · *LENINISM AND*
LENINISMS

Classical Marxism was a substantive social and political philosophy in the sense that it was developed as a theory that included ethical or ideal purpose. Marx thought that he had formulated a "natural science of society" that provided a general causal account of the main trends of human development, trends that culminated in the fulfillment of man in a society of rational freedom. This dual descriptive and normative character was implicit in the conceptual model of man that Marx adopted and adapted from Hegel. "Man is," Marx contended, "in the most literal sense a *zoon politikon*, not merely a social animal, but an animal that can develop into an individual only in society." Marx devoted himself to the study of material production because his model of man construed man as essentially a denizen of a *productive* community. Such a conceptual definition entails not only the presupposition of Marx's theoretical work, but also imparts to it a normative character. He postulates the individuality and fulfillment of man as a normative ideal attainable only in a rationally organized productive community.

Marx's conceptual model of man is here understood as a

descriptive frame of reference that suggests modes of general relations of the facts implicit in the descriptive terms employed. Such a model serves to identify and classify empirical data that the investigator can then employ in the construction of a theoretical system of verifiable experimental hypotheses. Such a conceptualization consists of a suggested definition or coordinated definitions that, as definitions, cannot be verified. The model itself makes no experimental claims. The claims are made only in the theoretical system constructed on the basis of the model. The model is a heuristic device that is justified pragmatically by its utility in organizing the wealth of observational data economically and fruitfully. In principle the conceptual model should always remain subject to modification, elaboration or even abandonment as a consequence of predictive poverty, a more adequate organization of data, or new analytic insights.

When a conceptual model is employed in constructing a theoretical system, the ordering of propositions indicates all the implications of the model. Particularly in the immature sciences, this drawing out of implications often necessitates alteration of the original conceptual model. This is especially true in a discipline as loose as sociology, in which concepts are defined in, and employ the syntax of, ordinary language. The most compelling virtue of such theorizing in a science like sociology is that the theory provides a parsimonious summary of actual or anticipated research results. Where observations do not satisfy anticipated results, we speak of disconfirmation, and alterations are undertaken within the body of theory or the conceptual model that served as a guide to the theory.

Much of classical Marxism suffers from methodological shortcomings. The original conceptual model is sufficiently vague to accommodate a multitude of alternate, and even mutually exclusive, explications. Essentially it is the conceptual model employed by Hegel but reoriented by a methodological empiricism and supplemented by a redefinition of man that construes him as a productive animal characterized by his ability to fashion tools. The theoretical system suggested by this redefinition is one that attempts to order empirical propositions by making an inventory of determinants and directing the strategy of research and explanation by isolating the prime variables. Such an ordering involves some sort of classificatory scheme to identify the variables. For example, variables are identified as belonging to the productive forces, to the relations of production, to the superstructure or to class interests—to specify only the most prominent categories. Changes in variables belonging to one or another category are related in a lawlike manner, indicating the direction in which variables influence each other. But many of the classificatory concepts of classical Marxism are notoriously ill-defined. The "productive forces," for example, are never clearly identified—nor is "class" defined with precision anywhere. Furthermore, the relations that obtain between variables in any reasonably well formulated theoretical system can be characterized as reversible or irreversible, deterministic or stochastic, sequential or coextensive, sufficient or contingent, necessary or substitutable. It is difficult to identify any of these relations between specific variables in classical Marxism. In critical cases the relationship between variables is described only in metaphor. We are informed that "conceiving, thinking, the mental intercourse of men, appear . . . as the direct efflux of their material behavior" and ideology is an "echo," a "reflex" of their material life process. "The phantoms formed in the human brain are also, necessarily, sublimates of their material life-process." It is impossible to formulate a testable hypothesis on the basis of such locutions. The very vagueness of many of Marx's propositions renders them intractable to any known empirical test.

The inordinate use of pictorial language, the lack of precise terminology, and the obscure relationships that purportedly connect variables all indicate that Ferdinand Tönnies was correct in characterizing classical Marxism as a fleeting outline of a theory.[2] To fill in the outline, it would at least be necessary to establish precisely the nature of the process by which the institutional, emotional, moral, philosophical, religious, political, and legal elements that animate a society are determined by the economic substructure. Such an attempt was never undertaken by the founders of classical Marxism. Much of the subsequent transformation of Marxism into Leninism is explicable on the grounds of the theoretical poverty of the original system. Vladimir Ilyich Lenin was faced with a dynamic and urgently real situation, and at critical junctures classical Marxism was a poor guide to action. Under the strain of one of the most demanding periods of man's history, classical Marxism underwent major revision and emerged as Leninism.

Leninism

• Lenin conceived of himself, and for all intents and purposes qualified, as an orthodox Marxist. He accepted the social and political philosophy of classical Marxism in its entirety and focused his attention on its scientific claims. His acceptance of Marxism entailed his acceptance of the Marxist model of man and society. Lenin committed himself to the conviction that "society [is] a living organism in its functioning and development" and rejected the contractualist view of "society being a mechanical aggregation of individuals. . . ."[3] The individual could be understood only as the product of his *social* being. The "sum of the strivings of all the members of a given society . . . stem from the difference in the position and mode of life of the *classes* into which each society is divided." The difference in position and mode of life of classes is, in turn, determined by the existing conflict between the social productive forces and the relations of production. Thus Lenin quoted Marx approvingly, "individual . . . consciousness must be explained . . . from the contradiction of material life. . . ." And he added, "all ideas and all the various tendencies *stem* from the condition of the material forces of production."[4]

. . . Marx's basic idea [is] that the development of the social-economic formations is a process of natural history. . . . By what means did Marx arrive at this basic idea? He did so by singling out the economic sphere from the various spheres of social life, by singling out production relations from all social relations as being basic, primary, determining all other relations.

Marxism, he continued, carried the analysis of the individual's ideas deeper, "to the origin of man's social ideas themselves; and its conclusion that the course of ideas depends on the course of things is the only one compatible with scientific psychology."[5] Once this is established, Lenin contends:

It is quite enough if, while proving the necessity of the present order of things, he at the same time proves the necessity of another order which must inevitably grow out of the preceding one regardless of whether men believe in it or not, whether they are conscious of it or not. Marx treats the social movement as a process of natural history, governed by laws not only independent of human will, consciousness and intentions, but rather, on the contrary, determining the will, consciousness and intentions of men. . . . If the conscious element plays so subordinate a part in the history of civilization, it is self-evident that a critique whose subject is civilization, can least of all take as its basis any form of, or any result of, consciousness.[6]

Employing this rationale, Lenin could reject "the absurd tale about free will," knowing that "consciousness is a thing which the world *must* acquire, whether it likes it or not." The primary agency of social development is the material life process and the "fact that the workers become united, welded together, and organized" in the struggle for a socialist society "is a derivative and secondary phenomenon."[7]

The substance of this analysis was common to the Russian Marxists of the turn of the century. Georgy Valentinovich Plekhanov, Lenin's intellectual mentor, had summarized the Marxist view in a variety of places. The conceptual model of man that Plekhanov employed in his account is that of Marx—man is essentially a social animal, a tool-making social animal. What man is, what man will become, is explicable and comprehensible only within a functional context that considers the individual as one element inextricably involved in a productive community. "Habits, manners, views, aspirations and ideals," Plekhanov contended, "will necessarily have to adapt themselves to men's way of life, to their mode of procuring their subsistence. The psychology of society is always expedient in relation to its economy, always corresponds to it, is always determined by it."[8] What a man is will reflect the conditions obtaining in the mode of production of the community of which he is a member. "Sociology only becomes a science," Plekhanov argued, "in proportion to the degree to which sociologists are able to understand the appearance of specific aims in social man (social 'teleology') as a necessary consequence of the social process, determined in the last analysis by the march of economic evolution," and "the principal cause of the social historical process is the development of the productive forces. . . ."9

These related propositions produced a theoretical sketch of man that "regarded man's nature itself as the eternally changing result of historical progress, the cause of which lies *outside* man," for "the forces of production are the outcome of a necessity determined by extant conditions external to man." Processes immanent in history itself produced changes in human consciousness. An understanding of the natural laws governing historical progression provided a corresponding appreciation of anticipated changes in human consciousness. Thus, Plekhanov could maintain that "when a class longing for emancipation brings about a social revolution, it acts in a way which is more or less appropriate to the desired end; and, in any case, its activity is the cause of that revolution. But this activity, together with all the aspirations which have brought it about, is itself the effect of economic evolution, and therefore, is itself determined by necessity." These theoretical convictions produced an assessment of human agents characterized by Plekhanov's description of a Marxist:

> The Marxist serves as an instrument of . . . necessity and cannot help doing so, owing to his social status and to his mentality and temperament, which were created by his status. . . . Since his social status has imbued him with this character and no other, he not only serves as an instrument of necessity and cannot help doing so, but he passionately desires, and cannot help desiring, to do so, [for] in the last analysis, everything depends upon the . . . development of productive forces and the mutual relations between men in the social economic process of production.10

Both Lenin and Plekhanov understood individual and class consciousness as dependent variables, derived as the necessary consequence of antecedent causes. This interpretation of classical Marxism is supported by specific factual claims advanced by Marx and Engels as well as by their entire theoretical orientation. In a variety of places both Marx and Engels construed the relationship between the economic base and collective consciousness as eminently simple. Marx spoke of consciousness as an "echo" and "efflux" of material conditions. In *Capital* he spoke of "the process of production" that "lays bare the mode of formation of his social relations, and of the mental conceptions that flow from them." Engels spoke of modern socialism as nothing but the reflex, in thought, of the conflict that had arisen between productive forces and productive relations. There is, of course, good internal evidence that both Marx and Engels later came to view the relationship between consciousness and objective, material conditions as more complex, but they never attempted a systematic explication that would yield a testable hypothesis.[11] What they left to their heirs was a collection of loosely worded and loosely formulated propositions that more than suggested that the working class would "spontaneously organize" and that "revolutions are not intentionally and capriciously made, but rather have universally been the necessary consequence of conditions completely independent of the will and leadership of the individual parties and entire classes."[12] But the relationship between being and consciousness was never clearly explicated. That proletarian life conditions should produce a proletarian consciousness seems at least intuitively plausible. But Marx also wished to maintain that a "communist consciousness" might arise among the other classes too through their recognition of the situation of the proletariat. In the *Communist Manifesto* he suggests that some members of the bourgeoisie can raise themselves to the level of theoretically comprehending the historical movement as a whole.

The relationship between being and consciousness can hardly be adequately represented as a reflex, an echo, or an efflux. Nor can consciousness be characterized as "flowing" from the mode of production. These metaphors obscure rather than clarify the putative relationship between the variables. For a theoretical system, such weaknesses are to be lamented, but their consequences for a developing *ideology* are, as will be suggested, onerous.

At the turn of the century Lenin found himself facing the tactical and strategic problems of directing a revolutionary movement. The question of proletarian consciousness was no longer a theoretical problem but a real and an urgent one. Many Russian Marxists had taken Lenin and Plekhanov at their word. Revolution would be the necessary consequence of the maturation of the objective conditions that develop with an in-

herent logic of their own. Class consciousness, class organization, and ultimately even revolution would be the spontaneous
consequence of the development of the productive forces. Since
consciousness could not precede this development, there was a
mild, somewhat detached, expectation that the proletariat would,
when conditions so determined, spontaneously organize itself.
If the working class did not feel disposed to organize, it could
only mean that objective conditions had not matured sufficiently.
Under the influence of these notions it was difficult to know
what the small revolutionary cadre of working men were obliged
to do besides wait.

In the spring and summer of 1894 Lenin had written *What
the "Friends of the People" Are*, in which the conscious element
was understood to play a subordinate part in history. By 1900
he argued that the working class movement would become "petty
and inevitably bourgeois" if isolated from the Social Democratic
party. This thesis gave the party added significance. In some
sense a strong, well-organized party was necessary in the class
struggle. By the end of 1901 Lenin was formulating the rationale
for a strong and active party organization. He maintained that

. . . the "ideologist" is worthy of the name only when he precedes
the *spontaneous* movement, points out the road, and is able ahead of
all others to solve all the theoretical, political, tactical and organizational questions which the "material elements" of the movement spontaneously encounter. . . . One must be able to point out the dangers
and defects of spontaneity and to *elevate* it to the level of consciousness.[13]

He argued that the spontaneous awakening of the masses must
be *led* by ideologists so well trained theoretically that there could
be no vacillations. These ideologists would constitute the conscious element necessary to direct the spontaneous element. By
the winter of 1901 Lenin defined the fundamental tactical problem that faced Marxist theoreticians as the definition of the
relationship between consciousness and spontaneity.

Lenin contended:

The history of all countries shows that the working class, exclusively by its own effort, is able to develop only trade-union con-

sciousness, i.e., the conviction that it is necessary to combine in unions, fight the employers and strive to compel the government to pass necessary labor legislation, etc. The theory of socialism, however, grew out of the philosophic, historical and economic theories that were elaborated by the educated representatives of the propertied classes, the intellectuals. According to their social status, the founders of modern scientific socialism, Marx and Engels, themselves belonged to the bourgeois intelligentsia. In the very same way, in Russia, the theoretical doctrine of Social Democracy arose quite independently of the spontaneous growth of the working class movement, it arose as a natural and inevitable outcome of the development of ideas among the revolutionary socialist intelligentsia.[14]

Lenin specifically rejected the thesis that the pure working class movement could produce a revolutionary ideology. A Social Democratic consciousness could only be brought to the workers from without. He proceeded to identify himself with the position assumed by Karl Kautsky. "Modern socialist consciousness can arise only on the basis of profound scientific knowledge. . . . The vehicle of science is not the proletariat, but the bourgeois intelligentsia. . . . Thus, socialist consciousness is something introduced into the proletarian class struggle from without, and not something that [arises] within it spontaneously." Lenin concluded that the spontaneity of the working class inevitably led it to bourgeois ideology. Social Democracy was therefore obliged to *"combat spontaneity . . . divert* the working class movement from this spontaneous, trade-unionist striving to come under the wing of the bourgeoisie. . . . *A fierce struggle against spontaneity* was necessary. . . ."[15]

The obscure propositions inherited from classical Marxism describing consciousness as a reflex and echo of objective conditions underwent an obvious and startling reformulation. Only a few years previously Lenin and Plekhanov had understood the theory to maintain that "life itself will make [the workers] revolutionaries." They now understood it to mean that the social status of an individual, which determines his mentality, produces *bourgeois consciousness* among the working class and a *revolutionary socialist consciousness* among elements of the bourgeois intelligentsia! The consciousness that flows from the life conditions of the working class is a bourgeois consciousness. Bourgeois social status produces, among select members of the bourgeoisie, a truly socialist reflex. In order to produce a revolutionary consciousness among the working class, specially endowed bourgeois intellectuals mobilized in a party organization that would permit no vacillations must carry it to people from without. The true consciousness of the working class finds expression in the ideological formulations of a select group of bourgeois intellectuals. The spontaneous consciousness of the working class would forever remain bourgeois without the intercession of social democratic ideologues. Just how consciousness, intentions, motives, and dispositions depend on the course of things becomes increasingly obscure. Certainly Marx and Engels conceived the relationship differently. Marx argued that the propertied class manifested a conservative consciousness and the proletariat a revolutionary consciousness. The workers, Marx argued, "are most painfully aware . . . that property, capital, money, wage-labor, and the like are [the] . . . very practical, very objective sources of their self-estrangement and that they must be abolished in a practical, objective way for man to become man. . . ."[16] The entire logic of the *Communist Manifesto* turns on the inevitability of the working class becoming a self-conscious class of men that perceives its own interests and soon learns *how* it has to go about realizing them. The proletariat alone is a really revolutionary class.

The failure of classical Marxism to specify the relationships between the objective conditions of life and the consciousness those relations somehow produce permitted Lenin to wedge in his notion of a true *proletarian* consciousness that could be articulated only by a small minority of declassed *bourgeois* theoreticians. The liberating consciousness of proletarian revolution was to be brought to the working class from without. Only the party led by Lenin could speak in the ultimate interests of the working class revolution and the ultimate liberation of man. This Leninist conception is incorrigibly *elitist*. The party leadership speaks in the ultimate interests of the working class, and the working class has the mission to liberate mankind. The party, therefore, speaks for mankind. Armed with historical materialism—the Marxist interpretation of history, the only scientific conception of history—the party leadership directed the course of man's struggle for liberation, for the creation of "a paradise on earth."[17] The responsibility for elevating the consciousness of the working class and of humanity rested upon a small coterie of party leaders and a party organization that was highly centralized and hierarchical. The party leadership had the responsibility of command, and the working class, possessed of only bourgeois potential, had the responsibility of obedience. They obeyed because in obeying they conformed, in the last analysis, to the dictates of their own ultimate and real will. The spokesmen of that will were the world historical individuals organized in the minoritarian revolutionary party.

The changes in the face of Marxism that Lenin effected did not go unnoticed among the Marxists of the period. As early as 1904, Rosa Luxemburg highlighted the change.[18] She argued that if class consciousness could not manifest itself among the workers under *any* objective conditions then Marxism becomes committed to a form of elitism that would make the central committee of the party "the only thinking element." Not only would the masses be subject to the conscious will of the party, but the party itself would be subject to "absolute and blind submission" to the will of the party center. Luxemburg argued that the liberation of man through socialism was predicated on the increasing social and political maturity of the entire proletarian class, which was a consequence of the development of society itself. Consciousness could not be brought in from without, it must be the spontaneous development of the urban working class itself. Lenin's conception would "enslave . . . [the] movement to an intellectual elite hungry for power. . . ." Only a politically self-conscious and self-reliant proletarian class could protect itself against the opportunist intrigue and personal ambition of such an elite. But such protection is possible only if the industrial working class is capable of developing an effective consciousness of its own interests; according to classical Marxism, this could only be the consequence of a matured consciousness that reflects the economic and social conditions of an *advanced* industrial community. This final point constituted the focus of Karl Kautsky's criticism of Leninism.

What are the prerequisites for the establishment of socialism? . . . The will to socialism is the first condition for its accomplishment. This will is created by . . . great industry. . . . This will first appears amongst the masses when large-scale industry is already much developed. . . . To the ripening of the conditions, the necessary level of the industrial development, must be added the maturity of the proletariat, in order to make socialism possible.[19]

There is much implicit in the arguments of Luxemburg and Kautsky against Leninism. Marx and Engels had certainly suggested that socialism presupposed the fullest maturation of the economic forces of society. In the *Anti-Duehring*, Engels specifically maintained that the separation of society into exploiting and exploited classes was "the necessary consequence of the deficient and restricted development of production." A class society is the necessary consequence of the insufficiency of production and can only be

. . . swept away by the complete development of modern productive forces. And, in fact, the abolition of classes in society presupposes a degree of historical evolution at which the existence, not simply of this or that particular ruling class, but of any ruling class at all, and, therefore, the existence of class distinction itself has become an obsolete anachronism. It presupposes, therefore, the development of production carried out to a degree at which appropriation of the means of production and of the products, and, with this, of political domination, of the monopoly of culture, and of intellectual leadership by a particular class of society, has become not only superfluous but economically, politically, intellectually a hindrance to development.[20]

Classical Marxism presupposed (1) a class capable of achieving spontaneously an economic, political, and intellectual maturity as a consequence of (2) the maturation of the productive forces of society. Consciousness was a dependent variable, determined by the socioeconomic conditions prevailing in a given society. In the *Manifesto*, Marx complained that German philosophers, would-be philosophers, and *beaux esprits* had attempted to import French socialist ideas into semifeudal Germany, not appreciating that French social conditions could not be imported along with them. The result could only be a caricature of socialism.

Leninism developed in a primitive economic environment in which the organization of the working class had only begun. With the single-mindedness of a man bent on revolution, Lenin committed himself to the proposition that a revolutionary consciousness could only be imposed on the working class by a disciplined cadre of party leaders. These leaders took on all the characteristics of Hegel's world historical individuals whose "particular purposes contain the substantial will of the World Spirit. . . . They see the very truth of their age and their world, the next genus, so to speak, which is already formed in the womb of time."[21] Their will is the real will of all, and it is only these great men who can bring the sleeping will of the rest of mankind to consciousness.

It has been suggested that Nicholas Chernyshevsky, the Russian author of *What Is to Be Done?* inspired Lenin's essay of the same name, which contains his mature convictions concerning the imposition of consciousness upon the elemental potential of the masses. Lenin, like Chernyshevsky, saw the advent of socialism as the consequence of the submission of the spontaneous will of the masses to the implacable will of the self-conscious and dominant minority of professional ideologists. Lenin could be said to be a disciple of Chernyshevsky. Chernyshevsky himself had been a careful student of Hegel, whose philosophical principles he found "broad, profound, and fruitful." Chernyshevsky owed an enormous intellectual debt to Herzen, who had himself maintained that the philosophy of Hegel provided the algebra of revolution—and traces of Hegelianism abound in Chernyshevsky's writings. Whatever the case, Lenin's reformulation of classical Marxism began to exhibit more and more of the features of its Hegelian ancestry.

The maturation of classical Marxism into Leninist ideology proceeded through the first two decades of the twentieth century. Chronologically, the next strategic issue that required an altered doctrinal posture was the position the Bolsheviks were to assume with regard to World War I. The war had broken over the social democratic movement in Europe like the crack of doom. The classical Marxists had argued that economic development had created the material base for a universal human ethics and the proletariat that represented the progressive elements of that material base were necessarily imbued with an internationalist moral sentiment. The politically and theoretically mature working class could never be driven to shed blood for bourgeois interests. A war of more than local scope was dismissed as a serious possibility because of the maturity of the internationalist proletarian movement. The outbreak of hostilities and dissipation of this fiction of working class internationalism was the last, but perhaps the most emphatic, of the influences that brought Leninism to full maturity. The official Soviet biography of Lenin informs us:

> The war served as a severe test for all trends in the working class movement. The West-European Social Democratic parties, which long before the war had been corroded by opportunism, betrayed the working class and began to help the bourgeoisie in their respective countries to incite the workers and peasants of the different countries to fly at each other's throats ostensibly in the interests of "national defense," but actually in defense of the interests of the bourgeoisie. The Second International collapsed. The leaders of the Second International and most of the Socialist parties supported the war and backed their respective imperialist governments. In this menacing situation, when the Socialist parties were rocked to their foundations by the severe crisis, and the leaders of the working class movement proved to be traitors and renegades, only Lenin . . . unflinchingly hoisted the flag of opposition to the imperialist war.[22]

The most concrete expression of Lenin's opposition was a short book entitled *Imperialism: The Highest Stage of Capitalism*, which he wrote between January and July of 1916.

Lenin faced the theoretical necessity of explaining how it was possible that precisely in those countries that were the most economically mature the working class appeared most anxious to identify with national interests in a catastrophic war that destroyed the international working class movement. He sought to explain how the utter betrayal of socialism was possible at the hands of the class whose mission it was to lead the world revolution. Lenin's theoretical supplement to classical Marxism maintained that "capitalism has grown into a world system of colonial oppression and of the financial strangulation of the overwhelming majority of the people of the world by a handful of 'advanced' countries." The bourgeoisie of these "world marauder" nations employ the "super-profits" plundered from the backward areas to "bribe the labor leaders and the upper stratum of the labor aristocracy" of their respective nations, producing a stratum of workers who "live in more or less petty-bourgeois conditions of life. . . . This stratum of bourgeoisified workers, or the 'labor aristocracy,' who are quite philistine in their mode of life, in the size of their earnings and in their outlook, serves as the principal prop of the Second International, and, in our days, the principal *social . . . prop of the bourgeoisie.* They are the real *agents of the bourgeoisie in the labor movement,* the labor lieutenants of the capitalist class, real channels of reformism and chauvinism. In the civil war between the proletariat and the bourgeoisie they inevitably, and in no small numbers, stand side by side with the bourgeoisie. . . . Not the slightest progress can be made toward the solution of the practical problems of the Communist movement and of the impending social revolution unless the economic roots of this phenomenon are understood and unless its political and sociological significance is appreciated."[23]

Lenin thus returned once again to the vexing theme of the consciousness of the working class. Classical Marxism had held that the inherent tendencies of the capitalist economic system would generate the very forces that would destroy it. The maturation of the capitalist system would drive the middle class into the working class, reducing society to two classes in irreconcilable antagonism. The increasing misery of the working class would drive them to revolution while the increasing organization and discipline of the struggle against their oppressors would produce the requisite class consciousness. Lenin attempted a similar but altered interpretation. Lenin held that capitalism did, in fact, produce the very forces destined to destroy it. But he shifted the focus of attention from the proletariat of the advanced industrial nations to the rural peasant masses of the yet undeveloped nations. The capitalists of the advanced countries were rapaciously exploiting the colonial areas and with their booty were bribing the leadership of the working classes at home. A venal aristocracy of labor confused the elemental consciousness of the working classes in the advanced capitalist countries, dissipated their revolutionary potential, and reduced the possibility of radical social change. On the other hand, the capitalist exploitation of the colonial and backward areas of the world provoked increasing resistance. As early as 1913 Lenin cited the increasing restiveness in the underdeveloped colonial and semicolonial areas of the world.[24]

By 1917 this implication of Lenin's analysis was made one of the most prominent programmatic changes in Bolshevik strategy. The party should

> . . . emphasize more strongly and . . . express more vividly . . . the prominence of the handful of the richest imperialist countries which prosper parasitically by robbing colonies and weaker nations. This is an extremely important feature of imperialism. To a certain extent it facilitates the rise of powerful revolutionary movements in countries that are subjected to imperialist plunder and are in danger of being crushed and partitioned by the giant imperialists . . . and on the other hand, tends to a certain extent to prevent the rise of profound revolutionary movements in the countries that plunder, by imperialist methods, many colonies and foreign lands, and thus make a very large (comparatively) portion of their population *participants* in the division of the imperialist loot.[25]

According to this assessment insurrectionary movements tend to arise *first* in underdeveloped countries. The revolutionary potential of the working classes of the more highly developed nations diminishes as a consequence of the laboring population's involvement in the looting of the peripheral areas. Where classical Marxism had postulated a *positive* correlation between the level of industrial maturation and a revolutionary working class consciousness, Leninism postulated a *negative* one. This inversion of the functional relationship between variables forced the *party* to assume a still greater burden of responsibility than Lenin had originally suggested in bringing class consciousness to an amorphous mass of insurgents. If workers in the capitalist countries were incapable of developing a revolutionary class consciousness without the intercession of the radical intelligentsia, how much more critical is the role of the party intellectual in backward economies in which there is no urban proletarian class at all.

Lenin's original modifications of the relationship between the material life conditions and the consciousness that they determined were disquieting to classical Marxists because the

party leadership seemed to assume an exalted role in the production of working class consciousness. Lenin's subsequent
doctrine of imperialism forced him to assign a still more emphatic role to that leadership. The original Marxist pronouncements had undergone so significant a change as to be no longer
recognizable. In 1890, in a new introduction to the *Manifesto*,
Engels maintained that "for the ultimate triumph of the ideas
set forth in the *Manifesto* Marx relied solely and exclusively
upon the intellectual development of the working class as it
necessarily had to ensue from united action and discussion."
That intellectual development was to be the necessary consequence of economic struggle against developed capitalism, for
only under such conditions would the working class develop
the political and social maturity that would make theirs a
liberating revolution. A people not subject to the rigors of such
a material struggle remain subject to the "idiocy of rural life,"
the barbarism that is the necessary consequence of a primitive
economy. Peasant revolutionary movements were always understood by both Marx and Engels to be narrow-minded and reactionary. Engels forever emphasized the completely different levels
of civilization of the various peoples and their therefore equally
different political needs. Whatever democratic sentiments these
backward peoples might possess (which reflected the thinking
of those who had acquired their education abroad) must inevitably dissipate because "the actual world, the real circumstances of their countries, offer no or merely imaginary points
of contact. . . ."[26] Engels insisted that the evolution of the conditions of existence for a numerous, strong, concentrated, and
intelligent proletarian class goes hand in hand with the development of specific material (that is, economic) conditions. The
historical movement must consequently be from West to East.
If the revolution was to have the emancipating character classical Marxism had described, it could not be the product of a
people whose social consciousness had been determined by
primitive social and economic conditions. Engels explicitly
maintained:

The time of surprise attacks, of revolutions carried through by small
conscious minorities at the head of unconscious masses, is past. Where
it is a question of a complete transformation of the social organization,

the masses themselves must also be in it, must themselves already have grasped what is at stake, what they are going in for with body and soul.[27]

Between 1900 and 1917 Leninism had developed gradually from one or two shifts in theoretical emphasis. The first was the reformulation of the relationship that supposedly existed between working class consciousness and prevalent socioeconomic conditions. Lenin (and Kautsky) contended that true socialist consciousness could only be brought to the working class through the agency of a revolutionary party. What had consistently seemed to be a *substitutable variable* for classical Marxism (the revolution would be "instinctive, spontaneous, irrepressible" and would occur *with or without* a party or an articulate leadership) suddenly became a *necessary condition* (without a party possessed of the "true" theory there could be no revolution). By 1917 Leninism, with its increasing emphasis upon revolution in the backward countries, began to *suggest* that a revolutionary party was not only a necessity, but also *the* necessary and sufficient condition for revolution. To complete its transformation, Leninism had but to traverse one final phase.

Lenin's *The State and Revolution*, written on the eve of the Bolshevik Revolution, has been called the most cynical book ever written. As a matter of fact, it would seem that its most memorable quality for our time is its tragedy. *The State and Revolution* reveals what Lenin *intended* his revolution to accomplish; what his revolution actually *did* accomplish provides the conclusion to the story of the maturation of Leninism as an ideology.

The most immediate feature of Lenin's treatise is its orthodoxy. Lenin outlines a theory of the state that reiterated every significant feature of classical Marxism. "The state," Lenin maintained, "is the product and the manifestation of the *irreconcilability* of class antagonisms. The state arises when, where and to the extent that class antagonisms objectively *cannot* be reconciled. And, conversely, the existence of the state proves that the class antagonisms are irreconcilable. . . . According to Marx, the state could neither arise nor maintain itself if it were possible to reconcile classes. . . . According to Marx, the state is an organ of class rule, an organ for the *oppression* of one class by another. . . ." Since the socialist revolution will end the oppression and exploitation of men by men, the historic task of the proletariat is to smash the machinery of the state. "The course of events compels the revolution to *'concentrate all its forces of destruction'* against state power and to set itself the aim not of perfecting the state machine, but of *smashing and destroying it.*"[28] The victorious proletarian revolution is destined, by the course of events, to destroy the machinery of the state.

The model for the proletarian dictatorship that was to immediately follow upon successful revolution was taken from Marx's account of the Paris Commune. Proletarian dictatorship was understood to be something that is no longer really the state—rather, it was a "semistate," an apparatus shorn of functions accumulated during the long epochs of class society. The revolutionary and transient form that the state as a proletarian dictatorship would assume would be "a very simple 'machine,' almost without a 'machine,' without a special apparatus. . . ." Lenin maintained that capitalism had created large-scale production, factories, railways, the postal service, and telephones, all of which had simplified the majority of the functions of the old state power to such a degree that they could be reduced to exceedingly simple operations of registration, filing, and checking—activities that could be performed easily by any literate person at ordinary workmen's wages. Thus, proletarian dictatorship would have no use for an elaborate bureaucracy. Any officials who functioned in the proletarian semistate (a state in the process of withering away) would be without exception elected and subject to recall at any time. Their salaries would be those of ordinary workers. The workers themselves would organize large-scale production on the basis of what capitalism had already created. They would rely on their own experience as workers, voluntarily submitting to the discipline required by production, while the role of the state officials would be reduced to that of simply carrying out the workers' instructions as responsible, revocable, and modestly paid foremen and bookkeepers. The workers would subsequently voluntarily amalgamate their productive communes into a nation in a process Lenin called "voluntary centralism."[29] This is what Lenin understood the workers must *start with* in accomplishing the proletarian revolution. This transitory situation was to be the inaugural of socialism. The proletarian dictatorship was to be a "fuller democracy," characterized by the rapid withering away of the state.

In March, 1918, after but a few months in power, Lenin was challenged by Bukharin to formalize the description of a socialist society, a society without a state. Lenin replied, "At present we certainly uphold the state and to say we should give a description of socialism in its developed form where the state will cease to exist—you couldn't do anything about that except say that then the principle would be realized: from each according to his ability, to each according to his needs. But this is still a long way off. . . ."[30] Less than a month later this departure from his original position became more explicit with his admission that it would be necessary to "compromise . . . the principles of the Paris Commune and of every proletarian power. . . ." The proletarian revolution had introduced what Lenin now called the "highest type of state—Soviet power," and what was lacking, he candidly admitted, were the material conditions for its existence. There was no nationwide accounting and control of production and distribution. The level of productivity was disastrously low. What was necessary was "Soviet government plus Prussian railroad efficiency plus American technology and organizations of trusts plus American public school education . . . etc., etc." In effect what was necessary was mature capitalism as the economic base for a socialist society! Russia's problem was her backwardness.[31]

To solve this problem Lenin suggested that the new proletarian state power arrange for "practically feasible, convenient and suitable forms of transition from fragmentary, scattered co-operatives to a single, national co-operative [to make] every citizen a member of a single nation-wide, or rather state-wide, co-operative." "To deprive," he went on, "the All-Russian center of the right to subordinate directly to itself all plants of a given branch of industry in all corners of the country . . . is . . . regional anarcho-syndicalism, not communism." He advocated "one-man managerial authority (which could be called dictatorial)" for industry, and added that in view of the fact that "the proletarian state sets about systematic creation of the socialist order . . . it is impossible to fulfill this task without coercion. We need the state, we need coercion." Socialism could come to backward

Russia only if Soviet power could be combined with the achievements of capitalism. "[S]tate capitalism would be our salvation;
if we had it in Russia, the transition to full socialism would be
easy . . . [but] that is exactly what we lack . . . and prevents us
from taking the very step on which the success of socialism
depends."[32]

Both Marx and Engels had argued that the transition from
capitalism to socialism would involve nothing more than strip-
ping away the capitalist integument from the matured productive forces. Capitalism would have created the socialized mode
of production that the proletarian revolution would simply
inherit. Capitalism would have matured the proletariat by disci-
plining it in the armies of labor and training it in the tasks
requisite to industrial efficiency and self-management. The revolution itself would have produced a communist consciousness
on a mass scale.[33] The proletarian masses, possessed of such a
matured class consciousness, would simply assume direction of
the matured forms of production. It would be little more than
transforming into socialized property what was already socialized
production.

A mature capitalism would have provided the economic base
for a socialist society as well as the mature consciousness that
could administer it. Lenin's tinkering with classical Marxist
theory had resulted in a theory that anticipated revolution in
the backward rather than the advanced economies. The class
consciousness was to be supplied not by the very processes of
industrial maturation, but by a small coterie of declassed intellectuals. A successful socialist revolution in a backward country
would find itself without an industrial base adequate to the
demands of socialism and a population innocent of the first
requirements of socialist discipline. Lenin was quite aware of
all this. "Given ideal class consciousness and discipline," he
argued, "on the part of those taking part in the common work,
. . . subordination would rather remind one of the mild leadership of a conductor of an orchestra. It may assume the sharp
forms of a dictatorship if ideal discipline and class consciousness are lacking. . . ."[34] The very backwardness of industry in
Russia made the ideal class consciousness upon which the
withering away of the state was predicated an impossibility.
This lack of maturity on the part of the working class made

sharp forms of dictatorship a necessity, not for the suppression of class enemies, but to ensure that thousands would subordinate their will to the will of one leader who foresaw the future trajectory of history. Originally, Leninism had assigned that vision to the cadre of the Bolshevik party, and their leadership was understood to constitute not dictatorship of the proletariat, but dictatorship *in the name of* the proletariat. After six months of power the dictatorship in the name of the proletariat became dictatorship *over* the proletariat to ensure its submission to discipline in the critical task of constructing an economic base for socialism.

The changes undertaken by Leninism could only increase the apprehension of thinking Marxists. Classical Marxism had argued that the revolutionary dictatorship would use an iron hand and iron rule against its *class enemies*. But in 1918 Lenin advanced the thesis that the repressive machinery of the revolutionary state, yielded by the party itself, was to be used against the *proletariat*. The simple commune-type state, which was really no state at all, suddenly developed into an enormously complex apparatus that reached into every branch of industry and commerce to coerce the strict and absolute unity of will of the working class itself. When Lenin's critics raised objections, he could only deplore their "slavish repetition of the slogans of yesterday" so inadequate to an "analysis of the altered conditions of the present period of history. . . . What has happened," he asked, "to these people that fragments of book-learning can make them forget reality?"[35] One of the books, fragments of which his critics had learned, was apparently his *The State and Revolution*, written less than six months before.

Although in retrospect it would seem that Lenin wrote with a cunning cynicism to cull support for his minoritarian revolution, all we know of the man suggests that he was convinced of the truth of what he wrote. He had intended just such a state—a state that would not be a state at all. He seemed to have believed that he could still rescue classical Marxism from Leninism—that the revolution would produce that realm of freedom, that universal emancipation that was the normative ideal of the social and political philosophy he had made his own. Almost immediately after the coming to power of the Bolsheviks in 1917 the "Draft Regulations on Workers' Control" and the "Draft Decree on the Right of Recall" were promulgated. In the maelstrom of historic events that filled those first few months of power in 1917–1918, Lenin seemed convinced that the revolution was giving birth to the state that he had envisaged in *The State and Revolution*.[36] Immediately after the October revolution, workers' organizations dominated industrial management. The syndical organizations managed their enterprises, including railroad and river transportation. Workers' productive communes were proceeding to "abolish the state."

But Lenin's departures from classical Marxism in the following months had become so fundamental that his detractors seemed to have had some grounds for considering him an unprincipled adventurer and political opportunist. Actually, a more complimentary interpretation can be given of his ideological development. Lenin's interpretation of the role of the party finds some doctrinal support in the classical Marxist texts. Marx had early written that "Material force can only be overthrown by material force; but theory itself becomes a material force when it has seized the masses. . . . Revolutions need a *passive* element, a material basis. . . . Just as philosophy finds its *material* weapons in the proletariat, so the proletariat finds its *intellectual* weapons in philosophy." In 1864 Marx maintained that although the working class possessed *numbers* as one element of success, "numbers weigh only in the balance, if united by combination and led by knowledge."[37] Finally, in a letter to Kugelmann on March 28, 1870, Marx indicated that "The English have all the material conditions necessary for a socialist revolution. What they lack is the spirit of generalization and the revolutionary passion."

While these random propositions ran contrary to the general theory, the theoretical structure was so open-textured that they could remain without obvious incongruence. The tactical necessities of creating a party in autocratic Russia prompted Lenin to utilize these elements, employing them in the renovation of the system. He reformulated loose sentiments into specific propositions. The working class would remain bourgeois unless a working class consciousness were brought to it by a revolutionary party composed of declassed bourgeois intellectuals. Social being no longer created social consciousness—social consciousness was created by a minority party that interpreted social being in accordance with Marxist theory. This reformulation, coupled with the reassessment contained in Lenin's *Imperialism*, provides the rationale for Leninism's emphasis on revolution in the backward countries.

Here again Lenin found suitable materials in the antecedent work of Marx and Engels. As early as 1845 Marx and Engels had indicated that big industry does not reach the same level of development in all districts of a country or all countries simultaneously. Nonetheless, the proletarians created by such industry can assume leadership of revolutionary movements and carry the whole mass along with them, for the workers excluded from big industry are placed by it in "a still worse situation than the workers in big industry themselves."[38] This could be understood to provide the classical Marxist substance for Leninism's conception of minoritarian revolution in underdeveloped areas in which the elemental masses, not yet capable of true consciousness, are carried forward in their own ultimate interests by a proletarian vanguard party led by bourgeois intellectuals. Such an interpretation would find further support in Engels' contention that England was creating for itself a bourgeois proletariat—a proletariat with a bourgeois social consciousness, the consequence of the capitalist distribution of plunder wrested from the colonies.[39] Should these conditions become general in a period of imperialism, this analysis would fit Lenin's account of the inevitable lack of mature social consciousness on the part of the proletariat of the advanced countries.

Such an analysis was certainly not advanced by classical Marxism. Both Marx and Engels saw a direct and immediate causal relationship between the development of an industrial society and the maturation of revolutionary consciousness. Engels, as we have suggested, had little patience with peoples afflicted with stunted industrial development. Both Marx and Engels favored the territorial expansion of "progressive capitalism," which was, for Engels, the equivalent of "the progress of civilization." They were convinced that capitalism alone could produce a revolutionary proletariat, that capitalism alone would create the material conditions requisite for the development of proletarian consciousness. They therefore generally supported the colonial expansion of capitalism and the establishment of larger economic units at the expense of national liberation movements that threatened to erect small economically non-viable enclaves incapable of producing large-scale industry. Thus, both Marx and Engels were somewhat chary of national liberation movements, and Engels had little sympathy with "the prattle about equal rights of nations. . . ." Engels argued that "peoples which have never had a history of their own, which from the moment they reached the first, crudest stages of civilization already came under foreign domination or which were only forced into the first stages of civilization through a foreign yoke, have no vitality, they will never be able to attain any sort of independence."[40] In his letter of September 12, 1882, to Karl Kautsky, Engels outlined what he understood to be the course of world revolutionary development. He realized that the English "workers gaily share the feast of England's monopoly of the world market and the colonies." The proletarian revolution, he thought, would therefore probably erupt in Germany and spread through the advanced industrial nations.

The colonies occupied by European populations would become independent, but in the colonies inhabited by a native population the proletariat would have to take over temporarily and lead the populace to independence as quickly as possible. Engels asserted that the reorganization of Europe would supply the model that the semicivilized countries would follow. Colonial independence would follow successful working class revolution in the advanced capitalist countries, for only that could release the enormous industrial power necessary to support a socialist society. Classical Marxism precluded the possibility that *all* the advanced capitalist countries would possess "bourgeois working classes." National uprisings and insurrection in backward areas were to be welcomed where they weakened the class enemy of the proletariat in the advanced countries, but socialism was always predicated on successful proletarian revolution in the mature economies. At best, revolution in the backward areas would act as a signal for the proletarian revolution in the West.

Only the coupling of revolutions in the backward countries with decisive proletarian revolutions in the advanced capitalist countries could make Leninism compatible with classical Marxism, and it was on this eventuality that Lenin rested his claim to Marxist orthodoxy. In his "Farewell Letter to Swiss Workers" he clearly indicated that "Single-handed, the Russian proletariat cannot bring the social revolution to a *victorious conclusion.*

But it can give the Russian revolution a mighty sweep that would create the most favorable conditions for a social revolution, and would, in a sense, *start* it. It can facilitate the rise of a situation in which its chief, its most trustworthy and most reliable collaborator, the European and American socialist proletariat, could join the decisive battles."[41] Lenin later added that since Russia was one of the most backward of European countries, it was impossible for socialism to triumph there directly and *immediately*. It may, however, constitute "a *prologue* to the world socialist revolution, a *step* toward it." Immediately before the seizure of power in 1917 Lenin admitted that "We do not know how soon after our victory revolution will sweep the West," but he did not doubt that it *would* sweep the West. The Russian situation was difficult because the revolution proved to be ahead of other revolutions, but he steadfastly maintained that the world revolution was beginning, and he continued to argue that the world revolution by "iron necessity" must soon make its appearance.

It is evident, then, that organizational and tactical necessities had driven Lenin to assume postures that seemed to violate the precepts of classical Marxism. He himself remained convinced that he was an orthodox Marxist. The revolution he led was to be the spark that would begin a conflagration in the advanced capitalist countries. With the decisive victory of the advanced proletariat of the West, Russia could make its rapid transition to socialism supported by the enormous material wealth of Western industry. *Revolution in the advanced capitalist countries of the West was the critical variable that would restore Marxist integrity to Leninism.* This recognition constituted the force of Trotsky's subsequent argument. "The socialist revolution," he wrote, "begins on national grounds. But it cannot be completed on these grounds. The maintenance of the proletarian revolution within a national framework can only be a provisional state of affairs. . . . The way out . . . lies only in the victory of the proletariat of the advanced countries." Thus Lenin had maintained that "it is impossible to pass from capitalism to socialism without breaking national frameworks, as it was impossible to pass from feudalism to capitalism without adopting the idea of the nation."[42]

Leninism could be restored as a variation of classical Marxism only if the Russian Revolution were not isolated as a *national* phenomenon. Lenin did, in fact, refuse to acknowledge such an isolation. He intoxicated himself with a vision of imminent *world* revolution. Neither he nor any of the Russian leaders of the first successful "Marxist" revolution conceived the possibility that their victory, won at so extravagant a cost, would be an isolated one. "The revolution has begun in the East," Trotsky wrote during this period, "but the revolution which we live through is a proletarian one, and the proletariat is strongest, most organized, most enlightened in the old capitalist countries."[43] Revolution there would fulfill Engels' prediction that the historic movement would be from West to East. For without such an accompanying movement, Russia, one of the most backward countries in Europe, would find itself with a socialist consciousness unsupported by an adequate material base—a circumstance that would reduce the Marxist analysis of reality to nonsense.

Leninisms

·   Lenin left all the elements of Leninism as a heritage to Stalin. He left Stalin the conception of the *party* as the ultimate arbiter of truth, a hierarchically organized and highly centralized party that brooked little opposition. It was a party not to be led by the masses whose mood was changeable and whose actions were unpredictable, but a party to be led only by the one, true theory that would "put an end to the opposition." He provided Stalin with a conception of the *state* that featured an expanding apparatus for inculcating discipline and effecting economic control. But for Lenin, it seemed that these components, so portentous in retrospect, were transitional, ahistorical because the revolution in the West would rectify them. The coupling of the Russian Revolution with that of the proletarian West would permit the fulfillment of the Marxist vision of the rational—and hence free—community of producers. Only the economically mature West could produce a correspondingly mature proletariat that had developed the full consciousness that, in Engels' words, "no longer needs any official organization, either public or private." Only mature capitalism could produce "the simple feeling of solidarity based on the understanding of the identity of class position"[44] that would make party and state superfluous and give reality to the classical Marxist dream.

The party and the state Lenin had created was a revolutionary necessity in circumstances that required the forced union of a lamentably small proletariat minority with the numerically overwhelming peasantry of primitive Russia. All knowledgeable Marxists were aware, at the time, of the anomaly of the Russian situation, and all assumed its rectification with the saving revolution in the West. In November, 1918, Stalin proclaimed, ". . . the eyes of all are naturally turned to the West. It is there, in the West, that the chains of imperialism . . . must first of all be smashed. It is there, first of all in the West, that the new, socialist life must vigorously develop."[45] He spoke with sincere conviction of the inevitability of a world proletarian revolution. Nor did all the failures sustained by insurrectionary attempts in Europe from 1917 until 1924 shake this conviction. As long as Lenin remained alive, the Bolsheviks sustained this fading image of the saving revolution. To forsake the image was to abandon the heart of classical Marxism. In May, 1924, four months after Lenin's death, Stalin reiterated, "The principal task of socialism —the organization of socialist production—has still to be fulfilled. Can this task be fulfilled, can the final victory of socialism be achieved in one country, without the joint efforts of the proletarians in several advanced countries? No, it cannot."[46]

Between 1917 and 1924 faith in the missing revolution gave the ideology at least the semblance of orthodoxy. Yet the Bolsheviks, grievously shaken by the lack of a revolution in Central Europe, began to draw the conclusions, already implicit in Lenin's work, that in our own time have defined Leninism as an ideology in its own right. Trotsky, for example, in his *The Lessons of October* concluded:

> After the revolution of October . . . it appeared that events in Europe would develop spontaneously. . . . But it is obvious that in the absence of a party capable of leading the proletarian revolution, that revolution becomes impossible. . . . For the proletariat . . . nothing can take the place of the party. . . . The fundamental instrument of the proletarian revolution is the party.[47]

Within the party it was the leadership that functioned with "exceptional and incomparable" influence. Lenin's heirs all agreed on this analysis, and the indispensability of the party and its exceptional leadership became an essential component of Leninism. The failure of the European revolution drove the Bolsheviks to assume a new strategic posture with respect to the mounting restiveness in China and India. Bukharin, in his *On the Theory of Permanent Revolution*, focused his attention on Lenin's concern (evident as early as 1913) with "advanced Asia" in contrast to "backward Europe." The revolutionary potential of the industrially underdeveloped, essentially peasant East began to occupy more and more of the Bolsheviks' theoretical concern. It was at this point that Leninism was first conceived as a new ideology, based on Marxism, but appropriate to a "new epoch," an ideology preoccupied with peasant revolutions. Rjazanov posed the dilemma that faced the victorious proletarian party of Russia: Should the party support itself on a peasant base or on the proletariat of Western Europe? A solution was proffered by Bukharin: The revolution had failed in the West, so the new Soviet state would receive the "assistance" of the primitive East. This constituted, for Zinoviev, the essence of Leninism, outside of which there could be no revolutionary Marxism.[48]

The subsequent development of Leninism into Stalinism was the consequence of the combination of all these elements. The doctrine of socialism in one country was already implicit in the abandonment of the faith in revolution in the West and in the reformulation of Leninism as a revolutionary ideology designed to direct, under the iron discipline of a Leninist party, the elemental revolutionary impulses of the peasant masses of the industrially backward East. In the autumn of 1924 Stalin announced, almost casually, his commitment to the development of socialism in one country—a commitment he had refused to make only a few months before. With that announcement Stalinism became the first fully matured Leninism: an ideology to support the rapid industrialization of a backward economy under the direction of a totalitarian party lead by a single, exceptional leader. By 1934 the first Leninism had come to fruition. In his "Report to the Seventeenth Congress of the Communist Party," Stalin revealed that Marxist theory would no longer be concerned with objective conditions. "The part played by so-called objec-

tive conditions," he announced, "has been reduced to a minimum; whereas the part played by our organizations and their
leaders has become decisive, exceptional." The voluntarism
always implicit in Leninism thus came to full fruition. The
classical Marxist thesis of man's consciousness being determined
by the material conditions governing his life was inverted. Man's
consciousness, represented by the party and its leaders, was to
create the material conditions of man's life. The influence of the
objective conditions of man's life diminished in direct proportion to the influence ascribed to the party and its leaders.

And that influence could only be effected through the machinery of the state. Stalin chided Marxists who insisted on
being "talmudists," who constantly referred to Marx or Engels
in their effort to orientate themselves with respect to the state.
Stalin suggested that they should rather further develop the
Marxist theory, for the classics had been written so long ago
that they could not anticipate "each and every zigzag of history."
Engels' formula on the withering away of the state could not
provide an answer to the problems that faced the Soviet state
of the twentieth century. Even Lenin's pronouncements in *The
State and Revolution* could not afford a definitive guide. Stalin
indicated that Lenin had indeed planned a further volume and
that "what Lenin did not manage to do should be done by his
disciples."[49]

Stalin did effect just such a "creative development." He gave
that development explicit expression in his report to the Sixteenth Congress:

> We stand for the withering away of the state. At the same time
> we stand for the strengthening of the dictatorship of the proletariat,
> which is the mightiest and strongest state power that has ever existed.
> The highest development of state power with the object of preparing
> the conditions for the withering away of state power—such is the Marx-
> ist formula. Is this "contradictory"? Yes, it is "contradictory." But this
> contradiction is bound up with life, and it fully reflects Marx's
> dialectics.[50]

The reflection of Marxist dialectics was purchased at the cost
of its substance.

The use of Marxian idiom, the concern with the metaphorical "withering away of the state" obscures important features of the voluntarism of Stalinism. The original use of the withering metaphor was applicable to a theoretical system that defined the state as a derivative of some more fundamental process. In classical Marxism the state was supposed to wither when the productive community produced *those material conditions, which alone could constitute the real basis of a higher form of society.* After the proletarian revolution the state would wither because capitalism would have developed all the productive forces for which there was room. The material conditions for its passing would have matured in the womb of the old society itself. But Leninism had captured an underdeveloped society in which Stalin proposed to *construct* a socialist economy. For the protracted process of construction the state was not derived or secondary, but fundamental and primary. It was the tool of party consciousness. The withering metaphor was originally employed in the context of a theoretical system that presupposed a causal connection between base and superstructure in which the former determines the rate and nature of changes in the latter. The relationship of the state to the economic base was one of dependency. Stalinist ideology *inverts* this relationship; the construction of socialism requires the state to effect industrialization. The relationship of the economic base to the state is one of dependency. By 1949 P. F. Yudin contended, "The Soviet state is the chief force, the principal instrument for the construction of a communist society. That is why the task of strengthening the Soviet state by all possible means is the main task both at the present time and in the future. . . ."[51]

Stalinism, the first relatively systematic expression of Leninism, made the party, a minority of declassed intellectuals, the motive force of history. Within the party the "exceptional" leader was made the vehicle of ultimate truth. As a consequence, the entire quasi-deductive theoretical system of classical Marxism was inverted. Where classical Marxism had argued that the material conditions of life spontaneously generated proletarian revolution, a spontaneity that manifested itself without leadership or party, without concrete rules or official organization, Leninism maintained that proletarian revolution was in principle impossible without the intercession of an authoritarian, hierarchically organized minority leadership of declassed theoreticians under the tight doctrinal control of an enlightened leader. Where classical Marxism had advanced the proposition that revolutions would no longer be carried out by small conscious minorities leading unconscious masses, Leninism defended the thesis that the party "sets the aims which the working class in their totality does not understand today but will understand tomorrow."[52] Where classical Marxism, and Lenin writing in its tradition, argued that the proletarian revolution and socialism could only come in and through the most advanced capitalist countries, Leninism was to insist that it could and would come independently in each underdeveloped nation. Where classical Marxism anticipated that the international proletarian revolution would simply inherit the capitalist technical base, Leninism pronounced that the national proletariat would construct it. Where classical Marxism still spoke with the voice of Lenin, it contended that "we Marxists are opposed to *every kind* of state" and "so long as the state exists there is no freedom," while Stalin's Leninism was to maintain that "the enormous and growing role which belongs to the Soviet state in the organization of communist construction requires its constant strengthening. . . ."[53]

For the convenience of the historians of Marxism and the revolutionary activists of the East, Stalin catalogued some of the most substantial changes in classical Marxist theory in the series of speeches he made immediately following the death of Lenin. Formerly, Stalin revealed, it was held that the working class undertakes revolution spontaneously with a clear consciousness of its own ultimate purposes. Formerly, the analysis of the prerequisites for the proletarian revolution was approached from the point of view of the economic development of individual countries. Formerly, it was the accepted thing to speak of the existence or absence of objective conditions for proletarian revolution in individual countries, or, to be more precise, in one or another industrially developed countries. Formerly, it was held that proletarian revolutions would first occur in countries where industry was more developed, where the proletariat constituted the majority, where there was more culture, where there was more democracy. These contentions, Stalin announced, were no longer tenable. Few Marxists had difficulty recognizing the views "formerly" held to be those of classical Marxism. Classical Marxism had become Leninism.

At about the same time that Stalin's Leninism was being systematized the Chinese Communist Party was beginning to organize the revolutionary nationalism that stirred the people of China. Among its organizers was the young but aggressive first-born son of a rich peasant, Mao Tse-tung. Ultimately he would become leader of the Communist Party, ruler of a united China, and founder of his own variant of Leninism. China was to become the focus of international attention as the scene of the most portentous "proletarian" revolution since 1917.

Conditions in revolutionary China were even more singular than those of revolutionary Russia. If Russia had a working class of no more than 2 percent of its population, China had virtually no urban working class at all. China was a seething mass of peasant unrest and nationalist resentment. Leninism had released revolutionary aspirants from any obligation to the classical Marxist commitments as to the course of revolution, its allies, its character, and the objective conditions that were its determinants. Maoism, Mao's "creative development" of Stalinist Leninism, took its point of departure from the Russian model but almost immediately introduced its own singularly non-Marxist (one might almost say anti-Marxist) elements.

Almost from adolescence Mao was an emphatic and vigorous nationalist. While serving as a librarian's assistant to Li Ta-chao in Peking, Mao was in a position to further cultivate, under Li's guidance, a combination of the most radical Western ideas and Chinese nationalism. Li had long been active in the Chinese nationalist movement, and when he embraced Marxism around 1920, he did so without divesting himself of his nationalism. At the same time Mao began to read more extensively in Marxist literature. Not much is known authoritatively about the maturation of Mao's thought during the period between 1917 and 1926, but what is known indicates that he remained preoccupied with the "historic greatness of the Chinese people" and the role in history of consciousness and will. These tendencies were probably cultivated by Li, who was convinced that because China was a rural nation any redeeming revolution would have to have essentially peasant support, but for China as a nation to be restored to her historic world position, it would be necessary for men of purpose to lead her restive masses against the exploiters, both national and imperialist. Li spoke of a *national* revolution in which the *whole nation*, led by the indomitable will of a minority, would rise up against its enemies. Whatever material survives from this period of Mao's political development reflect the influence of Li.[54]

Mao's insistence on the nature of the Chinese revolution as a national rather than an exclusively social one early characterized his thought as a distinct variant of Leninism. For all the obscurity and immaturity of Mao's early thought it is evident that he conceived the entire Chinese nation as a proletarian people. This was already implicit in Lenin's conception of imperialism. The class struggle had given way to national struggles after the debacle of the Second International. The proletariat of the advanced capitalist countries had been corrupted by imperialist profits, profits looted from colonial or semicolonial dependencies. The struggle for survival and profit had ceased to be class-bound and had become national. The masses of the backward nations had become the bearers of proletarian class consciousness, and the class struggle had shifted to a national plane. Mao's insistence that the Chinese people were the revolutionary class permitted him to wed Marxism with nationalism. It also destroyed the tactical and theoretical significance of "class" as a unit of analysis. Mao's analysis of classes, written in 1926, analyzes the revolutionary importance of classes in terms of the revolution for national liberation.[55] How little importance the specifically class character of the revolution had for Mao is revealed in his "Report of an Investigation into the Peasant Movement in Hunan," written in 1927.

All kinds of arguments against the peasant movement must be speedily set right. In a very short time . . . several hundred million peasants will rise like a tornado or tempest, a force so extraordinarily swift and violent that no power, however great, will be able to suppress it. They will break all trammels that now bind them and rush forward along the road to liberation. They will send all imperialists, warlords, corrupt officials, local bullies and bad gentry to their graves. *All revolutionary parties and all revolutionary comrades will stand before them to be tested, and to be accepted or rejected as they decide.*

He posed three alternatives to orthodox Leninists:

To march at their head and lead them? Or to follow at their rear, gesticulating at them and criticising them? Or to face them as opponents? . . . The fact is that the broad *peasant* masses have risen to fulfil their historic mission. . . . To reject them is to reject the revolution. To attack them is to attack the revolution. Their general direction of the revolution has never been wrong.[56]

Here Mao followed the lead of Li Ta-chao, who had, the year before, called upon the peasants to rely upon their own strength to liberate the nation. How radically Mao had departed from the Leninism of Stalin is evident in the role he ascribed to the peasant masses. They were to lead the revolution; they were to stand in judgment of the proletarian party. There was only one choice left for Mao—and that was to lead the peasant masses in the direction in which they wished to go! Here was a class with spontaneity and revolutionary resolve. But it was the wrong class.

Stalin, in a speech delivered before the Chinese Commission in 1926, had maintained that the role of leader of the Chinese peasantry must inevitably fall to the Chinese proletariat and its party. He went on to add that it was the proletariat who must rouse the peasants of China to revolution. It seems obvious that Mao ascribed a degree of leadership and initiative to the peasantry far beyond anything Lenin or Stalin had been willing to accord them.

Mao was not long to entertain such an advanced position. He lapsed into the Leninist idiom of the "hegemony of the proletariat" and similar locutions, but his tactical and organizational attention remained directed toward the peasantry. He set about creating an organization almost exclusively of peasant origin; nonetheless, he continued to call it the "party of the proletariat." Mao's strategy was to abandon the urban centers and their working class population and seek support in the peasant villages. "What the Party adopted was the mass line policy of resolutely *relying on the peasants' political consciousness* and organized strength. . . ."[57] Maoism's revolutionary strategy was to establish and consolidate strong Red political power in the countryside, to conduct an extended revolutionary struggle there, to surround the cities from the countryside, and finally to capture them. The vital positions for the Chinese revolution were the vast rural areas where broad masses of peasants lived. The peasants (not the proletariat) were to be the essential ingredients of revolution, and the revolution itself was to be *national*, not class, victory. It was a revolution of the Chinese people, in the service of national independence. The party conceived itself as the "concentrated expression of the *people's* will."[58]

Mao exploited the separation Lenin introduced between working class consciousness and the urban working class. That putative consciousness became completely detached from the working class in the Chinese revolution and was represented only in the convictions of Mao and his immediate party cadre. The "proletarian" party constructed by Mao and his subordinates carried proletarian consciousness to the insurgent peasant masses. The conjecture that this could be effected further dissipates the classical Marxist conviction that "particular political parties . . . [are] more or less adequate political expression of . . . classes and fractions of classes."[59]

Benjamin Schwartz has trenchantly observed that the experience of Chinese Communism casts a doubt on the whole organic conception of the relation of party to class.[60] The party became the incarnate *national* will, so much so that the four-class bloc composed of workers, peasants, petty bourgeoisie, and national bourgeoisie, proposed by Stalin as an interim united front, soon developed into a stable alliance of national forces. What appeared to be a tactic in defeating the Japanese in 1935 became, in 1949, a formal alliance. The broad masses that sustained the revolution were understood to be "all those who are oppressed, injured or fettered by imperialism, feudalism and bureaucrat-capitalism, namely, workers, peasants, soldiers, intellectuals, businessmen and other patriots. . . ."[61] The dictatorship of the proletariat had become the "people's democratic dictatorship," through which "the people throughout the country" are united, in which even the bourgeoisie can be "redeemed." It is now conceived frankly that the Communist Party "shares the destiny and life-breath of the Chinese *people*."[62] The identification of the party with the people, with "national regeneration," with the theory that China can advance to communism under a joint dictatorship of the four classes (even if ultimate power belongs to the Communist Party), indicates that Leninism has undergone significant, if not unanticipated, alterations. Mao's Leninism is a frankly *national communism*. Such an eventuality was already latent in Stalin's commitment to socialism in one country and his admonition that the Chinese revolution "assume a profoundly popular and pronouncedly national character."[63]

Mao is indebted to Lenin for the concept that political consciousness does not manifest itself spontaneously among the urban working class but must be brought from without through the agency of an elite vanguard. He is also indebted to him for the hierarchically organized, centralized political party. It was Lenin's theory of imperialism that gave Mao the theoretical basis for the conception of a union of all "progressive" classes in a "proletarian nation" against "imperialist nations" and, for all intents and purposes, identifying nations with classes. But Maoism has been advertised as something more than a Chinese application of Leninism. Mao Tse-tung has "creatively applied . . . the scientific theory of Marxism-Leninism"; he has made a "creative application of the revolutionary theories of Marx, Engels, Lenin, and Stalin to the actual conditions in China."[64]

Lenin identified his party with the true or ultimate will of the proletarian class. Certification for such an identification rested on the conviction that he, Lenin, possessed the one true science of society. Mao has made a similar identification. He and his immediate subordinates have not only identified themselves with the real will of the all but nonexistent proletariat of China, but with the people of China as well. Lenin outlined the tactics of national liberation and class collaboration, but as an international revolutionary he deplored the existence of national and class differences. Mao evinces all the species traits of one for whom nationalism is not a necessary evil but an authentic value in itself, who conceives it possible for China to proceed through socialism to communism under a joint dictatorship of the working class, the peasantry, the petty bourgeoisie, and the national bourgeoisie—even though the formula, "the hegemony of the proletariat," means that ultimate control rests with Mao and his party associates.

The conditions that prevailed and do prevail in China make Mao's voluntarism even more emphatic than that of Stalin, although both arise from the conviction that men must create an economic base compatible with their political and social vision. Lenin had made this inversion of the classical Marxist thesis a necessity by advocating revolution in backward countries. In so doing he advocated the priority of politics over economics. When Stalin committed Leninism to the creation of socialism in one country, the necessary corollary was man's independence of objective conditions. The Chinese revolution, therefore, undertaken in a country whose industrial backwardness made even primitive Russia seem advanced, could only be based on a voluntarism that saw man creating his own life conditions. Thus Chinese theorists could say:

Men are not the slaves of objective reality. Provided only that men's consciousness be in conformity with the objective laws of the development of things, the subjective activity of the popular masses can manifest itself in full measure, overcome all difficulties, create the necessary conditions and carry forward the revolution. In this sense, *the subjective creates the objective.*[65]

The singularity of Leninist voluntarism in its various guises is that it is the expression of an elite, a party hierarchy that possesses "the universal truth" of Marxism-Leninism and is therefore "most far-sighted." According to Liu Shao-chi, "Our mass movements are launched under the centralized guidance of the Party. Party guidance means integrating political work with economic work, integrating the political education of the masses with material incentives and *placing politics in command, making it the driving force.*"[66] The political elite, then, armed with "the great thought of Mao Tse-tung," united in the "voluntarily observed iron discipline" of a minoritarian revolutionary party,[67] is the motive force of historic change that mobilizes the elemental strivings of unconscious masses. The ultimate justification, then, for one-party rule is its monopoly on the truth, "the universal truth," of Leninism, with its insight into the "universal law of the development of human society. . . ."[68]

All these elements have received more emphatic development in the most recent of Leninist revolutions that has captured world attention—that in Cuba. Even before its self-identification as Leninist, the Cuban revolution displayed similarities with that of Mao Tse-tung. It was a rural-based, guerrilla insurrection. Its isolation from Cuba's urban proletariat was almost complete, even though the number of Cubans involved in manufacturing, commerce, and the service industries was larger than the number of Cubans employed in agriculture. The Cuban trade union movement claimed a membership of approximately 1 million in a nation of fewer than 6 million inhabitants. Nevertheless, the revolution was rural-based. Later Castro argued that the revolution had to be initially agrarian because the proletarian labor unions were afflicted with "economism," their privileges making them mere appendages and champions of the bourgeois system. On the other hand, he maintained, "The peasants possess a virgin mentality, free from an assortment of influences which poison the intellects of citizens in the city. The revolution works on these fertile intellects as it works on the soil." A cadre of declassed, revolutionary intellectuals can take up a position in the rural hinterland and *create* revolution by acting as a "sort of guiding angel" ("*una especie de angel tutelar*"), directing the virgin but fertile intellects of the peasant masses. Che Guevara, in his *La Guerra de Guerrillas*, indicated that "It is not always necessary to wait for all the conditions for a revolution to exist; *the insurrectional focal point can create them.*" Guevara identified his book as a "war against the pseudo-revolutionaires" whose quiescent attitude compels them to wait until all the objective and subjective conditions have been fulfilled before embarking on insurrection. Instead of waiting for the maturation of conditions, the insurrectional leadership composed of nonpeasant, nonproletarian bourgeois intellectuals can *create* them.[69] Under such circumstances the role of the leadership is "exceptional," "extraordinary." In 1954, when Castro discussed the logic of revolution, he argued that "a perfectly disciplined human nucleus" could provide "the force necessary to conquer power, whether it be by peaceful or by revolutionary means. . . . The indispensable conditions . . . are: ideology, discipline and leadership. The three are essential, but leadership is basic."[70] Castro's latter maxim, *la jefatura es basica*, epitomizes the entire course

of the Cuban Leninist revolution. Writers as varied as Theodore
Draper, Louis Conte Agüero, and Daniel James have identified
caudillismo, the leadership principle, as the distinguishing feature of Castroism.[71]

Leadership of the revolution was vested in what Guevara
called the "telluric force" of Fidel Castro. Leading an absurdly
small band of declassed intellectuals, he *created* (according to
Cuban theory) the conditions for revolution. He exercised his
will on the elemental restiveness of the peasants, who were un-
spoiled by urban sophistication and carried through the first,
agrarian, phase of a "permanent revolution," which rapidly
transcended to the "socialist" phase. Each phase commenced and
concluded in accord with his will. Socialism was *proclaimed*.
Only in 1961 were the Cuban masses told that their revolution
had in fact been a Leninist revolution. Faure Chomón, in a
public address on March 13, 1961, reported that Fidel Castro
by his act of will had "converted the entire Cuban people to
Communism." This most singular process has been conveniently
summarized by a not unsympathetic historian of the Cuban
revolution, J. P. Morray.

On December 14, 1960, Castro said that the working class *ought
to demand*, not crumbs from the capitalist table, but political power.
*In fact, the workers did not have to demand it. It was thrust upon
them by the intellectuals who were directing the revolutionary government. From their study of Marxism-Leninism they realized that the
proletariat is the class that must serve as the base and the vanguard
for a socialist revolution. The proletariat took power in Cuba through
the conversion to Marxism-Leninism of a government of lawyers. The
initiative came from above, not by insurrection from below.*[72]

The Leninist revolution in Cuba might as well be described
in the following manner:

Brought up in the school of conspiracy, and held together by the
strict discipline which went with it, they started out from the viewpoint
that a relatively small number of resolute, well-organized men would
be able, at a given favorable moment, not only to seize the helm of
state, but also by a display of great, ruthless energy, to maintain power
until they succeeded in sweeping the mass of the people into the

revolution and ranging them round the small band of leaders. This involved, above all, the strictest, dictatorial centralization of all power in the hands of the new revolutionary government.[73]

But this is Engels' description of *Blanquist* revolution—the kind of minoritarian revolutionary adventure against which classical Marxism inveighed so mightily. It is a revolution made by "great men" who impose their will upon history. It is a minoritarian revolution, leading unconscious masses to the seizure of the state machinery not in order to destroy it, but in order to elaborate upon it and to commit a captured nation to rule by hierarchical investiture. Marx had written that "nothing could be more foreign to the spirit of the Commune [which Engels and Lenin both identified with the dictatorship of the proletariat] than to supersede universal suffrage by hierarchic investiture."[74] In Cuba there is little disposition to substitute elections for the hierarchical investiture that has characterized the Cuban government since the revolution. Castro is trusted to solve the problem of creating new institutions of popular representation at some unspecified future time.

Castroism is the culmination of Leninism. Originally, Lenin maintained that class consciousness must be brought to the proletariat by declassed bourgeois intellectuals. He argued that this cadre of professional revolutionaries must maintain a highly centralized, hierarchical party devoted to the one "true science of society." He supplemented these convictions with the theory of revolution in economically backward areas where the enlightened party would lead insurgent peasant and petty bourgeois elements in the service of the political vision of the future. In economically impoverished Russia the party became the manifestation of the ultimate rather than the immediate interests of the proletariat. The party possessed of the true vision of the future could divorce itself from the express and immediate interests of the working class, not to speak of those of the peasantry and the petty bourgeoisie. With the advent of the theory of socialism in one country the party identified itself with the ultimate interests of the nation. Man's vision was to create the economic base in which that vision would be reflected. Men, disciplined by the single minoritarian party that had become guardian of that vision, were to be marshaled to construct a society that the masses could not yet envision. An elite is understood to represent the *real* will, as distinct from the *momentary* will of individuals taken singly or in aggregate.

In China the features remained essentially the same with the exception of the exaggerated emphasis upon peasant initiative (which was later modified to better accord with Leninist theory) and the increased commitment to voluntarism divorced from objective or material conditions. In Cuba the pretense that a class or a party possesses the true consciousness has been all but abandoned. A large and articulate working class existed there before the revolution. The revolution did not rest upon its support—nor was any attempt made to involve the urban working class in the deliberations of the Fidelistas. The peasant class provided some of the revolutionary force, but their intellects were virginal. Even the Partido Socialista Popular, the official Communist Party of Cuba, was not considered the bearer of true consciousness. True consciousness resided only with Fidel Castro Ruz. Freed of objective conditions, freed of involvement with the urban working class and their aspiring Communist Party representatives, *Castroism made a revolution in the name of one man's vision of the good society.* History is no longer moved by economic forces, the development of the productive forces. Leninism's priority of politics over economics had already made that evident. But neither class nor party seem to bear any intelligible relationship to the sequence of events. History moves, insurrections are undertaken, and revolutionary phases are initiated and closed upon the command of a world historical individual who speaks in the name of the real will of the nation, which only he can interpret.

Conclusions

•   Leninism as an ideology has undergone significant doctrinal development, but its course was already implicit in Lenin's original theses. Lenin did not intend that his innovations would promote an abandonment of classical Marxism. Until his death, he expected a saving revolution from the West that would restore the essentials of the orthodox tradition. Nonetheless, Leninism had inverted a number of critical classical theses in this tradition. "Consciousness," the appreciation of the *real* will of a collectivity, was not the possession of a mature working class. It was the possession of a self-selected and self-perpetuating body of revolutionary intellectuals. Furthermore, revolutionary potential increased in inverse proportion to economic development. Revolution would more easily manifest itself in proletarian nations, colonial or semicolonial dependencies where insurgent masses were necessarily lacking in the sophistication that would qualify them to rule. This lack necessitated the elaboration and perpetuation of state machinery to ensure the discipline and dedication requisite for the initial arduous phase of industrialization (after the hope of a revolution in the highly industrial West had been abandoned). The minority party comes to identify itself with the state and the state with the people. For it is the consciousness of the party, the manifestation of the universal truth of Marxism-Leninism, that guides the nation in the course of its *true*, that is, historical and imperative, goals. The license to rule is certified by the truth of Marxism-Leninism. Only Communists "armed with Marxist theory" can predict the general course of history.[75] Only Communists, therefore, are equipped with the truth necessary to lead mankind to the "paradise on earth" of which Lenin spoke and the "Great Harmony" of Mao. The test of so important a body of truth is *never* majority decision. The defense of truth is a difficult, demanding task, truth can only be won by a few, but "they *alone* are *the leaders of the people.* . . . It is not a question of numbers, but of giving correct expression to the ideas of the truly revolutionary proletariat."[76]

We have suggested that classical Marxism was a loosely textured collection of theoretical propositions in which some of the critical functional relationships between variables were not stipulated with care. Much of its language is metaphorical. As a consequence the interpretation of such a body of truths is always subject to dispute. Factional infighting has therefore been one of the characteristic features of Marxist parties. Such infighting has, on a variety of occasions, not only undermined the revolutionary potential but shattered the organizational fabric of Marxist movements.

Classical Marxism has given birth to a multiplicity of sects, each advancing itself as the truly orthodox heir of scientific socialism. Leninism has attempted to circumvent this ever-present hazard by institutionalizing hierarchy and banishing opposition. But this effort involves an elaborate system of substitutions. Classical Marxism spoke in the name of the real will of *mankind*, and the proletariat was the class that possessed the consciousness of that will. The proletariat was substituted for mankind. But Lenin argued that the proletariat was condemned to only a petty bourgeois consciousness unless guided by the revolutionary consciousness of the party leadership. The party was then substituted for the proletariat. But if the party leadership lapses into factions in the interpretation of the truth, its disputes can only be resolved by the intercession of some ultimate authority. The party leader was then substituted for the party. The *party leader* thus becomes the interpreter of the ultimate interests of mankind.

To avoid such a reductionist course, Leninism would have to abandon its claim that Marxism-Leninism is the sole source of truth. Its system would degenerate into a multiparty system that tolerates differences. But few revolutionary parties have shown themselves disposed to share power. Leninist parties have, because of their assumption of leadership in countries afflicted with backward economies, assumed tasks of such imposing magnitude that the disciplined unity of a one-party state seems to be essential to national survival. Thus in Leninist countries, party rule means a dictatorship that brooks no opposition, and inner-party democracy can never mean freedom of factional groups. "Inner-party democracy" means, according to Stalin, strengthening the unity of the party. Intraparty differences can only be resolved by fiat. Since Marxism, and Leninism as well, is such a loose theoretical structure (upon which, nonetheless, the party's ultimate right to rule must rest), judgments on what is to be understood as the truth must be decisive. Such decisions can only be made by a small collective leadership, or, more efficiently, by one man. Since that one man's judgment becomes the final arbiter of so critical a body of truth, his every dictum must bear the mantle of "genius." Thus the Soviet Union's *Brief Philosophical Dictionary* describes Lenin as the "theoretical genius and guide of the world proletariat"; Stalin is spoken of as "the genius who is continuing the great cause of Lenin"; Chinese Communists are admonished to arm themselves with "Mao Tse-tung's thinking"; Guevara informs Cubans that Castro is a "telluric force" possessed of "tremendous" personality. The cult of personality is a necessary consequence of a system whose ultimate justification rests on truths for which there is no known process of objective accreditation. As long as such determinations were to be made within a national context, the decisions could be rendered by the "genius" who controlled the party apparatus, but when Leninism captured a number of nations outside the effective control of Moscow, no final arbitration was possible and conflicting interpretations tended to generate national deviations. This has been the process that has transformed prewar Leninist monocentrism into postwar polycentrism.

In 1935 Nikolai Bukharin could still maintain that national rivalry between Communist states was, by definition, an impossibility. Today the confrontation between China and the Soviet Union, the frictions evident between Communist states are bitter realities. Leninism has become the creed of revolutionary *national* communisms. It is a revolutionary creed most suitably adapted for colonial or semicolonial areas. Its monolithic state structure seems designed to force rapid industrial development on the national level at whatever cost. The values to which it makes appeal are generally nationalist, an appeal for a place in the sun for nations that had hitherto languished as dependencies. The Cuban cry is "the fatherland or death." China's Communists appeal to the commitment to "national regeneration." Even Nicolae Ceausescu's appeal to the Rumanian people to industrialize more rapidly in order to "ensure national independence and sovereignty" is nationalist. Similar sentiments animate Leninists from Albania, North Korea, Indonesia, Poland, and a host of other nations. Lenin has proclaimed that "the aim of socialism is the elimination of the fragmentation of humanity in petty states and the individualism of nations, not only the coming closer of nations to each other, but their merger or fusion." In this endeavor Leninism has been notably unsuccessful. The Albanian Labor Party and the Chinese Communist Party have attacked what they call "Tito's national communism" and the Italian Communist Party's disposition to go "the Italian way" that must inevitably lead to "nationalism." The Czechoslovak Communist Party has attacked Communist China because of what it terms its "adventurism" and "nationalism." The

Chinese Communist Party has charged the Soviet Communist Party with falling "into the quagmire of great-nation chauvinism [and] other forms of bourgeois nationalism." The French Communist Party has maintained that the Chinese Communists have appealed to "nationalist movements." The Chinese Party has denounced the Indian Communist Party for what it terms a betrayal of Marxism-Leninism by "stirring up reactionary nationalist sentiment, fanatical national chauvinism." The Communist Party of China has charged the Communist Party of the United States with being addicted to "great-power chauvinism."[77]

The fact is that Marxism-Leninism was, at least in this one principal respect, the product of a nineteenth-century humanitarian optimism. None of its optimisms were more utopian or, as seems obvious, more doomed to failure, than its vision of proletarian internationalism. Stalin's doctrine of socialism in one country transformed proletarian internationalism into national communisms. Each subsequent independent socialist revolution has been animated by the same national purpose. Ours is an age of nationalism.

The development of Leninism as an ideology of national communism is the most eloquent testimony to the failure of classical Marxism's theoretical apparatus. This is nowhere more evident than in the abandonment of "class" as an analytic and theoretic concept. Classical Marxism had predicated proletarian internationalism upon an assessment of contemporary society that made class membership an ultimate determinant. Class consciousness was a function of class membership. Political parties more or less adequately represented classes. The state was machinery developed by one class for the oppression of other classes. All of these theses have been abandoned by Leninism. Class interest, class membership, and the class mission are all referred to with tedious regularity, but they are all used to mean some "ultimate" class interest, some "implicit" class membership, and some "ideal" class mission. Leninists have acceded to power in countries embarrassed by the absence of an urban working class. The party of the proletarian class has more frequently than not been a party of dissident intellectuals. In other countries where an urban working class is to be found, the Leninists, as in Cuba, have simply ignored it.

The abandonment of class as a serious theoretical, analytic, or tactical guide is most evident in contemporary Leninist discussions concerning the state. Classical Marxism had analyzed the state as the machinery of class oppression. Marx, Engels, and Lenin were all in substantial agreement that the existence of the state, *any* state, was indisputable evidence that society was riven by antagonistic classes. Where no antagonistic classes were to be found, no state would be found either. The future classless society, therefore, must necessarily be a stateless society, a *commune*, a *Gemeinschaft* or *Gemeinwesen*. In the long, acrimonious discussion between contenders for Marxist-Leninist orthodoxy much has been written by contemporary Leninists concerning the state. What has become increasingly obvious is that the analysis of the state, its nature, and its functions no longer bears any resemblance to that advanced by classical Marxism. In Khrushchev's comments on the program of the Communist Party revealed at the Twenty-second Party Congress it is plain that Leninism has suffered another "creative development." The victory of socialism in the Soviet Union, we are informed, has

. . . transformed the state of proletarian dictatorship into *a state of the whole people*. That, comrades, *is a fact unparalleled in history*! Until now the state has always been an instrument of dictatorship by this or that class. In our country, for the first time in history, a state has taken shape which is not a dictatorship of any one class, but an *instrument of society as a whole, of the entire people*. . . . The state develops from an instrument of class domination into an organ expressing the will of the whole people. The might of our society and state, far from diminishing, increases many times over in the course of its development from a dictatorship of the proletariat into a state of the whole people. . . . Every worker, every peasant, every intellectual can say: We are the state; its policy is our policy. . . . The state will remain long after the victory of the first phase of communism. The process of its withering away will be a very long one; it will cover an entire historical epoch. . . .[78]

In February, 1964, the Plenary Meeting of the Communist Party of the Soviet Union spoke flatly and frankly of the "future statehood in communist society." Classical Marxism denied the possibility of a "classless" state, an "all-people's" state, a state that is the expression of the will of a whole people. But contemporary Leninism has devolved so many responsibilities upon the state that nowhere is there any indication that Leninists intend to permit the state to wither away. They have decided to make a virtue of necessity. The state has necessary economic and organizational as well as cultural and pedagogical functions. What is particularly interesting is the increasing emphasis, in recent discussions, of the ideological or pedogogical responsibilities of the state as the executive arm of the Communist Party. The program adopted at the Twenty-second Party Congress states:

> In the struggle for the victory of communism, ideological work becomes an increasingly powerful factor. . . . The Party considers that the paramount task in the ideological field in the present period is to educate all the working people in a spirit of ideological integrity and devotion to communism. . . . Special importance is attached by the Party to the molding of the rising generation.[79]

The Party, through the machinery of an all-people's state, will inculcate a "new ethics"; for, true to the original Leninist commitment, the working class is incapable of spontaneously developing a communist consciousness. That consciousness can only be brought to the masses through the agencies of the state under the direction and guidance of the Party.

The "new ethics" to be inculcated derives its imperative force from the classical Marxist conviction that man is in essence an ensemble of social relations. Contemporary Leninists focus attention on the injunction implicit in the classical Marxist definition of man, which conceives him as an essentially social being.[80] What has masqueraded as a descriptive account and a set of informative propositions about man is now seen to have normative or evaluative character. Liberalism or individualism has proffered an account of man that is not only erroneous but immoral as well, because individualism alienates the individual from his essence. Contemporary Leninists conceive man as a living concentration of social relations. This conviction is advanced in the guise of a factual assessment. But such a factual proposition is understood, by Leninists, to generate an imperative. Man's existence *should* correspond with his essence. Characteristically, contemporary Leninists return to the early writings of Karl Marx, which are infused with moral imperatives: "The individual *is the social being.* . . . Man's individual and species life are not different. . . . In his *consciousness of species* man confirms his real *social life.*" The following pronouncements evince normative injunctions: "A social revolution," Marx contended, ". . . is a protest of men against degraded life, because it proceeds from the *standpoint of the real individual,* who reacts against his separation from the community, that *true* community which is the *human* essence.[81] The adjectival use of "real," "true," and "human" impart *normative* force to seemingly *descriptive* propositions.

Contemporary Leninists who increasingly charge the state, as the principal instrument of Party policy, with the responsibility of inculcating "Communist morality," return more and more insistently to the early writings of Marx, where the ethics of secular humanism are most emphatic. This preoccupation with imparting a Communist morality has become so imperative that the Party program describes the promotion of such an ethic as one of the most important functions of the state. Communist morality is described as

. . . the noblest and most just morality, for it expresses the interests and ideals of the whole of working mankind. Communism makes the elementary standards of morality and justice, which were distorted or shamelessly flouted under the rule of the exploiters, inviolable rules for relations both between individuals and between peoples. Communist morality encompasses the fundamental norms of human morality which the masses of the people evolved in the course of milleniums as they fought against vice and social oppression.[82]

Not only is such a commitment explicit, but it stands in stark variance with the conception of ethics that animated classical Marxism. Contemporary Leninists utter prescriptions and proscriptions that have taken on the character of absolute ethics. There is talk of "fundamental norms" evolved by the "masses of the people" (not even the "working" people much less the "proletariat," which certainly has not existed for the requisite millennia) in the course of time. Parallel to the class moralities of times past there existed a timeless morality developed by the masses of the people. The imperatives issued by this morality evolved in the course of millennia by the masses of the people include: "Subordinate private interests to the interests of the collectivity"; "Remain faithful to communism by maintaining faith in the Marxist Party, its leadership, and its authority"; "Maintain a high sense of public duty, intolerance of actions harmful to public interest, honesty and truthfulness, moral purity, modesty and unpretentiousness in social and private life, mutual respect in the family and concern for the upbringing of children, an uncompromising attitude to injustice, parasitism, dishonesty, careerism, and money-grubbing."

This incredibly bourgeois list could be extended to include an abundance of almost Victorian imperatives, including the necessity of an education calculated to invoke "patriotism, the love of one's people and fatherland." All of these prescriptions have been formalized in a "Moral Code for the Builders of Communism."[83] The Party and the state administer the code, guide the education that systematically inculcates it, and legislate its apparently variable content.

What has made its fulsome appearance in the Soviet Union— and it appears that other Leninist states are destined to produce functional analogues—is the pedagogical or ethical state. Such a state is conceived in some sense as expressing the real will, yet standing above the aggregate of citizens of which it is composed. Leninist protestations notwithstanding, the citizenry is understood to be incapable of ever developing Communist consciousness without the express and systematic intervention of the state, the executive agency of the Party. These theses are expressed in the following manner: ". . . the formation of the new man, the new communist moral does not proceed independently, spontaneously, but rather under the immediate influence of the organizational and pedagogical (ideological) efforts of the Marxist Party. . . ."[84] The ultimate ethical vindication of Party rule rests on the conviction that the Party is armed with universal and infallible truth in the form of Leninist theory. Historical materialism, it is insisted, is the *only certain* and *scientific solution* to the problems of social science. The Party possessed of such truth is led by "farsighted, clever and experienced leaders" without whom Communist victory cannot be achieved. The leadership of the Party is the "most important and decisive condition" for such victory. In effect, the leaders are world historical personalities possessed of both cognitive truth and moral vision.

Whatever imperative force these doctrinal statements have derives ultimately from the Leninist conception of man—that man is, in some ultimate sense, a social being. The individual is defined not in terms of some intrinsic properties but rather in terms of his relations to others. Apart from these social relations man has, strictly speaking, no human essence. These relations are constitutive of the essence of man and consequently constitutive of any individual insofar as he is human. In the final analysis it is society that produces man as man. Such a definition of man accords priority and intrinsic value to society vis-à-vis the individual. This conception stands at stark variance with the Christian, Kantian, or natural law conception, which conceives each individual as possessing intrinsic value and substantive rights independent of the society of which he is member. Because of this commitment, liberalism (as we have christened methodological and analytic individualism) conceives the real possibility of a conflict of interest between the individual and the society of which he is a member. It is this possibility that Leninist ideologues take great pains to reject. The principle of collectivism rests on the conviction of a substantial identity between individual and collective interests. Leninists observe that "the new type of individuality distinguishes itself from the old specifically in that it does not find itself in conflict with the collective whole."[85] Such a conviction is already implicitly contained in the recommended redefinition of man as an "ensemble of social relations." Such a proposition has both descriptive character and normative intent. The moral ideal of humanity is a society that creates social conditions in which the free development of man is the condition for the free development of all. Since man is an aggregate of concrete social relations, each of those social relations is constitutive of himself. In some vague sense it is contended that the individual cannot be in substantial conflict with elements of himself. The individual and society are in a literal sense one. Only a society based on the proposed redefinition of man can fully realize man's potential and permit his free development as a person through the establishment of unrestricted interpersonal relations. Only in such a society would man's essence correspond with his existence.

It is not our purpose here to pursue all the difficulties that afflict such a system of ethics. It is only necessary to indicate that in the final analysis the ideal entertained is far too vague to provide criteria for evaluating specific ethical injunctions. What can such a conception tell us about prescriptives enjoining "moral purity," "modesty," or "unpretentiousness in social and private life"? Ultimately the content of such a proposed moral code must derive from dicta issued by the Party and because of the hierarchical structure of the Party must ultimately derive from the "farsighted, clever and experienced leadership," who, in effect, tower independent over the code they fashion.

It seems that what Leninism has achieved is a literal restoration of the social and political philosophy of Hegel, couched in commonplace idiom and conjoined with a general social theory that issues judgments framed in terms of "inevitability," "universality," "necessity," and "absolute truth." That Leninism as an ideology has followed this course is the result of the fact that it inherited the normative components of classical Marxism, which were essentially those of Hegelianism. The theoretical elements of classical Marxism that pretended to talk in terms of positive science were so vaguely formulated that the effort to "creatively develop" them produced internal tensions that qualitatively transformed the original system. The sweeping assertions of classical Marxism that economic conditions determine the development and change of all other features of human society has informative or explanatory merit only insofar as it can be rendered precise by explicit laws which specify just what order of change in human affairs will regularly follow upon specific modifications in the material conditions of life. Leninism attempted to employ such general statements, usually advanced as metaphors and analogies, in its insurrectional and organizational activities. Under the stresses produced by prevailing conditions these assertions were given varied and various interpretations as the situation demanded. In themselves the assertions have little, if any, informative or explanatory power and were consequently discreetly jettisoned. What remains of classical Marxism is its normative element, and this is essentially Hegelian.

The normative core of Leninism is the proposed redefinition of man, and that definition was shared by Marx and Hegel.

The gradual abandonment of the theoretical machinery of classical Marxism has revealed the restoration of almost all the Hegelian categories. The "freedom" to which Leninists aspire is Hegelian freedom. It is a freedom that is characterized by the identity of the interest of the individual and the collectivity, and that collectivity has long since ceased to be one or another class. That collectivity is the socialist fatherland and the ethical or pedagogical state through which, as Hegel contended, the real interests of the *whole people* find expression. The entire force of Leninist reasoning is calculated to support a Hegelian presumption in favor of a rule-governed collectivity over and above the empirical individual. The rule-governed community, for the Leninist, is the socialist nation, and the promulgation of rules is the responsibility of the ethical state, the executive agency of the Party. Within such a context a procedural priority is accorded the rule-governed association and nonconformity *qua* nonconformity on the part of the individual requires justification. Nonconformity threatens the viability of the association, and since it is only in association that the individual becomes possessed of the qualities that characterize his humanity, nonconformity, in principle, requires justification.

Classical Marxism failed to accommodate some of the stark realities of our time. It conceived nationalism as a dependent variable at a time when its independent force was becoming increasingly apparent. It conceived the state as the executive arm of economic interests at a time when men were becoming increasingly conscious of its autonomous power. It refused to recognize the impact of singular, charismatic leaders on society at a time when restive masses were making more and more evident the potential force that awaited such leadership. Such grievous misassessments were the consequence of an unfortunate, if consistent, reductionism on the part of classical Marxism, a shortcoming that could not, whatever other afflictions it suffered, be charged to Hegelianism. Leninism, in turn, has been driven to restoring a place for each of these historical factors; as a consequence, it has taken on a singularly Hegelian appearance. Leninism, in fact, is Hegelianism couched in positivist idiom.

Notes

1. K. Marx, *Grundrisse der Kritik der Politischen Okonomie (Rohentwurf)* (Berlin: Dietz, 1953), p. 6. See also N. Rotenstreich, *Basic Problems of Marx's Philosophy* (New York: Bobbs-Merrill, 1965), particularly Chap. iv.

2. F. Tönnies, *Marx: Leben und Lehre* (Jena: Lichtenstein, 1921), pp. 117f.

3. V. I. Lenin, "What the 'Friends of the People' are and How They Fight the Social Democrats," *Collected Works [LCW]* (Moscow: Foreign Languages, 1960–), I, pp. 189, 142; see also p. 165.

4. "Karl Marx," *LCW*, XXI, pp. 56f.

5. "What the 'Friends of the People' are . . . ," *LCW*, I, pp. 137f., 139f.

6. *Ibid.*, p. 166.

7. *Ibid.*, pp. 185, 177.

8. G. Plekhanov, "The Development of the Monist View of History," *Selected Philosophical Works* (Moscow: Foreign Languages, n.d.), I, p. 690; see also p. 653.

9. G. Plekhanov, *Fundamental Problems of Marxism* (New York: International, n.d.), p. 93; *Selected Philosophical Works*, I, p. 693.

10. Plekhanov, *Selected Philosophical Works*, p. 652; *Fundamental Problems*, pp. 90, 92f.; *The Role of the Individual in History* (New York: International, 1940), pp. 17, 54f.

11. See A. J. Gregor, *A Survey of Marxism: Problems in Philosophy and the Theory of History* (New York: Random House, 1965), pp. 177–85.

12. K. Marx and F. Engels, "The Communist Manifesto," *Selected Works in Two Volumes [MESW]* (Moscow: Foreign Languages, 1955), I, p. 62; "Grundsätze des Kommunismus, *Werke [MEW]* (Berlin: Dietz, 1957–), IV, p. 372.

13. "A Talk With the Defenders of Economism," *LCW*, V, p. 316.

14. "What is to be Done?" *LCW*, V, p. 374.

15. *Ibid.*, pp. 375, 383f.

16. K. Marx and F. Engels, *The Holy Family*, trans. by R. Dixon (Moscow: Foreign Languages, 1956), p. 73. See also "The Communist Manifesto," *MESW*, I, p. 43; A. G. Meyer, *Communism* (New York: Random House, 1960), p. 39.

17. See "What the 'Friends of the People' are . . . ," *LCW*, I, p. 142; "Socialism and Religion," *LCW*, X, p. 87.

18. R. Luxemburg, *The Russian Revolution and Leninism or Marxism* (Ann Arbor: University of Michigan, 1962), pp. 81–108.

19. K. Kautsky, *The Dictatorship of the Proletariat* (Ann Arbor: University of Michigan, 1964), pp. 12f., 15.

20. F. Engels, *Anti-Duehring: Herr Eugen Duehring's Revolution in Science* (Moscow: Foreign Languages, 1962), pp. 386f.

21. G. Hegel, *Reason in History: A General Introduction to the Philosophy of History*, trans. by R. S. Hartman (New York: Bobbs-Merrill, 1953), p. 40. Copyright © 1953, by The Liberal Arts Press, Inc. Reprinted by permission of The Liberal Arts Press Division of The Bobbs-Merrill Company, Inc.

22. *Vladimir Lenin: A Political Biography*, prepared by the Marx-Engels-Lenin Institute, Moscow (New York: International, 1943), p. 138.

23. "Imperialism," *LCW*, XXII, pp. 191, 193f. See also "Opportunism and the Collapse of the Second International," *LCW*, XXII, pp. 108–20.

24. See "The Awakening of Asia" and "Backward Europe and Advanced Asia," *LCW*, XIX, pp. 85f., 99f.

25. "Revision of the Party Programme," *LCW*, XXVI, pp. 168f.

26. F. Engels, "Democratic Panslavism," *The Russian Menace to Europe*, ed. by P. Blackstone and B. Hoselitz (New York: Free Press, 1952), p. 72. See also *ibid.*, pp. 69, 71; "Hungary and Panslavism," *ibid.*, p. 58; Marx and Engels, "Communist Manifesto," *MESW*, p. 44; K. Marx, *Capital* (Moscow: Foreign Languages, 1954), I, p. 764, *n.* 1.

27. Engels' Introduction to Marx, "The Class Struggles in France 1848–1850," *MESW*, I, p. 134.

28. "The State and Revolution," *LCW*, XXV, pp. 387, 409.

29. See *ibid.*, pp. 419ff., 453, 463.

30. "Speech Against Bukharin's Amendment to the Resolution on the Party Programme," *LCW*, XXVII, p. 147.

31. "The Immediate Tasks of the Soviet Government," *LCW*, XXVII, pp. 248f. See also N. Gourfinkel, *Lenin*, trans. by M. Thornton (New York: Grove, 1961), pp. 141–50.

32. "Original Version of the Article, 'The Immediate Tasks of the Soviet Government,'" *LCW*, XXVII, p. 216; "Immediate Tasks . . . ," *LCW*, XXVII, p. 259; "Report on the Immediate Tasks of the Soviet Government," *LCW*, XXVII, pp. 294f.

33. K. Marx and F. Engels, *The German Ideology* [*GI*], ed. and trans. by R. Pascal (New York: International, 1947), p. 69. Copyright © 1947, by International Publishers Co., Inc. Reprinted by permission of International Publishers Co., Inc.

34. "Immediate Tasks . . . ," *LCW*, XXVII, p. 269.

35. "Original Version . . . ," *LCW*, XXVII, p. 215; "Report on the Immediate Tasks . . . ," *LCW*, XXVII, p. 293.

36. See R. Payne, *The Life and Death of Lenin* (New York: Simon and Schuster, 1964), pp. 411–22; L. Fischer, *The Life of Lenin* (New York: Harper & Row, 1964), Chap. xvii.

37. K. Marx, "Contribution to the Critique of Hegel's Philosophy of Right," *Early Writings*, ed. by T. Bottomore (New York: McGraw-Hill, 1964), pp. 52, 53, 59.

38. *GI*, p. 58.

39. Engels to Marx, letter dated October 7, 1858, in *Der Briefwechsel zwischen Friedrich Engels und Karl Marx: 1844–1883*, ed. by A. Bebel and E. Bernstein (Stuttgart: Dietz, 1913), II, p. 290.

40. Engels, "Hungary and Panslavism," *Russian Menace,* p. 64; "Democratic Panslavism," *ibid.*, p. 72.

41. "Farewell Letter to Swiss Workers," *LCW*, XXIII, p. 272.

42. L. Trotsky, *Permanent Revolution* (Calcutta: Gupta, Rahman and Gupta, 1947), p. 25, and *Stalin and Bolshevism* (New York: Pioneer, 1937), p. 15; B. D. Wolfe, *Marxism: 100 Years in the Life of a Doctrine* (New York: Dial, 1965), p. 89.

43. As quoted in I. Deutscher, *The Prophet Armed: Trotsky, 1879–1921* (New York: Random House, 1965), p. 455.

44. Engels, "On the History of the Communist League," *MESW*, II, pp. 355f.

45. J. Stalin, "Don't Forget the East," *Works [SW]* (Moscow: Foreign Languages, 1952–1955), IV, p. 174.

46. Stalin, citation in "Concerning Questions of Leninism," *SW*, VIII, p. 65.

47. L. Trotsky, "The Lessons of October," in G. Procacci (ed.), *La "revoluzione permanente" e il socialismo in un paese solo: 1924–1926* (Rome: Riuniti, 1963), pp. 35f., 85. For Trotsky's later views, see I. Deutscher, *The Prophet Outcast: Trotsky, 1929–1940* (New York: Random House, 1963), pp. 245f.

48. N. I. Bukharin, "On the Theory of Permanent Revolution," in Procacci, *op. cit.*, pp. 100f., 104, *n.* 1, 135; Zinoviev, "Leninism," in *ibid.*, p. 140.

49. J. Stalin, "Report to the Eighteenth Congress of the Communist Party," *Problems of Leninism* (Moscow: Foreign Languages, 1953), pp. 792–95.

50. "Political Report of the Central Committee to the Sixteenth Congress," *SW*, XII, p. 381.

51. As cited in I. Lapenna, *State and Law: Soviet and Yugoslav Theory* (New Haven: Yale, 1964), pp. 39f.

52. Quoted in A. B. Ulam, *The Unfinished Revolution* (New York: Vintage Books, 1964), p. 201.

53. Compare "The Tasks of the Proletariat in Our Revolution," *LCW*, XXIV, p. 85; "The State and Revolution," *LCW*, XXV, p. 468; and M. I. Piskotin, as cited in Lapenna, *op. cit.*, p. 69.

54. See S. R. Schram, *The Political Thought of Mao Tse-tung* (New York: Praeger, 1963), pp. 9f., 19f., 105f., 170f.

55. Mao Tse-tung, "Analysis of the Classes in Chinese Society," *Selected Works* [*MSW*] (New York: International, 1954–1956), I, pp. 13–19.

56. *MSW*, I, pp. 21f., 25, 32. Italics supplied.

57. Liu Shao-chi, *The Victory of Marxism-Leninism in China* (Peking: Foreign Languages, 1959), p. 5, italics supplied; see also p. 8.

58. "Resolution on Some Questions in the History of Our Party," *MSW*, IV, p. 206. Italics supplied.

59. Engels' Introduction to "The Class Struggles in France, 1848–1850," *MESW*, I, p. 119.

60. B. Schwartz, *Chinese Communism and the Rise of Mao* (Cambridge: Harvard, 1958), p. 191.

61. "On the Question of the National Bourgeoisie and the Enlightened Gentry," *MSW*, V, p. 207; see also "On the People's Democratic Dictatorship," *MSW*, V, p. 415.

62. Liu, *op. cit.*, pp. 15, 37.

63. For a discussion of this point, see Chen Po-ta, *Stalin and the Chinese Revolution* (Peking: Foreign Languages, 1953), p. 7.

64. "Resolution . . . ," *MSW*, IV, pp. 171, 174.

65. As cited in Schram, *op. cit.*, p. 80, italics supplied; see also pp. 78f.

66. Liu, *op. cit.*, p. 27. Italics supplied.

67. Liu Shao-chi, *On the Party* (Peking: Foreign Languages, 1951), pp. 2f. Liu gives the membership of the Communist Party as 1,210,000 in 1949 in a nation of 475,000,000 inhabitants.

68. Hou Wai-lu, *A Short History of Chinese Philosophy* (Peking: Foreign Languages, 1959), pp. 108f.

69. C. Guevara, *Guerrilla Warfare* (New York: Monthly Review, 1961), p. 15. Italics supplied. This has been retranslated to better accord with the original.

70. L. Conte Agüero, *Cartas del Presidio* (Havana: Editorial Lex, 1959), p. 60. Castro himself was the author of the *Cartas*.

71. As Cited in T. Draper, *Castroism: Theory and Practice* (New York: Praeger, 1965), pp. 75f., 8, 9; see also D. James, *Cuba: The First Soviet Satellite in the Americas* (New York: Avon, 1961), pp. 42–44.

72. J. P. Morray, *The Second Revolution in Cuba* (New York: Monthly Review, 1962), pp. 164f. Italics supplied.

73. Engels' Introduction to "The Civil War in France," *MESW*, I, pp. 482f.

74. Marx, "The Civil War in France," *MESW*, p. 521.

75. O. Kuusinen, *Fundamentals of Marxism-Leninism* (Moscow: Foreign Languages, 1961), p. 19.

76. "The Tasks of the Proletariat . . . ," *LCW*, XXIV, pp. 80, 82. Italics supplied.

77. *Marxist-Leninist Ideology Will Certainly Overcome Revisionism* (Tirana: Naim Frasheri, 1964), pp. 9, 159, 164; *The Differences Between Comrade Togliatti and Us* (Peking: Foreign Languages, 1963); *Workers of All Countries Unite, Oppose Our Common Enemy* (Peking: Foreign Languages, 1962), p. 4, 14; *Whence the Differences* (Peking: Foreign Languages, 1963), p. 3; *A Mirror for Revisionists* (Peking: Foreign Languages, 1963), pp. 1, 5, 7; *A Comment on the Statement of the Communist Party of the U.S.A.* (Peking: Foreign Languages, 1963), p. 11.

78. N. Khrushchev, *Report on the Program of the Communist Party of the Soviet Union* (New York: Crosscurrents, 1961), pp. 107–09. Italics supplied.

79. *Program of the Communist Party of the Soviet Union* (New York: Crosscurrents, 1961), pp. 118f.

80. D. Bergner, "Dialektischer Materialismus, Psychologie und Ethik," in G. Heyden (ed.), *Wissenschaft contra Spekulation* (Berlin: Akademie, 1964), pp. 208f.; K. Mácha, *Individuum und Gesellschaft* (Berlin: VEB, 1964), pp. 14, 19, 23, 271.

81. Marx, "Kritische Randglossen zu dem Artikel eines Preussen," *MEW*, I, p. 408. See also K. Marx, *Economic and Philosophic Manuscripts* (Moscow: Foreign Languages, n.d.), pp. 104f., and Mácha, *op. cit.*, pp. 272f.

82. *Program of the Communist Party*, p. 121.

83. *Die Grundlagen der kommunistischen Erziehung*, Soviet Academy for Pedagogical Science (Berlin: Volkseigener, 1964), p. 147.

84. A. F. Schischkin, *Grundlagen der marxistischen Ethik* (Berlin: Dietz, 1964), pp. 50f.

85. Mácha, *op. cit.*, p. 9. See also Schischkin, *op. cit.*, pp. 240, 252.

IV · *FASCISM AND FASCISMS*

The three decades between the death of Friedrich Engels in 1895 and the advent of Italian Fascism in 1922 include a remarkable period of intellectual activity in Italy. It was during this period that the major works of Vilfredo Pareto, Georges Sorel, Gaetano Mosca, and Roberto Michels appeared. In the first decade of the twentieth century the ideas of Pareto, Sorel, Mosca, and Michels found expression in the writings of representative syndicalist revolutionaries—Arturo Labriola, Giuseppe Prezzolini, Sergio Panunzio, and A. O. Olivetti—as well as in the writings of nationalist revolutionaries like Enrico Corradini. All these men, with the possible exception of Corradini, were in protracted and relatively intimate intellectual contact with each other. After World War I their thought became the basis of doctrinal arguments that supported the programmatic and organizational imperatives of the first Fascists.

These men were "protofascists" in that they provided the substance of the doctrine of Fascism, the set of loosely compatible ideas that served as an operational guide as well as a justificatory argument during its initial phases. The Fascists came to power in 1922. A decade later, with the publication of *La dottrina del fascismo,* they had developed a mature ideology. Thereafter, Fascism developed some doctrinal elaborations, such as a nationalist racism, and during its republican interlude (1943–1945) undertook substantial constitutional and socioeconomic innovations. But the *Dottrina* of 1932 remained its definitive ideological statement.

Protofascism and Fascist Doctrine

•   To identify Pareto and Mosca, perhaps the two most notable of those here considered, as protofascists is to say nothing more than that they contributed significantly to the doctrine of Fascism in that they (Mosca, probably indirectly) materially assisted Benito Mussolini in the formulation of his social and political thought. It is clear, however, that neither Pareto nor Mosca were ever Fascists in the literal sense of the word. In fact, Mosca was one of the small coterie of intellectuals who, under the leadership of Benedetto Croce, opposed the Fascist regime. Mosca was an anti-Fascist, but elements of his thought entered Fascist doctrine. Pareto, on the other hand, spoke of Mussolini, who had been his student in Switzerland,[1] with approval. Pareto was, in effect, a qualified supporter of the Fascist regime. This statement needs some qualification, for both Pareto and Mosca were essentially liberals (in the sense that we have identified liberals). Both men conceived society as an aggregate of individual atoms. Pareto was certainly a methodological individualist who conceived social phenomena as reducible, in principle, to individual psychology, and both men advocated institutional constraints on the collectivity in order to ensure individual freedom. In fact, one of Pareto's last articles, published in Mussolini's journal *Gerarchia,* was a defense of freedom of opinion and instruction against any governmental restraints.

The influence of Pareto and Mosca on nascent Fascism derives principally from (1) their critical analyses of classical Marxism as social science, (2) their general contribution to the antidemocratic tendencies of the first part of the twentieth century, and finally, (3) their respective theories of the functional role of "elites" in society. Both Pareto and Mosca focused their attention on historical materialism as a purportedly scientific enterprise. Both charged classical Marxism with simplism and reductionism in conceiving the relationship between material factors and superstructural elements as a determinate functional dependence of the latter on the former. While Engels admitted that the "ideological spheres," the "intellectual life process in general," might react on the economic factors "with a secondary effect," he insisted that the "material mode of existence is the *primum agens. . . .*"[2] Both Pareto and Mosca objected to this reductionist thesis. Pareto insisted that "there is a relationship of mutual dependence between economic conditions and the remaining social phenomena. . . . We find in this regard habitual error [on the part of Marxists], that of substituting for such mutual dependence a relationship of cause and effect." Mosca's criticism was essentially the same. "The error of historical materialism," he contended, "lies in holding that the economic factor is the only factor worthy of consideration as cause, and that all other factors have to be regarded as effects. Every great manifestation of human activity in the social field is at the same time both cause and effect of the changes that occur in manifestations of the same activity. . . ."[3]

The criticism was not, of course, original. Engels was well aware of it before he died. But both Pareto and Mosca emphasized the role of conviction, of dedication, of what might be termed the "belief systems" of the human participants in social action. Both considered the political and moral consciousness of human agents a dynamic determinant in society irreducible to strictly economic forces. For Pareto the decision of an individual or a group to undertake a course of action is governed by conviction. Often, if not always, the conviction rests upon nonlogical fictions, sincere illusions that provide the motive force of actions. These illusions and fictions become the derivations of Pareto's later, more mature *Trattato di sociologia generale*, written in 1915. These fictions serve to legitimize claimants to political and social power. In the perpetual struggle for dominance, society provides the arena for a succession of contending elites. There is a continual circulation of elites, each motivated by a belief system that coordinates action and legitimizes claims. Such legitimizing fictions tend to form relatively persistent nuclei, identified by Pareto as early as 1906 as sentiments that find expression in morality, religion, and patriotism. These sentiments are common dispositions that persist beneath variable surface manifestations. The dispositions find expression in the set of propositions—the belief system—that sustains and justifies the efforts of contending elites. The elites employ these systems of belief to mobilize the passive and diffident population in their support in the contest for power. What this meant for Pareto was that the economic factor could not be considered the *ultimate* determinant of social evolution. The relationship between economic and intellectual factors could not be construed as irreversible or unidirectional in the sense required by classical Marxism. The development in the economic base could not, in a simple and direct fashion, generate the consciousness needed to direct social change. The moral and intellectual qualities of men were no doubt *influenced* by economic factors, but they were not *determined* by them. And those moral and intellectual qualities, in turn, influenced economic factors. The relationship between the productive forces and consciousness was not irreversible, but rather a combination of reversible, sequential, and contingent relations: a relation of interdependency of variables in which moral and intellectual factors were of indeterminate but consequential weight.[4]

Mosca's analysis of the ruling class, which he had developed as early as 1881, was surprisingly similar to that of Pareto. He maintained that among the constant facts and tendencies to be observed in all political organisms, irrespective of classification, is a ruling class composed of a minority that exercises power and performs all political functions. It is to this minority that the majority defer. Such a minority rules because it acts in concert; it is organized. Its organization is sustained by a belief or ethical system that acts as both an operational guide and a vindication. Within a society social forces constantly contend for power, and the force that can mobilize the elemental potential of the masses prevails. Mosca calls the energizing belief system that mobilizes the masses a "political formula," a set of moral and juridical imperatives that have the appearance of rationality but are not subject to intersubjective certification. However, Mosca adds, this does not imply that political formulas are

. . . mere quackeries aptly invented to trick the masses into obedience. Anyone who viewed them in that light would fall into grave error. The truth is that they answer a real need in man's social nature; and this need, so universally felt, of governing and knowing that one is governed not on the basis of mere material or intellectual force, but on the basis of a moral principle, has beyond any doubt a practical and a real importance.[5]

The real need in man's social nature to which Mosca refers is the fact that all social groups are possessed of a set of beliefs, sentiments, habits, and interests that distinguish them from other groups, animating their cohesiveness and directing their disposition to pass and surpass. The ruling class mobilizes such sentiments in its own interests; but if it is to sustain its dominion, the political formulas employed by the ruling class must appeal to a viable combination of the forces operating within their particular social and economic environs. The formulas thus employed are never literally true; they are functional. Among the most functional of formulas are those that are religious, moral, and nationalist.

Mosca's conception of social causation was therefore neither unilateral nor monistic.

It seems altogether absurd to regard as mere effects, and never as dignified, respectable causes, the political doctrines and religious beliefs which constitute the moral foundations of state organisms. Penetrating deep down into the consciousness of ruling classes and masses alike, they legitimize and discipline command and justify obedience, and they create those special intellectual and moral atmospheres which contribute so greatly toward determining historical circumstances and so toward directing the course of human events. . . . Every moral force tries, as soon as it can, to acquire cohesion by creating an underpinning of interests vested in its favor, and every material force tries to justify itself by leaning upon some concept of an intellectual and moral order.[6]

Years later he analyzed historic changes through the operation of "two orders of forces . . . one which is intellectual and moral and the other material."[7]

Roberto Michels was considerably younger than Pareto and Mosca. He was, in fact, a disciple of Mosca and almost twenty years his junior. He and Mussolini (Michels was seven years older than Mussolini) had the same prewar socialist contacts. During this prewar period Mussolini referred to Michels' work and was apparently greatly influenced by him. And it was Michels who adapted most easily to the Fascist regime.

Michels' ideas reached maturity in his *Zur Soziologie des Parteiwesens in der modernen Demokratie* published in 1911 (published in Italy in 1912 as *La sociologia del partito politico nella democrazia moderna*). The ideas of concern to us are: (1) that humanity cannot dispense with minoritarian ruling classes because the masses, being politically indifferent, need guidance; (2) that successive dominant elites satisfy a variety of psychological needs on the part of the masses, among the most insistent of which is to supply the "necessary fictions," the "general ethical principles" that serve to mobilize their efforts in the service of ideal ends; and (3) that classical Marxism must be supplemented by a more sophisticated appraisal of the relationship of variables in functional relationships within society. In comparison to the growing body of analytic and empirical investigations of the relationship of consciousness to the productive forces, the original formulations of classical Marxism were deemed naïve. In the 1915 Italian edition of his *Zur Soziologie*, for example, Michels indicated that World War I had destroyed the Marxist illusion that the working classes of the world were united by economic, at the expense of national, interests.[8] The war brought about the reassessment of the relationship between the working class and the nation. The concept "nation" effectively replaced the concept "class" in theoretical as well as practical importance.

This remarkably similar collection of ideas found in the works of Pareto, Mosca, and Michels finds expression in the complex and often contradictory writings of Georges Sorel, a contemporary and intellectual companion of Pareto and an acknowledged master of Michels. Pareto, in fact, contended that Sorel and he, beginning from opposite points, had reached the same conclusions.[9] Sorel had argued that insurgent masses required special imperative expressions that would unite them by "evoking as an undivided whole the mass of sentiments [that] recur to the mind with the insistence of instincts [through which] men can reform their desires, passions, and mental activity."[10] Sorel calls these special language forms "myths." Such myths can weld together a special group—a nation, a people, or a class—

by arousing their most profound sentiments and at the same time directing their energies toward the solution of the real problems facing the group in its actual environment. Pareto understood Sorel's theory of the myth to be the consequence of a special application of his own theory of individual and group motivation.

Sorel was concerned with mobilizing the apathetic energies of the proletariat into a combined and directed vitality—to impart to a collectivity of men an absolute faith in their own strength. He systematically denied that such an eventuality was an automatic by-product of the economic process itself. Consequently, he also denied that classical Marxism was a universal social science capable of delivering general laws that could be employed to discern necessary and inevitable conclusions. He specifically inveighed against the thesis that the revolutionary consciousness of the proletariat could be an inevitable consequence of the maturation of the productive forces.[11] Sorel's thought moved irresistibly from objective factors in the social structure to the influence of private and subjective elements at work in the interplay of politics and economics. Sorel wanted to formulate a general theory of social action, and his preoccupation with proletarian violence was a special application of that theory of motivation. Men do not act because they have rationally assessed the nature and extent of their involvement in institutions or collectivities, but because they are committed to some myth. A political myth fosters and gives expression to collective endeavor, but a myth is a fiction because as a complex combination of thought and values, it can never be certified as "true" in an objective sense. Mythology has the function of generating the sense of unity that renders men capable of protracted communal endeavor.

Revolutionary mythology was to be employed to develop a proletarian "heroism"—proletarian dedication and selflessness. Sorelianism was a program for systematic moral regeneration, an ethical enterprise calculated to impart to man a new form of consciousness. Political mythology was a necessary organizational and ethical adjunct of that program.

The foregoing were the ideas current in Italy during Mussolini's formative years. The stages of his development from the anarchic, revolutionary socialism inherited from his father to the doctrine that brought him to power on October 28, 1922, were marked by his progressive assimilation and synthesis of these elements. His idiom remained, until the crisis of intervention, that of classical Marxism, but by that time the substance of his ideas had been significantly altered. Unlike the young Lenin, the young Mussolini was not a doctrinaire Marxist. As early as 1908 Mussolini enjoined socialists not to simply believe socialist doctrine

. . . with blind and dogmatic faith. . . . No. To believe is not enough; it is necessary to reason as well. . . . We are restive, inquiring spirits. We throw ideas—all ideas—into our intellectual furnace, and from the impure mass—through hard labor and in the purifying flame of passion—arises the idea freed of all heterogenous elements. . . . We wish to divest [socialism] of all Christian and humanitarian romanticism, and from the simplisms of petty bourgeois reformers, abandoning to the poets the imaginary social reconstructions of the future. Our socialist notions are free of all that is superfluous, vague, indeterminate, arbitrary, and which cannot resist the test of criticism.[12]

During this same period he maintained that that which is "decadent, sterile and negative in all philosophies is precisely the 'system,'" which is often nothing more than an "arbitrary and illogical" intellectualism.

At twenty-five, then, Mussolini had begun a massive revision of classical Marxism. As early as 1904, the year in which he reports that he studied social sciences with "a kind of passion" under Vilfredo Pareto, he made positive reference to Pareto's work, specifically his *Systemes socialistes*, describing it as "precise, clear, and mathematical" and embodying a "sane positivism."[13] Four years later he made specific reference to Pareto's theory of elites, referring to it as the "most ingenious sociological conception of modern times. History is nothing other than a succession of dominant elites."[14] It was in 1904, when he was twenty-one and under the immediate influence of Pareto, that Mussolini became a revolutionary syndicalist and separated himself from orthodox socialism by rejecting the "economic determinism" that "subjected man to inscrutable laws difficult to assess. . . ." He opted, instead, for that syndicalism which restored to history the "creative will of determinate and determining man, [man] who can leave the imprint of his modifying power on things and institutions which surround him, man who can 'will' in a given direction. Syndicalism does not reject 'economic necessity' but adds to it 'ethical consciousness.' "[15] In support of this conviction Mussolini made reference to the idealist political writings of Alfredo Oriani, who had specified that the task of every epoch was developing the human character. The task of syndicalism, for Mussolini, was to create "the new man, economically and morally." In order to accomplish that task determined men are necessary who will bring to the elemental energy of the masses a consciousness of purpose. Such men will constitute a "socialist vanguard," a Paretan elite that represents a new society in formation, a Sorelian force charged with *moral* purpose.

In the six years between 1904 and 1910 Mussolini forged a social and political doctrine substantially different from that of classical Marxism, whose language he still retained. Mussolini had become a revolutionary syndicalist and syndicalism remained the nucleus of his political convictions. The idiom remained Marxist; for the myth to which he appealed was still that of the class struggle and his sentiments remained internationalist. But his Marxism was voluntaristic and elitist, composed of a diversity of elements adapted from the thought of Pareto and Sorel. He had also been influenced by idealism and American pragmatism through the work of Giuseppe Prezzolini, Arturo Labriola, Sergio Panunzio, A. O. Olivetti, and Alfredo Oriani. By 1910 Mussolini was convinced that only an organized and dedicated minority, capable of heroism and sacrifice, could constitute a functional vanguard for a revolutionary mass movement. Only such a professional elite could forge from diffident and pliable human resources the "new moral consciousness" that could create "the spiritual unity of Italians."[16] With Prezzolini he rejected the thesis that this consciousness could be simply the reflex of economic conditions and conceived the revolutionary problem as one involving "ethical energy."[17]

Thus by 1911 Mussolini could justifiably maintain that he was not a "Marxist theologian." Marxism could not be read to the letter, he argued, it must be *interpreted*. He went on to indicate that all systems have their infirm elements—even Marxism. He did not interpret historical materialism as historical fatalism. Rather, he argued that the instruments of production and the development of productive forces are contingent upon the "intellectual capacity of man," a human factor of "incontestable importance." The "thought and action of man" were spoken of as independent determinants in social evolution.[18] As a consequence of this reformulation Claudio Treves identified Mussolini with an "absolute revolutionary idealism," and Benedetto Croce indicated that Mussolini had imparted a new spirit to Italian Marxism by introducing elements of Sorel, Bergson, and pragmatism as well as emphatic voluntarism and idealism.[19]

Mussolini's development was surprisingly similar to that followed by Lenin after 1900. The lawlike propositions of classical Marxism were tendency statements that could be used to little effect except in combination. Such a combination of statements necessarily involved some theorizing concerning the relative weights to be assigned to factors contributing to or reducing positive tendencies. Classical Marxism assumed its theoretical system was deductive in nature (events were "inevitable" and "necessary"). But a deductive pattern could be most economically achieved if a *single* factor were understood to enjoy almost exclusive subsumptive power. For classical Marxism that factor was the development of the instruments of production. Each statement in the lower level of theory could be derived, with the aid of appropriate minor premises, from some single statement of the higher level (for example, the invention of the steam engine and of the machinery for working cotton brought about an industrial revolution, a revolution that radically changed the whole civil society).

Lenin continued to treat classical Marxism as though it were such a deductive system. But he insisted that at some levels of the deductive system the statements generated must be corrected by a consideration of the influence of at least one extrinsic factor—the revolutionary consciousness of the organizational elite. Mussolini, in turn, rejected the entire monistic conception of classical Marxism. He introduced the influence of "the thought and action of man" on the level of the development of the productive forces themselves. Both Lenin's and Mussolini's interpretation of classical Marxism divested it of its monofactorial pretenses and assigned significant, if indeterminant, weight to human will and consciousness. Lenin's reinterpretation originally necessitated only peripheral theoretical adjustments. Mussolini's, on the other hand, literally transformed the entire system. From the time of the founding of the *Lotta di Classe* in 1910 (of which he was the editor) Mussolini began to express his own ideas. The principles that he was later to employ in founding Fascism began to manifest themselves in the guise of socialist ideas. He did remain, for the time being, the advocate of proletarian internationalism, of the irreconcilability of class antagonism, and of violent social revolution. But he was convinced of the incontestable efficacy of superior human will and determination and the pliability of the masses. As a consequence, he was an elitist, impatient with the principles of majority rule, and a voluntarist opposed to social or economic determinism.

In July, 1914, immediately before the outbreak of World War I, Mussolini made his position clear to his party comrades. He demanded the right to reinterpret the texts of classical Marxism. "You," he maintained, "see Marxism in the perspective of an evolutionary and positivistic interpretation, we see it . . . in the perspective of an *idealistic* interpretation, more modern."[20] Thus, with Europe poised at the edge of war, Mussolini made it clear that *his* Marxism had undergone fundamental revision. The war only accelerated an independent development begun ten years before.

The war found Mussolini the editor of the largest Socialist paper in Italy (*Avanti*) and one of the principal leaders of the Socialist party. The position he assumed, as a Socialist, during the months of July through October, 1914, was one of intransigent opposition to the war. His reasoning was clear. International war made *nations*, not *classes*, historic disputants. In international struggle the classes lost their autonomy and identified with collectivities; this defied the analysis of classical Marxism. "This is the reason," Mussolini contended, "that makes us detest the war. We are not . . . professional pacifists."

But throughout this period Mussolini was torn by grave personal doubts. His "absolute neutrality" vacillated. His private statements indicated that for him, as for Lenin, World War I, a war of unprecedented magnitude, created a doctrinal crisis. Beginning in October, 1914, Mussolini indicated that he was prepared to consider the international situation "from the *national* point of view." Finally, on October 18, he announced the necessity of shaking oneself free of "dogma," "eternal laws," and "iron necessity" in order to reassess the issue of national problems. Those Socialists, he argued, "who deny the existence of *national* problems are . . . blind and dogmatic. . . . *National* problems exist even for socialists." He rapidly reviewed the profound importance of national sentiments even within socialist parties themselves and suggested that the concept "nation" and its defense were very serious concerns.[21] At this point he resigned his editorship of *Avanti* but remained a member of the Italian Socialist party.

On October 25, in a letter to the *Corriera della Sera*, he specified his reasons for resigning his post. He maintained that he found it necessary to evaluate Italy's possible entrance into the war from a proletarian and national point of view. He went on to indicate, in fact, that his analysis was more national than proletarian. Finally, on November 10, 1914, the transition was completed. On that occasion he indicated that "the source of our psychological difficulty is this: we Socialists have never examined the problems of *nations*. The International never occupied itself with them. . . ." As a consequence the International was dead— overtaken by events. "We must find," he went on, "a conciliation between *the nation, which is a historic reality*, and class, which is a living reality. It is certain that the nation represents a stage in human progress that has not yet been transcended. . . . *The sentiment of nationality exists, it cannot be denied!*"[22] The class struggle should be postponed until after the war. National interest and national sentiment were to be accorded priority. For a voluntarist and activist like Mussolini, the vision of men from all classes and all walks of life united in one firm resolve was the vision of "spiritual unity" and "moral consciousness" that he had sought. He had discovered the political formula, the animating myth, with which to energize the masses.

Lenin, embroiled in the same doctrinal crisis, unable or unwilling to further modify the classical Marxism to which he had committed himself, resorted to the theory of imperialism to explain the willingness with which the proletariat embarked upon a program of systematic international carnage. As has already been suggested, Lenin's theory modified classical Marxism in its own way, for the focus of revolutionary potential was transferred to the backward countries. Mussolini, on the other hand, was prepared to admit national sentiment as a significant and independent determinant. His study of Pareto and his Sorelian voluntarism had already loosened the theoretical fabric of classical Marxism sufficiently to permit its inclusion.

Mussolini's decision to cast his lot with the interventionists of World War I reflected a significant doctrinal reorientation. Where his interpretation of history and his assessment of tactics had been hitherto governed by a *class* analysis, it was thereafter to employ *nationality* as the unit of interpretation. When Mussolini had founded his own journal in Forli in 1910 it was called *Lotta di Classe (The Class Struggle)*, but in 1914 when he founded an independent journal in Milan, it was called *Popolo d'Italia (The People of Italy)*. The political organization that arose to complement the new journal was called the Fasci di Azione Rivoluzionaria—the first Fascist political units. Fascism was born.

Mussolini's diary of the war between 1915 and 1917 is a record of the increasing explanatory force he attributed to nationality and national sentiment. "Italy appears, . . ." he wrote, "for . . . perhaps the first time, in the consciousness of so many of its sons, as a *single* and living reality, as the *common* fatherland. . . ." The nation is spoken of as a single unity, as a common homeland. Class distinctions play a smaller and smaller role in his assessments. The energy for prospective change is supplied not by a class, but by a *people*. To invoke and direct these elemental energies an elite was necessary. "The Italian people," Mussolini maintained, "is, at this moment, a mass of precious raw material." To make of it "a work of art, a government is necessary. A man. A man who possesses a hand with the delicate touch of an artist and, when necessary, the heavy hand of a warrior. A man sensitive and commanding."[23]

In 1914 he had argued that the class struggle should be postponed until after the war. By 1918, after the experience of the war itself, class was completely abandoned as a unit of meaningful analysis. *National* syndicalism replaced what had been *proletarian* syndicalism. It was a syndicalism predicated upon the reality of the nation and the sentiment that sustained it.[24]

The development of Fascism as national syndicalism was, from this juncture, sporadic and unsystematic. Like all doctrinal formulations, Fascist doctrinal statements were issued to support some organizational or tactical posture. Fascist syndicalism was composed of a loose body of descriptive propositions charged with the emotion of some common sentiments that provided the justificatory arguments in the support of a social action program. National syndicalism was a union of nationalist and syndicalist elements—an amalgam that Sorel maintained constituted evidence of Mussolini's peculiar political genius. While the elements were compatible, the resulting structure remained so loose that even Mussolini himself could not, at that time, draw out all its implications. Like many Italian socialists and syndicalists, he had always been something of an anarchist. As early as 1908 he had referred to the state in classical Marxist terms as "organized oppression at the cost of the individual."[25] As late as 1920, after he had made his transition to nationalism and a qualified idealism and was only two years away from the Fascist revolution, Mussolini could still proclaim that he was among the minority of individuals who were "in potential revolt against the state, not against this or that state, but against the state in itself. . . . Down with the state," he insisted, "in all its forms and incarnations. The state of yesterday, today, and tomorrow."[26] Like Lenin on the eve of the Bolshevik Revolution, he was still an anarcho-syndicalist. The end of the war, as he saw it, would bring a "sane and honest regime of *productive classes.*" There was the suggestion that the nation would be a free association of productive syndicates.

But even in making his statement of what he considered to be "religious consolation," Mussolini realized that anarchism was an absurdity. As early as 1909, Prezzolini, one of Mussolini's intimate syndicalist associates who had also been influenced by Pareto and Michels, had been led to ask, "Who would mediate the conflicts [between the proposed productive syndicates] and avoid the dissipation of force? If there is to be an arbiter, who is this arbiter to be?" As long as syndicalism was *proletarian* syndicalism, it was difficult to identify an arbiter for *general* proletarian interest as distinct from the interests of the proletariat of the railroad industry, the proletariat of the metallurgical industry, the proletariat of the automotive industry, and so forth. The proletarian syndicalism that aspired to abolish the political state would find itself constrained to reconstruct a central authority to mitigate the rivalry of the parochial interests of the industrial and agricultural components. The advent of *national* syndicalism, which committed itself to the conception of the nation as a historical, cultural, and spiritual reality, required a juridical or executive body that expressed the will and interest of that nation in its entirety, a juridical or executive body that did not speak in the name of any factional or class interests.

Less than eighteen months after his speech on the consolations of anarchism, in October, 1921, Mussolini published his programmatic outline for the Fascist party that was to "stabilize [the Fascist] . . . position with respect to the concepts of the nation, the state and humanity."[27] The nation was identified as the central analytic, theoretical, and political concept of Fascist doctrine. The nation was understood not only as the aggregate of individuals who live in a determinate territory in a determinate period of time, but also as an organism that includes an indefinite series of past, present, and future generations of which individuals are component but transient elements. The state, Mussolini argued, represents the interests of that historical and spiritual organism, and arbitrates and stabilizes the interests of the component classes and categories. The state thus assumed economic, political, juridical, and moral obligations. By November, 1921, the logic of national syndicalism became clear. Mussolini argued:

> We begin from the concept "nation," which for us is indefeasible and insuperable fact. . . . Beginning with the nation we arrive at the state, which is the tangible expression of government. . . . [We] wish to identify the nation with the state. . . . It is necessary that the state rediscover its authority, for without it there is only chaos.[28]

Thus, before the Fascist party's accession to power in 1922, a doctrinal position for Fascism had been formulated quite distinct from the classical Marxism and revolutionary proletarian syndicalism from which it had developed. A. O. Olivetti, another of the early intimates of Mussolini, argued that internal social and political developments must always "be subordinated to the supreme necessity of not jeopardizing the existence of the nation. . . . The nation is superior to classes, and every consideration of class must subordinate itself to the national interest."[29]

Early national syndicalist theoreticians developed the same argument but added an element that became increasingly recur-

rent in Fascist literature: The state not only arbitrated in the
national interest, but also had the obligation of fostering the
"national consciousness" of Italian productive classes; this consciousness, although based on instinct and sentiment, was nonetheless "sadly deficient." The state could conciliate interests
without coercion only if it undertook the systematic education of
the several productive classes in order to awaken a sense of
common purpose in them.[30] By 1925 Mussolini had given full
doctrinal accommodation to all these considerations, and in 1927
they became the justificatory arguments in the preamble of the
Carta del Lavoro, one of the most important pieces of Fascist
social and political legislation. In the same year Mussolini personally commended the doctrinal statement of national syndicalism contained in a work by Olivetti's son, Ezio Maria
Olivetti.[31] In his bibliography Olivetti cited the works of Vilfredo
Pareto, Gaetano Mosca, Roberto Michels, Sergio Panunzio, A. O.
Olivetti, and Georges Sorel. Fascism had fabricated its doctrine.

The Ideology of Fascism

·   During its initial phases Fascism underwent a *doctrinal* development. It was characterized by relativism and pragmatism
and its development was determined by the social and political
problems with which it contended. But at the same time Mussolini was aware of the fact that a mature ideology was composed
of three types of elements: ideal, doctrinal, and practical. On
August 26, 1921, he wrote to M. Bianchi that Fascism required,
"on pain of extinction," a body of doctrine which he did not
hesitate to call "the philosophy of Fascism." The orientation of
such a philosophy had already become obvious. Mussolini had
identified himself with the neoidealism that made its appearance
in Italy before the turn of the century. In 1921, before the Italian
House of Deputies, he tendered a confession of philosophic faith
that was an almost rank epistemological idealism.[32] He also
identified himself as an ethical idealist. The political events that
had marked the development of Fascism, he contended, were
"accompanied by a philosophic process: if it is true that matter
remained, for a century, on the altars, today it is spirit which
assumes that place. . . . Where one says that God returns, one
intends to affirm that the values of the spirit return."[33]

Thus, while he had reservations about the metaphysics and lyricism of neoidealism, it is clear that he accepted some form of idealist epistemology and an ethical idealism.[34] Mussolini's development had taken him from classical Marxism through the positivism of Pareto and Mosca, the romantic individualism of Nietzsche, and the moral idealism of Sorel. By 1920 Mussolini felt the need of a systematic social and ethical philosophy that would make Fascism an integral whole. The neo-Hegelian philosophy of Giovanni Gentile fulfilled that need. Years later, in speaking of the period immediately following World War I when he had been articulating a philosophic position for Fascism, he indicated that "Gentile prepared the road for those—like me—prepared to take it."

During the decade between 1922 and 1932, the Fascists attempted to develop a philosophical component that would complete their system. In June, 1932, a definitive statement of doctrine was published, *La dottrina del fascismo*, under Mussolini's name. It contained two sections, the first entitled "Idee fondamentali," which, in thirteen tightly written sections, set forth the social and political philosophy of Fascism; and the second, entitled "Dottrina politica e sociale," which contained an outline of the history of Fascism's development and a loose statement of its doctrinal position. The first section of the *Dottrina* was actually written by Gentile, the second by Mussolini. The entire *Dottrina* became the basis of the formal ideology of Fascism. During the Fascist period the actual author of the "Idee fondamentali" was never acknowledged, and many Fascist ideologues attempted to distinguish Fascist philosophy from the actualist philosophy of Gentile. But with the recognition of Gentile as the author of the philosophical glosses that precede the doctrinal statement by Mussolini, the distinction is hard to defend. The "Idee fondamentali" are patently actualist. Their author was the founder of actualism and identified himself as a Fascist. He conceived the Fascist state to be the embodiment of his principles. He worked for that state as a theorist and as a public administrator. As one of its last ideological apologists, he was assassinated on April 15, 1944.

Gentile's works provided the philosophic rationale for Fascism. The first full statement of Fascist social and political philosophy is to be found in Gentile's *Fondamenti della filosofia del diritto*, published in 1915. In this sense Gentile was a Fascist before there was a Fascism.[35] His last work, *Genesi e struttura della società*, posthumously published in 1946, was the last Fascist apologetic.

Giovanni Gentile and the Philosophy of Fascism

• Late in the Fascist period, Fascist theoreticians maintained that "every social and political theory . . . has as a foundation a particular manner of conceiving man, be it as an individual or in relation with his similars. Therefore, it is a matter of no small importance to understand the Fascist conception of the individual. . . ."[36] The philosophical conception of man that was the basis of Fascist doctrine was the antiliberal, neo-Hegelian conception of Gentile.

According to Gentile, indefeasible difficulties beset liberal political philosophy because the state and society are conceived as somehow antagonistic to the "self" or "true individuality" of man.[37] Thomas Paine and Jeremy Bentham, as cases in point, contended that every law was an evil and government a necessary evil because they conceived of law as a constraint on liberty and every constraint on liberty as a moral infraction. Under this interpretation "liberty" means nothing more than the absence of constraint. The definition entails a *recommendation* to so conceive liberty and, consequently, to assess law as a constraint on freedom. In this conception the absence of law is understood to afford the maximum *formal* occasions for freedom to act. According to Locke, for example, the complete absence of law would leave men in "a state of perfect freedom to order their actions and dispose of their possessions and persons as they think fit."

Gentile, in criticism, pointed out that these liberal theorists go on to argue that a certain minimum of this antagonistic constraint is the *sine qua non* of the full development of freedom, without which human life is at best "nasty, brutish and short." According to the contractualist thesis, when the "free individual" enters society, he is compelled to surrender some measure of his liberty to secure elementary rights. The issue, Gentile maintained, is whether there is any *effective* liberty without the security of elementary rights. Without freedom *from* violence, plunder and death, without freedom *from* circumstances that render each the enemy of all, is it at all meaningful to speak of freedom or liberty? Outside of society the putative "natural freedom" of individuals to order their actions and dispose of their possessions and persons as they think fit has very little real significance.

We are faced, Gentile contended, with a singular circumstance: Liberty (made significant by the acquisition of essential elementary rights) is enhanced, as it were, by subtraction, which suggests that liberty is not all of a piece like a bolt of cloth, but rather more like a plant that flourishes only with judicious pruning. If the analogy is appropriate, the pruning could hardly be conceived as destructive of liberty. Restraints that foster the increased *effective* freedom of the individual by insulating him from arbitrary and unpredictable violence and hindrance, by affording him certain securities, cannot seriously be deprecated as antagonistic to liberty. The paradox, Gentile suggests, arises out of the mistaken liberal conception that the claims of "others" upon the "self" are destructive of the individual's liberty and the neglect of the alternative thesis that the recognition of mutual claims *enhances* rather than diminishes the effective opportunity for life and development of individual freedom.

According to Gentile, the notion that man exists in perfect freedom anterior or exterior to society is simply a fiction. Actually, insofar as man is outside the organization of society with its system of reciprocal rules and obligations, he has no significant freedom. Outside of society man would be the subject of nature, not its master. He would be the enemy of all and friend of none. He would be threatened by persons and things alike. His would be a state of abject dependence. There would be no freedom, no security, no assurance of life, much less of liberty. The freedom that man is supposed to barter away in part upon entering society, in order to secure the remainder, is an imaginary possession, conveyed to society by an imaginary transfer.

Gentile objected that such a notion could arise only if the "individual" is conceived in a wholly abstract manner.[38] This abstract individual is not nourished and fostered by the rule-governed relations and obligations arising in society; he is ensconced in the recesses of an innermost particular self, a self that must be protected from a threatening external natural and

social world. The only possible outcome of this conviction was
the kind of speculative and pious anarchism that characterized
nineteenth-century liberal thought.[39] The egocentric recluse
Henry Thoreau was taken as a model of the fully developed self.
Society was held to be the father of monotony and uniformity,
the moral enemy of human nature.

Gentile argued that freedom from violence and depredation
was one of the *necessary conditions* of substantial freedom and,
furthermore, that the rule-governed association of men was not
only a necessary condition for freedom but that *freedom could
be meaningfully understood only as rule-governed behavior.* The
"human individual is not an atom. Immanent in the concept of
an individual is the concept of society. . . . Man is, in an absolute
sense, a political animal."[40] Man, as a spiritual agent, is an
essentially social animal who finds freedom only in a rule-
governed association with other men. Ethical idealists had long
argued that philosophers have always been implicitly committed
to this conception of man, for the concept of social man is entailed in the commitment to reason. Such a conception involves
a recognition of "the universal power" of reason that belongs
to all, those living and those dead, even those not yet born.
Reasoning necessarily appeals to intersubjective rules governing
truth ascription and moral assessment. It is the name given
to that rule-governed enterprise that involves all men who seek
to establish truth and vindicate moral decisions. That which
binds all men together is their humanity in rule-governed reason
—in thought. Outside of that spiritual community they are animals without a conception of truth or morality and without the
semblance of freedom.

For Gentile it is *thinking,* consequently, that uniquely characterizes man. Since thinking involves rule-governed language
behavior and must be "social" in that sense, Gentile's model of
man is "normic" in that it offers not only a collection of descriptive propositions characterizing what man *is,* but also a recommendation concerning what man *should* be. "Scrutinizing the
content of the moral law," Gentile argued, ". . . one provides
the most rigorous concept in the admonition: render yourself
human ('*sii uomo*'). But for clarity's sake it is preferable to
say . . . Think." Man cannot judge ". . . according to his own
private bias but as a man possessing the faculty of judgment that

is common and proper to all men—the universal power of reason. . . . For at the root of the 'I' there is a 'We.' The community to which an individual belongs is the basis of his spiritual existence. . . ."[41] Whether the concern is with truth or morality, the standards of correct thought and behavior arise only in a rule-governed association of persons that provides the individual with "an internal law to which his every word, his every action must conform at the moment of utterance or performance."[42] There is no rule without a standard by virtue of which correctness or incorrectness could be applied and no standard for the followers of rules unless there are those whose assessments provide the necessary conditions for the ascriptions "correct" and "incorrect."

Language is the essential and indissoluble link between men. As such, it is a paradigm of social interrelations. If thought is man's essence and language its expression, man can attain true humanity only in spiritual union with his fellows. Gentile finds the conception of man outside society not only a historical and empirical fiction, but literally senseless. An individual outside society would be either a god or an animal. Man to be truly man must respond to the imperious voice of reason, the voice of the spiritual community in which reason can be said to manifest itself. To reason is to show oneself disposed to submit to the procedural rules required by the concept rule-following. Ideally, reasoning is understood to be universal, but Gentile argued that the reasoning of men is always conditioned by historical circumstances. It is conditioned by the historical language of the spiritual community of which the empirical individual is a member. It is conditioned by the morality of that community. It is conditioned by the technical circumstances in which it is pursued. Ideally, all reasoning prescinds from personal and local limitations, but such reasoning is an aspiration, a moral ideal. In reality our thinking is always circumscribed by the brute facts of the world in which we live. Our actual thinking takes place in specific communities, in given familial, associational, and national circumstances.

A free individual does not undertake action out of impulse, instinct, or passion. We speak of individuals who are disposed to act impulsively or who are activated by instinct or passion as persons "dominated by impulse," or "compelled by instinct," or "in the grips of passion." Truly free actions are not capricious; they display elements of continuity and identity. There is a *point* to such acts. Behavior that is pointless is not free. It is lunatic. The point of human action resides in the *reasons* for which it is undertaken. But reasoning is intrinsically rule-governed, and rules are developed only in associations. In the modern world the most all-inclusive rule-governed association is the nation. Within its formal rule system all other associations, and the rules governing them, have their being. The nation, as the state, is sovereign and, in the last analysis, unconfined by any overarching association or rule system to which it must submit.

Gentile argued that even science, for example, although *ideally* universal, is in fact always historically particular and national. The ascription of truth status to specific scientific formulations always involves consideration of a determinate set of necessary conditions such as falsifiability (that is, some determinate empirical operation can either confirm or infirm the subject proposition), relevance (that is, the theoretical proposition answers the original question or applies to such a question), and predictive power (that is, such a proposition would reveal that specific matters of fact would prove to be the case which were not known to be the case when the original proposition was formulated). But scientific criteria alone are not sufficient for truth ascription. The fitness of a proposition or a set of propositions articulated as a theory to support desirable conduct of citizens or, more accurately, to support moral behavior has always served as a consideration in scientific truth ascription.

For Gentile such an understanding is essential to the appreciation of science as a *national* enterprise.[43] Philipp Frank has expressed this thesis in the following manner:

The conviction that science is independent of all moral and political influences arises when we regard science either as a collection of facts or as a picture of objective reality. But today, everyone who has attentively studied the logic of science will know that science actually is an instrument that serves the purpose of connecting present events with future events and deliberately utilizes this knowledge to shape future physical events as they are desired. This instrument consists of a system of propositions—principles—and the operational definitions of their terms. These propositions certainly cannot be derived from the facts of our experience and are not uniquely determined by these facts. Rather they are hypotheses from which the facts can be logically derived. If the principles or hypotheses are not determined by the physical facts, by what are they determined? We have learned by now that, beside the agreement with observed facts, there are other reasons for the acceptance of a theory: simplicity, agreement with common sense, *fitness for supporting a desirable human conduct*, and so forth. All these factors participate in the making of a scientific theory.[44]

A scientist must at some point in his enterprise *validate*, that is, accept or reject, a proffered hypothesis. Since no scientific proposition is ever completely verified, the scientist is required to tender a judgment of *sufficiency*, that is, he must at some point make a *value* judgment on the question of whether the evidence to support a scientific proposition is sufficiently strong to warrant a truth ascription. When such an ascription is made will depend upon the importance, in the *ethical sense*, of making such an ascription, and this is inevitably influenced by moral, political, religious, and esthetic considerations. In effect, science can never be independent of the *national culture* in which it flourishes.

The individual is born into a national association, a complex system of interrelated rule systems, including civil and criminal codes, rules governing truth ascription in science, inculpation and exculpation in moral conduct, evaluations in esthetic judgment, and vindications and condemnation in the political order. These rule systems give continuity and identity to the individual's actions. His actions are rational, and hence not impulsive or instinctive, when the community of which he is a member can fathom the *point* of them, that is, when his actions are in conformity with its rules. Since only actions that are rational and meaningful can be *chosen*, only rational acts are free. If freedom is acting in accordance with rules, then the meaning of freedom is logically dependent on a social context. That context, for Gentile, is the historical nation-state.

Freedom finds expression in action *chosen* because it conforms to explicitly or implicitly formulated rules. Reflex or instinctive action is not free and therefore not subject to inculpation or exculpation. Random or capricious action is not free because it does not conform to rules. If such action is judged immoral, it is because we assume that the agent behaved in such a manner in willful violation of his understanding of established rules. Only the agent's explicit exposition of the *reasons* governing what we felt to be his random or capricious behavior could justify his behavior or challenge our judgment concerning his guilt. Gentile is arguing that action in clear conformity with socially established rules is never questioned because such actions are expected. We never ask someone why he speaks the language correctly, why he persists in driving within the speed limit, or why he accepts a scientific proposition when it conforms to accepted criteria for admissibility. Nor do we consider his actions "coerced" when he acts in conformity to rules. He exemplifies what we mean by a free agent. He has chosen to behave in a certain way, and we see the point of it. It is when he behaves otherwise that we ask the point of it; we ask him to justify his actions as exemplifying rule-governed conduct. When a neologism is coined, reasons are given in its support. When someone speeds in traffic, he cites reasons for the violation of rules—and those reasons appeal to intersubjective criteria. His reasons appeal to a set of socially acceptable values that the agent believes reveal the point of his conduct. (For example, a man who speeds in traffic to bring an injured child to a doctor expects that the point of his conduct will be apparent to a traffic officer who stops him.) Apparent departures from rule-following conduct are justified only when they are revealed to be instances of such socially responsible conduct. If an individual fails to convince us of the legitimacy of his appeal, we charge him with moral infraction or intellectual perversity.

Codified law is sanctioned by its rationality, its "transparency," that is to say, the point of it. Gentile assumes that rules are established to further the development of man. The development of language enhances the development of man as a personality. The development of morality and science has the same effect. Each receives its sanction from the moral imperative "render onself human" (*"sii uomo"*). Society can compel conformity to rule and law because they are understood to be conducive to this end. There is in Gentile's system an initial presumption in favor of tradition, rule, and law. Those agents who choose to violate tradition, rule, and law are required to justify their infractions. Their justifications can appeal to changed conditions requiring alterations in tradition, rule, or law; or they can demonstrate that a tradition, rule, or law impairs self-development. But in any event, change must be justified before a communal court of appeals, before a court that follows the preestablished rules that license reasoning. Such procedures are always social. The individual who chooses a free and justifiable course of action never transcends the community, the "We" of which he is a member.

Thus, for Gentile, a "person" is conceived as a complex whole, an ensemble of relations exemplified in communications of intelligence and love, without which a person cannot be said to be other than a material thing. A human person can never exist or be understood apart from the communal life that his essence requires. Society is the unity of the universal and the particular and constitutes a whole that is greater than its immediate parts. Society is a rule-governed association that gives meaning to the parts that compose it at any particular time. Society, for Gentile and for Fascist ethicists in general, has a logical, factual, and moral priority over the individuals who compose it.[45] Such a conception accords an ethical priority to the rule-governed association and rests on a normic model of man as a rule-following animal. Violation of established law, a disobedience of rules, a thoughtless or willful neglect of responsibility always demands an accounting. Consequently, Fascist ethicists interpret the liberal, individualist principle "all restraint, *qua* restraint, is an evil" with its initial presumption in favor of an individual with "reasons," "rights," and "freedoms" peculiar to himself and independent of society as not only mistaken, but also profoundly immoral. It is a consequence, Fascists insist, of liberalism's radically egoistic model of man.

Following from his understanding of man, Gentile maintains that the individual who seeks to absent himself from rules and obligations laid upon him by positive law and social sanction in the historic community is *morally* required to justify his abstention. Man is conceived to be free only in the sense that his choices are rational, and rationality is understood to necessarily entail conditions that make rule-following possible. Thus, the existence of rule-governed associations in which those preconditions are realized is logically prior to the individual who accedes to rationality only within its confines. The community therefore enjoys a moral privilege, for its rules make cognitive and moral choice possible, and only choice can make man what he is and should be. The disposition to violate social rules and codified law and absent oneself from one's obligations demands an accounting. Such a formal or procedural maxim does not function as a premise in a deductive argument, which would permit us to decide whether any given justification is adequate, but it does indicate where the responsibility for justification lies. Outside the strict confines of social and political philosophy such a recommendation fosters a *doctrinal bias* in favor of the collectivity.

Central to Gentile's social and political philosophy is a recommended definition of man supported by analytic and factual argument that provides an initial presumption in favor of the collectivity, over and against the individual, as a focus of interest and privilege. Totalitarian systems, predicated on the priority of the collectivity rather than the individual, tend, as a consequence, to develop structuralist, functionalist, and organicistic conceptions of society. The nation is conceived as an organic or functional whole in which individuals find their place, in which they "define" themselves. The state is understood to be the express will of such an organic whole, a will transcending in scope and interest the will of individuals, classes, or categories. But it is a will that includes the express will of antecedent individuals, classes, or categories (the logical presupposition of *established* rules) and must attempt to assess the interests of the future collectivity (establishing the rules that will provide the basis for future choice).

Gentile, therefore, sees no necessary conflict between freedom and the obedience to the rules and laws of a given historical community. Rational laws and rules constrain only the momentary and immediate will. The hindrance to impulse is not a limitation of liberty; it is the necessary condition for the effective operation of the particular individual's true or rational will. It is a discipline required by the very conception of freedom. Rules and law are given; they are the preformed moral realm into which the individual is born. As aspects of the moral realm rule systems can be scrutinized, reassessed, and modified, but the entire system cannot be subject to question. The very logic of judgment requires that the critic would have to accept some, and in fact, much, of the preestablished rules (the rules of language, of truth ascription, of value judgment and so forth). In this sense Gentile, and Fascist ethicists in general, are traditionalist and conservative. Man commences his rational and moral life as the denizen of a specific historic community.[46] He rejects aspects of that community's prescriptions and proscriptions only when armed with sufficient reason. Man in the mythical state of nature, devoid of the rule system governing human association, is man devoid of human contacts, devoid of language, thought, and morality—and hence devoid not only of freedom, but of humanity itself. As men increase the complexity of their law-governed relations, they correspondingly increase their humanity and their freedom. Society is the discipline that affords true liberty because it constitutes the material and logical prerequisites of reason, without which there can be no humanity, much less freedom. As such, society speaks with authority and demands discipline. It is the authority and the discipline that man, as a true person, would lay upon himself. It is his rational will made concrete. In its concrete actuality that embodied will is the historical state.[47]

The state not only protects the individual's life and property; it is also the medium of transmission of the funded knowledge; the traditions, rules, and laws; the spiritual patrimony that makes man what he is. There cannot be, consequently, any consistent appeal to rights or freedoms apart from the state, for every such appeal must be couched in terms of reasons that appeal to the socially established rules licensing such reasoning. The claimant is not arguing that he possesses rights or freedoms apart from the community and its embodiment in the state. What he is arguing is that the historical, determinate state is not the *ideal* state. The claimant is advancing a virtual, or ideal, state against the existing state. The appeal he is making is not to anything apart from the state, but to a state that he conceives would more adequately embody the collective will. Thus Gentile (as do Fascist theorists in general) argues that rights and freedoms cannot be conceived apart from the state. Any alternative course, such as one conceiving individuals possessed of "inalienable" or "natural" rights, courts paradox and confusion. If men are understood to possess a "natural right" to "life, liberty, and the pursuit of happiness," it would be strange that the state can, in fact, oblige individual men to lay down their lives in the defense of the community, can imprison individual men for infractions of social rules, and can define the legitimate happiness that men can pursue. None of these "inalienable" rights are inalienable. They are concessions made by the state.[48]

The logic of Gentile's rationale requires (irrespective of qualifications) that the individual, the people, the nation, and the state are, in some sense, substitution instances of each other. In some sense it is legitimate to say that the individual *is* the collectivity as people, nation, or state. Fascist theorists express this with the contention that "in Fascist ethics the end of society is identical with that of man; the same reason which affords norms for individual life provides norms for social life. . . ."[49] In Gentile's words,

> The human individual is not an atom. Immanent in the concept of an individual is the concept of society. . . . Only this identity can account for the necessary and intrinsic relation between the two terms of the synthesis which requires that the concept of one term must involve the concept of the other. . . . I hope that the importance of this concept will escape no one, for in my judgment it is the keystone of the great edifice of human society.[50]

Political philosophers have long recognized the legitimacy of public restraint applied to the momentary zeal of individuals when it might involve the individual's own injury. The right to restrain individual action is sanctioned by the restraining agencies acting to effect what is understood to be the *real* will of the individuals involved. Those agencies compel the individual to act as he would act were his will not temporarily clouded by enthusiasm or passion. This real will, essential to the real or ultimate interests of the individual, is understood to be occasionally at variance with the individual's immediate impulse. The agencies of society have the moral right to act in the name of that will in restraining the individual. Conjoined with the conviction that a minority can speak for that real will, such an analysis produces the rationale of Fascism. The will of the state as expressed by a minority is understood to be, on such occasions, identical with the real will of the individual. That minority represents the real will of the individual—a will identical with the individual's own will were his reason not distracted.[51]

Similarly, the will of the state manifests the real will of an entire people divested of the contingencies of class and category—a will that attempts to express the real and ultimate will of the entire spiritual community. The minority of men who express this will as leaders of a particular historical community speak for their nation and for their epoch.[52] They are possessed of the "political genius" that commands the assent of the common rational will. They not only resolve the concrete problems of a given time and place, but are also inspired by a view of life that invokes the assent of the masses. This view of life is expressed in an appropriate "political formula," a formula that expresses the "will" of a "political elite."

Fascism advances a normic conception of man.

Man as Fascism conceives him (*"L'uomo del fascismo"*) is an individual who is at once nation and fatherland, the moral law which binds . . . individuals and generations. . . . [to] an objective will that transcends the particular individual and elevates him to conscious membership in a spiritual community. . . . Fascism is a historical conception in which man is not what he is except as a function of the spiritual process in which he participates, in his family and social group, in the nation and history. . . . Hence the great value of tradition in memories, in language, in rules of social life. Outside of history man is nothing. . . . Liberalism negated the state in the interests of the particular individual; Fascism reaffirms the state as the true reality of the individual. And if liberty is to be attributed to real man, and not to that abstraction of individualistic liberalism, Fascism is for liberty. It is for the only liberty that can be a serious thing, the liberty of the state and the individual in the state, since for the Fascist, all is in the state and nothing human or spiritual exists, or much less has value, outside the state. In this sense Fascism is totalitarian, and the Fascist State, the synthesis and unity of all values, interprets, develops, and gives power, to every aspect of the life of the people. . . . Grouped in accordance with their several interests, individuals are classes; they are trade unions according to their several economic activities; but they are first and foremost the state. The state is not therefore a mere aggregate, the sum of individuals composing the majority . . . [but] a people conceived . . . qualitatively, not quantitatively, as the idea which is more powerful because more moral, more coherent, truer, which manifests itself in the people as the consciousness and will of the minority, if not, indeed, of one. [This] idea tends to realize itself in the consciousness and will of all. . . . The nation as state is an ethical reality.[53]

Fascism by 1932 had thus developed its social and political philosophy, and it was to this social and political philosophy that Fascist legislation and Fascist policy made ultimate recourse. The doctrinal principles of the organismic conception of the nation, class collaboration, the unitary party, and totalitarianism find support in the justificatory arguments marshaled in the social and political philosophy here briefly reviewed.

Final Doctrinal Developments

· By 1932 Fascism had matured as an ideology. Its social and political philosophy was exemplified, as already indicated, in the work of Gentile, and its nationalist and syndicalist doctrines had been synthesized into a body of thought that displayed the characteristics of a relatively coherent ideological system. Whatever subsequent developments Fascism underwent took place on the doctrinal level—although, as in all politically active ideologies, these doctrinal changes did, at critical junctures, create tensions at the level of social and political philosophy.

The most prominent doctrinal development was that which is now generally identified as Fascist racism. While the doctrine is prominent in its notoriety, very little has appeared in English that provides any information concerning its character and content. Most frequently the doctrine is dismissed as a clumsy imitation of Nazism, which is not only essentially false, but which also obscures its relationship to contemporary forms of racism.

The racism that developed in Fascist Italy was essentially an Italian product. Long before the advent of National Socialist Germany the Fascists had developed a form of racism out of nationalist elements. "Race" had been identified by Italian precursors of Fascism as one of the collectivities with which men identified themselves. Pareto had even used race as an explanatory concept in his account of "residues" in the volume with which Mussolini was acquainted. Alfredo Oriani's book, which

Mussolini had commended as early as 1909, contained a long section on race in which he identified race as the first order of distinction among men.[54]

What is worthy of note is that pre-Fascist discussions of race tended to identify race with people and nation. This was true even of Pareto, who certainly was aware of the legitimate distinctions between them. It was also true of Roberto Michels, who spoke interchangeably of races, peoples, and nations.[55] Such usage abounds in the literature of the Fascist precursors. The works of Filippo T. Marinetti, the founder of the Futurists, exemplify this point.

At the time when Mussolini opted for intervention and began to collect around a nascent Fascism various interventionist groups, Marinetti, whose Futurists early entered the Fascist ranks, was writing appeals to the "Italian race." Such racial appeals had, in fact, appeared regularly in his exhortations since 1909. As early as April, 1915, Guglielmo Jannelli, one of Marinetti's followers, exhorted Italians to develop their "racial pride."[56] What is important to establish is that this racial pride was understood to signify a new *national consciousness*. The identification between pride of race and the Italian national consciousness was made specific as *coscienzo nazionale* and *il prestigio della nostra razza* were used interchangeably. Expressions like "our race," "the Italian race," "Italian blood," and "Italian people" were all used to mean the same thing. Thus Mussolini's statement of April, 1921, which maintained that "Fascism was born. . . . out of a profound, perennial need of this our Aryan and Mediterranean race," along with the pronouncement that Fascism had dedicated itself to making 50 million men a "great family" united in "one single pride of race,"[57] can only be understood to mean that the "Italian people" needed Fascism and that Fascism would instill in Italians a sense of collective identity. In fact, the expression "race" ("*razza*" or "*stirpe*") appears in Mussolini's writings and speeches at least thirty times between 1922 and 1932 and is always used as a synonym for the "Italian people," or the "Italian nation." It *never* refers to a biological or anthropological entity distinct from the Italian people.

The employment of race as an independent biological variable would violate the logic of nationalist and idealist doctrine. The distinction between a biological and a national "race" is clearly illustrated in the juxtaposition of statements contained in an authoritative Fascist doctrinal statement issued as late as 1936.

The subject of the state in Fascist doctrine is the people, not insofar as they are a population, that is to say a "multitude" of individuals, but insofar as they constitute a nation, that is, an enduring collectivity animated by its own sense of civilization. In this manner the state in the Fascist and national conception is the race *("stirpe")* itself. . . . Thus . . . Fascist doctrine of the state rejects the individualistic thesis . . . as well as racist infatuations that rest on ethnological and biological considerations.[58]

It is obvious that for Fascist theorists people, nation, and race denote the same aggregate and can be used interchangeably. A theoretical racism of the variety with which the modern world has become familiar would require that race be employed as an independent determinant in any adequate account of phenomena. For Fascists, on the other hand, the term race performs the same doctrinal and theoretical service as people or nation.

Mussolini's statements concerning race always function in the above indicated manner. Thus, in 1921 when he referred to the racial solidarity to which Fascism aspired, he rendered the expression specific by identifying it with "a union of free spirits in the Italian nation." In 1923 he referred to the "will of the entire Italian people" as an "Italian racial phenomenon."[59] There can be little serious doubt that the racism manifested by Fascism in its formative years was little more than a restatement of its nationalism. The expression "our race" was uniformly understood to designate all Italians, as distinct from Frenchmen or Englishmen, irrespective of anthropometric traits. Thus, in 1923 Mussolini said, ". . . before I love the French, the English, the Hottentots, I love Italians. That is to say I love those of my own race, those that speak my language, that share my customs, that share with me the same history."[60] The qualifications necessary for inclusion in the race were the same as the qualifications necessary for inclusion in the nation or people. Fascist racism was thus innocent of any specifically biological intention. Fascism, like Futurism and nationalism in general, was concerned with the collectivity—the Italian people or the Italian nation—and was understood to have certain moral, cultural, and historic traits. The nation or nationality was the critical doctrinal concept for Fascists. Race was only an alternate expression for people or nation.

During World War II, in a discussion with Bruno Spampanato, Mussolini characterized the racism of Fascism:

> I have occupied myself with racism since 1922 but a racism of my own. The health, the conservation of the race, its betterment, the struggle against tuberculosis, [the advocacy] of mass sport, children to camps—that was racism as I understood it. But there was also a moral racism that I advocated, the pride of belonging to this millenarian race born between the snows of the Alps and the fire of Etna. Our racism with respect to the outside world? The elevation of Italian prestige, of the genius of our civilization. . . .[61]

This kind of racism was, of course, compatible with Fascist doctrine. The logical equivalence of race with nation and their identification with the state is explicit in Mussolini's political thought even in 1921. He continued to use race with population as its referent throughout his political career. As late as 1944 he spoke of "the flower of the Italian race," and in one of his last interviews he spoke of the Italians as a race difficult to govern.[62]

Mussolini was equally explicit in his rejection of a racism that made race an independent determinant in theoretical and doctrinal analyses. As early as 1911 he mocked the racial speculations of Arthur de Gobineau, Ludwig Woltmann, Houston Stewart Chamberlain, and Vacher de Lapouge, all of whom we shall see were to figure prominently as precursors of National Socialist "Nordicism." Again in 1912 he repeated his objection to simplistic racial interpretations of history.[63] Later, as head of the Fascist state he repeated the same objections to Emil Ludwig.[64] Then in 1934 he pointed out that science "does not guarantee the 'purity' of anyone's blood" and that the "new 'civilizers' from the North [referring to the National Socialist racists] might well have unrecognized relatives even within the walls of Tel Aviv."[65] Mussolini's statements were sufficiently explicit to render any misunderstanding impossible. As late as 1942, Fascist theorists could write. "Benito Mussolini, a youth but already an acute journalist and student, early perceived the weaknesses of the simplisms [of Gobineau, Lapouge, Woltmann, and so on] and exposed their excesses to corrosive irony."[66]

It was clear that the elements constituting the Fascist doctrine of race were different from the kind of racism that made race an independent determinant in historical analysis and political assessment. Long before the advent of National Socialism in Germany, Fascist academicians had attempted to articulate a general synoptic doctrine that related the state, the nation, and the concept of race in a coherent whole. Fascist doctrine conceived national sentiment as a collective disposition (the result of man's essentially social or associative nature) to place general, collective interests before immediate private interest—a disposition expressed and reinforced against out-groups. Out of this and related sentiments an ethos was articulated that could integrate the various social and productive categories into a viable national unity convinced of its specific historical and cultural destiny. The will of such a community manifested itself in the state. It was into this conceptual scheme that the concept of race was to be accommodated.

The conception of race compatible with this scheme was one that construed race as a dynamic and historical constant, the ultimate product of geographic and social isolation, of attendant inbreeding, of natural and artificial selection, and of genetic mutation.[67] Those aggregates that anthropologists study as anthropometric races are polar or ideal types, abstractions employed in assessing the end product of a long historical and biological process, involving protracted inbreeding, differential birth rate, selection, and genetic variation. Within such a conception of race formation, any natural community that is endogamous, that practices inbreeding, is a potential race—a race in formation. Its degree of anthropometric uniformity will be a function of the length of its isolation, the intensity of selection it undergoes, the size of the breeding population, and the reproductive rate of its constituent subgroups. But no natural race would, of course, ever display anthropometric uniformity.

The races to which Fascist theoreticians referred were thus "historic" or "natural" races, rather than races factitiously defined in terms of uniform or ideal types. This conception was affirmed in the theoretical proposition "long-established nations

. . . can solidify themselves into races, becoming new races. . . ." In addition, "it is to be understood that the 'new races' . . . *are nations solidified into races*, that is to say, politico-cultural entities, solidified through time and intermarriage, into a unity of blood derived from a harmonious and stable fusion of several 'old races'. . . ."[68]

Within the context of this theoretical account the nation was conceived as a "race cradle," an essentially endogamous breeding circle whose political independence and internal mobility would tend to relate all constituent members to a common gene pool. This pool, given sufficient time, would produce a relatively distinct type, a new race.[69] Fascist racial doctrine thus assimilated the biological concept of race to a national, historical, and political reality in terms of peoples, nations, and states. The more sophisticated Fascist theorists identified the concept race with population, understood in terms of a national gene pool. Rather than the taxonomic or morphological conception of race, Fascist theoreticians advanced a notion of "natio-races," that is, politically defined breeding circles.

By 1938 Fascist theoreticians had assimilated the concept race into the doctrinal system of Fascism without creating internal tensions. It was in 1938, however, that the *Manifesto of Fascist Racism* was published, and its publication did introduce considerable confusion into Fascist doctrine. The stir caused by its publication constitutes *prima facie* evidence that extraneous forces were generating structural tensions in the system. The forces, of course, are not difficult to identify: the rise of National Socialist Germany and its *rapprochement* with Fascist Italy. During the first years of the National Socialist regime in Germany, Mussolini remained ambivalent. His first response was to deplore National Socialist excesses. In 1933 he even attempted to disabuse Hitler of his anti-Semitic postures. He advised Hitler that state anti-Semitism was dangerous and that while "every regime has not only the right but the duty to eliminate from posts of command elements in which it does not have complete trust, it is not necessary, in fact it can be disastrous, to make a question of race—Semitism and Aryanism—that which is simply a measure of defense. . . ."[70] His attempt was notably unsuccessful. Nonetheless, during the period from 1932 until 1936 Fascists generally deplored National Socialist racism as aberrant. It was during this period that Gaetano Mosca's scathing critique of National Socialist racism was published and Giovanni Gentile maintained that the "Italian ideal" could not be a "sordid racism." As late as 1939 Leone Franzi published an urbane but searching criticism of the National Socialist position on race.[71]

By 1936, however, Mussolini had become convinced that the race issue might seriously compromise attempts at Italo-German *rapprochement*, and the race question became one of singular tactical importance. Having failed to convince the National Socialists to abandon their racist postures, Mussolini decided to accommodate them by introducing specifically racist legislation—in effect, anti-Semitic legislation—into Italy. He considered it an offering to solidify the Italo-German alliance. "There is no doubt," De Felice has convincingly argued, "that Mussolini's decision to introduce . . . state anti-Semitism into Italy was determined, essentially, by the conviction that it was necessary to eliminate every marked difference in the politics of the two regimes in order to render the Italo-German alliance infrangible."[72]

But it is not our purpose to pursue the character of Fascist anti-Semitic legislation; it is sufficient to indicate that a certain bad conscience seems to have attended its anti-Jewish measures. There is ample evidence that well into 1943 Fascist officials systematically obstructed National Socialist attempts to transport Jews out of Fascist-occupied territory. Mussolini himself deplored the excesses of anti-Semitic propaganda as late as 1941, but he did nothing to stop it out of fear of alienating the National Socialists.[73]

Mussolini's personal relationships with Jews evidenced little systematic bias. His friendship with the Jews Angelica Balabanoff and Margherita Sarfatti (his first official biographer) was intimate and enduring. There were Jews present at the foundation of the Fascist party in March, 1919, and Jews served in many leading positions in the state. In 1941 Mussolini stated that he "could not forget that four of the seven founders of Italian nationalism were Jews."[74] He personally interceded in behalf of the French-Jewish philosopher Henri Bergson and "Aryanized" a number of Italian Jews for valor.

Mussolini's anti-Semitism and the singular racism introduced in 1938 were a consequence, then, of tactical, not doctrinal, considerations. The introduction of taxonomic racism into Fascist doctrine, with the official publication of the *Manifesto* in 1938, produced intolerable tensions in the ideological system of Fascism. The *Manifesto* is literally a confusion of two distinct conceptions of race, the static, or taxonomic, race concept employed by the National Socialists and the dynamic, or populationist, conception systematized before the advent of National Socialism by Fascist ideologues. Mussolini told Galeazzo Ciano that he himself had drafted most of the *Manifesto*.[75] If he did, he compromised the doctrinal integrity of Fascism, for the *Manifesto* introduced indigestible elements of biological determinism that Fascist voluntarism found impossible to assimilate. In fact, several years later, Mussolini specifically denied authorship and told Spampanato that

> . . . the *Manifesto on Race* could have been avoided. It is a scientific abstruseness of certain scholars and journalists, a German text translated into bad Italian. It is a long way from anything I have said, written or signed in fact. . . . I have always considered the Italian people an admirable product of diverse ethnic fusions on the basis of a geographic, economic, and especially spiritual unity. It has been the spirit that has put our culture on the byways of the world.[76]

All of this is quite true, but it does not explain the appearance of the *Manifesto*.

What is obvious is that the *Manifesto* contains two incompatible conceptions of race. On the one hand it speaks of the Italians as a "race" that has become "pure" through a historical process of systematic inbreeding with relatively little admixture of foreign "blood." Whatever this may mean, it obviously refers to a population, a breeding circle. It is a dynamic concept. Yet elsewhere in the document races are identified by strictly anthropometric traits and the classification is taxonomic, static. The races mentioned are those familiar to physical anthropologists: Nordics, Mediterraneans, Alpines, and so forth. To increase the confusion, the *Manifesto* begins with the disclaimer that "to say that human races exist is not to say a priori that there exist superior or inferior races, but only to say that there exist different human races." Then it goes on to proscribe certain interracial marriages, a proscription that could only be warranted by the fact that some races are inferior or by some evidence that the breeding of two equal but different races produces deleterious consequences. Further in the text, "Aryan," which could have only a cultural or linguistic meaning, is introduced. Besides making the document confusing, such concepts are incompatible with Fascist doctrine, which employs "nation" as its central analytic tool.

Space forbids any attempt at extended analysis. Here it is only necessary to indicate that the two incompatible concepts of race found in the *Manifesto* precipitated a polarization among Fascists during the final years of the regime. A group of so-called "intransigents" collected around Giovanni Preziosi, perhaps the only systematically anti-Semitic Fascist Italy produced, who attempted to reinterpret Fascist doctrine in terms of a biological and static racism, identifying specific aggregates of men as inferior on the basis of some metric or nonmetric anthropological criteria. The majority of Fascist theoreticians took a position with Carlo Costamagna, who, in his definitive *Dottrina del fascismo*, maintained that "criteria for evaluating one race superior to another . . . defied 'scientific' demonstration. . . ."[77] In September, 1940, Mussolini himself maintained that "there is no such thing as superior and inferior races."[78]

Gentile, of course, remained assiduously aloof from any form of biological racism that was inimical to his ideal of Fascism. He befriended Jewish scholars who had been driven from Germany, assisted some in escaping from Italy when anti-Semitic persecutions began, and, in 1941, when the anti-Semitic campaign was well under way, courted personal risk in paying public homage to his Jewish teacher, Alessandre D'Ancona.[79]

By the time of the Fascist instauration in the north in 1943 the two factions had polarized. Fascism had split along lines that followed the race question. The Fascist intransigents openly renounced Gentile and advocated the reconstruction of doctrine on the basis of National Socialist biologism. Preziosi, an intimate of Alfred Rosenberg and a vocal critic of Mussolini, was considered a substitute for Mussolini by the National Socialists. Preziosi's opposition to Gentile was so violent that in 1943 Gentile at first refused to participate in the Fascist republican government. Only a personal appeal by Mussolini persuaded him to assume the presidency of the Fascist Italian Academy.

From 1943 until the destruction of the Fascist republic Mussolini's authority papered over the dissension. It was only with the assassination of Gentile in April, 1944, that Mussolini finally submitted to National Socialist pressure and appointed Preziosi, whom he found "repulsive," Inspector General for Race. At the same meeting in which he announced the death of Gentile Mussolini announced the appointment of Preziosi. This marked the last and most tragic phase of anti-Semitism and biological racism in Fascist Italy and opened a breach in Fascist doctrine that threatened the integrity of the entire system. It remains an embarrassing and unassimilable adjunct to Fascist ideology. The most systematic neo-Fascist authors today identify it as alien to Fascism, an aberrancy that undermines the coherency of the system,[80] just as the concept of consciousness introduced from without undermined classical Marxism.

The remaining doctrinal developments pursued their course during the brief life span of the Fascist Social Republic. Perhaps the most significant development is that resulting from the searching criticism that the Fascists leveled against themselves. The *Manifesto of Verona* of November, 1943, which served as the constitution of the republic, contains the judgment that Fascist Italy's electoral experience had been negative and that the head of the republican government would be elected every five years by the entire citizenry. This reassessment is of critical importance. What the Fascists of Verona indicated was that an elite must be in a position to license its rule. Leninism attempts to produce such a license by claiming that the elite possesses a theory composed of universal and necessary truths. Fascists have made no such claim. But if an elite is to rule, some legitimizing procedure seems to be required. That the Fascist republicans of Verona made recourse to periodic elections seems to indicate that they understood rule to be legitimized by the consent of the ruled. This interpretation seems fully borne out by Gentile's doctrine of toleration spelled out in his final Fascist apologetic, *The Genesis and Structure of Society*. Gentile argued that humanity cannot be divided, on the basis of simple exclusive alternatives, into the elected and the damned. Consensus can legitimately be obtained only by an on-going dialogue in which all men, at least initially, are accepted as equal. The right of some to speak for all must be licensed by the consent of the ruled, who are convinced that the rulers are qualified for their position.[81] The importance of such a principle is obvious. The analysis of the conditions that would make implementation of the principle effective is the task of political scientists. But that the Fascists of Verona were aware that at least some of the conditions had to be established is indicated by the fact that the Verona *Manifesto* included specific provisions for the liberty of person ("No citizen arrested *in flagrante,* or detained for preventive measures, can be detained over seven days without an order from the judicial authority"), protection from domicilary search ("Except in cases *in flagrante,* an order from the judiciary is necessary for domicilary search"), and entrenched freedom for the magistrature ("In the exercise of its functions the magistracy will act in full independence").

On the other hand, the Fascist Republican party remained the sole and indivisible repository of the responsibility for the "people's education." The Jews were still spoken of as a race and were declared foreigners. The latter was qualified by the amendment that such was to be the case for the duration of the war. The Verona *Manifesto* contained no other reference to race, and, in fact, as early as June, 1942, Mussolini had made it clear that he could not conceive of biological racism surviving the war.[82]

Finally, the social and economic doctrinal statements contained in the Verona *Manifesto* indicated that it was largely the work of Mussolini himself[83] and marked a return to the syndicalist and socialist origins of early Fascism. His speech of December, 1944, indicated that Mussolini himself thought of it as a return. During the last year of his life he spoke of the Fascism of the Verona *Manifesto* as a Fascism relieved of much of the "tinsel" that impeded its march, freed of the many "compromises required by contingencies"—a Fascism "returned to its revolutionary origins. . . ." He spoke of the implacable internal opposition of "industrial and financial groups," which had deformed Fascism, and of Italy as a "proletarian nation" opposed by capitalist nations.[84]

Socialization became one of the social and economic preoccupations of the republic with the direction of industry the joint responsibility of workers and managerial committees in a literal reinvocation of the early Fascist demands for industrial "committees of competence."[85] Mussolini did not hesitate to refer to these developments as "true socialism," a nonmaterialist or *Fascist* socialism, resting on the interests of the people and the nation. The nation thus remained the irreducible theoretical and analytic tool of Fascist ideology. Fascist socialism was supplemented by a conviction that labor in all its manual and intellectual forms was essential to the full development of man, a conception Fascists identified as a "humanism of labor." And labor could only be conducted in a social context, a national context. Man could fulfill himself only in society and his fulfillment was the embodiment of human liberty, for liberty was understood as the free choice of rule-governed behavior calculated to achieve man's maturation as man. The rule-governed relations found in the family, in class association, in participation in categories of productive labor were all synthesized in the nation-state.[86] It was a conception essentially Platonic and Hegelian. Plato's *Republic*, in fact, was a volume to which Mussolini returned again and again during this last period, and it was during this period that he identified the Fascist conception of the ethical state with that of Hegel.[87]

The Fascism of the final period received its fullest philosophical explication in Gentile's posthumously published *The Genesis and Structure of Society*, written immediately prior to the founding of the Fascist republic. There seems little doubt that Gentile's last thoughts reflected Fascism's final ideological reflections. This volume has provided the only coherent expression of contemporary neo-fascism, and it is to this final period of Fascism, to the ideological system constructed in its final days, that contemporary neo-Fascists have turned for the truth of Fascism.

Fascisms

• The fascisms that arose as indigenous developments in a variety of countries—the corporativism of Vichy France, the National Union of Portugal, the Falangism of Spain, the Justicialismo of Peron's Argentina—remained essentially *immature* ideological systems. Most of them developed a doctrinal coherence that displayed overt fascist features: a pronounced ethical idealism, the theoretical and sentimental emphasis on the nation, the advocacy of minoritarian rule in a strong, integralist state, the collaboration of classes within the nation, and a one-party political system. Some emphasized specific doctrinal components at the expense of others, but all were related in a family of regimes sharing some features of the paradigmatic model. Pétain's France displayed an emphatic corporative structure that reflected Italian Fascist institutions; nonetheless, it was rooted in a long French intellectual tradition, which included the mixed heritage of Sorelian thought. It incorporated the corporativist thought of Emile Durkheim, who performed the services for the Vichy theoreticians that Vilfredo Pareto had performed for Mussolini. Durkheim had emphasized the sentiment of sodality, the solidarity created by "collective consciousness." He spoke of such a consciousness as transcending that of the individual who participated in it. Any society that failed to utilize, protect, and foster such a sentiment threatened the individual with *anomie* (a pervasive sense of detachment), which reduced him to impotence and society to a mere aggregate of individuals stripped of the belief system that animated it. A viable society required such belief systems, and individuals required society to develop into persons.

Although elements of fascism characterized Vichy France, it was essentially a regime created to meet contingencies. Its brief span of life did not permit the maturation of a coherent doctrinal position, and its elitism seemed to have been little more than expediency. The role of the state was never clearly defined, and all the parliamentary machinery of the liberal past was retained.

Salazar's regime in Portugal displays many of the same features. Its corporativist features obviously reflect fascist influence, and Salazar's long tenure in office gives the regime a spurious elitist appearance. At best, Portugal can be identified as a "clerical-fascist" regime, so strong is the influence of the Catholic Church. Its "integralist" conception of society stops short at identifying man as essentially a political or social animal who finds fulfillment only within the ordered relations of a rule-governed community. As early as 1930 Salazar maintained that the individual is possessed of certain inalienable rights that the state or society cannot abridge. Mihail Manoilescu, one of the most articulate of the prewar fascist commentators, characterized

Salazar not as a fascist but as the "embodiment of the Catholic spirit [and] Catholic morals. . . ."[88] The Roman Catholic conception of man is, in fact, radically incompatible with fascism, and a wedding of convenience, such as that effected in Portugal, can only result in a sacrifice of one to the other. Salazar has chosen to sacrifice fascism. Mussolini chose to sacrifice Roman Catholicism. Salazar's clerical-fascism has much more kinship with Dollfuss' clerical-corporativism than with Mussolini's Fascism.

Franco's Spain represents a fossil fascism. On the other hand, Falangism, the political movement founded by José Antonio Primo de Rivera, had all the features of paradigmatic Italian Fascism. Its doctrinal development displayed the entire syndrome of fascist traits. It had even begun to complete its ideological system with the formulation of an articulate social and political philosophy when it was cut off with the execution of José Antonio. The selection of Francisco Franco as *Caudillo* of the revolution was not the consequence of his Falangist convictions but a matter of expediency. José Antonio had, in effect, no intellectual successors. Spanish fascism remained an immature ideological system. But of the several fascisms, that of José Antonio (irrespective of his disclaimers) most closely approximates Mussolini's paradigmatic model. The nation was chosen as the unit of analysis. The selection was specifically calculated to counter a class or category analysis. The nation was conceived as animated by a national sentiment, an elemental energy that could be invoked by an elite, conceivably by a single "hero," who was sensitive to the needs of a historic community. National sentiment integrates all individuals and classes in a transcendent synthesis motivated by ends that transcend those of narrow egotism but that are completely harmonized with the real and ultimate interests of man as an object of intrinsic value. That value, however, can only be realized when man recognizes himself to be the product of the real relations he establishes with others in familial, local, and syndical association. The ultimate effective medium of the complex of relations that constitute the human personality is the fatherland, and its express will is the totalitarian state in which all relations are synthesized.[89] "The individual and the state, integrated in a total harmony . . . have a common goal, a common destiny, a common course. . . ."[90]

The economic correlative of these doctrinal and quasi-philosophical pronouncements was the advocacy of a nationwide syndical system, what José Antonio called a "national syndicalism," in which vertical syndicates of worker and entrepreneurial membership could be integrated in an organic corporativism. Such programmatic and organizational suggestions were calculated to overcome the opposition of productive classes and categories and their antagonism toward the state. In effect Falangism opposed both political *and* economic liberalism.

The execution of José Antonio in November, 1936, brought the ideological development of Spanish fascism to an end. Thereafter Falangism became the political tool of the clerical conservatism of Spain.[91] Spanish fascism has remained in this somnambulent state into our own time.

Conclusions

• Fascism as an ideological system rests upon a normic model of man that construes the individual a by-product of a social process, a complex of relations established in a rule-governed community. While such a model has a long philosophical heritage, its immediate progenitor was Hegel. It is significant to note that Giovanni Gentile, in his *Filosofia di Marx*, written before the turn of the century, analyzed Karl Marx's conception of man as one radically Hegelian. Gentile took no objection to the *form* of Marx's analysis—what he drew attention to was its *content*. He accepted the thesis that man was, in effect, an ensemble of relations, but he objected to Marx's reductionist program that made the ultimate relations economic. Gentile argued that social development was the consequence of an elaborate interdependency of variables, among which "ethical and sentimental motives" remain irreducible to simply economic causes.[92] This, of course, constituted the logic of Mussolini's revision of classical Marxism. But this same qualification, in attenuated form, provided the logic of Lenin's revision as well. In fact, Lenin had read Gentile's critique, and although the author was recognized as an idealist, Lenin recommended these essays to his readers as "noteworthy"! The development of Leninism followed a trajectory surprisingly similar in many respects to that followed by Italian Fascism. The functional role of elites, the development of a national socialism, the collaboration of classes, the one-party state, the conception of the state as the express will of a people rather than a class, the ethical and pedagogical responsibility of the state, are all doctrinal features common to both mature Leninism and fascism. Both are anti-liberal and expressly opposed to the atomic conception of individuality. Both invest minoritarian leadership and exceptional personalities with prodigious powers and responsibilities. Both conceive an ultimate identity of interests to obtain between the individual and the state. The doctrinal distinctions between Leninism and fascism have become so vague that Fidel Castro is said to be able to deliver some of the speeches of José Antonio Primo de Rivera by memory so much had they impressed him, and among his "preferred reading" was an eight-volume collection of *Mussolini's* speeches.[93] It seems likely that a Fidel Castro in 1940 would have been identified, without hesitation, as a fascist of sorts. It has only been the world situation and the continued disintegration of Leninism that led him to cast his lot with the Marxists of our time.

Neo-Fascist theoreticians have been quick to highlight these developments. Ugo Spirito, a student of Gentile and one of the most aggressive of the ideologues of fascism, has traced the principal features of Leninist development and found them to be those of mature Italian Fascism, particularly the Fascism of the Republic of Salò. The entire ideological edifice of contemporary communism rests upon an identification of the individual with a collectivity, in this case with the state, for Leninism has literally abandoned the concept of class as an analytical or theoretical instrument. Leninism has produced a "classless state" that expresses the will of an entire people rather than a specific class. That state, ethical because it is understood not to subserve the interests of class or category, is the operational will of an elite that embodies the real will of the masses. In sum, Leninism is understood to be an ideologically inconsistent fascism—an involuntary fascism—a fascism in spite of itself.

Fascist ideology is in a substantial sense Hegelian. The revision of classical Marxism, undertaken independently by Gentile, Mussolini, and Lenin, restored much of the critical elements of Hegelianism. There seems to be no small measure of truth in Spirito's judgment that "the revolution effected by Hegel in the history of thought has not yet been seen in the immensity of its reach and its necessary consequences have not yet been gauged with proper understanding."[94] Some of the most effective radical ideologies of our time have impressed upon us the vitality and permanence of the principles first enunciated in Hegel's *Philosophy of Right*.

Notes

1. H. S. Hughes is not correct when he suggests that Mussolini may not have attended Pareto's courses at Lausanne. (*Consciousness and Society* [New York: Random House, 1958], p. 271.) Pareto, in a letter to C. Piacci of January 5, 1923, specifically stated that "Mussolini remained for a time in Lausanne and attended my courses. . . ." (R. De Felice, *Mussolini il rivoluzionario* [Turin: Einaudi, 1965], p. 38.)

2. Engels' letter to C. Schmidt, August 5, 1890. K. Marx and F. Engels, *Selected Works in Two Volumes* [*MESW*] (Moscow: Foreign Languages, 1955), II, p. 486.

3. V. Pareto, *I sistemi socialisti* (Turin: Unione Tipografico, 1954), p. 517, and *Manuale di economia politica* (Milan: Libraria, 1919), p. 38; G. Mosca, *Ruling Class*, trans. by H. Kahn (New York: McGraw-Hill, 1939), p. 443.

4. V. Pareto, *Corso di economia politica* (Turin: Einaudi, 1949), II, p. 24.

5. Mosca, *op. cit.*, p. 71.

6. *Ibid.*, pp. 444f.

7. G. Mosca, *Storia delle dottrina politiche* (Bari: Laterza, 1951), p. 9. See also J. Burnham, *The Machiavellians* (Chicago: Regnery, 1943), p. 93; A. Livingston's Introduction to Mosca, *Ruling Class*, pp. xvi, xxx.

8. R. Michels, *Political Parties*, trans. by E. and C. Paul (New York: Dover, 1959), pp. 15f., 60, 393; see also pp. 18f.

9. J. Meisel, *The Genesis of Georges Sorel* (Ann Arbor, Mich.: Wahr, 1951), p. 294.

10. G. Sorel, *Reflections on Violence*, trans. by T. E. Hulme and J. Roth (New York: Free Press, 1950), pp. 140, 142.

11. G. Sorel, *Saggi di critica del marxismo* (Milan: Sandron, 1903), pp. 16f., 59–94.

12. B. Mussolini, "Socialismo e socialisti," *Opera Omnia* [*Opera*] (Florence: Fenice, 1951–1963), I, p. 138; "La filosofia della forza," *Opera*, I, p. 174.

13. B. Mussolini, *My Autobiography* (London: Paternoster, 1936), p. 27 (this book was actually written by Arnaldo Mussolini); " 'L'individuel et le social'," *Opera*, I, pp. 73f.

14. "Intermezzo polemico," *Opera*, I, p. 128.

15. "Le teoria sindacalista," *Opera*, II, pp. 125, 128.

16. De Felice, *op. cit.*, p. 77; see also pp. 40, 63, 88.

17. G. Prezzolini, *La teoria sindacalista* (Naples: Perrella, 1909), pp. 48, 57.

18. "Profeti e profezie," *Opera*, III, p. 313; "Ciò che v'ha di vivo e di morto nel Marxismo," *Opera*, III, p. 365.

19. B. Croce, *Storia d'Italia dal 1871 al 1915* (Bari: Laterza, 1942), pp. 279f.

20. "Intermezzo polemico: battute di preludio," *Opera*, VI, p. 273; compare "Battute polemiche," *Opera*, III, pp. 321f.

21. "Intermezzo polemico," *Opera*, VI, p. 384; "Dalla neutralità assoluta alla neutralità attiva ed operante," *Opera*, VI, pp. 393-403.

22. "La situazione internazionale e l'atteggiamento del partito," *Opera*, VI, pp. 427, 428. Compare with "Nazionalismo," *Opera*, III, pp. 280f. See also "La neutralità socialista: una lettera del Prof. Mussolini," *Opera*, VI, p. 421.

23. "Diario di guerra," *Opera*, XXXIV, p. 32; "I nostri postulati: per la storia di una settimana," *Opera*, X, p. 87.

24. "Il sindacalismo nazionale: per rinascere!" *Opera*, XII, pp. 11-14.

25. "La filosofia della forza," *Opera*, I, p. 175.

26. "Divagazione: L'ora e gli orologi," *Opera*, XIV, pp. 397f.

27. "Le linee programmatiche del partito fascista," *Opera*, XVII, pp. 174f. See also "Programma e statuti del partito nazionale fascista," *Opera*, XVII, pp. 334f.

28. "Il programma fascista," *Opera*, XVII, p. 219.

29. A. O. Olivetti, *Il sindacalismo come filosofia e come politica* (Milan: Alpes, 1924), pp. 81f.

30. G. Pighetti, *Sindacalismo fascista* (Milan: Imperia, 1924), pp. 136-42.

31. Mussolini, letter to A. O. Olivetti, November 22, 1927, *Opera*, XXIII, p. 301. See also E. M. Olivetti, *Sindacalismo nazionale* (Milan: Monanni, 1927); V. Zangara, *Rivoluzione sindacale: lo stato corporativo* (Rome: Littorio, 1927); S. Panunzio, *Che cos'è il fascismo* (Milan: Alpes, 1924), *Stato nazionale e sindacati* (Milan: Imperia, 1924), *Lo stato fascista* (Bologna: Cappelli, 1925).

32. "Per la vera pacificazione," *Opera*, XVII, p. 298. See also A. Carlini, *Filosofia e religione nel pensiero di Mussolini* (Rome: Istituto Nazionale Fascista di Cultura, 1934), p. 14.

33. "Da che parte va il mondo?" *Opera*, XVIII, pp. 70f.

34. See "Il primo discorso alla camera dei deputati," *Opera*, XVI, p. 440; "Al congresso delle scienze prima del quarto attentato," *Opera*, XXII, p. 251. See also L. Volpicelli, *Motivi su Mussolini* (Rome: Istituto Nazionale Fascista di Cultura, 1935), p. 22.

35. G. Gentile, "Discorso agli Italiani," *Giovanni Gentile: la vita*

e il pensiero (Florence: Sansoni, 1954), IV, p. 67; see also A. Carlini, *Studi gentiliani* (Florence: Sansoni, 1958), pp. 106, 115. For exhaustive and interesting discussions of Gentile's relationship to Fascism, see V. Vettori (ed.), "Introduzione a Gentile," *Giovanni Gentile* (Florence: Sansoni, 1954), pp. 5–67, and H. Harris, *The Social Philosophy of Giovanni Gentile* (Urbana: University of Illinois, 1960), Chap. vi.

36. O. di Giamberardino, *L'individuo nell'etica fascista* (Florence: Vallecchi, 1940), p. 5.

37. See G. Gentile, *Genesi e struttura della società* [*GS*] (Florence: Sansoni, 1946), p. 14; *Fondamenti della filosofia del diritto* [*FD*] (Florence: Sansoni, 1955), p. 103; M. Aebischer, *Der Einzelne und der Staat nach Giovanni Gentile* (Freiburg: Kanisiusdruckerei, 1954), p. 56.

38. See G. Gentile, *Riforma dell'educazione* [*RE*] (Florence: Sansoni, 1955), pp. 20f.; *GS*, pp. 60, 65f., 109f., 115.

39. *FD*, p. 105; see also p. 108.

40. *GS*, pp. 33, 38.

41. *Ibid.*, pp. 15, 44.

42. *Ibid.*, p. 16.

43. *RE*, pp. 8–16.

44. P. Frank (ed.), "The Variety of Reasons for the Acceptance of Scientific Theories," *The Validation of Scientific Theories* (Boston: Beacon, 1956), pp. 13f. Italics supplied.

45. See also G. Pannese, *L'etica nel fascismo e la filosofia del diritto e della storia* (Rome: La Voce della Stampa, 1942), pp. 149f.; C. Costamagna, *Dottrina del fascismo* (Turin: UTET, 1940), pp. 337–65.

46. See also V. Bellezza, *L'esistenzialismo positivo di Giovanni Gentile* (Florence: Sansoni, 1954), Chap. x.

47. *FD*, pp. 67, 80f.; *GS*, p. 57. See also G. Maggiore, "Il problema del diritto nel pensiero di Giovanni Gentile," *Giovanni Gentile: la vita e il pensiero* (Florence: Sansoni, 1952), I, p. 236.

48. Pannese, *op. cit.*, p. 161.

49. *Ibid.*, p. 158.

50. *GS*, pp. 32, 34, 39.

51. *Ibid.*, p. 48.

52. G. Gentile, *Origini e dottrina del fascismo* (Rome: Littorio, 1929), pp. 9f.; see also Harris, *op. cit.*, p. 219.

53. "Dottrina del fascismo," *Opera*, XXXIV, pp. 117–20.

54. "La teoria sindacalista," *Opera*, II, p. 128; see also A. Oriani, *La rivolta ideale* (Bologna: Cappelli, 1943), pp. 111–13.

55. Pareto, *Corso*, II, pp. 387–92; R. Michels, *Lavoro e razza* (Milan: Vallardi, 1924), p. ix.

56. Jannelli as cited in F. T. Marinetti, *Futurismo e fascismo* (Foligno: Campitelli, 1924), pp. 174f.; see also pp. 25, 198f.

57. "Discorso di Bologna," *Opera*, XVI, pp. 239, 240.

58. *L'ordinamento dello stato fascista* (Rome: Libreria dello Stato, 1936), pp. 22f., 24.

59. "Discorso di Bologna," *Opera*, XVI, p. 243; "Al popolo di Piacenza," *Opera*, XIX, p. 272.

60. "Agli operai del Poligrafico," *Opera*, XIX, p. 115.

61. B. Spampanato, *Contromemoriale* (Rome: Illustrato, 1952), II, p. 131.

62. "Alle camicie nere della brigata nera 'Aldo Resega,'" *Opera*, XXXII, p. 116, "Conversazione con Maddalena Mollier," *Opera*, XXXII, p. 159.

63. "Il Trentino veduto da un socialista," *Opera*, XXXIII, pp. 153-61; "Da Guicciardini a . . . Sorel," *Opera*, IV, p. 172.

64. E. Ludwig, *Colloqui con Mussolini* (Verona: Mondadori, 1932), p. 71.

65. "Fallacia Ariana," *Opera*, XXVI, p. 298.

66. A. Capasso, *Idee chiare sul razzismo* (Rome: Augustea, 1942), p. 27.

67. For the clearest accounts of Fascist racial doctrine, see C. Gini, *Nascita, evoluzione e morte delle nazioni* (Rome: Istituto Nazionale di Cultura Fascista, 1930); M. F. Canella, *Lineamenti di antropobiologia* (Florence: Sansoni, 1943) and *Razze umane estinte e viventi* (Florence: Sansoni, 1942); G. Acerbo, *I fondamenti della dottrina fascista della razza* (Rome: Ministero della Cultura Popolare, 1940), p. 26.

68. Capasso, *op. cit.*, pp. 21, 23. Italics supplied. See also G. Landra, "La razza Italiana nella teoria dell'ologenesi," *Difesa della Razza*, II, 11 (April 5, 1939), 10.

69. Canella, *Lineamenti*, p. 8. See also G. Maggiore, *Razza e fascismo* (Palermo: Agate, 1939), pp. 204f.; R. Biasutti, *Razza e popoli della terra* (Turin: UTET, 1941), I, pp. 300f.

70. Mussolini as cited in R. De Felice, *Storia degli ebrei italiani sotto il fascismo* (Turin: Einaudi, 1962), p. 148.

71. Mosca, *Storia della dottrina politiche*, Chap. xxxix; G. Gentile, *Memorie Italiane e problemi della filosofia e della vita* (Florence: Sansoni, 1936), p. 384; L. Franzi, *Fase attuale del razzismo tedesco* (Rome: Istituto Nazionale di Cultura Fascista, 1939).

72. De Felice, *Storia*, p. 286.

73. V. De Begnac, *Palazzo Venezia: storia di un regime* (Rome: La Rocca, 1950), p. 643. For the Fascist relationship with the Jews, see De Felice, *Storia*, pp. 509f., 659; J. Tanenbaum, *Race and Reich: The Story of an Epoch* (New York: Twayne, 1956), pp. 293-99.

74. De Begnac, *op. cit.*, p. 643.

75. G. Ciano, *Ciano's Hidden Diary* (New York: Dutton, 1953),

p. 136. The complete text of the *Manifesto* can be found in the preface to Capasso, *op. cit.*

76. Spampanato, *op. cit.*, II, p. 132.

77. Costamagna, *op. cit.*, p. 193.

78. De Begnac, *op. cit.*, p. 642.

79. Harris, *op. cit.*, p. 245.

80. See M. Bardeche, *Qu'est-ce que le fascisme?* (Paris: Les Sept Couleurs, 1961), pp. 30, 32.

81. *GS*, pp. 134–36.

82. De Felice, *Storia*, p. 293; G. Pini and D. Susmel, *Mussolini: l'uomo e l'opera* (Florence: La Fenice, 1955), IV, p. 145.

83. Pini and Susmel, *op. cit.*, IV, pp. 364f. The full text of the Verona *Manifesto* can be found in E. Cione, *Storia della repubblica sociale italiana* (Caserta: Cenacola, 1948), pp. 167–75.

84. "Rivoluzione sociale. Primi sintomi," *Opera*, XXXII, p. 267; "Soliloquio in 'libertà' all'Isola Trimellone," *Opera*, XXXII, p. 171; "Colloquio con il giornalista Cabella," *Opera*, XXXII, p. 180. See also "Il discorso al 'Lirico' di Milano," *Opera*, XXXII, p. 129; "Soliloquio . . . ," *Opera*, XXXII, p. 180; Message of June 4, 1944, *Opera*, XXXII, p. 228.

85. For these developments, see G. Perticone, *La repubblica di Salò* (Rome: Leonardo, 1947); Pini and Susmel, *op. cit.*, IV, Chap. vii.

86. "Della vera libertà," *Opera*, XXXII, pp. 271–73; see also "Le basi della nuova economia," *Opera*, XXXII, p. 295.

87. Pini and Susmel, *op. cit.*, IV, pp. 145, 216, 424, 462.

88. M. Manoilescu, *Die einzige Partei* (Berlin: Stollberg, 1941), p. 163.

89. José Antonio's philosophy is set forth in his *Textos de doctrina politica* (Madrid: Españolas, 1952). For his discussion of the points stressed here, see in particular pp. 43–48, 53, 65–69, 85–93, 215, 281, 335f., and 559.

90. "Ante una encrucijada en la historia politica y economica del mundo," *ibid.*, p. 507. See also pp. 483–507.

91. For an excellent discussion of Spanish fascism, see S. Payne, *Falange: A History of Spanish Fascism* (Stanford: Stanford University, 1961) and B. Nellessen, *La rivoluzione proibita: ascesa e tramonto della Falange* (Rome: Volpe, 1965).

92. *FD*, pp. 173–86.

93. D. James, *Cuba: The First Soviet Satellite in the Americas* (New York: Avon, 1961), p. 34.

94. U. Spirito, *La filosofia del comunismo* (Florence: Sansoni, 1948), p. 42.

V · NATIONAL SOCIALISM

Almost a generation has passed since the death of Adolf Hitler and the dissolution of the National Socialist German Workers party, yet it is still difficult to deliver a brief and objective account of National Socialist ideology. One is initially ill-disposed toward the undertaking, so charged with negative emotion has the entire historical and political phenomenon become. Neither Leninism nor Mussolini's Fascism inflamed the emotions to such a degree. On the other hand, the rise of National Socialism and the accession to power of Adolf Hitler are without doubt unique and momentous events of our century. They are unique in that they constitute essentially *one* event. National Socialism was Adolf Hitler, and Adolf Hitler was National Socialism. National Socialism lived, achieved maturity and power, and as a political system, died with him.

Almost from his adolescence, National Socialism was the focus of Hitler's life. Between 1909 and 1913, during Hitler's sojourn in Vienna, the collection of ideas that became National Socialism was finally drawn together into a loosely framed and loosely jointed structure that remained remarkably constant throughout Hitler's life. In *Mein Kampf* he reported that "in this period there took shape within me a world picture and a philosophy which became the granite foundation of all my acts. In addition to what I then created, I have had to learn little; and I have had to alter nothing."[1]

Mein Kampf was written during Hitler's imprisonment in Landsberg Fortress after the unsuccessful Munich *Putsch* of November, 1923. Hitler referred to this period years later as the time in which he sought to provide his philosophy with a natural, historical foundation. Prior to that time, we are told, he acted by intuition.

Intuition does not, of course, provide the contents of a philosophy, but it may assist in selecting elements out of available material. Apparently, this is what Hitler intended. In 1924 his imprisonment in Landsberg afforded the opportunity of expressing his intuitions in some coherent manner. There is no doubt that Alfred Rosenberg, who has been called the philosopher of National Socialism, materially influenced the articulation of Hitler's ideas; both the first and second volumes of *Mein Kampf* give evidence of Rosenberg's racist formulations. But the ideas themselves were those that Adolf Hitler had developed years before in Vienna. The Vienna period is a time in which he was characterized as a voracious reader, but curiously enough we have no record of the specific books he read. Hitler himself mentions only a few by name in his writings and speeches. We do know that he read something of Schopenhauer, that references to Nietzsche are frequent in his speeches and writings, and that in *Mein Kampf* he specifically acknowledged his debt to Houston Stewart Chamberlain. Beyond these few we can only conjecture what other writers or writings contributed to the formulation of National Socialist ideology.

Our ignorance of the specific influences on Hitler coupled with the fact that his arguments were so loosely formulated renders exposition and analysis difficult. That Hitler never chose to document his sweeping assertions in *Mein Kampf* understandably creates problems, for there is no way to identify his sources of information. That his arguments were elliptical, employing vague and ambiguous terminology, further complicates reconstruction. And Hitler's disposition to simplify complex issues, to appeal to "intuition" and "instinct" rather than to "abstract reason" permitted the surface features of his ideas to appear unchanged although significant tactical shifts were being made. Hitler repeatedly insisted that "theoretical knowledge" should be "put [into] a form suited to the receptivity of the broad masses, which is and remains exceedingly limited. . . ." He maintained that "the receptive powers of the masses are very restricted, and their understanding is feeble. On the other hand, they quickly forget. Such being the case, all effective propaganda must be confined to a few bare necessities and then must be expressed in a few stereotyped formulas."[2]

Hitler did, of course, draw the necessary distinction between scientific propositions, which are qualified (*vielseitig*), and propaganda slogans, which are "more modest [in their] intellectual ballast." What is difficult to determine is whether Hitler ever thought he was uttering strictly scientific propositions. *Mein Kampf* does not appear to have scientific pretentions. Universal and unrestricted generalizations such as "All great cultures of the past perished only because the originally creative race died out from blood poisoning" are unsupported by argument or documentation. Such claims are neither self-evident nor generally accepted. Even in 1925 it would require elaborate historical, ethnographic, sociological, biological, and psychological data to support them. The best support that Hitler offered was vague references to instances of race mixture that seem, at least initially, to support his thesis that cultures decline as a consequence of miscegenation (neglecting the host of alternative explanations). Hundreds of similar claims, all tendered with the same lack of qualification and supporting evidence, could be culled from Hitler's speeches and writings. It is therefore difficult to trace development in Hitler's thought. The same statement, in fact, can literally mean two different things on two different occasions; at times, he even seemed to entertain two distinct and incompatible theses. In *Mein Kampf* he speaks on one page of the Jewish "race" ("*Rasse*"), on the next of the Jewish "people" ("*Volk*"), and on another of Jewish "nationality" ("*Volkstums*").[3] In 1928, in an unpublished manuscript, he maintained that "Jewry is a people with a racial core that is not wholly unitary." Yet in 1941 he referred to them as a racial community and as a race. Throughout his active political life he alternated between the various characterizations. Under such circumstances it is difficult to trace doctrinal developments, much less make exposition coherent.

Similar difficulties attend the use of expressions like "Aryan," "Germanic," and "Nordic." In the text of *Mein Kampf* Hitler uses the term Aryan and the term "Nordic-Germanic" (*"nordisch-germanisch"*) to identify his "culture-creators." In 1928 the term Nordic was employed with apparently the same meaning. In the table talks of 1941 through 1944 all three expressions are used interchangeably. It is hard to understand how the terms Aryan, Germanic, and Nordic could be used to refer to the identical class of individuals. In *Mein Kampf* Hitler speaks of the peoples of Europe and America as Aryans. This could only include millions who could not be classified as Nordic in any anthropological sense. However, by 1941 and 1942 "Nordic racial policy" seems to have involved only subjects from *part* of Europe —Norway, Sweden, Denmark, and the Netherlands—and Germanic seems to refer to individuals who are fair and blue-eyed.[4]

The vagueness of such critical expressions permits reformulations of doctrine without corresponding changes of vocabulary. The ideology appears remarkably constant, yet the collection of constituent ideas, subject to constant reinterpretation, can be in perpetual change. As a matter of fact, the ideology *was* in perpetual change. That change took place on the doctrinal level. The social and political philosophy is reducible to a few general and inflexible precepts.

The Foundation of National Socialist Ideology

• Historians of ideas have attempted to trace the intellectual origins of National Socialism to Romantic, conservative, and Darwinian sources. Peter Viereck, George Mosse, and Fritz Stern[5] have traced such influences with admirable clarity. That men such as Paul de Lagarde, Julius Langbehn, Arthur de Gobineau, Richard Wagner, Vacher de Lapouge, Houston Stewart Chamberlain, and Möller van den Bruck influenced National Socialism and prepared Germany for its reception can hardly be gainsaid. And yet, for purposes of exposition and analysis, National Socialism as a political and historical phenomenon must be distinguished from the specific complex of ideas that constituted the National Socialism of Adolf Hitler. Hitler's central convictions evinced a simplicity that cannot be traced to any of the individual authors cited, nor found in the writings of those thinkers who represent the broad stream of German "volkish" or nationalist thought. What will be argued here is that the central precepts of Hitler's social and political thought derive, in fact, from an elementary Social Darwinism. Hitler maintained:

> Things are as they are, and we can do nothing to change them. Providence has endowed living creatures with a limitless fecundity; but she has not put in their reach, without the need for effort on their part, all the food they need. All that is very right and proper, for it is the struggle for existence that produces the selection of the fittest.[6]

This collection of propositions provides the foundation of National Socialist ideology. Seemingly descriptive, these propositions have primarily normative and imperative functions. In their simplicity they are qualitatively different from almost anything to be found in the writings of Hitler's most frequently cited predecessors. Their simplicity is only apparent. Even the most elementary analysis reveals a host of difficulties not easily resolved.

The rational reconstruction of Hitler's core conceptions is tedious and difficult. The course of his arguments are almost always psychological rather than logical, and equivocation regularly resulted as a consequence of the employment of vague and ambiguous terms. In the development of his arguments Hitler frequently used the word "species" ("*Arten*") as though it were synonymous with "races" ("*Rassen*"). He would begin a typical argument referring to species and conclude with references to races. Such equivocations regularly invalidated his arguments. In one instance he argued that "a fox is always a fox, the goose a goose, the tiger a tiger, etc., and the difference can lie at most in the varying measure of force, strength, intelligence, dexterity, endurance, etc., of the individual specimens."[7] From this he obviously wished to conclude that races are inherently different. But foxes, geese, and tigers do not constitute races—they are species. Whatever can be said of species cannot, without argument, be applied to races. Much of his subsequent arguments trafficked on these initial equivocations.

Hitler's intentions were obvious. He was attempting to establish the existence of some finite set of natural laws governing species formation *and* racial formation. He was attempting to demonstrate that interspecific competition, the struggle for survival, ensures the survival of only the fittest species and consequently provides for progressive specific evolution. It would be necessary to disinter the suppressed premises that would relate races and species to reconstruct the argument calculated to demonstrate that the same laws obtain in *intra*specific as well as *inter*specific competition. The struggle for existence among races, like the struggle between species, ensures the survival of the fittest.

What Hitler had attempted is to identify races with clearly demarcated traits, traits as clearly demarcated as those distinguishing foxes from geese. In the competition for space and sustenance these races enter into conflict. The race that survives the struggle is the fittest and provides for the progressive development of mankind. Hitler's argument proceeded in somewhat the following manner:

[1] True genius is always inborn and never cultivated, let alone learned. . . . This applies not only to the individual man but also to the race. [2] If we were to divide mankind into three groups, the founders of culture, the bearers of culture, the destroyers of culture, only the Aryan could be considered as the representative of the first group.[8]

Each race has a genetically determined endowment. One is capable of creating culture, others only of sustaining it, and still others destroy it. From this Hitler concluded:

All great cultures perished only because the originally creative race died out from blood poisoning. The ultimate cause of such a decline was their forgetting that all culture depends on men and not conversely; hence that to preserve a certain culture the man who creates it must be preserved. This preservation is bound up with the rigid law of necessity and the right to victory of the best and stronger.[9]

This constitutes nothing more than a literal transposition of Darwinian laws, operative in organic and biological evolution, to a social and cultural context. That such an application cannot be made without considerable supplementary argument is obvious. In nature the test of fitness is survival. To say that the fittest survive is to say nothing more than that those who survive, survive. Hitler, on the other hand, wishes to apply this principle to social and cultural contexts. If this is to be effectively accomplished, fitness would have to be defined independently of survival, for to say that those who survive are fittest would not satisfy Hitler. He argues:

> When man attempts to rebel against the iron logic of nature, he comes into struggle with the principles to which he himself owes his existence as a man. And this action against nature must lead to his own doom. . . . The man who misjudges and disregards the racial laws actually forfeits the happiness that seems destined to be his. He thwarts the triumphal march of the best race and hence also the precondition for all human progress . . .[10]

Thus, the "best" race can perish if man does not heed the "iron logic of nature," and the iron logic of nature does not ensure that the fittest will survive. It is possible for the unfit to survive and halt the "triumphal march of the best race."

Reconstructed, Hitler's argument would pursue the following sequence: In nature there is a tendency for the rate of reproduction to exceed the limits of subsistence. As a consequence there is a struggle for survival conducted by species, races, and individuals. Those that survive are the fittest. At this point Hitler introduced the contention that races are distinguished by the possession of disinct endowments. One race is gifted with the ability to create culture. Here the transition becomes difficult. It is not self-evident that those capable of creating culture are necessarily the fittest in the sense of having a high survival potential. Hitler was apparently intuitively aware of this because he spoke of the highest attainments of man being the consequence of a "unique pairing of the brutal fist and the intellectual genius. . . ."[11]

Hitler is obviously not trying to illustrate anything about the logic of nature's laws. What he is doing is *recommending* a course of action. The term culture has a strong commendatory force, and assigning the capacity to create cultures to one race recommends the protection of that race. If life is a constant struggle against competitors for space and sustenance and only one race can create culture, then it is imperative that the creative race should be preserved if one values culture. The normative character of this conclusion rests upon the empirical truth as well as the persuasive character of the antecedent propositions. But the injunction would lose force if the survival of the fittest were a necessary consequence of the operation of nature's laws. It is evident that Hitler is aware of this qualification, but this does not deter him from arguing: "By means of the struggle, the elites are continually renewed. The law of selection justifies this incessant struggle, by allowing the survival of the fittest. . . . That's in accordance with the laws of nature."[12] There are a number of suppressed premises in the elliptical argument as it is stated. If the struggle is justified because only the fittest survive, then one cannot deplore the outcome of any struggle. Whoever survives the struggle is, by definition, the fittest. Apparently this is not at all what Hitler intends to say, yet the same garbled argument appears and reappears in his writings and speeches. In 1928 he insisted that "man has become great through struggle. The first fundamental of any rational *Weltanschauung* is the fact that on earth and in the universe force alone is decisive. Whatever goal man has reached is due to his originality plus his brutality. . . ."[13]

Again the argument harbors critical ambiguities. Is force *alone* decisive? If so, why then is "originality" introduced in the next sentence? Is originality an independent variable, or is force defined as originality plus force, that is, the "unique pairing of brutal fist and the intellectual genius"? What Hitler was doing, in fact, was issuing a recommendation. If the original, the creative, the intelligent wish to survive, they must become brutal in this world of constant struggle. The descriptive propositions with which he articulates his argument are all borrowed from the evolutionism of his day. Their truth claims are certified by observations made upon the world. At best Hitler's arguments are argument sketches. In order to make them even interesting, it is necessary to disinter suppressed premises and define terms. When this is done, an elementary form of Darwinism is revealed, for all of Hitler's theses are biological (to which covert normative statements are conjoined). The struggle to which Hitler

regularly refers has nothing in common with the *Sturm und
Drang* of German Romanticism. It is a struggle for biological
survival—a Darwinian struggle for existence. As late as 1942
Hitler made this abundantly clear. "As in everything," he contended, "nature is the best instructor, even as regards selection.
One couldn't imagine a better activity on nature's part than
that which consists in deciding supremacy of one creature over
another by means of a constant struggle."[14]

Basically, Hitler was neither a Romantic nor a conservative.
He was committed to a Social Darwinism of a simplistic sort.
The ultimate source of his ideas is the work of the anthropological racists of the end of the nineteenth and the beginning of the
twentieth century—racists such as Vacher de Lapouge and Ludwig Woltmann. To the Darwinism he inherited, Hitler added
select elements found in the Romantic and mystical work of
Houston Stewart Chamberlain. Of the many anthropological
and cultural racists with whom Hitler might have been familiar,
it was probably Woltmann who exercised the decisive influence.

Popular in the Pan-Germanic circles frequented by Hitler
during his Vienna period were the publications of J. Lanz von
Liebenfels, the founder of the anti-Semitic and Nordicist Ostara
association. Ostara, founded in 1905, was dedicated to the philosophy of "Aryan aristocracy" and provided a series of racist
pamphlets devoted to a range of subjects, each of which was
calculated to advance the contention that Nordics were the sole
originators of everything of value created by man. Ostara also
featured the constellation of ideas common to the Social Darwinism of the period. Central to Liebenfels' doctrine was what he
called nature's "aristocratic principle," which governed the
"struggle for existence of the diverse races of men." This notion
was reflected in Hitler's identical conviction that an "aristocratic
principle" governs nature.[15] Liebenfels went on to argue that
each of the races in constant competition differed in intrinsic
merit with the "Ario-heroic" being the sole culture-creating race,
the remaining races having, at best, a "reproductive intelligence" (*"rein reproduktiven Intellekt"*). Such a conjecture fits
surprisingly well with Hitler's distinction between "culture-
creating" and "culture-bearing" races.[16] What is interesting,
moreover, is that Liebenfels had identified the swastika as the

symbol of his culture-creators as early as 1907 and had traced their origin back to the sunken continent of Atlantis, a belief Hitler seems to have entertained as late as 1941.[17]

Ostara's publications were distributed by Friedrich Schalk in Vienna during Hitler's years in that city, and it is extremely doubtful that as both an anti-Semite and a pan-German he would not have been familiar with them. What is more significant for our purposes is the fact that Liebenfels made available in easily accessible form the ideas of Lapouge and made frequent references to the work of Woltmann as well. The writings of Woltmann that would have interested Hitler were published between 1903 and 1907 and were easily obtainable in the lending libraries and bookshops that we know Hitler frequented in Vienna. In point of fact, almost all of Hitler's mature ideas are to be found in more systematic and expanded form in Woltmann's *Politische Anthropologie*, published in 1903. Hitler had the disposition to reduce problems to almost stenographic formulations, and the arguments presented above seem to be little more than an elliptical and garbled presentation of Woltmann's more detailed arguments in the *Politische Anthropologie*.

That Woltmann was the *principal* source of Hitler's social and political ideas cannot be advanced with absolute assurance since, of course, Hitler never identified *any* specific source. That Liebenfels was an *initial* source for many of his ideas seems probable, and that Liebenfels' mysticoreligious extravagancies drove Hitler to more substantial references seems likely. Liebenfels was given to Biblical exegesis, theosophy, and phrenology, concerns with which Hitler was not in the least occupied. Woltmann, on the other hand, was a substantial and popular exponent of all the ideas that Hitler made his own. In 1911 when Mussolini undertook the study of pan-Germanism in the Trentine, he found Gobineau, Lapouge, Chamberlain, and Woltmann the most popular authors among its exponents.[18] The same theoretical material was available to pan-Germanists in Vienna during this period. Gobineau had been made popular by the Wagner circle, but he was a pre-Darwinian. Lapouge was a Darwinist, but his books were not, at that time, available in German. Chamberlain was popular, and his books were easily accessible, but many of his basic ideas were not compatible (as we shall try to indicate) with the ideas that characterized Hitler's mature thought. Only the works of Woltmann, particularly the *Politische Anthropologie*, contain all those ideas. Any number of other German sources contained elements that Hitler might have synthesized, but only Woltmann advanced literally all of Hitler's Darwinian and quasi-Darwinian convictions, and it is to Woltmann that one must turn for the insights that make Hitler's arguments at all coherent.

Ludwig Woltmann, Marxism, and the Ideology of Hitler

• Ludwig Woltmann began his intellectual and political career as a classical Marxist. One of his early major works, published in 1900, was *Der historische Materialismus: Darstellung und Kritik der Marxistischen Weltanschauung*, a Marxist work sufficiently noteworthy to merit Lenin's recommendation.[19]

In *Der historische Materialismus* Woltmann traced the development of Hegelianism through Feuerbach to Marx. Marx, according to Woltmann, had made the development of technology and the instruments of production the ultimate determinants of world history. The juridical, political, and philosophical superstructure of human history was uniquely, although in a complex fashion, determined by its economic substructure. What Woltmann sought to explicate were the circumstances governing the development of technology and the instruments of production. He contended that Marx's treatment of the logic of technological development was unconvincing. Technology does not develop itself. The instruments of production do not simply appear. Marxism's treatment of technology as an independent variable was, Woltmann argued, *prima facie* implausible. He argued that the instruments of production and the development of productive forces were contingent upon the creative and intellectual activity of men.

The economic theory of history, if it is to afford a compelling and complete account of human history, must be supplemented by a coherent explanation of the organic evolution of man and the development of the physical basis of creativity, the human brain.[20] Marx, Woltmann maintained, had neglected the organic basis of man's development. Woltmann, quoting from *Capital*, revealed that Marx *had* indicated that the productiveness of labor, and by implication all subsequent social history, was "fettered by physical conditions. . . . all referable to the constitution of man himself (race, etc.) . . . ," but he had failed to pursue the insight.[21] The development of the productive forces, Woltmann went on to argue, was not an independent, but a dependent, variable, determined by the differential creative potential of the races of man. The materialist interpretation of history must be augmented by a biological and anthropological supplement, which could be found in the works of Darwin and his followers. To this end Woltmann pressed into service all the theoretical machinery of the Social Darwinism of his time.[22] Engels, Woltmann maintained, had attempted just such a synthesis after Marx's death by indicating that "according to the materialistic conception, the determining factor in history is, in the last resort, the production and reproduction of immediate life. . . . On the one hand, the production of the means of subsistence . . . on the other, the production of human beings themselves, the propagation of the species. . . ."[23] Alongside material *production* Engels sought to insinuate biological *reproduction*. Woltmann construed Marx's reference to race as a determinant and Engels' insinuation of reproduction into the base of the materialist interpretation of history to be license for advancing Darwinism as a necessary supplement to the materialist interpretation of history. Before a coherent explanation of man's social development through the evolution of productive forces can be forthcoming, an account of the differential capacity of individual men and individual groups to generate and support such an evolution must be explained. In order to accomplish this the Darwinian conceptions of variation, adaptation, heredity, and selection involving individuals and collectivities must be employed.[24] All of these conceptions are inconceivable without the central notion of the individual and collective struggle for existence (*"Kampf ums Dasein"*).[25]

Man is the only tool-making animal; it is only he, of all animals, who creates his means of subsistence. Classical Marxism must, in the last analysis, explain man's uniqueness by recognizing him as a more highly developed organism, with a more complex central nervous system and a thicker cerebral cortex, qualitatively different from creatures of a lower order. The ultimate explanation of man's social history lies not in material production but in biological evolution.[26]

Woltmann insisted that human history required an explanation in terms of historical process laws that employed Darwinian concepts like the struggle for existence and natural and artificial selection. By the time he wrote *Politische Anthropologie* in 1903, he had become convinced that the economic interpretation of history could only serve as an adjunct to Social Darwinism. "The biological history of the races of man," he maintained, "constitutes the real and essential history of states."[27] World history is but a fragment of the law-governed organic history of biological evolution whose subjects are races, which develop and decline under the regularities governing variation and heredity, adaptation and selection, inbreeding and miscegenation. Woltmann considered this interpretation the legitimate heir of the idealist and materialist interpretation of history, which he identified with Hegel and Marx, respectively. What he called the "anthropological conception of history" was the result of the impact of natural science, specifically Darwinism, on these antecedent conceptions.[28]

The central explanatory presupposition that Woltmann advanced was that of Malthus: Organic life has an inherent tendency to reproduce itself beyond available subsistence. Each animal community, impelled by an instinct for survival, finds itself involved in a perpetual struggle for sustenance. That struggle requires an internal cohesiveness, a group solidarity, a consciousness of kind that has high survival potential. Woltmann identified that consciousness of kind as "race consciousness," a "natural instinct" to find satisfaction in the company of an association of like kind, an internal sympathy that generates a sense of distance and antipathy toward outgroup members. Ingroup amity and outgroup enmity are both the causes and the consequences of group struggle. The struggle for existence necessitates internal sodality and a drive toward mastery over outgroups. In order to survive, each group must wage a pitiless struggle against real and potential competitors. Groups without internal unity and a drive for mastery are either destroyed or dominated by those that are. When defeated outgroups cannot serve the interests of the conquering community they are exterminated. But when these conquered peoples can be put into the service of their conquerors, they are made subordinate members of a new, more complex community. Each community, motivated by a drive to mastery ("*Herrschaftstrieb*"), succeeds to dominance or succumbs to domination or destruction in an unremitting struggle for survival. "Mastery and submission are the natural facts of the world. . . . [They] rest on force and serve force." Such a process exemplifies the natural laws of progressive evolution. "Those that survive, those who are victorious . . . are the best."[29] Nature knows no abstract "right to life"—rights are established, allotted, and rendered effective only by force in the universal struggle for existence governed by the infrangible laws of nature.

Woltmann advanced a set of descriptive and theoretical propositions that were common to the Social Darwinism of his time, and it was this common set of propositions that gave structure to Hitler's social and political philosophy. Hitler argued that the unrestricted fecundity of animal life necessarily outstripped the means of subsistence generating a "struggle for existence that produces the selection of the fittest. . . . By means of the struggle, the elites are continually renewed. The law of selection justifies this incessant struggle, by allowing the survival of the fittest."[30] He went on to argue that every people has self-preservation as its driving force. The most "patent" principle governing the struggle of communities for survival, each animated by the natural instinct of self-preservation, is "inner segregation," a "herd" or "racial" instinct that disposes the individual not to "transgress against the principle of blood purity." The conflict of such self-regarding communities can only result in the subordination of one to the other. The ultimate arbiter is force.

According to the laws of nature the soil belongs to him who conquers it. . . . By virtue of an inherent law . . . riches belong to him who conquers them. . . . It's success that justifies everything. . . . The stronger asserts his will; it's the law of nature. The world doesn't change; its laws are eternal. . . . Men dispossess one another, and one perceives that, at the end of it all, it is always the stronger who triumphs. Is that not the most reasonable order of things? If it were otherwise, nothing good would ever have existed. If we did not respect the laws of nature, imposing our will by the right of the stronger, a day would come when the wild animals would once again devour us. . . .[31]

Hitler had voiced these convictions as early as 1923.

This collection of propositions might have been culled from the works of any number of Social Darwinists writing at the turn of the century. Even Houston Stewart Chamberlain, certainly not a Darwinist in the strict sense, maintained that "the hypothesis of evolution has accidentally got hold of a truth—the importance of the struggle for existence," a struggle, he contended, that meant destruction for the fundamentally weak race and a steeling of the strong.[32] Lapouge, self-characterized as a "strict Darwinist," maintained that "there is no such thing as human rights. . . . The notion of justice is a delusion. There is nothing but force. . . . There is no right that prevails against force."[33] Passages in Woltmann suggest the same conception: "The struggle for existence becomes a struggle for social power. The struggle for rights is therefore originally, and in its general significance, a struggle for the rights of the stronger. . . . Law or right is, therefore, the 'politics of force,' to use Jhering's expression. . . ."[34]

All these conceptions have a superficially descriptive character. They are advanced as assessments of facts. It is only when they are tacitly or explicitly coupled with value judgments that they generate the injunctions of social and political philosophy. The propositions that Hitler employed were infused with value judgments. For example, the struggle for existence is "justified" by the process of selection understood to attend it—a process that affords the superior human material upon which all development is contingent. This would require, as we have suggested, that superiority could be defined independently of survival. If it is not, the attempted vindication for the struggle for existence would fail, and one could only maintain that those that survive, survive. The use of the persuasive term "fittest" conceals the vacuity of such a proposition. The proposition "the struggle for existence provides the circumstances for survival of the fittest" becomes a vindication for struggle only if fittest has as a reference class some collection at least potentially other than the class of those that survive. Hitler never seemed to make this distinction clearly. On the one hand, he couples "best and stronger," "the brutal fist and intellectual genius" as though they can, in fact, be distinguished and as though the "best" people might find themselves weak before their inferior but stronger opponents. This seems to be the substance of his appeal for a German revival. Yet, on other occasions, he seems to have identified the best with the stronger, making one term a logically substitutable instance of the other. Speaking to Albert Speer in March, 1945, Hitler said of Germany, "The nation has proved itself weak, and the future belongs solely to the stronger Eastern nation."[35] In 1941, in discussing the war then in progress, he said that one side must succumb and added that "it's all in the natural order of things—for it makes for the survival of the fittest."[36] It seemed that survival certified superiority. This would make intelligible Hitler's statement, "In my opinion, that an inferior people should triumph over a strong is a negation of the laws of nature." "Inferior" seems to have been employed as the opposite of "strong." In this case Hitler seems to have equated "strong" with "superior." That the triumph of the inferior over the superior contradicts a law of nature could only mean that Hitler understood the "law" of the survival of the fittest to mean that those who survive are superior. It would then be a rank contradiction to say that the inferior survive, since in that case the inferior would, by definition, be the superior.

To reconstruct with assurance what Hitler meant to say, particularly by scrutinizing his casual table conversation, is well-nigh impossible. There are a sufficient number of counterexamples in which he distinguished strength and superiority to give us pause. At one point he spoke of the "duel between intellect and strength" in which he suggested that the outcome would always be decided to the advantage of the strong.[37] Superiority in terms of strength and superiority in terms of intellect are certainly distinguished. What Hitler seems to have intended is the issuance of an injunction. In order to realize their potential, the superior, the best, must be prepared to acknowledge and ruthlessly apply "Nature's stern and rigid laws. . . . Those who want to live, let them fight, and those who do not want to fight in this world of eternal struggle do not deserve to live. Even if this were hard—that is how it is!"[38] The superior must make themselves strong.

Postulating the unlimited reproductive capacity of peoples,

their mutual hostility, and limited means of subsistence, Hitler could safely conclude that "life is a cruel struggle." In the struggle the will to survive of competing groups is tested. If that will is coupled with superiority, mankind has progressed. If the will is lacking among the superior, the inferior will triumph and mankind will lapse back into savagery. Should this be correct, it would make little sense to say that men should recognize the privilege of force and strength. Rather, strength or force could only be construed as a necessary safeguard for intelligence, creativity, or superiority (defined independently of strength or force). Hitler seems to have implicitly recognized this because he defines Aryan superiority independently of survival (since he illustrates instances when the race failed to survive). He defines Aryan superiority in terms of scientific and technical achievements, intellectual imagination, creative power, organizational capacities, and cultural attainments, identifying Aryans as the "founders," perhaps the *sole* founders, of culture.

In Woltmann's work the distinction is quite explicit. "The right of the stronger," Woltmann cautioned, "need not always be the right of the superior any more than adaptation signifies increasing perfection in either the organic or the social world. The ethical justification for right requires first a proof of superiority."[39] The arguments in *Mein Kampf* are elliptical and confused, as we have stressed previously. When they are reformulated with the suppressed premises restored, they are revealed as the Social Darwinist arguments fully developed in Woltmann's principal work. Few of these arguments, in either an elliptical or a fully articulated form, are found in the pamphlets of Liebenfels or in Chamberlain's *Foundations of the Nineteenth Century.*

What is more significant for our purposes is that Woltmann advances a conceptual model of man which is essentially that of Hegel and Marx. Woltmann maintained that man lives not in isolation, but within a historical and social community ("*Gemeinschaft*"). The individual conceived outside society is an abstraction. Liberal social and political theory failed to adequately appreciate this essential consideration. Man evinces an "elemental, inborn social drive" that requires membership in a community for fulfillment, and that membership is not the consequence of choice but of biological origin. The individual's manifest traits are those of his biological community, his race. The life of the individual is explicable only in terms of his racial provenience.

Woltmann explicitly rejected methodological individualism. The individual could only be explained by reference to the whole and as an exemplification of his race. Any account of individual behavior required antecedent propositions referring to his racial membership. For Woltmann, observed individual behaviors could only be accounted for by subsuming them under traits common to a racial confraternity developed in the course of organic evolution governed by the struggle for existence. Woltmann argued that the entire history of humanity is a transparent proof of the significance of race, a significance that the theoretician cannot neglect if his concern is with the causes and laws of historical development.[40] Where Marx had seen the surface features of history as a struggle between economic classes, Woltmann tended to conceive them as instances of struggle between races. Years later in the works of Liebenfels this idea was expressed in the proposition, "Not class, but race struggle is the content of world and cultural history," and in *Mein Kampf* it appears as "all occurrences in world history are only the expression of the races' instinct of self-preservation. . . ."[41]

The Social Darwinism expressed in Woltmann's work fosters a presumption in favor of the biological collectivity. Whatever is good is the product of law-governed natural process. Nature has produced races, and the individual is what he is only because he is a member of a specific biological community. These are the considerations in terms of which Hitler justifies a presumption in favor of the collectivity.

. . . True idealism is nothing but the subordination of the interests and life of the individual to the community, and this in turn is the precondition for the creation of organizational forms of all kinds, it corresponds in its innermost depths to the ultimate will of Nature. . . .

Here the instinct of knowledge unconsciously obeys the deeper necessity of the preservation of the species, if necessary at the cost of the Individual. . . .

[The] forces which create culture and values are based essentially on racial elements and . . . the state must, therefore, in the light of reason regard its highest task as the preservation and intensification of the race, this fundamental condition of all human cultural development.

As a consequence, Hitler could argue:

> If I accept a divine commandment, it's this one: "Thou shalt preserve the species." The life of the individual must not be set at too high a price. . . . What is important . . . is . . . the maintenance of conditions that enable science constantly to renew itself. . . . I dream of a state of affairs in which every man would know that he lives and dies for the preservation of the species. It's our duty to encourage that idea. . . .[42]

Hitler's argument seems to be (1) everything of value is ultimately based upon race (ignoring the evident equivocation involved in frequently confusing species with race); (2) the preservation of the race requires the sacrifice of individuals; (3) therefore, if cherished values are to be defended, it is necessary that individuals be prepared to sacrifice themselves for the race.

By a series of substitutions Hitler identified the future of humanity and the German people with the continued existence of a specific race, at the same time identifying the German people with the state, the state with the party, and the party with himself.[43] Hitler thus licensed himself to speak not only for the interests of the German people, but for the ultimate interests of humanity as well. Employing this rationale, that biological collectivity enjoys moral priority over the individual, he could issue imperatives binding on individuals. This finds expression in the National Socialist slogans *"Gemeinnutz vor Eigennutz"* ("Collective interest before individual interest") and *"Alle für einen, einer für alle"* ("All for one, one for all"), which were predicated upon the conviction that "The individual is nothing when not a member of a community (*"einer Gemeinschaft"*)," for "Man is a communal being" (*"Der Mensch ist Gemeinschaftswesen"*). Since Hitler spoke for the racial community, he spoke in the *ultimate* interests of the individual components of that community.

This justificatory argument, formulated to support the issuance of imperatives, rests upon two critical considerations:

(1) the real superiority of a specific racial aggregate that is understood to constitute the ultimate source of humanity's values; and (2) an explication of what it means to say that the ultimate interests of the individual and the community are one and can be expressed in the pronouncements of a single man.

Hitler never argued the first thesis; he issued pronouncements. In *Mein Kampf* he maintained, "Everything we admire on this earth today—science and art, technology and inventions —is only the creative product of a few peoples and originally perhaps of *one* race." In Liebenfels this is rendered, "[The] blond race . . . is . . . the sole culture creating and culture sustaining race . . . ," which echoes Woltmann's judgment, made years before, that "the Nordic race is the natural bearer of world civilization" whose "special interests are identical with the highest interests of mankind."[44]

Liebenfels' pamphlets are dotted with references to the work of Woltmann. Wherever Liebenfels lapsed into a semblance of rationality, he employed material culled from Woltmann. In fact, whole sections of his pamphlets are literal plagiarisms. Years later, in 1933, when Karl Weinlaender wrote his *Rassenkunde, Rassenpädogogik und Rassenpolitik*, whole paragraphs of his text that he attributed to Liebenfels were taken word for word from Woltmann's *Die Germanen in Frankreich*.[45] It is Woltmann who developed the argument that the civilizations of Malaya, Polynesia, India, China, Central America, Persia, Greece, Rome, Babylonia, and Egypt were the products of Nordic creativity.[46] Hitler not only reflected Woltmann's arguments, but employed his vocabulary. Woltmann used Aryan, Nordic, Germanic, and the peculiar hyphenated Nordic-Germanic to identify his culture-creators, just as Hitler did. Liebenfels, although he objected to the employment of the term, sometimes used Aryan, but more frequently employed blond race or clumsy hyphenates like Nordic-heroic, or Ario-heroic, and specifically abjured Nordic-Germanic or Germanic. Neither the arguments that ascribe the cultures of Asia and the New World to the Nordic race nor the corresponding vocabulary appear in the work of Chamberlain. Chamberlain argues that the Germanics, who made their entrance into history with the decline of antiquity, are not to be confused with other races, and he speaks of such different and distinct (though related) races as the

Greeks, Romans, Franks, Swabians, Italians, and Spaniards. His
dynamic conception of race and race formation would not accommodate the notion that *all* these peoples constituted *a* race
or that a Nordic race, which was the putative creator of all the
world's culture, persisted through historical epochs. Chamberlain did speak of the "hypothetical Aryans" as "blood related
peoples," but it is clear that he did not conceive them to be a
uniform anthropological race.[47] He does not seem to have employed the term Nordic at all.

There is little point in pursuing an extrinsic criticism of the
thesis that the race of tall, long-headed, blond, and blue-eyed
men are the sole creators of the world's culture. There is an
abundant literature devoted to analysis and criticism of the truth
claims of the Nordic hypothesis.[48] For the purposes of this
exposition it is only necessary to indicate that because there are
so many substantive parallels between Hitler's arguments in
Mein Kampf and the major work of Woltmann, it seems almost
certain that this work is the source of Hitler's Nordic convictions. For example, in *Mein Kampf* Hitler argued that "The road
which the Aryan had to take was clearly marked out. As a con-
queror he subjected the lower beings and regulated their practical activity under his command, according to his will and for
his aims." Although these contentions were couched in the past
tense, it was clear that Hitler intended them to characterize the
future relations of Aryans and non-Aryans, for he went on to
indicate, "We all sense that in the distant future humanity must
be faced by problems which only a highest race, become master
people and supported by the means and possibilities of an entire globe, will be equipped to overcome." How the master
people will accede to such dominion is equally clear. It will be
*"based on the victorious sword of a master people, putting the
world into the service of a higher culture."* This is a consistent,
but perhaps less candid, rendering of Woltmann's revelation
that "the Nordic race is destined to mastery of the earth, to
exploit (*"auszubeuten"*) the wealth of nature and labor-power
and employ the passive races as servitors (*"dienendes Glied"*) in
[Nordic] cultural development."[49]

One of the most critical theses of Hitler's justificatory argument, the literal dependence of world culture on the prevalence
of Nordics, is found in its most consistent and explicit form in

Woltmann's work. The remaining considerations, the explication of what National Socialism meant in maintaining that the individual's ultimate interests are those of his community, is also found in the work of Woltmann. Hitler's own thought reflects that of Woltmann, as does its amplification found in the work of National Socialist theoreticians like Helmut Nicolai and Carl Schmitt.

The central conception by which Woltmann related the individual to his biological community was that which made mentality and all the attributes of spirit the necessary and determinate consequence of the possession of some finite set of racially specific hereditary factors. The individual who is a member of a pure race, a race that has been subject to protracted selection in isolation, is the heir of a constellation of harmoniously integrated psychic traits. A pure race contains members who share, with a limited range of variability, this constellation of traits. A community composed entirely of members of a pure race is one in which the individual, surrounded by a like-minded fraternity of congeners, finds the maximum opportunity for self-development and self-realization. Such a society is truly an organism in which the component members, by obeying the laws of their own preservation, growth, and development, enhance the survival potential, expansion, and cultural advance of their community.[50] Membership in such a social organism affords the individual freedom in the sense of fostering self-realization in accordance with the common laws governing his own and his community's physical and psychic life. Any division of labor within such a racial community would follow the lines dictated by the natural variation found within any biological collectivity, variations based upon sex, age, and natural gifts. But all members of a racially homogeneous community would share the essentials necessary for a harmonious communal life. The interests of the individual and the community are one—certified by the unity of blood.

The intuitive awareness of a unity of sentiments, aptitudes, and aspirations in a racial community composed of like members generates a group unity, a racial instinct that fuses the individual to the community. This sense of unity has high survival value in the struggle for existence. It is only when conquest or alliance bring together two communities that are composed of dissimilar racial stocks that this original harmony is destroyed. The first and predictable attempt at accommodation of unlike racial elements is slavery or a caste system in which the conquering race attempts to socially isolate the conquered. Protracted involvement in the same community enterprise tends, however, to erode the social restrictions that isolate the various racial components, and there is a gradual infusion of alien blood into the superordinate caste. The result is an increment of intrasocial friction as a consequence of the increasing contact of individuals possessed of divergent psychic traits. The most doleful consequence is the racially mixed individual who no longer exemplifies the harmonious constellation of physical and psychic traits that is the heritage of pure racial ancestry. The racially mixed individual manifests a "disharmonious and unstable character." The individual and society become subject to tensions and real and potential conflicts, which reduce not only the opportunity for self-realization in freedom for the individual but also threaten the existence of the community as well.

This is precisely the argument Hitler presents in *Mein Kampf*, and parts of it reappear constantly in writings and speeches throughout his life. Hitler speaks of the "racially unified being" making "correct, that is, unified decisions" while the "racially divided one" remains "uncertain." It is the

. . . lost purity of blood alone [that] destroys inner happiness. . . . Peoples which renounce the preservation of their racial purity renounce with it the unity of their soul in all its expressions. The divided state of their nature is the natural consequence of the divided state of their blood, and the change in their intellectual and creative force is only the effect of the change in their racial foundations.[51]

It is the unity of expression common to all members of the community of blood that permits a minority, perhaps one man, to speak with the voice of all. It is the unity of blood that demands unity in an integrated political organism. "One blood demands one Reich."

How consistently Hitler adhered to this conception of psycho-physical harmony, which provided the theoretical foundation for his conceptions of freedom and the identity of the individual and his biological community, is illustrated by his proposals concerning the future National Socialist magistracy. This magistracy was to be "as homogeneous as possible. Let the magistrates present a certain uniformity from the racial point of view—and we can expect the magistracy to apply the conceptions of the state intelligently." The judges, he continued, must be Nordic. "We Germans," he proposed, "must arrive at the result that every judge resembles every other judge even in his physical appearance." These judges were to be given wide discretionary powers. "But the condition of this discretionary power which is granted to the judge is that the magistrature should be racially so homogeneous that the smallest sign should be sufficient to make it understand us."[52] The logic of such sentiments is that if the individual is a member of a racially homogeneous community, he can operate with the widest discretionary power, unrestricted by codified restraints or social sanctions. All members of such a community would understand each other because they have the same values and sentiments. Freedom would mean the identification of the individual with his community.

These conceptions were employed by Carl Schmitt in what was perhaps the most coherent theoretical exposition of the National Socialist conception of the state. In his *Staat, Bewegung, Volk*, written early in the National Socialist period, Schmitt maintained that leadership (*"Führung"*) in the National Socialist state was predicated on "the absolute equality of race (*"Artgleichheit"*) between the leader and his following. Upon this racial homogeneity is founded the continuous and infallible contact between the leader and his following as well as their reciprocal fidelity. . . . Without the principle of the identity of race, the National Socialist state could not exist and its juridical life would be unintelligible. . . ."[53] The fundamental element that makes totalitarian leadership possible and that justifies the unitary party is the unity of race, which makes nation, party, and state one. As Helmut Nicolai indicates, this makes a conviction in the scientific merit of the laws of human heredity central to the entire argument. Those laws confirm the reality of the innate community of sentiment and will (*"angeborene Übereinstimmung des Fühlens und Wollens"*) that unite the leader with his people. These conceptions, Nicolai argued, reveal the poverty of liberal notions of freedom, which conceive the individual as a reality divorced from the community of blood

(*"Blutsgemeinschaft"*) of which he is a natural member. Freedom is not caprice; it is action governed by the rule system generated by a particular racial community—a rule system that
answers the spiritual and intellectual needs of a specific historical
and biological aggregate of men.[54]

The National Socialist movement in Germany ultimately
absorbed an almost infinite number of elements. There is no
doubt that the volkish, Romantic movement so active around
the turn of the century lent much of its vocabulary as well as
many of its activists to the National Socialist movement. But
Hitler himself was very critical of the volkish elements that
coquetted with his movement. For Hitler, the concept "volkish"
was vague and subject to unlimited interpretation, and he rejected it as a possible basis for his movement. It was, in fact,
around this concept that much theoretical tension was to ac-
cumulate.

Alfred Rosenberg, commonly regarded as the philosopher of
National Socialism, is credited with far too much influence in
the articulation of Hitler's ideology. It is true that, in a discussion with Gregor Strasser, Hitler is reported to have recommended Rosenberg's book as "the most tremendous achievement
of its kind," and the book was given prominence in National
Socialist Germany. But in his candid table talks Hitler stated:

> I must insist that Rosenberg's *The Myth of the Twentieth Century*
> is not to be regarded as an expression of the official doctrine of the
> Party. . . . There is, indeed, no question of confronting the conceptions
> of the nineteenth century with the so-called myth of the twentieth. A
> National Socialist should affirm that to the myth of the nineteenth cen-
> tury he opposes the faith and science of our times.

He went on to indicate that, like most members of the party,
he had merely looked through Rosenberg's major work.[55] The
reason is not far to seek. Rosenberg admitted that his book was
not a biological treatment of the race issue. In his memoirs he
indicated that when he undertook to write the *Mythus* he knew
"little about modern biology." His starting point was "artistic
experience."[56] Hitler, on the other hand, conceived his own
philosophy to be *scientific*. He was a Social Darwinist of a simplistic and reductionist sort. His ideas are as scientific as those

of Woltmann; they are as Romantic and volkish as those of Woltmann; they *are*, in fact, the transmogrified Hegelian and Marxist ideas of Woltmann.

Finally, if Hitler was an advocate of *Realpolitik*, as everything we know of him clearly indicates, and *Realpolitik* is understood to mean a ruthless national power politics, it is not necessary to rummage through the works of Fichte, Hegel, and Treitschke for his inspiration. Certainly, the prevalence of these ideas in Germany assured Hitler's advocacy greater chance of success. The justification Hitler gives for power politics is clearly advanced in his unpublished work of 1928. There Hitler argued:

> Countless are the species of all the earth's organisms; unlimited at any moment in individuals is their instinct for self-preservation as well as the longing for continuance, yet the space in which the whole life process takes place is limited. The struggle for existence and continuance in life waged by billions upon billions of organisms takes place on the surface of an exactly measured sphere. The compulsion to engage in the struggle for existence lies in the limitation of the living space; but in the life-struggle for this living space lies also the basis for evolution.[57]

This is the entire rationale for Hitler's *Realpolitik*. It stands behind the National Socialist demand for "living space." It is the justification of struggle. Its sustaining value is evolution. It is simply a Social Darwinism that could be found in a number of places, but was most probably derived from the work of Ludwig Woltmann.

All this is not to say that Hitler was not influenced by Wagner, Chamberlain, or Liebenfels. His pathological preoccupation with the Jews can hardly find its source in Woltmann. Woltmann did identify the Jewish question as an *anthropological* question of significance and he characterized the Jews as "an alien race" (*"einer andersartigen Rasse"*).[58] But Hitler's concern has features more akin to those found in the tracts of Liebenfels than the more respectable work of Woltmann. In this respect Hitler's ideas are similar to, although more virulent than, those of Chamberlain and Wagner. But it is difficult to speak with any confidence concerning the origin of ideas that are essentially pathological.

Doctrinal and Theoretical Developments

•   In retrospect it is possible to reconstruct the essentials of the social and political thought of Adolf Hitler with considerable confidence. But there remain certain significant elements that, during the period of National Socialist hegemony and even into our own time, defy full explication. One of these problem areas is the relationship of the concepts "nation" and "volk" to that of "race."

One of the programmatic intentions of the National Socialist party was to create a national people's community in which national consciousness would take precedence over class consciousness. Hitler sought to obviate the influence of those class and professional prejudices that fragmented the unity of the German nation. National interests were to be given precedence over parochial or class interests. National Socialism conceived itself obliged to "uproot all those trackless and often indefinable feelings and emotions which in human society spring from pride of descent or class consciousness. . . . [All] these social and personal traditions [have] to go, and the common element in the people's life (*"das volklich Gemeinsame"*) [has] to be brought to the foreground." The transcendent unity in which all personal, class, regional, and professional differences were to be mediated was the volkish community, the nation. Within such a conception socialism and nationalism merged. Nationalism united the individual and his nation in an organic community of interest.

Every truly national idea is in the last resort social, i.e., he who is prepared so completely to adopt the cause of his people that he really knows no higher ideal than the prosperity of this—his own—people, he who has so taken to heart the meaning of our great song *"Deutschland, Deutschland über alles,"* that nothing in this world stands for him higher than this Germany, people and land, land and people, he is a socialist. . . . [He] is not merely a socialist but he is also national in the highest sense of that world.[59]

The central concepts of the National Socialist *Weltanschauung* appear to have been the volkish or national community (*Volksgemeinschaft*). Germans of every class and occu-

pation were members of the volk, the national community of
blood (*Blutsgemeinschaft*), and the state was conceived as a
volkish organism. In this sense National Socialism incorporated
the essence of volkish philosophy as it was represented in the
movement that traced its origins back to Paul de Lagarde and
Julius Langbehn. It found clear expression in innumerable passages in Rosenberg's *Mythus*, in which the nation and the state
are united in mystic union with the volkish collectivity (*Volks-
gesamtheit*).[60] In this sense Hitler proclaimed himself "a German nationalist." "This means," he went on, "that I proclaim my
nationality. My whole thought and action belongs to it. I am a
socialist. I see no class and no social estate before me, but that
community of people who are linked by blood, united by language and subject to the same general fate." In this same sense
he could maintain years later, "I believe blindly in my nation."[61]

Hitler, and the National Socialists in general, made seemingly
effortless transitions from nationality to volk and race as though
the relationships between these concepts were completely transparent. In the works of Schmitt volk and race are used interchangeably. Nicolai bridges the evident distinction between a
volk, which is composed of diverse racial elements, and a homogeneous race by maintaining that the German volkish community had received the "strong imprint" of the Nordic race.[62]
If the distinction is made, any argument to support the claim
of any identity of interests between the individual and the
collectivity (when the collectivity is described as a homogeneous
race) cannot also be used if the collectivity in question is described as a volk (which is heterogeneous) without supplementing
the original argument. This difficulty attends most discussions
throughout the National Socialist period. We have indicated that
Hitler consistently referred to the Jews both as a volk and as a
race as though both terms had the same denotation. His use of
the term Aryan harbored the same ambiguity.

When the National Socialist state began promulgating laws,
the question of the reference class denoted by "Aryan" became
one of urgent practical significance. In the deliberations in 1933,
the Akademie für deutsches Recht decided that "German and
cognate blood" should be substituted for "Aryan" in all relevant
places in National Socialist legislation.[63] This echoed the National Socialist judgment, made years before in the party pro-

gram, that only those of German blood could be members of the nation (*Volksgenosse*). The term Aryan became equivalent in denotation to the class of individuals of German blood, but National Socialist legislation never seems to have been fully capable of stipulating with precision the scope of application of the phrase. When proof of "German blood" was required for official purposes, the process involved no more than establishing by documents or sworn statement that the applicant had neither parents nor grandparents of Jewish provenience. As National Socialist theorists indicated in 1934, the word "Aryan" had come to have only negative racial or volkish connotation; it meant little more than non-Jewish.[64]

To be non-Jewish permitted one to be a member of the volkish community. But Hitler had used the term Aryan with obvious racial intention: It was only his vagueness in applying the concept that obscured the fact that National Socialism as a system harbored radically incompatible elements. The reference class of the term Aryan is different from that of non-Jewish, and the reference class of the term German is different from either, while the reference class for the expression German volk is patently different from all of them. This problem in distinctions threatened a doctrinal crisis of a magnitude that involved the entire ideological system. The critical issues collected around the use of the words "volk" and "race."

The German Romantics and the volkish philosophers had always used the term volk in vague and ambiguous ways. It was Hitler who sought to give the term a specifically racial character. "[National Socialism] must set race in the center of all life," and yet at the same time the function of the volkish state is to foster "national pride."[65] Now either volkish pride is identical with national pride and racial pride and the three expressions are substitution instances of each other, or there were perhaps three sorts of pride that National Socialism sought to foster. In the former case Aryan refers to German volkdom, German nationality, and some specific race, and all these expressions have the same scope of predication. In the latter case the German volk was something other than German nationality, and the race that was the center of all life was conceivably different from both. The negative definition of Aryan as non-Jewish left the issue unresolved. If all non-Jews were Aryans, then Negroes and Orientals were Aryans. But several references in National Socialist legislation precluded this interpretation. The Japanese had to receive special dispensation in order to avoid some of the Aryan clauses in National Socialist legislation and "Negro blood" is specifically mentioned as disqualifying an applicant for Aryan status in the Reich Homestead Inheritance Law of September, 1933. Hitler had referred to a unity of language as one of the necessary qualifications for membership in the German community. This established a cultural criterion that he elsewhere rejected—not language, but blood, must be decisive.[66] None of which clarified the issues.

When *Mein Kampf* was published, Hitler had made an attempt to unravel these issues. He stated:

> German nationality, unfortunately, is no longer based on a unified racial nucleus. . . . Not only are the basic racial elements scattered territorially, but on a small scale within the same territory. Beside Nordic men, Easterners (*"ostische"*); beside Easterners, Dinarics (*"dinarische"*); beside both of these, Westerners (*"westische"*); and mixtures in between.[67]

Woltmann had pointed out that the German volk could not be identified with a homogeneous racial type, but Hitler's nomenclature, which identified European racial entities as *ostische*, *dinarische* and *westische*, indicates that he had apparently already read H. F. K. Günther's *Rassenkunde des deutschen Volkes*, which appeared in 1922. Woltmann's anthropological vocabulary designated the Eastern race as Alpine, and the Western race as Mediterranean. He had no designation for the Dinaric race. As early as *Mein Kampf* National Socialist race theory had apparently begun to assimilate the notions of Günther.

The works of Günther were attractive to National Socialist theoreticians beset as they were by the necessity of systematizing the highly unstable mixture of volkish and Social Darwinian elements that made up Hitler's thought. As National Socialism expanded in membership and influence, there was an increasing demand that its theoretical house be put in order. Günther's works seemed to suit the purpose admirably well.

Günther's ideas can be briefly summarized in the following

definitional and theoretical propositions: (1) A race is a biological collection of human beings that, breeding true, distinguishes itself from its neighbors by constant hereditary physical
and psychic traits. (2) The psychic traits possessed by the various
races differ qualitatively. (3) In almost all mental traits the
Nordic race (tall, slender, fair-skinned, blond, blue-eyed,
leptoprosopic [narrow-faced], leptorrhine [narrow-nosed], doli-
chocephalic [long-headed]) is superior—Nordics being sage in
judgment, truthful, energetic, independent, realistic, bold,
courageous, clean, inventive, tenacious, prudent, steadfast in
duty, competitive, justly respectful of the property of others,
knightly, individualistic, and possessed of the gift of narrative,
depth of character, an inquiring mind devoted to natural science,
roguish humor, a capacity for statesmanlike achievements, and
a talent for leadership, music, art, and philosophy. (4) European culture (not to speak of world culture) is positively correlated with the presence and prevalence of members of the
Nordic race.[68] "When we survey the fall in each case of the great
empires and creative cultures from India to the West," Günther
maintained, "this much is always clearly to be seen: that every
'fall' of a people of Indo-European speech is brought about
through the drying up of the blood of the creative, the Nordic
race."[69]

There had always been a tendency among those in volkish
and nationalist circles in Germany to identify themselves vaguely
with the Aryan creators of culture. Germans were in some sense
Aryans. Günther's books had the merit of disabusing Germans
of these romantic—but unscientific—notions. First and foremost,
Günther indicated that the term Aryan was a linguistic term and
tended to obscure rather than enlighten. He counseled its abandonment and advocated the uniform use of the anthropological
term Nordic to identify the race of culture-creators with which
National Socialism was so much concerned. Günther insisted
upon being painfully specific. He warned that one must not con-
fuse Germans with Nordics. The German volk was a composite of
at least five European and two extra-European races. Germany's
total Nordic genetic patrimony was, at best, 45 to 50 percent.
Still more disconcerting was the fact that, using Günther's
cephalic, facial, and nasal indexes and pigmentation and stature
charts as a guide, only 5 percent of the German volk commu-

nity could be classified as pure Nordic types. The use of terms like Aryan and Germanic race, Günther argued, obscured such facts and tended to produce a false conviction of the unity of the German volk. For those who understood the truth, yet refrained from bruiting it about for fear of sundering the unity of the volk, Günther could only provide a biblical allusion: "The Nordicists have not come to bring peace. . . ."[70] In fact, Nordicists are in the unhappy position of having to identify the vast majority of Europeans (and Germans as well) as mixed bloods, bastards (*Mischlinge, Bastarde*). Moreover, Günther indicated that there were entire regions of Germany occupied by Alpines (*"die ostische Rasse"*), "small, dark, intellectually stunted men, similar to Mongolians, who have never produced a gifted individual."[71] Günther had very little to say about Alpines that was complimentary. The fact that they were members of the German volk did not obviate the fact that they were racially inferior. The racial worth of the components of the German volk varied on a hierarchical scale, the most worthwhile being the Nordic.

By the early thirties all of Günther's conjectures had passed into National Socialist literature. Pamphlets and party handbooks were replete with his charts, photographs, and anthropometric indexes—as well as with his conclusions. "Race" began to receive a priority that rapidly decreased the theoretical and doctrinal significance of "volk."

This eventuality was implicit in Hitler's social and political thought as early as 1928, for even at that time he said that Germany was composed of unequal racial elements. He went on to identify those members of the volkish community who possessed the "best blood." They were the "Nordic elements," who were responsible for the technical, cultural, and civic-political superiority of Germany. It was they who had the "greatest capacity for resistance, who [were] the boldest and most determined." These were the most valuable members of the national community.

This notion characterized Hitler's political and tactical postures throughout his life. His assessment of people (barring Jews) turned more and more consistently on their physical attributes—their blondness and their blue eyes. These physical features became diagnostic of membership in the *Germanic race*. The term

Germanic had an imprecise but exclusively racial reference. That his reference became increasingly racial rather than national or volkish is indicated by the fact that in 1942 Hitler advocated a Greater Germanic State (*Das grossgermanische Reich*) as distinct from a Greater Germany (*Grossdeutschland*). The Greater Germanic State would be a union of Germanics, a union of Nordic racial elements from any country. The swastika flag was not to be the flag of the German volkish community, but of an internationale of blonds! Each country in Europe that fell within the confines of that Greater Germanic State was to be led by Germanic, that is, Nordic, elements. This is what Hitler correctly understood as "methodically" pursuing a racial policy. As a consequence of that policy, there were Swedes, Danes, and Norwegians, members of enemy nationalities, that were conceived superior to Germans—if those Germans were members of inferior racial stock. It must be understood that Hitler was *not* referring to Jews, Negroes, or Mongolians. He was referring to non-Jewish Germans, members of what used to be considered the unified volkish community. He specifically referred to the "objectionable" racial types to be found in Greater Germany around Vienna, Munich, and Berlin.[72]

The entire National Socialist movement became infatuated with blondism. Prospective members of the elite SS troops (Schutzstaffel) were subjected to cranial measurements and osteometric examination, which, coupled with their degree of depigmentation, ensured their membership in the Nordic race. Only blond and blue-eyed men over six feet tall qualified for membership in Hitler's bodyguard, the Leibstandarte Adolf Hitler. Heinrich Himmler is known to have given special dispensation to concentration camp inmates who displayed the constellation of physical traits understood to characterize Nordic provenience.

The principle governing these tactical and doctrinal postures was racial discrimination within the volkish community. Preference was to be accorded non-volk elements if those elements met specific metric and nonmetric racial criteria. National Socialism revealed itself as a racial rather than a volkish movement. The decisive community of which the individual was conceived to be a member was racial, not national. Hitler's fundamental social and political thought revolved around Social Darwinian and Nordicist notions. The entire racial ideology of the SS was calculated to provide a master class (*Herrenschicht*) of "pure Nordic-Germanic manhood" ("*reinen nordisch-germanischen Menschen*") to rule the lesser peoples of the Greater Germanic State. This was Heinrich Himmler's avowed purpose. It sought to fulfill the racist vision of Adolf Hitler and that of Ludwig Woltmann before him.

The National Socialist movement had developed in Germany with the avowed intention of restoring the unity of the volkish community (by dissolving the divisive confessional, professional, and regional distinctions within Germany) only to manifest itself as a racial movement that advocated distinctions more penetrating and permanent than class or regional lines had ever been. Men have sometimes risen above their class, their regions, and their professions, but no man can escape his degree of pigmentation or his cranial index. Fascist theoreticians in Italy were not slow to point out what had, in fact, transpired in Germany. In 1939 Leone Franzi indicated that National Socialism threatened the integrity of the German community with the creation of castes with individuals assigned their places according to possession of a syndrome of metric and nonmetric physical traits. Guido Landra, one of the architects of the Fascist *Manifesto on Race* contended, "It is pernicious to divide a people into various races on the basis of a typology that uses certain somatic characteristics as sorting criteria, particularly when the different types are to be assigned diverse ranks on a hierarchical scale." Aldo Capasso pointed out that to attempt to assess the merits of individuals on the basis of an index of physical traits undermined the unity of the national community in the service of a caste system and laid the foundation for a racist internationalism as pernicious to nationalism as class internationalism.[73] Fascism sought to accommodate racism to nationalism while National Socialism had abandoned nationalism for a consistent racism.

At its very inception National Socialism was a highly unstable mixture of volkish and racist elements, a fact obscured only by the vagueness and ambiguity of National Socialist vocabulary. Chamberlain's tomes were compatible with volkish sentiments because he systematically rejected what he deprecated as "objective" scientific techniques for the identification of race. For Chamberlain it was the nation that created the conditions for race formation, a process that required the mixture of various but related racial components with protracted social or geographic

isolation and the consequent inbreeding subject to arduous natural or artificial selection. The races so formed cannot be distinguished solely by physical criteria. Chamberlain rejected the
thesis that fair hair and blue eyes constitute necessary conditions
for the ascription Germanic. Still less could craniometry assist in
separating Germanic from non-Germanic by metric formulas. For
him, these would constitute artificial classifications advanced by
men with little creative intuition. What Chamberlain suggested
was a technique by virtue of which "we must ascertain precisely
what groups actually exist as individualized, morally and intellectually distinguishable races, and then see whether there are
any anatomical characteristics which will aid us in classification."
It is thus the "mental element" which permits one "to separate
the Germanic from the non-Germanic, and at the same time
thereby to recognize the physical element and value it at its true
worth."[74]

For Chamberlain the nation remained the fundamental unit
of analysis. The collectivity with which the individual identified
was the living *Volkstum* in which he develops in the course of
the nation's historical and cultural evolution. In this sense Chamberlain was in the romantic and volkish tradition, and for a
time National Socialism attempted to incorporate that tradition.
Chamberlain hailed Hitler as a prophet and joined the young
National Socialist movement. But if Hitler was a prophet, he
was one in the service of another man's vision. Chamberlain's
conception of race was dynamic and historic. Races were never
pure; they were purified within the volkish confines of a politically organized community defined by the state. Chamberlain
could maintain that men do not make the state, rather the state
makes men—outside the state man is an animal. "Outside the
state is neither speech, nor civilization, nor culture, neither law,
nor art, nor science, nor religion. . . ."[75] But more than that,
the state is the will that defines the volkish community, an endogamous breeding community in which a race is fashioned. At
critical points in time a purified race appears as the culmination
of a protracted historical process, and the world enjoys a rare
spectacle of compelling creativity.

Chamberlain was essentially a volkish theoretician and a nationalist. Hitler was essentially a biological racist. Both their
"philosophies" remained in unhappy combination throughout

the National Socialist period. Even though the National Socialist hierarchy opted for a consistent racism of the sort advocated by Woltmann and Günther, there remained an irrespressible volkish tendency that sought to defend national values. Thus, even in the strictly anthropological literature of the period there were academicians who conceived the relationship between volk and race as one in which a "volk is a race in formation." The volk was understood to constitute a new biological unity within which race-building factors tend to produce a new anthropologically uniform race. Similar arguments in the defense of the volkish community were attempted throughout the National Socialist period. As late as 1943, it was still maintained that a volk was, in fact, a breeding community that tended—given appropriate conditions—to constitute a new race out of elements of preexisting related races. The defense was sometimes coupled with arch criticism of the racial theories of Günther, whose notions were understood to provide spurious arguments that engendered an unfounded race pride that could disintegrate the unity of the German people.[76]

It is not our purpose here to inspect the scientific credibility of this alternate volkish tendency any more than it is to inspect the Nordicist hypothesis. All we have attempted to establish is that two distinct and mutually incompatible tendencies in National Socialist thought existed in reality, although that mutual exclusivity was often obscured by Hitler's systematic ambiguity of expression. The confusion was further compounded by Hitler's indisposition, for obvious tactical reasons, to base an individual's merit exclusively on his anthropological characteristics. "One cannot," Hitler maintained, "only infer from the fact of race that certain capacities will be present, one can also start from the capacities and infer the race." Rosenberg similarly maintained that "nothing would be more superficial than to measure a man's worth by his physical appearance. . . . A far more accurate measure of worth is conduct."[77] These qualifications appeared and reappeared in National Socialist literature. In mid-1936 the *Nationalsozialistische Korrespondenz* could maintain, "From his deeds one can recognize the Nordic man—not from the length of his nose and the color of his eyes."

The tactical necessity for such qualifications were obvious. National Socialist literature identified Hitler as a Nordic-Dinaric, and Goebbels (who had precious little of the Nordic in his appearance) as a Nordic-Mediterranean cross. Some theorists went so far as to suggest that the amount of Nordic blood an individual possessed meant nothing in the Nordic scheme of things because "it has often enough been the case that men of extremely mixed race (*"stark gemischter Rasse"*) have conceived and more powerfully grasped these notions than the predominantly Nordic."[78] These pronouncements, conjoined with Hitler's public statements that the Nordic "core-people" who had conquered the land that was to become Germany had merged with the conquered to create a single, unified community, had given heart to thinkers in the volkish tradition.

The fact that these two conflicting traditions persisted unresolved throughout the National Socialist period made exposition and analysis of doctrine extremely difficult, even for National Socialists themselves. There were some interesting attempts to synthesize the two. Among the best perhaps was Lothar Stengel von Rutkowski's *Was ist ein Volk? Der biologische Volksbegriff.* As late as 1942 Rutkowski could indicate that "race and volk are the very foundations of the Third Reich" and yet go on to illustrate that the relationship between the two critical concepts remained problematic and confused in the theoretical literature. The entire National Socialist concept of leadership and the unity of the individual and the community, which afforded substance to its concept of freedom, rested on a meaningful account of race and volk and their conceived interrelationship. If either concept were conceived as primary and determinant with the other secondary and derived, the entire structure of justificatory argument was fundamentally altered. If *racial* identity were fundamental, political leadership could only represent members of the same racial fraternity, and members of the national community who were not members of the core-people would have to be relegated to second-class citizenship. If *volkish* identity were fundamental, then the concept of leadership rested on the credibility of the evidence that established the uniformity of will and feeling in the volkish community that licensed one man to speak for that community. Moreover, if membership in the volk were determined by conduct rather than anthropological characteristics, how could Jews who behaved in the best volkish manner be legitimately excluded from the historic community? For most volkish thinkers, the answer was simple. They were not. Chamberlain argued:

> One does not need to have the authentic Hittite nose to be a Jew. . . . the term Jew rather denotes a special way of thinking and feeling. A man can very soon become a Jew without being an Israelite; often he needs only to have frequent intercourse with Jews, to read Jewish newspapers, to accustom himself to Jewish philosophy, literature, and art. On the other hand, it is senseless to call an Israelite a "Jew," though his descent is beyond question, if he has succeeded in throwing off the fetters of Ezra and Nehemiah, and if the law of Moses has no place in his brain, and contempt of others no place in his heart. "What a prospect it would be," cries Herder, "to see the Jews purely humanized in their way of thinking!" But a purely humanized Jew is no longer a Jew because, by renouncing the idea of Judaism, he *ipso facto* has left that nationality. . . .[79]

For Chamberlain, the volk (nationality) was the primary unit of analysis and the focus of value. And for that reason his work was more favorably received in Fascist Italy than much of the National Socialist material. There are, in fact, striking similarities between his work and the Fascist racism that found half-articulated expression in the *Manifesto of Fascist Racism* of 1938.[80] It is obvious that Hitler opted for a form of biological racism that reduced nationality to a derived product of historical racial conflict. All the elements of such a position were already contained in Woltmann's major work. Hitler's political misalliance with volkish elements in Germany obscured the true character of his social and political convictions. Only his accession to absolute power fully revealed the implications of the Social Darwinism and biological racism fundamental to his social and political thought. Only then did it become obvious that his commitment was to a racial community he called Germanic (or Nordic-Germanic) in the same descriptive vocabulary found in Woltmann's work, rather than to a national or volkish community called Germany.

Many authors have indicated the similarity in formal structure between the arguments advanced by Hegel and those of Marxists, Fascists, and National Socialists.[81] For Hegel the state was the embodiment of reason with which all individuals could identify without loss of freedom because the state embodied all that was of value for them. For Marx and the classical Marxists the state as society was the embodiment of the interests of a liberating class, interests that made men what they were, interests that constituted the foundation of everything that was of value to them. For Fascists the state was the embodiment of reason and interest outside of which the individual could realize nothing of value. For Woltmann and the National Socialists the state and the community were the embodiment of racial potential, a potential that constituted the full value of individual personality. Both Marx and Gentile were neo-Hegelians. Both Mussolini and Woltmann were neo-Marxists. All were methodological collectivists. All believed that the individual was, in some essential sense, only an element in some collectivity, a historically determined national community, a class, or a race. For all of them the value of the individual is derived; the individual is a sort of cellular element in a social whole. The logical and moral priority of the collectivity accord it an intrinsic value—it can make moral assessments and issue imperatives. To maintain that the whole has moral precedence over its elements is the consequence of adopting a specific theoretical model of man. The use of the recommended model is supported by factual and analytic arguments. The use of persuasive terms (freedom, personality, culture) in the description of the model impart to it a normative potential. Such terms can be employed in propositions that serve as major premises in justificatory arguments used to generate moral judgment and normative injunction.

To sustain the entire program, the model advanced must have the support of intersubjectively compelling arguments. National Socialist theoreticians were at least intuitively aware of this requirement, and their response was sufficiently unique to require a brief assessment.

One fundamental characteristic came to distinguish National Socialist arguments—the ultimate appeal to some form of intuition. Rosenberg gave the most characteristic expression to this technique when he argued that there were no sciences without presuppositions, the presuppositions of any science being ideas that are racially conditioned (*"bedingt"*). He maintained that only the abstract individualism of liberal thought could conceive of a science without presupposition. The liberal system was constructed in terms of an abstract human thought whereas in fact human thought is always conditioned by membership in a racially determined community.[82] The techniques for truth ascription must include reference to the racial membership of the investigator. Thus the Nobel Prize winner in physics Philipp Lenard could maintain that there was a Nordic or an Aryan physics as distinct from other sorts of physics. Lenard rejected the thesis of an international science on the grounds that such a notion rested on an error. "In reality," he maintained, "science, like all things produced by man, is conditioned by race and blood." Günther maintained, in turn, that "each race has its own manner of thinking. . . . Even when people of diverse race employ the same language, they must misunderstand each other." The same argument is advanced by Curt Brenger, who insists that there can be no international science since science is an expression of the "race soul" (*"Rassenseele"*) of individual communities. There is a physics and a chemistry that is the product of men of Nordic derivation (*"nordisch gaerteten Menschen"*).[83] Intersubjective truth conditions can be understood to obtain only within the confines of a specific racial (or racially conditioned) community.

The difficulties that beset this conviction are immediately evident. Of itself, the conviction that men of different races do not understand each other requires confirmation. If two men undertook the resolution of a problem in nuclear physics and gave all conceivable operational indications that they understood each other, could they then be characterized as sharing the same "racial soul," even if one displayed the physical features of one of the Mongoloid races and the other the features of a Caucasian? Or would the possession of epicanthic eye folds and lank black hair be necessary and sufficient evidence that the one did not understand the other even if the Mongolian had passed every operational test for "understanding"? The problem was not an abstract theoretical issue in National Socialist Germany. It was a matter of *urgent* practical importance. Once having made the possession of a particular "racial soul" a necessary condition for perceiving truth (and not being able to certify the possession of that soul independently of perceiving truth), perceiving the truth became the evidence for the possession of the particular racial soul. The entire system collapsed in a vicious circle that had onerous political consequences. If one did not intuit the truth of National Socialist pronouncements, this was considered *prima facie* evidence that one did not possess the requisite racial soul, even if one's metric and nonmetric anthropological traits were Nordic.[84]

One of the significant evidences advanced for certification of Aryan character in National Socialist Germany became political conformity. Rosenberg made it clear that the racist *Weltanschauung* of National Socialism reflected the life process of the race. *Weltanschauung* itself was not a "logically developed philosophy, nor the result of a development that conformed to natural laws, but rather the articulation of a mystic synthesis, a spiritual activity, that cannot be explicated by reason nor conceived as a causal process."[85] This conception relieved National Socialism of any dependence upon formal or factual techniques for the certification of its truths. A mystic truth could be pronounced, licensed by nothing more than its pronouncement—and conformity would be required if the individual did not wish to be identified as racially alien.

This notion of mystic truth would seem to be part of National Socialism's legacy from Germany's Romantic past. It appears and reappears in German prose in many guises and finds characteristic expression in statements like that expressed by Otto Dietrich, Director of the national press services in National Socialist Germany: ". . . life is only understood by life and National Socialism is perhaps the best and living proof for this conception." Dietrich went on to object to the abstract and exact sciences as obstructions to the full and free expression of the "living strength of the spirit and the soul." In this sense Goebbels could maintain that "the intellect is a danger to the education of the character. We are not on earth to have our heads crammed with knowledge. That is at best secondary when it has no relation to life. We must fulfill our destiny."[86]

Destiny or life seem to speak a mystic tongue meaningful only to the possessors of the requisite soul. Hitler referred to mystic intuitions with sufficient regularity to indicate that he felt they constituted a legitimate source of wisdom. He spoke of an "inner conviction" that commands action. He talked of acting on the basis of intuition and instinct. He denied that a nation could expect to play a significant role in world history if it is governed by "people who weigh and analyze everything," and suggested that a man should "intuitively establish the connection between . . . facts, thus showing exact science the path to follow." He maintained that until he was thirty-five his own social and political ideas were based upon instinctive feeling and insisted that "in political matters feeling often decides more correctly than reason."[87]

Cognitive propositions are normally understood to be subject to appraisal by means of which their truth status can be established. The truth condition that confirms or infirms a descriptive proposition is some determinate state of affairs. If a truth claim is made by a descriptive proposition, its truth could be established by referring to some intersubjective state of affairs understood to establish its truth. To maintain that a statement is confirmed would be to say that some finite set of observations have been made that bestow some degree of probability on the statement. Truth or falsehood can only be discovered by making observations that are in principle public and neutral. A formal truth or a logical truth, on the other hand, is true by virtue of its logical form, and its truth is a function of the logical elements it contains and not of the meanings of descriptive terms. The comprehensive explanatory systems employed in science are a combination of empirical laws and/or unrestricted generalizations logically interrelated to provide predictive power. Nowhere within the range of the cognitive enterprise has a place been found for the special truths of mysticism, intuition, or instinct that seem to have been required by all too many National Socialist theoreticians. A scientist or a mathematician may have a "brilliant insight" into the resolution of a problem, but the merit of his answer is established not by the quality of the inner experience, but by his ability to subsequently meet the requirements of intersubjective empirical or formal tests of truth.

Conclusions

· Hitler was his own philosopher. He was aware of the distinction between what he identified as a general philosophy of life and a definite political faith—philosophy and doctrine. He referred to the "abstractly correct spiritual conception, which the theoretician has to proclaim" as being distinct from the "definitely delimited, tightly organized political community of faith and struggle, unified in spirit and will," which, coupled with specific formal or informal tactical measures, constitute what we have identified as ideology.[88] The general philosophy of life that Hitler articulated was taken almost entirely out of the work of Ludwig Woltmann. As a result, the form that Hitler's justificatory arguments took reveal the structure common to Hegelianism, Marxism, and Fascism. The content was, of course, radically different. For Hitler, race became the unit of analysis and the repository of value. The logic of his central argument is common to that of Social Darwinism and the Nordicism of the turn of the century, which characterized itself as strictly scientific. Whatever their vices, academic Social Darwinists assumed that their accounts were always subject to reappraisal. Hitler, on the other hand, combined the Social Darwinism he had adopted with a romantic and mystic epistemology. In this respect he had more in common with Chamberlain and Rosenberg than he had with Woltmann. Woltmann may have been a poor scientist but he never advanced the claim that he had privileged insights into mystic truth. Chamberlain, and more emphatically Rosenberg, made frequent appeals to instinct and intuition in order to establish their truth claims. Rosenberg maintained that the ultimate truth for men was implicit in a racial myth that was not "scholastic-logical-mechanical" but "living and organic." His myth was a necessary faith, or inspiration, or unifying mass longing, a folk tale truer than truth. As Julius Evola indicated, in a sympathetic commentary written in Italy in 1937,

. . . rather than as a conception that is properly scientific, philosophic, or historical, subject to objective evaluation, . . . the theory of race, or racism, that has taken form in Europe during the last quarter of a century has come to identify itself . . . as a "myth." . . . an idea that receives its force, primarily from nonrational elements.[89]

Only by pressing into service this peculiar epistemology was it possible to operate with a social and political doctrine that attempted to incorporate volkish elements into a fundamentally racist system. When Rosenberg identified National Socialism as an organic-racist-volkish *Weltanschauung*, whatever organic qualities it possessed were imparted by the obscurity of the mystic epistemology, for racism, as Hitler understood it, was radically incompatible with volkish nationalism. Ultimately the unstable mixture precipitated out the racist elements that were always fundamental to Hitler's world view. The influence his simplistic racial views had on the conduct of the global conflict in which Germany was involved can be documented in any history of the period. Here it is only necessary to give one example—the conviction that the "lower races" of Russia be subjected to systematic insult and deprivation *did* subordinate political tactics and Germany's military self-interest to Hitler's Nordicist notions. Goebbels had advocated a "positive" policy in the East in order to capitalize upon the good will with which the Russian Ukrainians pathetically welcomed the advancing troops of National Socialist Germany. Even Rosenberg, convinced as he was of the "spoiled blood and poisoned soul" of the Russians, seems to have advocated a moderate policy calculated to win Germany some advantages in the East. But Hitler's Nordicist and Social Darwinist conjectures prevailed, and a program of calculated brutality and humiliation bolstered flagging Russian resistance until it became an important factor in breaking the strength of the Germany army.

It is doubtful if any single account can provide an exhaustive explication of the system of ideas that constituted National Socialist ideology. That it was essentially a terrible simplification of the Social Darwinism common among a group of thinkers at the turn of the century seems apparent.[90] That the volkish elements which collected around it were merely tactical adjuncts to the central system and were later largely abandoned seems equally evident.[91] That the primary source of Hitler's own ideas was the work of Ludwig Woltmann is probable. But that such a collection of ideas could capture the allegiance of millions of rational men and women will perhaps always remain something of a mystery.

Notes

1. A. Hitler, *Mein Kampf* [MK], trans. by Ralph Manheim (Boston: Houghton Mifflin, 1943), p. 22.
2. *Ibid.*, pp. 99, 180f. The latter quote is the author's own translation from the German; see *Mein Kampf* (Munich: Eher, 1942), p. 198.
3. *MK*, pp. 300, 302, 306, 307. See also the German edition, *op. cit.*, pp. 329, 331, 335, 337.
4. *MK*, pp. 286–300; A. Hitler, *Hitler's Secret Book* [*HSB*] (New York: Grove, 1962), pp. 102, 107f.; *Hitler's Secret Conversations, 1941–1944* [*HSC*], trans. by N. Cameron and R. H. Stevens (New York: Signet, 1961; London: Weidenfeld & Nicolson), pp. 53, 576.
5. P. Viereck, *Meta-politics: The Roots of the Nazi Mind* (New York: Capricorn, 1961); G. L. Mosse, *The Crisis of German Ideology: Intellectual Origins of the Third Reich* (New York: Grosset & Dunlap, 1964); F. Stern, *The Politics of Cultural Despair: A Study in the Rise of Germanic Ideology* (Garden City: Anchor, 1965).
6. *HSC*, p. 150.
7. *MK*, pp. 284, 285.
8. *Ibid.*, pp. 293, 290.
9. *Ibid.*, p. 289.
10. *Ibid.*, pp. 287, 289.
11. *Ibid.*, p. 299.
12. *HSC*, p. 76.
13. A. Hitler, quoted in G. Prange (ed.), *Hitler's Words (1923–1943)*, (Washington: American Council on Public Affairs, 1944), pp. 8f.
14. *HSC*, p. 377.
15. Compare J. Lanz von Liebenfels, *Die Ostara und das Reich der Blonden* (Magdeburg: Ostara, 1922), p. 9 (see also *n*. 6 for references dating back to 1905) and *MK*, p. 65.
16. Compare J. Lanz von Liebenfels, *Die Blonden als Schöpfer der technischen Kultur* (Mödling-Vienna: Ostara, 1913) and *Die Ostara*, pp. 10, *n*. 7 and 12, with *MK*, pp. 290f.
17. For Hitler's relationship to J. Lanz von Liebenfels, see W. Daim, *Der Mann, der Hitler die Ideen gab* (Munich: Isar, 1958), pp. 70–74. Compare J. Lanz von Liebenfels, *Das Geschlechts und Liebesleben der Blonden und Dunklen* (Rodaun: Ostara, 1910), *Die Ostara*, p. 8, and *HSC*, p. 103.
18. B. Mussolini, "Il Trentino veduto da un socialista," *Opera Omnia* (Florence: Fenice, 1951–1963), XXXIII, pp. 153–61.

19. V. I. Lenin, "Karl Marx," *Collected Works* (Moscow: Foreign Languages, 1960–), XXI, p. 87.

20. L. Woltmann, *Der historische Materialismus* (Düsseldorf: Michels, 1900), pp. 337f., 340; see also pp. 321–30.

21. K. Marx, *Capital* (Moscow: Foreign Languages, 1954), I, p. 512; Woltmann, *op. cit.*, pp. 326f.

22. L. Woltmann, *Die Darwinsche Theorie und der Sozialismus* (Düsseldorf: Michels, 1899).

23. F. Engels, "The Origin of the Family, Private Property and the State," K. Marx and F. Engels, *Selected Works in Two Volumes* (Moscow: Foreign Languages, 1955), II, pp. 170f. Woltmann discusses this in *Der historische Materialismus*, pp. 220–25.

24. Woltmann, *Die Darwinsche Theorie*, pp. 6f., 27f.

25. Woltmann, *Der historische Materialismus*, pp. 323, 353, 361.

26. L. Woltmann, *System des moralischen Bewusstseins* (Düsseldorf: Michels, 1898), pp. 318ff.

27. L. Woltmann, *Politische Anthropologie* (Leipzig: Doerner, 1936), p. 35.

28. L. Woltmann, *Die Germanen in Frankreich* (Leipzig: Doerner, 1936), pp. 17f.

29. Woltmann, *Politische Anthropologie*, pp. 156, 223.

30. *HSC*, pp. 150, 76. For a full account of this Malthusian thesis, see *HSB*, p. 6.

31. *HSC*, pp. 261, 76, 64, 65.

32. H. S. Chamberlain, *The Foundations of the Nineteenth Century* (New York: John Lane, 1911), II, p. 218; I, p. 276.

33. G. Vacher de Lapouge, *Der Arier und seine Bedeutung für die Gemeinschaft* (Frankfurt am Main: Diesterweg, 1939), pp. 339f.

34. Woltmann, *Politische Anthropologie*, pp. 179f.

35. Cited in A. Bullock, *Hitler: A Study in Tyranny* (New York: Harper & Row, 1952), p. 707. See also *HSC*, p. 439.

36. *HSC*, p. 78.

37. *Ibid.*, p. 256.

38. *MK*, pp. 288, 289.

39. Woltmann, *Politische Anthropologie*, p. 180.

40. Woltmann, *System*, pp. 272f.; *Die Germanen in Frankreich*, pp. 18, 23.

41. Compare Lanz von Liebenfels, *Die Ostara*, pp. 9f.; see also *n.* 6 and *MK*, p. 296. Hitler is reported to have said to Gregor Strasser: "There are no revolutions except racial revolutions." (N. Baynes [ed.], *The Speeches of Adolf Hitler, April 1922–August 1939* [New York: Oxford, 1942], II, p. 988.)

42. *MK*, pp. 299, 391; *HSC*, pp. 157, 160. See also *MK*, pp. 407, 423.

43. *MK*, pp. 288, 383, 397f., 449; *HSB*, p. 33; *HSC*, p. 184.

44. Compare *MK*, p. 288, Lanz von Liebenfels, *Die Ostara*, p. 7, and Woltmann, *Politische Anthropologie*, pp. 225, 341.

45. Compare K. Weinländer, *Rassenkunde, Rassenpädagogik und Rassenpolitik* (Weissenburg: Orion, 1933), p. 105 and reference 30 on p. 504 with Woltmann, *Die Germanen in Frankreich*, p. 24.

46. See Woltmann, *Politische Anthropologie*, pp. 342–45; *Die Germanen und die Renaissance in Italien* (Leipzig: Dörner, 1936), pp. 39f.

47. See Chamberlain, *op. cit.*, I, pp. 266n., 276, 294.

48. For example, see M. F. Ashley Montagu, *Man's Most Dangerous Myth: The Fallacy of Race* (New York: Harper & Row, 1952); J. Barzun, *Race: A Study in Superstition* (New York: Harper & Row, 1965); G. Dahlberg, *Race, Reason and Rubbish: A Primer of Race Biology* (New York: Columbia, 1942). For a balanced account, see I. Schwidetzky, *Das Problem des Völkertodes* (Stuttgart: Enke, 1954), and A. J. Gregor, "Nordicism Revisited," *Phylon*, XXII, 4 (Winter, 1961), 351–60.

49. *MK*, pp. 295, 384, 396; Woltmann, *Politische Anthropologie*, p. 355f.

50. See Woltmann, *Die Germanen und die Renaissance*, pp. 45f.; *Die Germanen in Frankreich*, pp. 19, 24, 26f., 44f.; *Politische Anthropologie*, pp. 39–43, 113–21, 147.

51. *MK*, pp. 400, 327, 394.

52. *HSC*, pp. 124, 125, 149.

53. C. Schmitt, *Principii politici del nazionalsocialismo* (Florence: Sansoni, 1935), pp. 226, 227. See also J. Figalkowski, *Die Wendung zum Führerstaat: Die ideologischen Komponenten in der politischen Philosophie Carl Schmitts* (Cologne: Westdeutscher, 1958), pp. 151f., 164f.

54. H. Nicolai, "Nationalsozialismus und Straatsrecht," *Verwaltungsakademie* (Berlin: Späth & Linde, n.d.), I, Sec. 2, No. 14, pp. 8, 11, 12f.

55. Baynes, *op. cit.*, II, p. 989; *HSC*, p. 400.

56. S. Lang and E. von Schenck (eds.), *The Memoirs of Alfred Rosenberg* (New York: Ziff-Davis, 1949), p. 126.

57. *HSB*, p. 6.

58. Woltmann, *Politische Anthropologie*, pp. 369, 371.

59. Baynes, *op. cit.*, I, pp. 90, 35f. See also *MK*, pp. 339f.; J. Goebbels, *Das kleine ABC des Nationalsozialisten* (Elberfeld: NS Briefe, n.d.), pp. 3–5; G. Feder, *Das Programm der NSDAP* (Munich: Eher, 1933), p. 29, and *Der Deutsche Staat auf nationaler und sozialer Grundlage* (Munich: Eher, 1932), pp. 47–49.

60. A. Rosenberg, *Der Mythus des XX. Jahrhunderts* (Munich: Hoheneichen, 1933), pp. 534–62.

61. *HSB*, p. 44; *HSC*, p. 180.

62. Nicolai. *op. cit.*, p. 9. See also A. Helbok, "Zur Frage: Was ist ein Volk," *Zeitschrift für deutsche Bildung*, XII, 9 (September, 1936), 418.

63. M. Weinreich, *Hitler's Professors* (New York: YIVO, 1946), p. 38.

64. E. Rüdin, *Erblehre und Rassenhygiene im völkischen Staat* (Munich: Lehmanns, 1934), p. 48. See also G. Jacoby, *Racial State: The German Nationalities Policy in the Protectorate of Bohemia-Moravia* (New York: Institute of Jewish Affairs, 1944), pp. 76–92.

65. *MK*, pp. 403, 426.

66. See *HSB*, p. 44, and *MK*, pp. 433–41. Goebbels (in *Das kleine ABC*, p. 3) maintains that the criteria for admission into the German volkish community include that one be "productive, possessed of German blood, manifesting German customs or morals (*"Sitte"*) and speak German." Gottfried Feder indicates that the term "German" must be given specific volkish, or "sharper still," racial reference. To be a German one must possess German blood, be a member of the German cultural community, and be involved in its destiny. Then he goes on to indicate that one must also in some sense be a bearer of "Nordic thought." All of which does not seem to help in the slightest. (Feder, *Das Program*, pp. 35, 42.) Feder regularly hyphenated "volkish-racial" as though this resolved the problem.

67. *MK*, p. 396. See also Woltmann, *Die Germanen in Frankreich*, pp. 18–20; *Die Germanen und die Renaissance*, pp. 32f.; and particularly *Politische Anthropologie*, pp. 82f.

68. H. F. K. Günther, *Rassenkunde des deutschen Volkes* (Munich: Lehmanns, 1929), pp. 14f., Chaps. v, xii; *Racial Elements of European History* (London: Methuen, 1927), p. 3, Chap. ii, Sec. A, Chap. iii, Sec. A.; *Kleine Rassenkunde des deutschen Volkes* (Munich: Lehmanns, 1943), pp. 10f., Chap. ii, Sec. A, Chap. iv, Sec. A.

69. Günther, *Racial Elements*, p. 198; see also p. 184.

70. H. F. K. Günther, *Der nordische Gedanke unter den Deutschen* (Munich: Lehmanns, 1927), p. 22; see also Chap. ii.

71. H. F. K. Günther, *Ritter, Tod und Teufel: Der heldische Gedanke* (Munich: Lehmanns, 1920), p. 135.

72. *HSC*, pp. 53, 266, 317, 384, 490f., 504; see also Daim, *op. cit.*, pp. 194f.

73. L. Franzi, *Fase attuale del razzismo tedesco* (Rome: Istituto Nazionale di Cultura Fascista, 1939), pp. 44f.; G. Landra, "Il concetto di razza," *Difesa della Razza*, II, 9 (March 5, 1939), 12; A. Capasso, *Idee chiare sul razzismo* (Rome: Augustea, 1942), p. 27.

74. Chamberlain, *op. cit.*, I, pp. 533, 538; see also, pp. 522–26, 532.

The German edition reads: "Whoever behaves as a German is, whatever his origins, a German." (*Die Grundlagen des Neunzehnten Jahrhunderts* [Munich: Bruckmann, 1941], I, p. 574.) For a discussion of Chamberlain's views, see J. Real, "The Religious Conception of Race: Houston Stewart Chamberlain and Germanic Christianity," in M. Baumont, J. Fried, and E. Vermeil (eds.), *The Third Reich* (New York: Praeger, 1955), pp. 242–86.

75. H. S. Chamberlain, *Politische Ideale* (Munich: Bruckmann, 1916), pp. 46f.

76. See E. von Eickstedt, *Die rassischen Grundlagen des deutschen Volkstums* (Cologne: Schaffstein, 1934), p. 12; O. Kleinschmidt, *Rasse und Art* (Leipzig, Armanen, 1933), pp. 14–19; A. Pöschl, *Das Gesetz der geschlossenen Blutkreise als Grundgesetz der Stammes-, Rassen-und Volksentwicklung* (Steiermark: NS Gauverlag, 1943), pp. 315ff., 363; H. Weinert, *Biologische Grundlagen für Rassenkunde und Rassenhygiene* (Stuttgart: Enke, 1943), p. 166.

77. Baynes, *op. cit.*, I, p. 469; Rosenberg, *Mythus*, p. 596.

78. H. Eichenauer, *Die Rasse als Lebensgesetz in Geschichte und Gesittung* (Leipzig: Teubner, 1934), p. 136.

79. Chamberlain, *Foundations*, I, pp. 491f.

80. See G. Marro, *Primato della razza italiana* (Milan: Principato, 1940).

81. See Viereck, *op. cit.*, pp. 201f., 231; E. Cassirer, *The Myth of the State* (Garden City, N. Y.: Doubleday, 1955), pp. 311–13; G. Franceschi, *Totalitarismos* (Buenos Aires: Difusion, 1945), I, pp. 20f., 208.

82. Rosenberg, *Mythus*, pp. 119f.; "Freiheit der Wissenschaft," *Gestaltung der Idee* (Munich: Eher, 1936), pp. 207f.

83. P. Lenard, "Deutsche Physik," in W. Hofer (ed.), *Der Nationalsozialismus: Dokumente, 1933–1945* (Frankfurt am Main: Fischer, 1957), p. 98; Günther, *Ritter, Tod und Teufel*, p. 137; C. Brenger, *Die Welt im Spiegel der Rassenseele* (Breslau: Hirt, 1938), pp. 10f.

84. See L. Stengel von Rutkowski, *Grundzüge der Erbkunde und Rassenpflege* (Berlin: Langewort, 1944), p. 43.

85. Rosenberg, *Mythus*, p. 117.

86. J. Goebbels, *Michael: Ein deutsches Schicksal in Tagebuchblättern* (Munich: Eher, 1933), p. 14.

87. *HSC*, pp. 127, 251; *MK*, p. 173. See also *HSC*, pp. 46, 58, 284, 290.

88. *MK*, p. 381; see also p. 99.

89. J. Evola, *Il mito del sangue* (Milan: Hoepli, 1937), p. ix.

90. Thus, I do not contend that books such as those by Mosse, Stern, and Viereck are wrong. They must be supplemented and quali-

fied. National Socialism was an enormously complicated phenomenon. It is true, for example, that National Socialism was a crude Social Darwinism, as I have repeatedly stated, and that an ideologue like Möller van den Bruck was in this tradition. But it must be added that Möller was not a racist. He was essentially a nationalist. Similarly, Chamberlain was a Social Darwinist, but a nationalist as well. Woltmann was a Social Darwinist *and* a consistent racist and, consequently, a *direct* forebear of National Socialism.

91. This has become evident to contemporary "neo-Nazis," cf. M. Koehl, "Adolf Hitler: German Nationalist or Aryan Racist?" *National Socialist World,* 4 (Summer, 1967), pp. 13–22.

VI · APARTHEID

Apartheid as a *specific* social and political ideology made its appearance in the years that marked the end of the first half and the beginning of the second half of the twentieth century, although it did incorporate elements of "traditional" South African racial policies and attitudes. In this chapter the term "apartheid" will refer to a relatively mature synthesis of the following three components: a philosophical basis, doctrinal convictions, and an applied program. N. J. Rhoodie and H. J. Venter characterize the ideology that had developed in South Africa by 1950 in the following manner: "The apartheid *idea* is the synthesis from which the present [South African] Government's *policy* of apartheid originated and is therefore indirectly the source of all the practical *measures* which have been passed in the implementation of this policy."[1]

In this sense apartheid is a secular social and political ideology typical of the twentieth century. It advances its own normic model of man and society, defends its model by appeals to science and experience, and employs that model in justificatory arguments in support of policy. Although the apologists of apartheid argue Biblical support for its policies when they address themselves to a domestic audience, such arguments do not function as essential parts of its mature rationale. In arguments developed in the public forum, ideologues and apologists have rarely indulged in the luxury of theological disputation. For example, in his regular arguments in defense of apartheid before the United Nations, the former foreign minister of South Africa, Eric Louw, never once made appeal to Divine sanction.[2] Nor have the state attorneys of South Africa included Biblical references in their *Reply* and *Rejoinder* to the *Memorial* of the government of Liberia in the South-West Africa case before the International Court of Justice. The exposition provided below will indicate that while Afrikaner apologists and ideologues may be convinced that apartheid is fully compatible with their religious convictions, their ultimate appeal is to secular arguments. In this respect apartheid is one with Leninism, Fascism, and National Socialism. It is a secular ideology that animates a mass movement.

Apartheid is the secular ideology of the Afrikaner volk. Rhoodie and Venter are correct in identifying apartheid as "the common spiritual possession of the Afrikaner people . . . a part of the Afrikaner's national philosophy of life."[3] Since 1948 the National party of South Africa has come to represent that philosophy, and its appeal is to the totality of Afrikanerdom. The "dissident" Afrikaners have gradually abandoned the bilingual United party, the ephemeral Conservative party, and more intransigent Afrikaner party to take their place within the ranks of the Nationalists, rendering it, in effect, a party of solidarity. It has become a movement of the Afrikaner volk rather than a party of representation in the sense of Western parliamentarianism; and as such, it demands total loyalty, defining its allies and its enemies in terms of that loyalty. An Afrikaner outside the party is thought of as a traitor to his volk.

That the National party has failed to create a totalitarianism in the Republic of South Africa is a consequence of unique historical and social circumstances as well as ideological considerations. Even though apartheid as a radical social and political system animates a united volk, it does not manifest itself as a frank, integralist totalitarianism because the Republic of South Africa is composed of diverse peoples—white, colored, Asian, and Negroid. Apartheid affects English-speaking colored, Asian, and Negroid peoples in South Africa, but does *not* seek to unite them or incorporate them into the volk. It is strictly an expression of the life style of Afrikanerdom. As a consequence, very little Afrikaner ideological literature is available in English—much less in any of the indigenous Bantu languages. The popular support the National party has sought has been found among Afrikaans-speaking South Africans, and within the Afrikaner volk life, it is surprisingly totalitarian. Apartheid ideology permeates the religious, economic, and cultural life of the Afrikaner. It cuts across class lines and religious subdivisions and has the all but unanimous support of Afrikaner intellectuals.

This characteristic does not in itself distinguish apartheid as an ideology from Italian Fascism or German National Socialism, both of which were also little concerned with attempting to convert outside groups. What distinguishes apartheid from Italian Fascism in this instance is that for Fascism the terms "people" and "nation" had an identical reference class. The Italian people constituted the Italian nation. In South Africa the nation represents a political unity of diverse peoples; apartheid is a volkish, not an orthodox, nationalist ideology. Apartheid has committed itself to a policy that seeks to erect in the Republic of South Africa a federation, a confederation, of separate people—if not nations. W. W. M. Eiselen has referred to this programmatic goal as a "co-operative South African system based on the Commonwealth concept, with the Union Government gradually changing its position from guardian and trustee to become instead the senior member of a group of separate communities."[4] This is implicit in the conception of separate or autogenous development *("eiesoortige ontwikkeling")* central to the ideology of apartheid. The National party is not totalitarian in the customarily understood sense of the term because it does not aspire to reduce the differences that separate population elements and unify them within the political confines of the nation. Instead it intends to make those differences more emphatic. Its totalitarianism, like its appeal, is restricted to the Afrikaner community.

Apartheid is a contemporary reformulation of concepts traditional with the Afrikaner volk. It is this traditionalist character that makes apartheid unique among contemporary ideologies. Although other contemporary radical ideologies include traditional elements, they are *revolutionary* in the sense that they anticipate significant social and economic changes in the old order. Apartheid, on the other hand, has a continuity not exemplified in any other radical ideology. Apartheid's development as a secular belief system has been relatively recent, but that development as yet reveals no significant departure from its traditional heritage. An adequate appreciation of apartheid requires, therefore, a consideration of its historical background.

The Historical Origins of Apartheid[5]

· The term "volk" best characterizes the Afrikan people because the term "people" in English is generally taken to mean any aggregate that takes up a particular political allegiance. The term volk involves an entire constellation of cultural and social attitudes as well as a vague biological relationship. It would be all but impossible for a non-Dutch immigrant to the Republic of South Africa to find a place among the Afrikaner volk simply because he took up South African political allegiance. So much of Afrikaner volk membership is made up of historical and cultural elements that outsiders are all but completely excluded.

The history of the Afrikaner volk began with the establishment of a victual station at the Cape of Good Hope in the year 1652—a logistic necessity for Dutch vessels traveling between Holland and the East Indies. Five years later, members of the Dutch East India Company, permitted to settle as free burghers, ensconced themselves as permanent settlers at the southernmost tip of Africa. In 1658 the first slaves were imported to serve as menials for the settlers, and a complex pattern of intergroup relations developed. The first contacts between the groups were characterized by obvious and enduring differences that were not unique. There was diffidence, occasional mutual hostility, ethnocentric judgments, and an insistent sense of social distance.

The insistent need for labor, the shortage of white women, and the exigencies of a growing economy, however, drew elements of the aboriginal population into the orbit of the white community. Jan van Riebeeck, founder of the victual station and early opponent of dealings with the natives, ultimately found himself sponsoring the marriage of Pieter van Meerhoff to the sister of Chief Harry of the Hottentot Gorihaiconas. But by 1678 the Political Council of the settlement proclaimed an official prohibition on miscegenation and concubinage. The evolution of a stable class of free burghers and the increased availability of women of their own provenience tended to further increase the sense of social distance between the whites and the indigenous peoples. East India Company officials, on the other hand, motivated by tactical considerations, tended to assume less rigorous postures with respect to what has since become known as the "native question" (*"die Naturellevraagstuk"*). In the presence of an increasing number of Negroid slaves, freedmen, Hottentots, transient European seamen, temporary company officials, and settled farmers (Boers), a single pattern of intergroup relations simply did not obtain.

There is evidence, though, that the attitudes which are now understood to characterize the Afrikaner were already evident among the settled farmer community. The Boer population, as distinct from the townsmen, was far more homogeneous in race, life circumstance, and general outlook. Even before the turn of the eighteenth century, the *vry landbouwer*, (the Boer-Afrikaan of European—Dutch, German, French—descent) was ascendant in the agricultural community and had begun to formulate a uniform code to govern his own interracial relations. Although still small in number, the Boer community was already beginning to develop characteristics of its own. Subjected to a demanding agrarian existence, isolated from the town dwellers at the Cape, the Boer, stimulated by the increasing demands of the Cape market for meat, moved east across the Hottentots-Holland Mountains to establish large cattle farms and to develop there the traits that still, in part, characterize the volk.

These pioneer farmers (*Trekboere*) with their superior technology, animated by an implacable conviction in the truth of their Calvinist faith and threatened by imminent aboriginal attack, developed a pervasive color consciousness, for color was a ready index of technological inferiority, a corrupt Calvinism at best, and real danger. Under such conditions the compelling group identity (*"sterk groepsinstink"*), the racial consciousness (*"rasseselfbewussyn en rassetrots"*), of which contemporary Afrikaner historians speak, had a high survival value.[6] A rigid system of social stratification based upon racial traits became firmly established. The rationale that supported the system was essentially religious, and the fundamentalist Boers sought Biblical justification for the maintenance of social distance and white supremacy. L. E. Neame has written:

> The Boers were an Old Testament people who regarded themselves as a Chosen Race and fashioned their life upon Biblical patterns. They were glad to avail themselves of the labor of the sons of Ham; but their society was based upon the principle that there was "no equality between White and Black in Church or State."[7]

During this initial expansion, the pioneering *Trekboere* moved into a vast and sparsely inhabited land area. It was only during the second half of the eighteenth century that the Boers made contact, on a large scale, with the Negroid Bantu peoples who were migrating into the territory south of the Limpopo. Both Boer and Bantu probably entered the territory that is now the Republic of South Africa at essentially the same time. As early as 1702 the Boers clashed with Bantu pastoralists and hunters, but regular conflict with organized Xhosa groups began about 1778. The regularity and ferocity of the struggle only exacerbated the racial consciousness of the pioneer farmer communities.

In 1795 the British undertook their first occupation of the Cape, but they did not establish themselves there permanently until 1806. The racial policy of the Cape under Dutch administration had been far more relaxed than that of the *Trekboere*, and with the advent of the British that policy became increasingly "liberal." The presence of Christian aborigines and freedmen, the influence of missionaries charged with the ideals of equality and brotherhood, and the heterogeneity of the urban Cape community all conspired to produce a "city-bred liberalism" alien to the racial consciousness of the pastoral Boer community. The fact that the British sought support from the indigenous population in their political struggle with the resident white population provided no small incentive for the ultimate extension of the franchise and a variety of attendant social privileges to nonwhites. "With outstanding exceptions," van den Berghe maintains, "that no amount of cynicism can dismiss, the English, as a group, have only shown liberalism (carefully minimized at that) when it suited their interests as opposed to those of the Afrikaners."[8]

The accommodating value system that differentiated the Cape townsmen from the Boer volk thus became more emphatic under the influence of the English. In 1820, 5,000 English immigrants settled in the Cape area, and the differences between the resident white communities became increasingly marked. There were cultural (linguistic and religious) differences, differences in attitudes (the English considered themselves an outpost of England while the Boers felt no such allegiance), as well as differences in their respective approach to the nonwhite population. The Boers became increasingly restive. Ordinance No. 50 of 1828, by which the Hottentots and coloreds (any nonwhite and white hybrids) were to be granted equal rights with whites, precipitated an explosive reaction on the part of the Boers. In 1835 the sense of grievance prompted sections of the Boer volk to undertake the Great Trek into the interior. Piet Retief's manifesto of 1837 indicated that the Boers intended to "adopt such regulations as will maintain the proper relationship between master and servant" in their new country. Retief's sister, Anna Steenkamp, maintained in her memoirs that the principal reason for embarking on the perilous trek was not so much the English freeing of the slaves "as their being placed on an equal footing with Christians, contrary to the laws of God, and the natural distinctions of race and color, so that it was intolerable for any decent Christian to bow down beneath such a yoke; wherefore we rather withdraw in order to preserve our doctrines in purity."

Impressed by the vast cultural differences between themselves and the indigenous peoples, convinced of the indefeasible truth of their religion, the peoples of nascent Afrikanerdom assigned themselves a special task and a special status. The technological inferiority of the aboriginal population and their paganism were invariably associated, particularly in the interior, with racial traits of high visibility. The outward sign of the Chosen Ones of the Lord became manifest physical differences. What is important for our purposes is the recognition that the nonwhites never became members of the Boer volk. They remained forever strangers—"the children of Ham"—in the Dutch-speaking European community.

The pioneers of the Great Trek founded the Boer republics—the Republic of Natalia, the Transvaal Republic, and the Orange Free State—in which membership in the volk was re-

stricted to Boer whites. The republics were agrarian communities with sparse and widely dispersed populations. In a series of
wars against the Kaffirs (Negro tribes), the republics attempted
to stabilize their borders. The pervasive tension of the presence
of hundreds of thousands of surrounding Bantu did nothing to
abate Boer racial consciousness. There was an attempt to maintain geographic segregation, and the Republic of Natalia designated a specific territory for Bantu occupancy. The Free State
attempted to establish a permanent border between itself and
the Basuto. The Transvaal Republic, in the effort to break the
military threat of the surrounding Bantu, subdivided the
aboriginal population and settled them on "locations," small
geographic areas scattered in a half circle around the Republic.

This tendency toward territorial separation was countered
by insistent Boer demands for Bantu labor. And thousands of
Bantu dispossessed by intertribal wars made themselves available as laborers, so that by 1881 there were about 700,000 Bantu
in the Transvaal Republic alone. The indenture system and in
some cases a cash levy drew increasing numbers of Bantu into
the economic system of the republics. In effect, attempts at
vertical geographic segregation were abandoned, and horizontal
segregation became the *modus operandi*. It permitted the Boers
to maintain social distance without forgoing economic benefits.
Among themselves the Boer inhabitants constituted a community
of virtually complete equality of wealth and condition. The
government of the Orange Free State, for example, has been
described as a "natural democracy," with an elected legislative
assembly, an elected president, and an independent judiciary.
Freedom of the press and the individual was guaranteed by the
constitution. These rights were accorded, however, only to recognized members of the volk—the Dutch-speaking Europeans.
Bantu in the Boer republics were squatters, refugees, or laborers—and always foreigners.

During this period England was extending her dominion over
the southern and eastern extent of South Africa. There were
desultory attempts to organize the Boer republics into a federation with the Cape Colony, which led ultimately to the first
armed struggle between the Boers and Britons. It was this war,
the Transvaal War of Independence of 1880–1881, that created
a sense of unity among the Boer communities and led Afrikaans-

speaking people throughout South Africa to begin to conceive themselves as a single volk. The Afrikaners of the Cape Colony might well be "liberal," but they were members of a South African volk possessed of a common history and a belief in a common destiny. The constant struggle with the aboriginal population and the resistance to the British "imperial factor" hammered bonds of unity that fashioned a volkish community that extended beyond the borders of the Boer republics.

The discovery of diamonds and gold provoked increasing pressure from England and finally resulted in the Anglo-Boer War that ended with the Treaty of Vereeniging in 1902, but not before Afrikanerdom had been created as a self-regarding entity. Eight years later, when the Union of South Africa was launched, it was beset by a multitude of problems, but the most urgent was the question of the nonwhite franchise. The liberal Cape elements (which included moderate Afrikaners) advocated a general franchise, conditioned by a "fixed level of civilization" as the qualification for the vote. Northern or radical Afrikaner elements refused to consider nonwhite enfranchisement. What resulted was a compromise that permitted each section to retain its own electoral system with a parliamentary color bar enacted by statute. It was a highly unstable mixture of temporarily reconciled but conflicting interests of the two superordinate European population groups with moderate Afrikaners supporting the more liberal policy of the south. The English effectively controlled the growing industrial economy while the Afrikaners remained essentially agrarian. The artificial Union, therefore, shared no value consensus with respect to the most imperative national problem and could neither formulate nor implement a uniform policy with respect to the nonwhite population.

Throughout the Union the constant demand for cheap labor continued to prevent any resolution of the conflicting views on the status of nonwhites. For example, by 1894 the number of nonwhites working in the mines had grown from 1,500 in 1886 to more than 40,000, and in 1899 it had reached 96,000. The demand for nonwhite labor led to recruitment of "foreign" nonwhites from Portuguese East Africa and areas to the north. In 1904 the labor shortage had become so urgent that Chinese coolies were imported to work in the mines. Before the repeal of the Chinese Labor Importation Ordinance, 63,500 Chinese had been imported, and in 1907 they constituted about 25 percent of the labor force in the mines. With so urgent a demand for labor there was little chance that vertical, or territorial, segregation could be maintained. Nonetheless, Afrikaner political leaders like General J. B. M. Hertzog continued to advocate territorial separation of the population on a racial basis. As a member of the first Union cabinet (1910–1912) Hertzog proposed a comprehensive segregation system involving territorial separation. Throughout the period dating from the organization of the Union to the outbreak of World War II Afrikaners of the National party advocated various forms of segregation based on the principle of political and social separation between the white and nonwhite population, and in some cases, even advocated segregation that "had as its ideal the development of the native along his own lines in his own territory."[9]

The Afrikaner ideal, however, continued to conflict with the needs of a rapidly developing economy. Both Afrikaner *plattelanders* and English industrial interests were not prepared to do without nonwhite labor. In 1932 the Native Economic Commission unequivocally stated that "full economic segregation would mean that the Europeans and the Natives would be put into separate areas and that they would not be allowed to work for each other. Nobody advocated this. It would be impossible, and uneconomical even if possible. . . ."[10] The various Native Land acts, which stabilized 41 million acres for nonwhite occupation, did nothing to stem the influx of nonwhites into white areas, the white farm lands, and the white industrial urban centers. The situation was further complicated by the development of a poor white problem.

In keeping with the worldwide phenomenon of urbanization, increasing numbers of unskilled rural whites (almost exclusively Afrikaners) made their way to the urban centers. The closing of the frontier, a phenomenon familiar to American historians, forced indigent Afrikaner labor to seek employment in the developing industrial complexes of the Rand. The English, who almost exclusively represented the manufacturing and mining interests of South Africa, welcomed the availability of cheap nonwhite labor (to the extent of importing hundreds of thousands of nonwhites), but the Afrikaner who had to compete in the open labor market found himself disadvantaged in the competition with the low-wage nonwhite laborer. By 1932 the Carnegie Commission estimated that about 20 percent of the entire white population of South Africa were to be regarded as "poor whites," with 12 to 16 percent of the total white population to be regarded as "very poor." The whites, equipped with the franchise, demanded a solution to so immense a problem, and in the twenties the "civilized labor policy" was adopted. This policy institutionalized the color bar and the differential wage in industry.

The economic and psychological consequences of the rapid downward mobility of the Afrikaner after the last of the Anglo-Boer wars does much to explain his attitudes with respect to the question of race relations. To the Afrikaner, the nonwhite who had been his enemy during expansion into the interior now became an ominous economic threat during industrial relocation. For members of the English-speaking elite the nonwhite had on critical occasions been an ally in the Cape Colony against Dutch opposition and an economic necessity in the effort to reduce operating costs and thereby increase profit margins in the period of intensive industrial expansion. The British, furthermore, long maintained a mother-country loyalty. This permitted them to conceive of their residence in South Africa as far less precarious than did the Afrikaners. The attitude of the English as a community (with the notable exception of its working class) toward the nonwhite population was, therefore, understandably different from that of the Afrikaner.

Out of differing attitudes, the compulsion of economic forces, and disparate traditions, a complicated and often contradictory pattern of race relations developed in South Africa. In the *platteland* the nonwhite labor force posed no threat to the essentially Afrikaner community. It had a juridically, economically, and socially defined "place." In the urban centers, on the other hand, nonwhite labor was a constant threat to white labor in open competition. The cry of "separation of the nations" was regularly heard. General Louis Botha, the first prime minister of the Union, insisted that territorial separation was the only feasible solution to South Africa's racial problems. The Native Land Acts of 1913 and 1936 were unsuccessful attempts to stabilize the nonwhite population within the confines of the reserves that could not remedy the insistent demand for cheap labor and the rapid decline in agricultural productivity of the reserves.

By 1936 there were more than a million nonwhites resident in the urban areas, almost double the 1921 number, whereas the number of whites in these areas had increased only 55 percent during the same period. This process was intensified by World War II. By 1946 there were 1¾ million nonwhites in the urban centers alone—an increase of 60 percent in ten years. Over half the nonwhites in the Union thus lived in the white areas. And by then only 40 percent of the total urban population was white.

For the English-language community from which the entrepreneurial class was almost exclusively drawn, the influx of nonwhite labor was essential to the maintenance of an attractive profit structure. To the Afrikaner community, recently urbanized, the nonwhite influx constituted a persistent threat to their wage levels and traditions. As early as the twenties the Afrikaner National party had made common cause with the predominantly English Labor party to entrench white employment privileges under the slogan: "Workers of the world unite and fight for a white South Africa!" The incompatibility between the white workers' interests and those of the entrepreneur was particularly emphatic in the secondary industries where there was a real demand for stable and relatively well-trained workers—preferably those who would accept a low wage and be in abundant supply—that is, the nonwhites. Since 1911 there has been a restrictive color bar, and this bar, at least in part, has minimized the direct competition of white and nonwhite. Over the years, nonwhites collected by the hundreds of thousands in shantytowns in and around the industrial centers of the Union without the least semblance of community control.

The United party, which governed South Africa between 1939 and 1948, represented the sentiment of the English-speaking community and, as a consequence, that of the business community. Its native policy and racial practice was influenced by a paternalism tempered by business pragmatism. The National party, which during the years of World War II became more and more the voice of the Afrikaner volk, directed its attention toward the economic, social, and political threat it saw posed by the increased incidence of nonwhites, particularly in the urban areas. The Afrikaner tendency to perceive the nonwhite as an economic and status threat fortified his traditional attitudes. By 1948, South African politics had crystallized along language lines. In the election of that year the United party under Jan Christian Smuts won every seat in the English-speaking areas, and the National party led by Malan, in league with the Afrikaner party, won every seat in the Afrikaans-speaking areas. Although the National and Afrikaner parties had a minority mandate (100,000 fewer votes than those cast for the United party), they won a simple plurality of seats in the government because of the weighted rural vote. The Afrikaner volk had acceded to the governing of the Union of South Africa. Since that time the National party has increased its Afrikaner support to the extent that it can legitimately claim to represent the community will of the Afrikaner volk.

The Development of Apartheid as an Ideology

•   It was against this background that apartheid as a social and political ideology developed. It is the heir of the most complicated interracial and interethnic complex in the world. One need go no further than a cursory perusal of English- and Afrikaans-language newspapers to receive the impression that one is reading fact and opinion perceived and construed from radically divergent points of view. When nonwhite groups are considered, the substantive differences in perspective are more fundamental still. Over half a century of union has not, for example, resolved the differences that separate the Afrikaner from the English-speaking South African. J. C. G. Kotze has remarked that "here we have to do with a very intimate, almost organic, development in which even the Afrikaners and the English [have] met with no success for centuries. For that they too greatly lacked a common binding way of life—in ideals and in practice."[11] This judgment is supported by experimental evidence and informed opinion.[12] South Africa is, in a significant sense, a culturally pluralistic society, malintegrated in all but partial political and economic aspects. In effect, it is a political union of diverse and divergent social aggregates mutually involved in a single economic enterprise under a single political administration.

Apartheid is the ideology of the politically dominant Afrikaner volk and is the all but exclusive product of the Afrikaner intellectual and academic community. That community has been responsible for the articulation of its rationale, for the systematic and coherent synthesis of traditional and contemporary elements that made its appearance immediately before, during, and after World War II. The Afrikaner churches and the Afrikaner press formulate and support its doctrinal statements, and a legislature, over 80 percent of which are Afrikaners, enacts its legislation.

The Afrikaner volk was born of conflict—an irridentist demographic, cultural, and political minority in the only land it knew. As a consequence, it developed into a highly integrated community in which *Afrikaner Volkseenheid* (Afrikaner volkish unity) took precedence over class or regional differences. An elaborate network of economic, cultural, and religious organizations knit the community into a society of remarkable solidarity. Each organization of Afrikanerdom shares its leadership with other organizations so that the entire community is infused with the thought and spirit of an interlocking directorate of personalities. The solidarity of the Afrikaner community is thus the result of rule by an elite of professional, academic, and religious leaders who hold prominent positions in a variety of Afrikaner organizations and mutually reinforce each other. The most important leaders of the National party, for example, are members of the Broederbond, a select group of Afrikaners drawn from the clergy and from the teaching and professional group, as well as from the growing Afrikaner entrepreneurial community. Whether the National party is controlled by the Broederbond, as has been suggested, is a proposition that cannot be documented and need not detain us. What is significant for our purposes is that an agency such as the Broederbond can act as a coordinating agency for formulating Afrikaner opinion. It shares membership with the clergy of the Dutch Reformed Churches, the Federasie van Afrikaanse Kultuurverenigings, the Reddingsdaadbond, the Institute for Christian National Education, and the South African Bureau for Racial Affairs (SABRA). Each group reinforces the other and the totality of Afrikaner volk life is infused with a common sentiment, a common *Weltanschauung*. The prevailing Afrikaner consensus is expressed in religious tracts, behavioral and biological science texts, historical writings,

Afrikaner press accounts, and political sentiments. There are, of course, notable exceptions in the writings of B. B. Keet and P. V. Pistorius[13] (to mention only some of the most widely acknowledged), but such men tend to be consistently treated as traitors to the volk. For the purposes of exposition it is only necessary to indicate that Rhoodie and Venter are essentially correct when they maintain that the apartheid idea constitutes a "broad fundamental synthesis based on the collective views of the Afrikaner. . . ."[14]

The formulation of the ideology of apartheid was, and is, the task of a self-conscious class of Afrikaner intellectuals both within and outside the formal structure of the National party. In this they are no whit different from the ideologues of Leninism, Fascism, or National Socialism—with the exception that no single individual or group of individuals can be identified specifically as the authors of the social and political philosophy of apartheid. It is a product to which many groups and individuals have contributed—but for all that it is a body of related ideas evincing a remarkable consistency.

Nonetheless, the specific *origins* of apartheid can be traced to the organization of the Suid-Afrikaanse Bond vir Rassestudie, a group of Afrikaner specialists in the social and biological sciences who broke away from the liberal South Africa Institute of Race Relations in the mid-thirties. In 1936 the Bond opposed the compromise policies of General Hertzog's segregation proposals and advocated a consistent policy of *rasse apartheid* as the solution to South Africa's racial problems.[15] The Bond was the forerunner of the present South African Bureau of Racial Affairs (SABRA). Despite its short-lived institutional existence, the Bond can be regarded as the original source of the social and political philosophy of apartheid. Its first proposals were quickly echoed in the publications of the Federasie van Calvinistiese Studente Verenigings, and their subsequent development constitutes a complex feedback phenomenon involving SABRA, the Afrikaans churches and cultural institutions, as well as the National party in power.

That apartheid includes historical Afrikaner values and related policies, and is in part to be explained by historical references, can hardly be gainsaid. That much of antecedent legislation provides some of the administrative machinery for its policies cannot be denied. But apartheid as an ideology arose only when a coherent program was evolved for a nationwide policy that sought to provide a final solution to the problems besetting South Africa. Only within the last generation has apartheid fully developed into the secular ideology of a movement of solidarity. Its maturity is evidenced by what Rhoodie correctly identifies as its sociopolitical philosophy in which doctrine and practice find their ultimate justification.[16] Within the confines of the traditional Afrikaner community, practices were justified by appeals to Scripture, but since World War II, South Africa's increased involvement in the community of nations and the continued and continual scrutiny of its policies by international critics have forced the Afrikaner intellectual to develop a coherent body of related propositions that serve as a secular argument for his nation's policies. Apartheid, like Italian Fascism, was originally a pragmatic posture and like Fascism only developed a mature ideology after it had been in power almost a decade. By 1960 apartheid had developed its rationale, a social and political philosophy by which its doctrine and legislative measures are ultimately justified.

The Ideology of Apartheid

• Apartheid is self-characterized as a fundamentally antiliberal doctrine.[17] It rejects the conception of the individual that makes him a significant unit of analysis for scientific or philosophical inquiry. Apartheid, as a theoretical system, focuses on a collectivity of which the individual is understood to be an organic member. In 1959 the Afrikaner intellectual community published its first handbook devoted to the science of man, *Inleiding tot die Algemene Volkekunde (Introduction to General Anthropology)*. It is particularly significant as an illustration of the conceptual model of man central to the Afrikaner world view. The first sentence reads: "Man is not a solitary being; he lives and realizes his existence in community with others" (*"in sosiale verbande"*). He is understood to be an animal with creative potential, a potential realized *only* in a community possessed of a culture. The cultural entity in which he realizes himself is an organic unity (*"organiese eenheid"*), a whole that is more than the mere sum of its parts, a unity of which he constitutes a component cell.[18] Elsewhere, in a specifically political context, P. J. Coertze, editor of the handbook, reaffirms the same collection of propositions and explains its implications by using the historic "organic phenomenon" of the Afrikaner volk in illustration. Man is not solitary. He attains the fullness of self only in association with other men in an interactive process, a process by virtue of which the community literally becomes the most significant and substantial part of himself. Should his organic relationship to that community be undermined, the individual suffers alienation (*"vervreemding"*).[19] This organic, collectivist conception recurs with regularity in Afrikaner prose. It is developed in N. P. Van Wyk Louw's *Liberale Nasionalisme* and A. B. Du Preez's *Inside the South African Crucible*.[20] "Man," Du Preez maintains, "does not stand apart from his world—his home and the community in which he lives are part of him." He attains self-realization only in a community with which he can identify, outside of which he is alienated. It follows that

. . . one has the right to protect the identity of one's people because it carries within it a spiritual treasure that has been entrusted to one's people. . . . [It] is the particular duty of man to protect these gifts against alienation. . . . Man cannot stand apart from his world, his background, his home [—and] to his spiritual home his nation too belongs. . . . Man is never born as an individual with no particular family, people, and country. . . . If one gives up one's identity there is always a danger of destroying one's own life.[21]

This constitutes an element fundamental to the core conception of apartheid. So characterized, apartheid bears significant resemblances to the radical collectivist ideologies of our time. Apartheid is opposed, as is Leninism, Fascism, and National Socialism, to the abstract humanitarianism of liberal individualism. "Man," Rhoodie maintains, "attempting to exist as a 'pure' or 'absolute' individual lives in an unnatural state. For all practical purposes man's existence only gains content and meaning when he comes into contact with others. . . ."[22] That the individual gains significance only within a community implies a rejection of the notion of inalienable and natural human rights, however they are conceived. The Dutch Reformed Church of South Africa has specifically inveighed against such a concept.

The Nederduits Gereformeerde Kerk, the principal Afrikaner Dutch Reformed Church, has, in its *Fundamental Principles of Calvinist Political Science*, forthrightly maintained that "rights" issue from God's commands ministered by the ordained terrestrial state in sharp and avowed contradistinction to the liberalism that maintains that "the sovereign individual with his own interests is the highest good."[23]

In a vague and unsystematic fashion liberal critics have raised objection to this explicit collectivist rationale. Keet indicated that "at the root of . . . apartheid-thinking . . . lies the supreme fallacy . . . in which the group is regarded as an entity with a personality of its own—the personification of the group. . . . All this leads to a cynical disregard of the individual and the chain of unfortunate consequences that result from this line of thought. . . . To treat the group as a magnified individual, apart from its constituent members, is an abstraction that leads to the most disastrous consequences, as is so manifestly proved by the inhumanities of Fascism and Communism. . . ." Against such group pretensions he insists that "there are certain fundamental human rights that cannot be withheld from any man whatever his status may be."[24] Pistorius has similarly focused his objections on the "group demands" that characterize Afrikaner social and political thought. J. K. Ngubane refers to the Afrikaner's disposition to see men from a "group perspective," and S. Patterson alludes to the Afrikaner's "rigorous Christian collectivism."[25]

The significance of such criticisms does not necessarily lie in their substance, for they do little more than recommend an alternate definition of man. Rather, their significance is that they draw attention to the central philosophical and ideological issue: the normic model of man calculated to support the moral injunctions and social policies of apartheid. Afrikaner theoreticians *do* tend to treat the group as a magnified individual. Van Wyk Louw repeats Plato's epigram "The state is the individual writ large," and J. C. G. Kotze insists that the individual as a "fallen man has no rights."[26] The volk, on the other hand, has a God-given right to exist, and whatever rights the individual enjoys derive from the collectivity. The Afrikaner tends to conceive the individual fused with a collectivity, identified with its destiny. The fact is that apartheid exemplifies the species-properties of a specific manner of conceiving man and society. Afrikaner ideologues have proposed a collectivist redefinition of man supported by empirical, analogical, and analytic argument. The normic model that results is characterized as "organic" to distinguish it from what has here been identified as the liberal model. Afrikaner justificatory arguments ultimately appeal to just such an organic model to support imperatives. The assessment of justificatory arguments requires an account of the conception of man and society that subtends those arguments. The counterposition of alternative models can only be effectively undertaken after such an assessment.

The normic model recommended by the ideologues of apartheid has familiar features—it is essentially the model advanced in the *Politics* of Aristotle. Man is, by nature, a social animal. He finds fulfillment only within a community. The manifest evidence of man's social nature is speech, which provides the foundation for the community of reason in which man creates his substantial self. Until man has attained the full measure of citizenship in a historically constituted community, he has not attained the full stature of manhood. For Aristotle, as for Hegel, Marx, Lenin, and Gentile, complete *humanitas* implies *civitas*—every man, insofar as he is man, is a member of a community.

As we have seen, this conception tends to support a *prima facie* presumption in favor of a rule-governed collectivity over the empirical individual. Thus, for Aristotle the state comes before the family and the individual. The conception and the presumption it supports dispose theoreticians of such persuasion to employ organic analogies in describing the relationship of the individual to the community. This is true for Aristotle (and Plato), Hegel, Marx, Lenin, and Gentile. And it is so much a part of Afrikaner thought that the analogy appears in official government publications. Thus, in the *Report of the Commission for the Socio-Economic Development of the Bantu Areas within the Union of South Africa*, the Tomlinson Commission report that provides programmatic suggestions for the application of apartheid in South Africa, there is constant reference to "the growing European national organism" and to "social organisms" in general.[27] The consequence of this manner of conceiving man is to focus attention on groups rather than individuals. The fate of the individual and his organic community is, in a substantial sense, the same. This is apparent in the following propositions: "Man can attain happiness only when he is harmoniously integrated in a [collective] organism. . . . In the realization of the community (*"Bestätigung der Gemeinschaft"*) the individual realizes himself."[28] That this is the case tends to foster an explicit or implicit totalitarianism. John Herman Randall speaks of the totalitarian implications of Aristotle's social and political thought in the sense that there is not, in principle, any sphere of individual interest or activity insulated against the intercession of the politically organized community.[29] This is to be contrasted with the general liberal view that the individual is somehow invested with rights or concerns that are essentially "self-regarding" as distinct from those that are "other-regarding" and the appropriate object of community concern.

Apartheid satisfies all the preliminary requirements of a totalitarian social and political philosophy that functions as the ultimate source of justificatory arguments in support of a value-orientated mass movement of solidarity. There is no internal evidence that apartheid was directly influenced by the thought of Hegel, Gentile, or Aristotle, although Afrikaner intellectuals (for a variety of historic reasons) were for some time under the influence of National Socialist thought and its organic and collectivist biases. Apartheid, rather, seems to be an autogenous development of the Afrikaner community under the stress of crisis conditions, a supposition to which we shall have occasion to return later.

Apartheid as a theoretical system is distinguished from other radical ideologies only when the collectivity with which the individual is identified is specified. Leninism originally identified that collectivity as economic *class*; Fascism identified that collectivity as the *nation-state*; National Socialism identified it as a biological *race*. Apartheid, on the other hand, has identified that community as the historically constituted *volk*.

In the past there has been a lamentable inconsistency in Afrikaner theoretical literature with respect to the concepts "race," "nation," and "volk." In the course of the protracted conflict between the English-speaking and Afrikaans-speaking communities, for example, that conflict was regularly referred to as the "race question." Relations between whites and nonwhites (specifically the Bantu peoples) were referred to as the "native question." Equally prominent were the "coolie" or "Indian question" and the "colored question." Only in fairly recent times has there been an attempt to put the theoretical house in order by assigning specific meanings to the expressions race, nation, and volk. Among the most recent and coherent attempts have been those of Kotze's—*Ras, Volk en Nasie in terme van die Skrif (Race, Volk and Nation in Scripture)*—and Coertze's *Inleiding tot die Algemene Volkekunde (Introduction to General Anthropology)*. Attempts at standardized usage are found in G. Eloff's *Rasse en Rassevermenging (Race and Race Mixture)* and C. C. Nepgen's *Die Sosiale Gewete van die Afrikaanssprekendes (The Social Conscience of the Afrikaner)*.[30] Nonetheless, even contemporary sociologists lapse into locutions that suggest that "local white groups" in South Africa constitute *a single nation* as opposed to resident nonwhite groups, and politicians regularly refer to the "white nation" of South Africa composed of *a* volk that includes *both* Afrikaans- and English-speaking constituents.[31]

The analysis of arguments cannot rest at the level of ordinary discourse, nor can the rational reconstruction of justificatory argument be made solely with doctrinal statements uttered by practicing politicians. Doctrinal statements are themselves generally couched in ordinary language in the effort to communicate with as broad a public as possible. Recourse must therefore be made to theoretical or philosophical literature for an accurate and objective account of justificatory argument. In the case of apartheid this is not only an intellectual exercise; there is substantive evidence that such arguments are literally the basis of policy, finding explicit, elliptical, and partial expression in official government documents provided not only for United Nations councils but for the International Court of Justice as well.

Because of its peculiar characteristics the Afrikaner community displays a remarkable solidarity. A specific if ill-defined intellectual elite provides a common leadership for the Afrikaner political, religious, and academic communities. Since the justification for apartheid must meet the requirements of international and cross-cultural publicity and neutrality, Afrikaner arguments must aspire to meet the minimal requirements governing rational discourse. For this reason religious justifications have tended to be reduced to the level of doctrine that serves only as the ingroup basis of belief. These justifications provide, in effect, consensus support for those already committed to social policy (for whatever reasons). Efforts like those of S. du Toit that seek to rest public policy on the interpretation of Scripture are particularly unsatisfactory simply because the vast majority of religionists reject such interpretation.[32] The justificatory arguments for apartheid have become, as a consequence, increasingly secular and represent a significant shift from doctrinal to theoretical and philosophical language. The academic and professional elite provide such arguments. They are characteristically secular arguments composed of analytic and descriptive propositions ordered in such a fashion as to produce a relatively coherent body of thought—a body of thought that, because of the homogeneity of the intellectual elite, is surprisingly uniform in expression.

Afrikaner theoreticians, for example, distinguish between the concepts race, nation, and volk by conceiving race as having a biological community as referent, nation as having a political community as referent, and volk as having a historical and cultural community as referent.[33] The distinctions are made, however, only for didactic purpose. When the concepts are used in explanatory accounts, they reveal themselves dynamically interrelated. In such accounts the central explanatory and analytic concept is always the volk. A "volk" is an organically integrated multitude animated by a common language, culture, and history, as well as a pervasive and persistent sense of common destiny. The individual is born to such a community—a rule- and custom-governed association of men, characterized by distinctive conventions and mores, laws and institutions. Exposure to these formative influences is inescapable. The volk culture, acting upon inherited dispositional traits, furnishes the substructure of personality. The individual is, essentially, what his hereditary potential and his society make of him. He is heir to a specific historical and cultural patrimony. During critical stages in personality development this heritage exercises decisive influence. Given such a conviction, tradition becomes endowed with intrinsic value, for it is not only something prior to the individual, but is also essential to the development and integrity of the self. Of this traditional heritage language is of particular significance, for it constitutes the medium of thought. It is the most effective medium for the social transmission of moral and intellectual values—it "enshrines the psyche of the group."[34] It effects the transmission of belief systems. Such traditional belief systems not only make social life possible, but also constitute the most essential parts of individual human personality. They are transmitted with relative uniformity from generation to generation and qualitatively distinguish the whole from the aggregate that comprises its membership at any specific time. In this sense the volk is prior to the individual; whatever is of value in and to the individual—his skills and his capacity to make intellectual, esthetic, and moral judgment—is derived. The techniques of truth ascription, esthetic evaluation, and inculpation and exculpation, not to speak of performance skills, are learned. Whatever the extent of individual genius and personal enterprise, the acceptance, in large measure, of prevailing tradition is presupposed. Moreover, the elements of inherited traditions, belief systems, norms, and usages are seldom transmitted without being charged with positive emotional valence. Rules are not transmitted as neutral stimuli. The distinction between what norms are and what attitude children should take toward them is seldom made. Departures from tradition, the violation of custom and usage, are always lamented and must be justified. Recourse, on such occasions, must be made to appropriate argument—and the appropriateness of the argument, its relevance, and its truth are determined by the rules governing what is understood *by the volk* to constitute reasoned discourse.

A volk can arise out of a variety of circumstances—by alliance of smaller associations bent on defense, by a common interest in the exploitation of nature, by conquest and subsequent amalgamation, or by simple population increase. A population that shares a common territory (at least originally), history, language, and tradition comes to conceive itself bound by a common destiny. Its members are united by marriage and, given sufficient time and protracted isolation, tend to become a biological unity ("*biologiese eenheid*") that under special conditions can ultimately produce a population possessing a gene pool sufficiently diverse in the relative frequencies of some of their genes to constitute a biological race.[35] J. D. J. Hofmeyr and G. Eloff have developed these conceptions in an essay entitled "Some Aspects of Raciation with Special Reference to the Bantu Population of South Africa." They maintain:

Dynamic anthropology provides an integrative view of the process of raciation. Elements of this essentially biological process are plainly sociological in implication. . . . [A] population . . . gradually weaves itself together with national sentiment, common language, and culture, producing breeding circles of reasonably well-defined limits. National sentiment is an isolating factor of the prime magnitude. Common sentiment, preferential breeding tend to produce, ultimately, a particular physiognomic phenotype.[36]

The volk, in effect, is a race cradle, what is called a "bio-cultural volk organism."[37]

Should such a unified volk accede to political dominion over a specific geographic area, it constitutes itself a nation. Under special circumstances, therefore, volk, race, and nation *can* have the same reference class. More frequently, a political union is a combination of peoples and races. South Africa itself is an example, composed as it is of at least two major anthropological races (three in South-West Africa) and at least eight relatively stable breeding circles involving at least the Afrikaans- and English-speaking communities; the colored community; the Indian community; and the Neguni, Sotho, Venda, and Tsonga ethnic communities, all subdivided into smaller ingroup units. Empirical studies indicate restricted gene flow among all these various ethnic volk, evidenced in phenotypic differences in facial features, head form, and serological and dermatoglyphic differences.[38]

What is significant for Afrikaner theoreticians is that such volkish communities *do* obtain and that they are each animated by an elemental consciousness of kind (*"saamhorigheidsgevoel"* or *"volksbewussyn"*), by a sense of group sentiment, by a sense of belonging (*"groepsbewussyn"*), by a disposition toward preferential association, an object instance of ethnocentricity (*"etnosentrisme"*). That such volkish communities exist within the political confines of South Africa is, for Afrikaner theoreticians, a fact of primary social and political significance. South

Africa is a collection of volkish communities at various levels of biological, economic, and cultural development, each animated, in varying measure, by ethnocentric sentiment. In this view South Africa constitutes a unique plural society in which various social organisms live in symbiotic relationship. Each socio-cultural and biogenetic unit is animated, in varying degrees, by a self-regarding group consciousness.

The degree of ethnocentricity they display is a function of a variety of factors. E. F. Potgieter and N. J. Rhoodie, for example, indicate that a community that is threatened by out-groups possessed of demographic superiority and characterized by a more rudimentary culture will be characterized by more emphatic ethnocentric behavior than a similar group that identifies with an overseas homeland.[39] The obvious reference here is the intergroup response patterns that distinguish the Afrikaans- and the English-language communities. On the other hand, status-deprived or partially demoralized communities, like the nonwhite communities of South Africa, tend to be accommodative, often xenocentric, outgroup orientated, rejecting their own cultural background in the effort to identify with the more prestigious or economically advantaged outgroup. The consequences, for demoralized volkish communities, is evidenced in individual personality profiles characterized by confused and conflicting values combining outgroup and ingroup cultural patterns. As a result, there is intro- or extrapunitive aggressiveness.[40] This is particularly the case with urban Bantu, who, irrespective of protracted intergroup contact, remain, according to J. C. De Ridder, tribally biased.

. . . tribal affiliation [is] still the fundamental individual association amongst the vast majority of urban Africans. . . . [They are] characterized by feelings of tribal difference and motivated by traditional isolationistic attitudes. . . . An analysis of the fantasy productions of urban Africans as a group has revealed: (1) the existence of a definite religious bewilderment; (2) the presence of strong tribal influences and biases amongst these people; and (3) the existence of a strong belief in witchcraft and the power of magic. . . . The urban African even today is very tribally biased. Complete detribalization, while it may exist, is definitely the exception rather than the rule. . . . The urban

African sees himself as a member of a particular tribe and he recognizes his fellows according to their tribe. He has adopted European dress and many of the white man's customs, but he has retained many of the beliefs, cultural mores and practices, peculiar to his particular tribe.[41]

The protracted contact of volkish communities distinguished by marked differences has, as a consequence, portentous significance. It fosters, in the case of South Africa, a marked sense of distance. The privileged white community considers the numerically superior nonwhites, possessed of a more rudimentary culture, a threat to its well-being and existence. On the other hand, the Africans, such as the urbanized Bantu, are beset by divergent cultural and moral imperatives. They find themselves in protracted and intimate contact with members of diverse ethnic and tribal groups. They must contend with cultural differences of compelling magnitude. As self-regarding (if demoralized) communities, they still resist intertribal marriages. They attempt to maintain a relatively emphatic sense of distance between themselves as corporate entities.

Afrikaner theoreticians and apologists insist that liberal thinkers fail to understand the nature of human groups and the problem that group dynamics creates for a political union whose constituent elements include fully developed, partially developed, and demoralized volk communities. Van Wyk Louw and Katzew argue that "classical European Liberalism had its origin in countries with homogeneous race or volk compositions; it was almost mechanically introduced into multi-national South Africa without any fresh thinking from the beginning about the application of its principles." Liberals are charged with developing abstract arguments appropriate, in fact, only for homogeneous nations.[42] "Is [the liberal]," Potgieter inquires, "under the mistaken impression that we did have a single nation somewhere in the past, or is he merely failing to see that we have different societies and the remnants of different peoples in this country in the present?"[43]

That the Republic of South Africa is, in fact, composed of diverse peoples each possessed of a different pattern of life is a consideration emphasized and reemphasized even in formal government publications.[44] The existence of diverse volk communities and the identification of the individual with his community

and its specific culture constitute the core of the rationale understood to support apartheid. The critics who have brought their
case against South Africa before the International Court of
Justice have clearly understood this and have indicated that

> . . . [a] rigid tendency to categorize by group designation is the
> recurrent theme of the metaphysics of Apartheid. . . . A striking indica-
> tion of Respondent's [South Africa's] attitude is revealed by the fact
> that . . . Respondent attributes to individuals qualities and charac-
> teristics which may only properly be assigned to groups.[45]

In effect the criticism implies an alternative conception of man
than that entertained by the theoretician of apartheid. The
ideologue of apartheid has argued that the individual is in some
significant sense the group of which he is the product. The individual is essentially the denizen of a community of limited compass. It is the spiritual endowment protected, nurtured, and
transmitted by the group that constitutes the essentials of his
personality. Therefore, the identification of the individual with
his group, they argue, is a requisite for rational and ethical
policy.

Since this conception occupies such a critical role in the
justificatory arguments for apartheid, Afrikaner theoreticians
have been driven to state their case with relative clarity. As has
been suggested, the concept of ethnocentricity, sometimes referred
to as volkish sentiment (*volksgevoel*), shoulders an imposing
theoretical burden in their exposition. Mankind is represented
as a complicated, segmented reality divided along biological,
cultural, and political lines. These distinctions divide men into
partially or fully exclusive associations of preference that, in
varying degrees, foster among their respective members a sentiment of identity, a consciousness of kinship.

Similarities of sentiment, religious beliefs, value systems, customs, language, economic interests, accouterment, appearance,
history, and geographic residence not only provide the essentials
of personality development but also foster bonds of association
that afford the individual a sense of being among his kind. During the long period of biological dependence in childhood these
values and norms are induced in the individual organism by a
process variously identified as socialization, enculturation, intro-

jection, imitation, and empathy, which in ordinary discourse refers to the acquisition of skills, attitudes, values, norms, and the disposition to conform. The successful completion of this process produces an individual possessed of a viable self-system, a conception of self enhanced by a sense of personal worth because the self reflects the skills, attitudes, values, and norms of the society that he has learned to consider as valued. The process by which a social inheritance is transmitted is accompanied by high emotional salience. The skills, attitudes, values, and norms transmitted are valued; proficiency in them is approved, and failure to conform deplored. Thus the normal process of maturation generates in the individual a positive bias favoring his own community. Such a bias functions to heighten the survival potential of the group, since under its influence the individual is disposed to sacrifice for his community, conform to its injunctions, and entertain its preferences. Communities fortified with such members are favored in the struggle for survival that has characterized the microevolution of the species. Under these circumstances, such a dispositional trait complex has become universal.

The phenomenon of preferential association among men is . . . a generally accepted and scientifically established fact. . . . This sense of similarity, or "sentiment of identity," is often referred to in social science literature as a "shared consciousness of kind." This "conscious-ness of kind" constitutes, in the words of one of the founders of the science of social psychology, Professor William MacDougall, "the principal force underlying all human associations." It has its counterpart in what has been called "a consciousness of difference," and it has been stated by Professor I. D. MacCrone . . . that the stronger the identification between the members of a group, the stronger the feeling against "alien" groups:

> The identification which lies at the basis of group psychology, while leading to the development of those attitudes and impulses without which a genuine group life would be impossible, at the same time, and necessarily, gives rise to those veiled or overt manifestations of hostility directed against others which constitute the essence of the psychology of group prejudice. The greater and more intense the group feeling, that is, the stronger the identifica-

tion between members of a group, the greater is the strength of the prejudice against the alien group and against those who are not members of one's own group. Social psychology may, or may not, have its laws, but there can be little doubt about the existence of that principle of group psychology according to which the feeling for one's own group and the feeling against some other group tend to wax and wane in direct proportion to one another.

Social scientists teach that the differences which give rise to group preferences and prejudices can be of many kinds, and that they can, depending on circumstances, have different consequences. It has been said in this connection that

> . . . the differences which are the basis for selective association are of indefinitely large variety, of all degrees of visibility and subtlety, and vastly different in social consequences, . . .

and that

> . . . group antagonisms seem to be inevitable when two peoples in contact with each other may be distinguished by differentiating characteristics, either inborn or cultural, and are actual or potential competitors. Only by eliminating the outward evidences of distinction, such as color, dress, or language, or by removing the competitive factor, may racial antagonisms be destroyed.[46]

Contact situations in which groups characterized by manifest and enduring differences of an inherited or induced variety meet are potential conflict situations, particularly when they threaten competition for survival, status, and general well-being.

The greater the differences between human groups, the more clearly the group consciousness reveals itself, the more strongly the central seeking influence of the group acts and the more powerfully the member identifies with that particular group. The smaller and less numerous the differences and the greater overlapping between groups, the weaker the identification process and the slighter the conflict potential in the event of contact. The conflict potential is normally considerable when, in a contact situation, two or more groups are characterized by an *accumulation* of differences. The conflict potential, however, is very much increased if there are *physically recognizable traits* or *sensory perceptible symbols* that lead to the easier *recognition* or *identification* of the particular group's members. . . . Apartheid policy cannot be divorced from the . . . universal pattern of "human relations—human differences—differentiation—grouping." . . . [These] groups attach significance [to] a common cultural heritage, social and political institutions, race, religion, and survival as national entities and united, free peoples—in any possible combination. The more numerous the objects of value for the group, the greater the group consciousness and the more violent the resistance to any threat from outside.[47]

Those threats can be political, cultural, or biological. Each is understood as jeopardizing the integrity of the self-regarding community.

The theoreticians of apartheid maintain that the presence in South Africa of a highly civilized white community among indigenous peoples characterized by emphatic cultural and physical differences has created a unique social and political situation. The white community, composed of English- and Afrikaans-speaking volk, established itself, largely as a consequence of the real differences that separated it from the indigenous population, as a white political association in which outgroup members were accorded little more than residence rights when they entered the service of the new political community. Both white volkish constituents of this political community were agreed that the nonwhite population would never be accorded full membership in the nation. *No* white political party (with the exception of extremely small splinter parties) advocated anything remotely suggesting such a policy. But economic expansion and the attendant urbanization and immigration of nonwhites made the situation explosive. As a consequence, the traditional white policies crystallized into apartheid as a social and political ideology. It was the product, almost exclusively, of the Afrikaner intellectual community—but it was not incompatible with the sentiment and policies of the established English-speaking community. It was advanced as a comprehensive solution to South Africa's vexing intergroup problem. That solution was equitable separation (*regverdige Apartheid*).

One of the earliest accounts of apartheid as a coherent ideological system (containing an exposition of values, a collection of doctrinal statements, and policy suggestions), as distinct from the vaguely formulated and irregularly administered policy of "segregation" that governed race relations in South Africa before 1948, is that contained in G. Cronje's *Regverdige Rasse-Apartheid (Equitable Racial Separation)*, published in 1947. In a section entitled "The Ideal Solution," Cronje indicated what Afrikaner theoreticians conceived to be the essence of a comprehensive solution to South Africa's most critical problem. "The ideal solution to the race question in South Africa," he maintained, "will result from the territorial separation of the diverse racial groups, permitting each community to pursue its own socio-economic evolution and develop its own form of government. . . ."[48] Cronje's language, unfortunately, is imprecise. He speaks of the "racial question," of "diverse racial groups," and of "each community" and then proceeds to indicate that the "different communities" to which he refers include "probably three or more Bantu communities" distinguished by "ethnic" differences. Cronje's ideal solution is not concerned with the "racial question" but with what might be more appropriately identified as the "volk question" of South Africa. The units he identifies are volk rather than racial units—what more contemporary apartheid theoreticians call "biocultural entities." Once this ambiguity is resolved, we receive a simple statement of the core concept of apartheid, a concept that has remained central in all discussions devoted to the issue. Cronje's presentation is a simple statement of radical or vertical apartheid, the complete territorial separation of the diverse volk of South Africa. It envisages a gradual and systematic disentanglement of volkish communities. As early as 1943, P. J. Coertze, J. Language, and B. I. C. van Eeden characterized the policy as one that sought "gradual separation in all spheres, with total separation (*"apartheid"*) both territorially and socially, as the ultimate aim."[49]

The rationale for apartheid includes a conviction that volkish sentiment is of critical significance in any responsible assessment of individual and collective life. This conviction is buttressed by explanatory (or theoretical), descriptive, and normative accounts. Afrikaner theoreticians maintain that the organic evolution of man (raciation as a biological process), involves the existence of *social isolates*, self-regarding endogamous communities of limited compass in which hereditary traits develop and are naturally or artificially selected. The rapidity of developmental change in evolutionary time indicates that such isolates could not have included very large populations. Groups that tended to retain an optimum size would evolve more rapidly and because of higher survival potential would displace less highly evolved communities. This would tend to make the disposition to maintain relatively small breeding communities an essentially universal trait. Ethnocentrism would come to characterize man as a social animal.

Group cohesiveness has always had a high survival value. It has had such a value in the evolutionary past, and the disposition to identify with one's community is understood to have come to constitute part of man's social nature. Afrikaner theoreticians maintain that the process of psychosocial development provides ample evidence that normal maturation involves, through socialization, the identification of the individual with his community and its skills, norms, and values. The acquisition of these skills, norms, and values and the differences that distinguish groups are never indifferent concerns.

Descriptive accounts, as we have indicated, make regular reference to the universality of ingroup and outgroup phenomena throughout historic time.

"Consciousness of kind" and "consciousness of difference"—particularly if deeply seated differences are at stake—form the breeding ground of . . . conflict. Thus . . . conflict is a latent danger in any situation where dissimilar . . . groups meet. Open conflict is practically unavoidable in cases where the more highly developed group is, at the same time, also the minority group. Now we are not dealing with artificial human behavior, but with a fundamentally human phenomenon which enjoys universal validity.[50]

Differences, particularly where those differences are fundamental, enduring, and/or of high social visibility, are initial loci of conflict. This is particularly true when large groups with basic differences are found together in the same community. Where cultural and racial differences are coupled with a disparity of numbers of a magnitude such as that of South Africa, the conflict potential is explosive. Of the total population of 15,850,000 in the Republic in 1960, there were 10,810,000 Bantu and 3,068,000 whites (the remainder being composed of the Asian and colored communities). If the United States, employing all the machinery of the

judiciary, the legislature, and the executive, has had tragic difficulty attempting to reduce the group sentiment that separates
whites and Negroes in the United States, where Negroes constitute approximately 12 percent of the population, what is to be
expected in South Africa, where the ratio of nonwhites to
whites is forty times greater? In both cases the nonwhite community aspires to upward mobility and political influence. In
both cases the conjunction of evident differences between the
groups and the conceived threat to the status and integrity of
the white community generate conflict. In the United States the
significant difference between the groups, which are one in language and culture, is essentially high social visibility. In South
Africa social visibility is an index to a multiplicity of far-reaching differences. The magnitude of the differences coupled with
the magnitude of the relative demographic strength in South
Africa generate a pervasive fear of literal extinction on the part
of the white community.[51]

Let us now recapitulate the main points that have been made
thus far. Normative implications are implicit in these accounts,
and conjoined with theoretical, analytical, and descriptive propositions, they generate recommendations and imperatives. For the
Afrikaner, man, as man, is a denizen of a cultural, historical, and
ultimately biological entity called a volk. Alienated from the
volk, or afflicted by membership in a demoralized volk, the individual fails to achieve the fullness of self without which life itself
becomes meaningless. For the Afrikaner, therefore, self-realization requires membership in a specific historic community united
in common purpose in a sense of common destiny. The Afrikaans
word nasionaal rests on the concept nasie or volk, a word for
which English has no precise equivalent. It refers to an organic
cultural, historical, and biological unit rather than a mechanical
aggregate of individuals in political union. Thus, "apartheid's
architects argue that it is the God-given right of every people
or nation on earth to develop against its own background."[52]
The Afrikaner, therefore, conceives the solution to the dilemma
of South Africa in a political union, a composite commonwealth
of volkish communities each developing separately in a system
of "vertical apartheid."[53]

This "ideal solution" is to be undertaken by the National
party, which represents the effective political arm of Afrikaner-

dom, for it is a solution that Afrikanerdom can entrust only to itself as a mature volkish community. The English-speaking white community continues to feel itself culturally and, in some vague sense, politically part of another overseas community.[54] The Bantu-speaking peoples suffer from the impact of an alien, but technologically advanced, civilization that has succeeded in demoralizing their historic and cultural integrity. As a consequence even the schooled Bantu, torn by the trauma of cultural alienation, cannot be conceived as understanding his real as distinct from his immediate interest. His immediate interests are outgroup determined. He seeks to identify with the technologically, culturally, and economically privileged community without an appreciation of the negative impact upon himself, for "major frustration and personality impairment occur precisely in circumstances of attempted but unaccomplished integration with a more developed group."[55]

The individual, even if distinguishable by nothing more than a manifest difference in appearance and in this instance by racial characteristics of high visibility, will encounter enormous tensions in attempting to find his "place" among an alien volk. He is circumstanced somewhat like a gifted individual with a gross physical deformity, pitied, perhaps applauded, but always stigmatized.[56] Impaired by an inadequate self-image, divorced from the community with which he shares inescapable affinities (if only overt physical appearance), he fails to attain fullness of self. In the pursuit of economic or status mobility he alienates himself from his historical, cultural, and biological community, only to become the restive marginal personality of the urban centers. Although status mobility and economic advantage are immediate interests of such an individual, they are really subsidiary to his ultimate interest—the creation of a fullness of self without which social mobility and economic advantage become meaningless. The individual cannot uplift himself if it is at the expense of alienating himself from the community with which he is identified. That identification is the consequence of shared similarities among which, in interracial contact situations, racial similarities have proved to be among the most compelling.

Given such convictions, the Afrikaner considers himself equipped, indeed obliged, to exercise "guardianship" over dependent (that is, demoralized and culturally and technologically retarded) groups—to undertake their uplift as organic *groups* rather than treat them as simple aggregates of individuals who individually can take up and leave off group membership in the pursuit of immediate real or conceived adavantage. Only groups that have attained volkish maturity and have attained the cultural and technological level requisite to the twentieth century can fully exericse self-determination. When they find themselves in contact situations involving deprived communities, their responsibility is to uplift such communities *as a group*. The alternate attempt to uplift *individuals* threatens personality dislocation in the individuals the well-intentioned effort is calculated to assist (particularly when such individuals have permanent characteristics that readily identify them as "different" in the host community). This creates tensions in the organically interrelated benefactor volk.

Theoreticians and apologists for apartheid regularly point to the situation in the United States and Africa for graphic illustration. The American Negro, who shares all the cultural attributes of the white community, never succeeds in identifying with it. He fails to attain an "identity," irrespective of whatever social or economic benefits he might obtain.

[The] Negro's unattainable wish to be white becomes the source of serious inner conflict. Professor Gunnar Myrdal said of this conflict that it produced "a personality problem for every single Negro. And few [American] Negroes accomplish an entirely successful adjustment." . . . [An] individual cannot attain a coherent and viable self-concept, which is necessary for healthy personality development, without a sense of group belonging. . . . [An] individual who identifies himself with a group which commands his respect and allegiance is able to attain psychological maturity with far less hazard than one who lacks such a sense of group identity. . . . [V]arious leaders of African thought have in recent years expressed themselves about the detrimental and demoralizing effect which an unsuccessful attempt at adopting white ways and notions—including color notions—has on Africans, and . . . they have emphasized that a healthy group sentiment serves to establish self-respect and a sound self-image on the part of the individual. Professor W. E. Abraham, Associate Professor of Philosophy at the University of Ghana, comments on the "tension" and "near neurosis" affecting the African who has managed to achieve only a superficial imitation of European culture, and whom Professor Abraham calls "a truly displaced man." He writes:

> The man of two worlds, the man who has been exposed in no consistent or radical fashion to a milieu which is different from that to which he belongs, though the latter continues to surround him, is a truly displaced man. His mastery of the new culture is not comprehensive enough, it is self-conscious, and, such as it is, it is generally in conflict with *mores* into which he was born, and which he has never truly uprooted from his system. He is a cultural ambiguity, not cultural ambivalence, for it is characteristically accompanied by misgivings. These misgivings, this tension, this near neurosis, can be most tragic. The man of two worlds, uncomfortably striding both, is the real displaced man.[57]

Technologically, socially, and psychologically impaired volk, nascent or demoralized volk, require the "guidance," the "guardianship" (*"voogdyskap"*), of advantaged volk. This is the secular expression of the Afrikaner conviction that his volk is obliged by a special "calling," that Afrikanerdom has an ordained "mission" to accomplish. It is a frank elitism that seeks to justify the political paramountcy of a numerical minority over a political union of 16 million persons. Only when each embryonic or demoralized volk in South Africa attains its maturity or rehabilitation will the Afrikaner's "mission" be accomplished and each community have undertaken self-determination (*"selfbeskikking"*), including "complete independence."[58]

This constitutes the essentials of the ideological system of apartheid as it has matured over the last quarter of a century. It is the volkish ideology of Afrikanerdom, the animating rationale for a movement of solidarity. It provides the arsenal for justificatory arguments employed by the National party of South Africa and influences the political and social history of our time as well as the lives of millions of men.

Doctrinal Problems

• One of the central doctrinal issues that has occupied both protagonists and detractors of apartheid is the question of the conceived differences that obtain between groups. Specifically, it is the question of whether apartheid rests on the conviction of racial "superiority" and "inferiority." In the not too distant past E. P. Dvorin could maintain:

The implication of [apartheid] is that the existence of a "natural," "common," or "universal" man is denied and that men are conceived as only members of different races. . . . The Dutch South African spirit of the Afrikanervolk bears a striking similarity to the European idea of the *Volk*. . . . The ideal of the *Herrenvolk*, or "master-race," a people with a common past, common language, and biological superiority . . . destined by physical and mental superiority to dominance over other races. . . .[59]

Actually, such an account is in error in several ways: (1) apartheid is a *volkish* and not a consistently *racist* ideology; (2) while commentators may *interpret* apartheid to *imply* a conviction in the biological inferiority of one race and the biological superiority of another, official policy *explicitly* rejects the contention that apartheid measures are predicated upon such a conviction.

P. J. Coertze, who has been influential in the articulation of apartheid thought, has maintained that science has not *established* the innate differences between biological races (nor has it *established* that such differences do *not* obtain).[60] What has been established to the satisfaction of apartheid theorists is that differences, either biological or cultural, are of primary significance in intergroup relations. Differences themselves are group-building and group-distinguishing factors. These differences are historical and cultural, and their importance is essentially psychological and not biological. The fact that biological race differences—skin pigmentation, hair form, and facial features—are traits possessed of high visibility and are, consequently, important factors in group dynamics is central to apartheid thought. This does not entail that those traits are conceived as indexes of *innate* inferiority or that alternate traits are conversely indexes of *innate* superiority. Thus, official South African statements include assertions such as these:

[It is] stated positively that [the] policy of separate development is not based on a concept of superiority or inferiority, and [the South African Government] . . . rejects . . . allegation[s] that it must, nevertheless, necessarily be implied that the policy is based on an assumption "not only that some 'groups' are inferior, but that individual members thereof are 'permanently and irremediably inferior.'" . . . [The] policy of separate development is not based on the concept of inferiority or superiority on the part of any group. Whilst the policy no doubt takes account of the present stages of development of the respective population groups, it does not rest on any assumption of innate, or biological, differences in the potential sociocultural ability of those groups. If it should be a scientific fact—[and it is not contended that] it is a fact—that observed differences in the cultural development and achievements of different groups are, wholly or in substantial part, the consequence of irremediable biological, or hereditary determinants governing cultural development, science would lend support to a policy which took proper account of such differences and factors. But, and [this is] the point, whilst the existence of such determinants could, if established, provide further evidence of the desirability of a policy of separate development in circumstances as existing in Southern Africa, the absence of such biological, or hereditary, determinants does not in the slightest degree affect the argument for separate development.[61]

The theoreticians of apartheid repeat these contentions in a number of places.[62] In 1958 J. P. Bruwer, a member of the editorial board of the influential SABRA publication, *Journal of Racial Affairs*, explicitly maintained: "[The] concept of race as it is biologically conceived deals only with physical traits. It has nothing to do with intelligence, innate characteristics or abilities, and certainly does not express an opinion as to the superiority or inferiority of varying somatic types."[63] Even contemporary critics acknowledge the distinction apartheid theoreticians attempt to draw. L. Kuper indicates that "Apartheid, in theory, rests on difference, not on inferiority. . . . and the inability of scientists, no matter how adequately motivated, to establish racial inferiority."[64]

Although this is clearly the case with respect to current *official* opinion, there remains a strong current of Afrikaner counteropinion. There is still a marked tendency among Afrikaner thinkers to base an invidious assessment of groups on anthropometric criteria. The identification of nonwhites as innately inferior has a long history among the Afrikaners, and this disposition was furthered by Afrikaner sympathy for National Socialist Germany prior to, and during, World War II. While this sympathy rested on essentially negative grounds, that is, the opposition to Britain, there was a tendency to accept some National Socialist representations bearing on the race question. Thus, G. Eloff's *Rasse en Rassevermenging* supports a view of the innate and irradicable differences between biological races with references to National Socialist literature, including the works of H. F. K. Günther (see Chapter V). Eloff went so far as to claim that the racial "foundations" of the Boervolk in South Africa was essentially "Germanic," a race composed of "creators and bearers of Western culture,"[65] and that a policy of racial separation was required to protect their racial potential from impairment. There are still echoes of these contentions in the most contemporary of Afrikaner works. Thus, T. E. W. Schumann speaks of the "inherent differences in intellectual and cultural capacities" between the races of man, maintaining the innate superiority of the group he sometimes seems to identify as "Aryan."[66] Even Cronje, in his book *Regverdige Rasse-Apartheid*, which is so important in the articulation of apartheid as an ideology, maintained that the innate differences between the races of man in intellectual and cultural potential were demonstrably established. Similar arguments can be found in the contemporary works of G. D. Scholtz and J. H. Grobler.[67] The books of G. M. Mes also enjoy considerable popularity. His arguments, although somewhat different, are essentially arguments seeking to support racial separation on the grounds that the several races of man possess incompatible "genetic determinants" that preclude the possibility of uniting them in a single society.[68]

It is clear that Afrikaner thinkers are not all of one mind on this sensitive issue. This difference is not simply theoretical, for it seems to be reflected in policy statements made by government representatives. If the Bantu-speaking peoples of South Africa are considered, in fact, to be incapable of creating a modern technological civilization, it would mean that the "Christian guardianship" of the Afrikaner volk would be perpetual—they would forever remain second-class citizens fashioned by the Almighty (or evolution) to serve as hewers of wood and drawers of water for their superiors. Sometimes there is more than a suggestion of this in Afrikaner policy statements. W. W. M. Eiselen, as an influential government spokesman, said (as late as 1959) that separate development envisaged

> . . . the utmost degree of autonomy in administrative matters, [but that this] . . . will stop short of actual surrender of sovereignty by the European trustee, and there is therefore no prospect of a federal system with eventual equality among members. . . . [The] maintenance of white political supremacy over the country as a whole is a *sine qua non* for racial peace and economic prosperity in South Africa.[69]

This clearly seems to imply that the Bantu-speaking peoples of South Africa will never be equipped to be masters in their homelands. Yet, at almost the same time that Eiselen's article was being published, the late Dr. H. F. Verwoerd, in reply to an opposition question in Parliament, maintained:

> [If] it is within the power of the Bantu and if the territories in which he now lives can develop to full independence, it will develop in that way. Neither he nor I will be able to stop it and none of our successors will be able to stop it, whether our policy is accepted or whether the policy of the United Party is accepted.[70]

Verwoerd went on to entertain the possibility that in the South Africa of the future there would be a white state and various Bantu national units and areas or states, independent nations, just as in Europe. The entire discussion was predicated on the supposition that there would be fully independent Bantu states, "linked to white South Africa by common interests," in an unspecified but foreseeable future.

There is apparently an intransigent Afrikaner faction within and without the National party. The prevailing Afrikaner opinion, however, is clearly volkish, jealously guarding the Afrikaner volk but providing for full equality between the English-speaking and Afrikaans-speaking communities. Apartheid, as has been stressed, is based theoretically, upon the intrinsic value of each and any historical and cultural community. Distinction in allocation of rights and duties are based upon considerations of manifest group differences in cultural development and the putative necessity of the individual to identify with his community. Racial differences of high visibility are simply one of the insistent differences that serve as a factor in making the integration of communities inadvisable. In principle, such a view provides for the ultimate attainment of complete independence of the various Bantu volk now maturing or being rehabilitated in the political confines of the republic. There is another view, articulate and apparently influential, which holds the racist conviction that the Bantu-speaking peoples of the republic are inherently incapable of the white level of civilization; therefore, rights can be legitimately withheld forever. The latter view would conceive of a perpetual white elite ruling a subservient mass of nonwhite laborers and would radically revise the ideology of apartheid until it became a more or less consistent racism.

Policy Problems

•   Although our present task is limited to an exposition of the rationale for apartheid, it is necessary to speak briefly of specific policy problems. Few critics have devoted much time to a serious attempt at examining and explaining the philosophical and doctrinal bases of apartheid largely because criticism focuses on the ability of the National party of South Africa to effect the ideal of vertical separation between the peoples of South Africa. Apartheid is most regularly dismissed as an "illusion," a "utopia," as impossible to implement.[71] The traditional "Bantu homelands," for example, at the present time and for the foreseeable future, are incapable of maintaining their population at minimum subsistence levels. The land surface is exhausted; the area overpopulated and overgrazed. Enormous sums are required simply to stabilize the land, an effort to which the national government has applied itself with admirable diligence—but an effort, no matter how admirable, that has not stopped the flow of Bantu labor to the urban centers. In Ellen Hellmann's judgment:

Despite the rigidity of the legislative framework designed to prevent the emergence of a permanent urban African community and to promote the policy of "separate development," urban African development is proceeding in precisely the opposite direction. The antithesis of what the Government is aiming at is actually taking place. The African urban population is increasing in size.[72]

The movement of the Bantu to the white urban areas continues unabated to the present time. Between 1951 and 1960, during nine years of National party control, the number of Bantu in urban areas increased by 45 percent (over 1 million persons). Today over 60 percent of the Bantu live or work as migratory urban or rural laborers in the white areas. The rapidly expanding economy of South Africa that requires a continuously increasing nonwhite labor force thus works at cross purposes to the policy of vertical apartheid. The result is a system of *horizontal* apartheid in which the upward mobility of the various nonwhite groups is frustrated by an elaborate system of restrictions of various kinds. For example, there is a wage discrepancy of approximately 15 to 1 between whites and Bantu in the mining industry and 5 to 1 in secondary industries—with whites, who constitute less than 20 percent of the population, accounting for about 67 percent of the national income and earning a per capita income of 850 Rand a year compared to 78 Rand a year for Bantu.[73] The living conditions of the Bantu in South Africa do compare more than favorably with those of Africans living in the African states to the north, but the Bantu of South Africa do not compare their standard of living with that of Africans in the Congo or Ethiopia. Their standard of reference is the privileged white community in which they must labor. The consequence can only be heightened tension and frustration. A partial solution would be the rapid industrialization of the Bantu homelands, but the national government has been little disposed to undertake programs of any appreciable magnitude. The Tomlinson Commission Report of 1955 envisaged a vast scheme of industrialization of the Bantu areas and anticipated the creation of at least 50,000 new employment opportunities in a decade. There is little evidence that employment opportunities in the Bantu areas have developed at anything like the rate requisite to stop the flow into the white areas.[74]

The rapid industrialization of the land area of South Africa reserved for the Bantu population (13 percent of the total area) would require massive allocation of resources to nonwhites and would tend to alienate white support so necessary for the maintenance of the National party in power. Although the government has made attempts to stimulate the development of "border industries" adjacent to the Bantu areas (investing $252 million in such industries between 1960 and 1965), they have apparently had only marginal influence on the urbanization of the Bantu, which has been characteristic of South Africa since the turn of the twentieth century. As a consequence an increasing number of Bantu are becoming completely detached from their traditional culture and must be considered, for all intents and purposes, permanent urban workers. In fact, the vast housing schemes undertaken by the national government, which have done much to alleviate the incredible conditions in which the urban Bantu lived under the *laissez-faire* policies of the past, has made the urban areas still more attractive to the Bantu. These Bantu, working at a bare subsistence minimum in a highly developed economy, beset by innumerable restrictions on their movement, family life, and political expression, constitute what appear to be an insuperable obstacle to vertical apartheid.

If the goal of apartheid is the fulfillment of the self for the Bantu as well as for the white man, it requires for its realization viable Bantu communities. The continued existence of Bantu involved in, and yet not part of, the white volk can hardly fulfill that aim. Even the development of meaningful local self-government for the Bantu in the white urban areas and full political rights in the Bantu homelands cannot provide a satisfactory solution. Realization of the ideal of apartheid requires that the 264 Bantu enclaves in South Africa become viable economic units capable of supporting at least the bulk of the Bantu population in stable communities and that these communities be allowed to develop a culture and a network of institutions compatible with the twentieth century. If the only solution to South Africa's unique problem of intergroup relations is separate development (and separate development requires for its ultimate realization immediate discrimination and injustice), it would seem to be incumbent upon the promoters of such a policy to prove that their program is, in fact, feasible. It is on the feasibility of apartheid as an effective program that attention is legitimately focused.

Conclusions

•   Apartheid is the ideology of a value-orientated movement of solidarity, and in this respect it shares certain features with

Leninism, Italian Fascism, and National Socialism. These movements advance a radical normic model of man that entails significant departure from the liberal conception of a universal humanity and of individual man as endowed with intrinsic rights and intrinsic value. Such a model fosters the issuance of normative injunctions that guide social action. As a seemingly descriptive account of man and man's relation to man, they generate, in fact, generalized belief systems that influence behavior and legitimize conduct. Apartheid as a value-orientated movement seeks the massive reorientation of values that is consequent upon its redefinition of man and society and as such envisions a corresponding reconstitution of subordinate values and the redirection of policy.

With the advent of the National party to power in 1948, a party spokesman characterized the differences between the contending parties (the United party and the National party) in the following fashion:

> What is at issue is two outlooks on life, fundamentally so divergent that a compromise is entirely unthinkable. . . . On the one hand we have nationalism, which believes in the existence, in the necessary existence, of distinct peoples, distinct languages, nations and cultures, and which regards the fact of the existence of these peoples and these cultures as the basis of its conduct. On the other hand we have liberalism, and the basis of its political struggle is the individual with his so-called rights and liberties. . . .[75]

The first distinction between the ideology of apartheid and the remaining ideologies of solidarity of the twentieth century is that the object of solidarity for the Afrikaner is the Afrikaner *volk*. When the Afrikaner ideologue, politician, or churchman speaks of his nation, he is referring to the Afrikaner *nasie*, the Afrikaner volk. The solidarity he seeks is that of the Afrikaner volk, an organic unity of the historical, cultural, and ultimately biological elements that constitute Afrikanerdom. This is evident in everything written by Afrikaner intellectuals and is particularly imperative in Afrikaner pronouncements on education. In 1948 the Institute for Christian National Education (Christelik-Nasionale Onderwys) issued a pamphlet that enunciated its program. Article One states as the "basis" of Christian National Education:

All white children should be educated according to the view of life of their parents. This means that Afrikaans-speaking children should have a Christian-National education, for the Christian and National spirit of the Afrikaner nation must be preserved and developed. By Christian, in this context, we mean according to the creeds of the three Afrikaner churches; by National we mean imbued with the loves of one's own, especially one's own language, history and culture.

It is obvious that the solidarity sought is a volkish solidarity to distinguish it from the solidarity sought by the nationalism of Fascism (and that of contemporary Leninism). Fascism sought to unify all Italians, obviating regional, class, or language differences. Apartheid seeks to obviate class or regional differences only within the Afrikaner volk. National Socialism, on the other hand, ultimately transformed itself into a movement of racial solidarity and sought to unite all Nordics and intimately related peoples irrespective of national origins. All these ideologies seek to unify the individual and some collectivity. Entertaining a dynamic conception of race, Afrikaner theoreticians have spoken of the Afrikaner volk as a sociocultural entity that has, through three centuries of social isolation and consequent endogamy, begun to solidify as a new race. This conception is surprisingly similar to the dynamic conception of race that supported the volkish philosophy of Houston Stewart Chamberlain and that is found in the scientific work of Egon von Eickstedt.[76] It bears a distinct family resemblance to the dynamic theory of race and raciation found in Fascist doctrine. (There is little direct evidence that Fascist theoreticians had any influence in the develment of this aspect of apartheid doctrine. J. D. J. Hofmeyr and G. Eloff [77] refer in one specific instance, however, to the work of Corrado Gini, who was very influential in the scientific life of Fascist Italy.) The sociocultural unity of the Boervolk is conceived as a new race, in effect subordinating the concept race to that of volk. The volk is primary; race is a derived product of volkish integrity and continuity. The concept nation, understood in its political sense, has become a commonwealth of nations under the impact of volkish preference. Nation is thus subordinated to volk. The critics of apartheid are essentially correct when they indicate that for the Afrikaner ideologue "there must be no attempt to form a single nation with a single outlook and a single loyalty."[78] South Africa is conceived to be a collection of autonomous nations or, more precisely, autonomous volk.

These peculiar features of apartheid ideology explain why South Africa is not a one-party state. Movements of solidarity tend, in fact, to create one-party states, and yet South Africa tolerates a multiparty parliamentary apparatus. What is reasonably clear is that *the Afrikaner volk has its one party*. The National party is the only Afrikaner party that remains in South Africa. The remaining parties represent the English-speaking volk. The National party (its protestations not withstanding) does surprisingly little to win the English-speaking electorate to its membership (although crisis conditions have tended to create more unanimity between the two language communities in the immediate past). The bulk of the National party's literature is published in Afrikaans, its meetings and rallies are conducted in Afrikaans, and its candidates run in Afrikaner-dominated constituencies. The solidarity sought by apartheid has been achieved in the *eenheid*, the unity of the Afrikaner volk, and that achievement is reflected in an undisguised unanimity of opinion among Afrikaner churches, cultural organizations, academic institutions, student organizations, the press, and the National party. There is no political party that pretends to express dissident Afrikaner opinion. The few Afrikaners who do not identify with the apartheid policies of the National party find their place (in decreasing numbers) in the United party.

Within the confines of the volk the National party as the state is essentially totalitarian in the sense that the state does not recognize any aspect of public life as, in principle, excluded from its influence. Thus, there is very little that the Afrikaans-speaking South African can read that does not have, directly or indirectly, the explicit approval of the National party (although the opposition English-language press is largely unrestrained). The totalitarian aspects of apartheid are particularly apparent in education, where principles are formulated in terms of what is called Christian National Education. In effect, education is conceived as a program for inculcating the generalized belief system of Afrikanerdom; consistent with its volkish bias, it "rejects the generally accepted European view that the interests of the child are supreme. Instead the child is regarded as an instrument to further the interests of the volk." This is pursued with such application that Afrikaner parents in Afrikaner-dominated provinces who would rather have their children educated in a dual-medium school are not permitted a choice.

The single medium or language apartheid school, where Afrikaans, English, or a Bantu language is the medium, is therefore the ideal form that national-minded Afrikaner educationalists have set out to achieve. It is however an ideal which not all parents in a given language group share. So the old Boer principle of parental choice has had to yield to the view that the "state knows best."[79]

Economics, similarly, are subordinated to apartheid principles, and industries are deployed into areas bordering on the reserves to serve the political program. Verwoerd, "like earlier Nationalist leaders, . . . [felt] that *laissez-faire* economics must bow to the higher social good, which in this case is the preservation of the Afrikaner volk."[80] In fact, totalitarian movements tend to systematically subordinate economics to the interests of policy, and while state control of certain sectors of the economy is common to capitalist countries, in few of them is it as extensive as in South Africa, where the state owns or effectively controls land and forests, the means of communication and transportation, as well as a host of other public services. In South Africa the state has entered the field of private industry in electric power generation (Escom), printing, the manufacture of arms and ammunition, the production of iron and steel (Iscor), heavy engineering (Vecor), insecticides (Kipfontein Organic Products), oil, gas, and chemicals from coal (Sasol), and fertilizers (Foskor). The state also controls the Industrial Development Corporation, which has become, together with private capital, a permanent shareholder in a host of industries.

Finally, the state maintains relatively strict censorship rights over all cultural, recreational, and news media and, armed with various defensive measures (for example, the Suppression of Communism Act), can suppress publications, banish individual dissidents, and restrict the movements of others. It has even extended its influence into church affairs with various enactments governing interracial church attendance.

The ideologists of apartheid identify it with a *volksbeweging*, a people's movement of Afrikaner solidarity.[81] Its leaders are

volksleier, volk leaders. There is talk of a "true Afrikaner sentiment" to which such leadership can give expression and which
finds manifestation in such slogans as "We honor our volk leader
—you lead—we follow." That the leadership has been patri-
archal rather than charismatic is characteristic of Afrikaner
political expression. Apartheid is not a revolutionary ideology
seeking to subvert existing belief systems. Rather, it is attempting,
in a world of rapid change, to sustain the essentials of a belief
system developed in the nineteenth century. It seeks to ensure
the perpetuity of a historic volk, not create or enhance a new
national solidarity (as was the case with Fascist Italy). Apartheid
seeks to restore the Boer republics that British imperialism,
armed might, and money succeeded in subverting. Its totalitarianism is negative in one sense because one of its purposes
is outwardly directed. It conceives itself as a benefactor, restoring
the integrity of "alien" residual or demoralized volk who are not
conscious of their ultimate interests. Its restrictions are imposed
not to create a solidarity within the nation of South Africa, but
in the conviction that it is dividing South Africa into diverse
volkish components. This purpose is to be effected without the
consent of such disenfranchised volk. Within its own volk, on
the other hand, its totalitarianism is positive in the sense that a
pervasive sense of group belonging effectively unites Afrikaners
into a unitary Calvinistic collectivism.

In the present climate of Afrikaner nationalism . . . it is increasingly
difficult for an individual to be a good Afrikaner or for an association
to pursue truly Afrikaans aims without being associated with the
tenets of the political party that claims to be the only political representative of Afrikanerdom.[82]

The National party seeks to articulate, foster, and defend a
single, relatively coherent social and political philosophy based
on an explicit rejection of the classical liberal theses in which
the primacy of the atomic individual is affirmed and in which
society is construed as a convenience whose importance is essentially negative insofar as it serves only to remove obstacles that
might prevent individuals from achieving complete satisfaction.
For classical liberalism the relationship between individuals and
society was understood as an external one, with the individual

and his native faculties as given and with society as an arrangement of convenience.

Apartheid advances a radically different conceptual model of man, based upon a finite set of descriptive sentences constituting a vague theoretical system capable, in principle, of generating verifiable experimental hypotheses. But more than that, these propositions, conjoined with implicit values such as the fulfillment of self, are deemed capable of supporting social policy and compelling assent. This is evident in the frequency with which apartheid ideologues employ imperative and normative language and on the doctrinal level maintain that their policy enjoys God's sanction. The National party seeks to foster a systematic generalized belief system, and to that end it directs education, employs censorship, and suppresses opposition. What Afrikanerdom has sought to create is what was early called a *Weltanschauung* state, a pedagogical or ethical state—a state that is not indifferent to value, a state that seeks to create solidarity on the basis of an explicit belief system.

Apartheid, in exemplifying a *volkish* movement of solidarity, is committed, in principle (if not in fact), to the ultimate dismemberment of a nation. It has successfully synthesized *race* and *state* with the *volk*, and it has fully identified the individual with this historic community. Until the realization of its ultimate ideal of vertical apartheid, the National party considers that it possesses the right to rule the majority of the population occupying the territorial confines of South Africa. Should such vertical apartheid ever be realized, it appears obvious that white South Africa would continue multiparty government, but ideally Afrikaners would have only *one* party, the National party, which would represent the volk will of their community. A select elite of that community, through an array of interlocking organizations, would effectively control all aspects of Afrikaner life. This is not to suggest that such elite rule is oppressive in the ordinary sense of the term. As is true for all value-orientated movements of solidarity, the ideal sought is an identification of individuals and factions with the collectivity. Unequivocal acceptance by the vast majority of people (effectively implemented by education and fostered by control of the media of communication) would provide a docile if highly centralized democratic basis for power. This factitious consensus is termed "democratic centrism" in

Soviet parlance, "authoritarian democracy" and "people's democracy" in Fascist and National Socialist jargon. White South Africa would, nonetheless, continue to maintain at least a two-party system because each party would, consistent with apartheid theory, represent the will of two diverse volk.

If the ideology of contemporary Leninism can be described as an inconsistent national Fascism and that of National Socialism as a consistent racial collectivism, apartheid can be suitably described as a consistent volkish collectivism. Its specific philosophical uniqueness is that it appears to be an autogenous product of Afrikanerdom. Nonetheless, it exemplifies the principal species characteristics of philosophical collectivism. It tends to identify the individual with the rule-governed association of virtual equals of which he is a member and as a consequence identifies his ultimate (as distinct from his immediate) interests with that of his community. The singularity of apartheid is that the elite, licensed by this rationale to rule, exercises its "guardianship" over outgroup as well as ingroup members. It is the rule of a mature volk over demoralized volk. But for all its content differences and special applications, the formal structure of the rationale is Hegelian.

Notes

1. N. J. Rhoodie and H. J. Venter, *Apartheid: A Socio-Historical Exposition of the Origin and Development of the Apartheid Idea* (Pretoria: HAUM, 1960), p. 19. See also N. J. J. Oliver, "Apartheid: A Slogan or a Solution?" *Fact Paper*, 30 (March, 1957), 8.

2. E. H. Louw, *The Case for South Africa* (New York: MacFadden, 1963).

3. Rhoodie and Venter, *op. cit.*, p. 20.

4. W. W. M. Eiselen, "Harmonious Multi-Community Development," *Optima* (March, 1959), p. 7. See also Louw, *op. cit.*, pp. 58f.

5. There are any number of good historical accounts of South Africa. The following section rests heavily on the accounts of P. L. van den Berghe, *South Africa: A Study in Conflict* (Middletown, Conn.: Wesleyan, 1965), Chap. ii; Rhoodie and Venter, *op. cit.*, Chaps. iii–viii; L. E. Neame, *The History of Apartheid* (London: Pall Mall, 1962), Chaps. i–v, *White Man's Africa* (Cape Town: Stewart, 1962); L. Marquard, *The Peoples and Policies of South Africa* (London: Oxford, 1962); S. Patterson, *The Last Trek: A Study of the Boer People and the Afrikaner Nation* (London: Routledge & Kegan Paul, 1957); W. M. Macmillan, *Bantu, Boer and Briton*, rev. ed. (New York: Oxford, 1963); H. Jenny, *Afrika ist nicht nur Schwarz* (Vienna: Econ, 1963), Chaps. iv, v.

6. C. C. Nepgen, *Die Sosiale Gewete van die Afrikaanssprekendes* (Johannesburg: C.S.V. Boekhandel, 1938), p. 230; see also A. Cryns, *Race Relations and Race Attitudes in South Africa* (Nymegen: Janssen, 1959), pp. 39–42.

7. Neame, *White Man's Africa*, p. 32. See also G. D. Scholtz, "The Origins and Essence of the Race Pattern in South Africa," *Fact Paper*, 61 (July, 1958), 4–6.

8. van den Berghe, *op. cit.*, p. 35.

9. O. Pirow, *James Barry Munnik Hertzog* (Cape Town: Timmins, 1957), p. 128.

10. As cited in Neame, *History of Apartheid*, p. 61.

11. J. C. G. Kotze, *Principle and Practice in Race Relations* (Stellenbosch: SDA Publishers, 1962), p. 53.

12. See I. D. MacCrone, *Race Attitudes in South Africa* (Johannesburg: Witwatersrand, 1957), and S. Pienaar and A. Sampson, *South Africa: Two Views of Separate Development* (New York: Oxford, 1960), p. 7.

13. B. B. Keet, *Suid Afrika Waarheen?* (Stellenbosch: Universi-

teits-Uitgewers en Boekhandelaars, 1956), *The Ethics of Apartheid* (Johannesburg: South African Institute of Race Relations, 1957); P. V. Pistorius, *No Further Trek* (Johannesburg: Central News Agency, 1957).

14. Rhoodie and Venter, *op. cit.*, p. 19.

15. See SABRA, *Die Naturellevraagstuk* (Stellenbosch: Pro Ecclesia, 1950), p. 7.

16. N. J. Rhoodie, *A Sociological Analysis of South Africa's Policy of Separate National Development* (an unpublished manuscript made available by the author), p. 45.

17. See H. Verwoerd, "Geloftedagrede by Bloedrivier, 16 December, 1958," in A. N. Pelzer (ed.), *Verwoerd aan die Woord* (Johannesburg: Afrikaanse Pers-Boekhandel, 1964), pp. 189–91.

18. P. J. Coertze et al. (eds.), *Inleiding tot die Algemene Volkekunde* (Johannesburg: Voortrekkerspers, 1961), pp. 11, 35.

19. See P. J. Coertze, in *Volkskongres oor Kommunisme* (Potschefstroom: Volkskongres, 1964), pp. 193f.

20. N. P. Van Wyk Louw, *Liberale Nasionalisme* (Johannesburg: Nasionale Boekhandel, 1958); A. B. Du Preez, *Inside the South African Crucible* (Pretoria: HAUM, 1959).

21. Du Preez, *op. cit.*, pp. 86, 56, 89, 110, 118–19, 121.

22. Rhoodie, *op. cit.*, p. 2.

23. G. Carter, *The Politics of Inequality: South Africa Since 1948* (London: Thames and Hudson, 1954), p. 273.

24. Keet, *Ethics of Apartheid*, pp. 7, 8, 14.

25. See Pistorius, *op. cit.*, p. 63, *passim*; J. K. Ngubane, *An African Explains Apartheid* (New York: Praeger, 1963), p. 12; and Patterson, *op. cit.*, p. 178.

26. Van Wyk Louw, *op. cit.*, p. 24; Kotze, *op. cit.*, p. 18.

27. *Summary of the Report of the Commission for the Socio-Economic Development of the Bantu Areas within the Union of South Africa*, U. G. 61/1955 (Pretoria: Government Printer, 1955), Chap. ii, Para. 77, Chap. iii, Para. 1.

28. H. G. Schütte, *Weisse Ismen, Schwarze Fakten* (Vaterstetten: Arndt, 1963), p. 63. I have taken some liberties with translation. In the first sentence Schütte refers to *Stammesorganismus*, but the remainder of the paragraph indicates that he does not wish to restrict this contention to tribal groups but to extend it to all significant collectives (the author).

29. J. H. Randall, *Aristotle* (New York: Columbia, 1960), p. 255.

30. J. C. G. Kotze, *Ras, Volk en Nasie in terme van die Skrif* (see Note 11 for English translation); Coertze, *Inleiding*; G. Eloff, *Rasse en Rassevermenging* (Bloemfontein: Nasionale Pers, 1942); Nepgen, *op. cit.*

31. See Rhoodie, *op. cit.*, p. 78; Verwoerd, "Boodskap aan die volk van Suid Afrika," in Pelzer, *op. cit.*, pp. 148–51; D. F. Malan, "Wat is Afrikaner-Volkseenheid?" *Afrikaner-Volkseenheid: En my Ervarings op die Pad Daarheen* (Cape Town: Nasionale Boekhandel, 1961), pp. 45–48.

32. S. du Toit, *Holy Scripture and Race Relations* (Potchefstroom: Pro Rege-Pers, 1960). There is an enormous literature devoted to Scriptural interpretation and social policy in South Africa. A representative sample would include: J. J. Buskes, *South Africa's Apartheid Policy—Unacceptable* (Roodeport: SA Fellowship of Reconciliation, 1956); D. E. Hurley, *Apartheid: A Crisis of the Christian Conscience* (Johannesburg: South African Institute of Race Relations, 1964); S. P. Freeland, *The Christian Gospel and the Doctrine of Separate Development* (Pretoria: Christian Citizenship Department, 1961); and the publications of B. B. Keet. Counterarguments are to be found in L. J. Du Plessis, *Apartheid: Ja of nee of janee* (Potchefstroom: Pro Rege-Pers, 1957); in the essays contributed by W. Nicol and E. P. Groenewald in G. Cronje, *Regverdige Rasse-Apartheid* (Johannesburg: CXV, 1947); and in the works of A. B. Du Preez referred to in the text. For a general discussion of the relationship of the various churches to South Africa's policies see L. Cawood, *The Churches and Race Relations in South Africa* (Johannesburg: South African Institute of Race Relations, 1964).

33. Kotze, *Principle and Practice*, pp. 44–49; Eloff, *op. cit.*, p. 27; Coertze, *Inleiding*, pp. 11, 12, 15.

34. H. Katzew, *Apartheid and Survival: A Jewish View* (Cape Town: Simondium, 1965), p. 47. See also Van Wyk Louw, *op. cit.*, p. 28; Du Preez, *op. cit.*, pp. 55, 114, 121f.

35. Eloff, *op. cit.*, p. 27; Coertze, *Inleiding*, pp. 11, 15; Rhoodie, *op. cit.*, p. 12.

36. J. D. J. Hofmeyr and G. Eloff, *Some Aspects of Raciation with Special Reference to the Bantu Population of South Africa* (an unpublished manuscript provided by the authors), pp. 3, 7.

37. Schütte, *op. cit.*, p. 63.

38. R. Elsdon-Dew, "The Application of Blood Grouping to South African Ethnology," *South African Journal of Science*, XXXIII (1936), 976–92; R. A. Dart, "Racial Origins," in I. Schapera (ed.), *The Bantu Speaking Tribes of South Africa* (Cape Town: Maskew Miller, 1956).

39. Rhoodie, *op. cit.*, p. 41; E. F. Potgieter, "The Problem of Objectivity in the Study of Ethnic Relations in South Africa," *Journal of Racial Affairs*, VIII, 3 (April, 1957), 128.

40. See J. C. De Ridder, *The Personality of the Urban African in South Africa* (London: Routledge & Kegan Paul, 1961), pp. 66, 84, 86,

94; S. Biesheuvel, *Race, Culture and Personality* (Johannesburg: South African Institute of Race Relations, 1959), p. 19.

41. De Ridder, *op. cit.*, pp. 95, 96, 105, 106, 160.

42. Katzew, *op. cit.*, p. 44; Van Wyk Louw, *op. cit.*, p. 107.

43. Potgieter, "The Problem of Objectivity . . . ," *op. cit.*, p. 126. See also Schütte, *op. cit.*, p. 84.

44. *Summary of the Commission Report*, Chap. ii, Para. 73.

45. *Reply of the Governments of Ethiopia and Liberia.* South West Africa Cases (Ethiopia and Liberia v. The Republic of South Africa). International Court of Justice (June, 1964), pp. 149, 150.

46. *Rejoinder filed by the Government of the Republic of South Africa.* South West Africa Cases (Ethiopia and Liberia v. The Republic of South Africa). International Court of Justice (1964), I, pp. 444f., 446. See also J. E. Holloway, *Apartheid: A Challenge* (Johannesburg: Afrikaanse Pers, 1964), p. 28.

47. Rhoodie, *op. cit.*, pp. 4, 5, 7, 83. See also R. C. Haw, *No Other Home: Co-existence in Africa* (Bulawayo: Stuart Manning, n.d.), Chap. iii.

48. Cronje, *op. cit.*, p. 155.

49. P. J. Coertze, J. Language, and B. I. C. van Eeden, *Die Oplossing van die Naturellevraagstuk* (Johannesburg: Publicite Handelreklamediens, 1943), p. 11. See also N. J. J. Olivier, "Is Separation the Answer to S. A. Race Problem?" *Fact Paper,* 16 (August, 1956), 17; "The National Party of South Africa: Programme," 1952, in D. W. Krueger (ed.), *South African Parties and Policies, 1910–1960* (Cape Town: Human and Rousseau, 1960), pp. 97f.; H. F. Lass, "Der burische Nationalismus," in F. Duve (ed), *Kap ohne Hoffnung oder die Politik der Apartheid* (Hamburg: Rowohlt, 1965), pp. 108–10.

50. Rhoodie, *op. cit.*, pp. 101f.

51. See G. D. Scholtz, *'n Swart Suid Afrika?* (Johannesburg: Nasionale Boekhandel, 1964), pp. 83ff.

52. B. Marais, *The Two Faces of Africa* (Pietermaritzburg: Shuter and Shooter, 1964), p. 11.

53. J. H. Coetzee, "Nationalism and the Future of South Africa," in H. Spottiswoode (ed.), *South Africa: The Road Ahead* (Cape Town: Timmins, 1960), p. 72.

54. *Ibid.*, p. 68; Potgieter, "The Problem of Objectivity . . . ," *op. cit.*, p. 128.

55. *Rejoinder*, pp. 470f.; see also Du Preez, *op. cit.*, Chap. iv, Sec. 4.

56. Du Preez, *op. cit.*, pp. 186ff.

57. *Rejoinder*, pp. 472f.

58. H. F. Verwoerd, *Hansard* (January 23–30 and May 18–22, 1959), Cols. 65 and 6520; see also Rhoodie, *op. cit.*, p. 40.

59. E. P. Dvorin, *Racial Separation in South Africa* (Chicago: University of Chicago, 1952), pp. 57f.

60. Coertze, *Inleiding*, p. 41.

61. *Rejoinder* . . . , pp. 451, 453f. See also *Summary of the Report*, Chap. ii, Paras. 77–82.

62. Rhoodie and Venter, *op. cit.*, p. 159; Kotze, *Principle and Practice*, p. 73; Du Preez, *op. cit.*, pp. 41, 49f., 88; Rhoodie, *op. cit.*, p. 81; H. F. Verwoerd, *The Truth about South Africa* (National Party Information Service. Pretoria, n.d.), p. 8.

63. J. P. Bruwer, "Theories Based on the Concept of Race," *Journal of Racial Affairs*, IX, 3 (April, 1958), 124.

64. L. Kuper, *Passive Resistance in South Africa* (New Haven: Yale, 1957), p. 31.

65. Eloff, *op. cit.*, p. 69; see also pp. 30f., 38–49.

66. T. E. W. Schumann, *Die Abdikasie van die Witman* (Johannesburg: Afrikaanse Pers, 1962).

67. Scholtz, *op. cit.*, pp. 100f.; J. H. Grobler, *Africa's Destiny* (Johannesburg: Book of the Month, 1958), pp. 117f.

68. G. M. Mes, *Mr. White Man, What Now?* (Johannesburg: Afrikaanse Pers, 1965), pp. 24, 46f., 108, 113, 117f., 121–23; *Now Men and Tomorrow Men* (Johannesburg: Afrikaanse Pers, 1964), pp. 3, 45, *passim*.

69. Eiselen, "Harmonious . . . ," *op. cit.*, p. 8.

70. H. F. Verwoerd, *The Choice: A Racially Integrated Fatherland or a White South Africa* (Bloemfontein: Merlo, 1959), p. 11. See also A. G. Mazerik (ed.), *Apartheid in the Republic of South Africa* (New York: International Review Service, 1964), pp. 6f.

71. A. Sampson, "Apartheid als Illusion," in Duve, *op. cit.*, pp. 37–47; Kuper, *op. cit.*, p. 37; see also C. M. Tatz, *Shadow and Substance in South Africa* (Pietermaritzburg: University of Natal, 1962).

72. E. Hellmann, "The Application of the Concept of Separate Development to Urban Areas," *African Affairs*, X (1961), 143.

73. *Apartheid in South Africa* (New York: United Nations, 1963), p. 26.

74. M. Horrell, *Reserves and Reservations: A Comparison of Plans for the Advancement of Under-Developed Areas in South Africa and the United States* (Johannesburg: South African Institute of Race Relations, 1965), p. 20. For a review of the discussions concerning the Tomlinson Commission Report, see "The Sequel to the Tomlinson Commission Report," *Supplementary Fact Paper*, 506 (January, 1957); S. T. Van Der Horst, "A Plan for the Union's Backward Areas: Some Economic Aspects of the Tomlinson Commission's Report," *South African Journal of Economics*, XXIV, 2 (June, 1956), 89–112; com-

pare *Business Report* (Information Service of South Africa), VI (April 14, 1966), 15, where it is stated that between 1960–1965, 41,000 Bantu have found employment in "border industries" adjacent to the reserves.

75. Dr. Diederichs as cited in B. Bunting, *The Rise of the South African Reich* (Baltimore: Penguin, 1964), p. 162.

76. Both Eloff (*op. cit.*, p. 30) and Coertze (*Inleiding*, p. 49) refer to the works of von Eickstedt.

77. Hofmeyr and Eloff, *op. cit.*, p. 5.

78. Bunting, *op. cit.*, p. 200.

79. Patterson, *op. cit.*, pp. 224f. See also Bunting, *op. cit.*, pp. 193–204.

80. Patterson, *op. cit.*, p. 175.

81. Rhoodie and Venter, *op. cit.*, p. 15.

82. Patterson, *op. cit.*, p. 271.

VII · AFRICAN SOCIALISM

The second half of the twentieth century has seen the appearance of a new doctrine identified by its exponents and adherents as African socialism. The term *socialisme africain* was probably first used by President Léopold Sédar Senghor of Senegal, when he broke from the Senegalese section of the French Socialist party to establish his own political party. His party, which ultimately became Senegal's party of solidarity, the Union Progressiste Sénégalaise, distinguished itself by maintaining that it would be based on African rather than European socialism. In the late nineteen-fifties George Padmore, mentor and confidant of the former president of Ghana, Kwame Nkrumah, wrote "A Guide to Pan-African Socialism," which laid down the general doctrinal guidelines for Ghanaian African socialism. Since that time the term has been used increasingly as an identification of a general doctrinal position that animates many of the newly independent African states. Nkrumah, Senghor, President Sékou Touré of Guinea, President Julius Nyerere of Tanzania, and President Modibo Keita of Mali have made African socialism the doctrinal basis of indigenous mass movements of solidarity. Although each doctrinal expression differs, they do reflect a core of common elements that permits a synoptic characterization. Without doubt, African socialism constitutes the most important single attempt on the part of African politicians to come to grips with the political problems of the continent. As a doctrine African socialism attempts to provide the belief system for the mass mobilization of human resources in the service of political enterprise. It therefore has specific significance in politically and economically underdeveloped communities and is, as a consequence, an intrinsically interesting and important contemporary political phenomenon. More than that, it may, as a totalitarian rationale, provide special insight into one of the most significant features of our century: the rise of the mass-based unitary party.

African Socialism as a Doctrine

· The cataclysmic changes that have swept over Africa since the end of World War II were no less traumatic than those that beset Europe after World War I. Since the end of hostilities in 1945, more than thirty-five new nations have appeared where hardly more than a decade ago there had been only European dependencies. Because effects of these changes will continue to influence the development of the African continent for the foreseeable future, any prediction of the course of events is extremely hazardous. The newly emergent nations of Africa are committed to a program of social development unparalleled in the history of man—a direct leap from various stages of readiness into the atomic age. The structural tensions to which African society will be subject and the individual and collective psychological dislocations that will occur will produce results difficult, if not impossible, to calculate. Nonetheless, the most intellectually aggressive of Africa's new political leaders have begun to formulate a relatively coherent political doctrine intended to animate the masses of their various communities at least during the initial stages of this proposed transition.

The most salient, and the most readily comprehensible, aspect of the doctrine is directed to Africa's economic development. All African socialists insist that their various nations, and the African continent in its entirety, attempt to close the enormous gap separating them and it from the developed nations of the earth. In order to accomplish this, they universally reject capitalism as the sole industrial system and advocate socialism in its stead. What this means in actual practice, however, is not at all self-evident. None of the African socialist countries accept as a model the economic system of either the Soviet Union or China. Instead, they advocate a mixed system of various "private," "cooperative," and "state" sectors of the economy with public initiative, investment, and enterprise prepared to satisfy national economic imperatives when private capital or enterprise is found wanting. There has been little disposition to alienate foreign capital investments by threatening nationalization. In fact, all the African socialist countries not only have found it expedient to accept extensive private capital investment and aid from foreign capitalist governments, but have welcomed it. Foreign investment has been given extensive legislative guarantees in Ghana and Tanzania, for example, albeit with restrictions on the investors' freedom to transfer earnings and with provision that some portion of the accrued profit remain in the host country. The right to nationalize has been explicitly or implicitly reserved with the understanding that compensation, in such an eventuality, would be forthcoming.[1]

The newly emergent African socialist states, preoccupied with economic development, conceive the world as divided among privileged and underprivileged nations. For them, the international contest is drawn not along the class lines of the international proletariat versus the international bourgeois class, but between proletarian (*nations proletaires*) and privileged nations. Both Padmore and Senghor argue that the "colonial masses" constitute the true "proletariat" and that the struggle between have and have-not nations constitutes the "class struggle" in its "acutest form."[2] It is obvious that class has ceased to be a serious analytic or theoretical concern. The protagonists in the African socialist "class struggle" are proletarian nations whose members are not identified by class characteristics but merged in an all-encompassing category—the people. Senghor explicitly maintains that his attempt "to define an 'African road to socialism' [is predicated on] *national* values and [starts] from *national* realities." Thus, African socialism seeks to create a nation (a people), in which "each individual will identify himself with the collective whole and vice versa."[3] Touré, the most Marxist of the

African socialists, nowhere affirms that the Guinean proletariat is the prime mover of national reconstruction; instead he constantly alludes to the historic role of the *people* of Guinea rather than to a determinate class or social stratum. The entire people are conceived as the prime movers of historical development; they are both objects and agents of historical progression. Senghor specifically maintains that it is necessary to subordinate the proletarian revolution to the national revolution, and Nkrumah enjoins the "entire people" of Ghana, including those of "whatever . . occupation or status . . . farmers, fishermen, masons, lawyers, doctors, the laborers, businessmen, engineers, architects, traders, teachers and students," to devote themselves to the production of the "wider and fuller life for our nation."[4] Specific economic nostrums like nationalization, *per se*, are of but secondary concern. The primary concern is the rapid industrial development of the nation.

That African socialism has seen fit to borrow Marxist vocabulary must be explained on grounds other than doctrinal commitment. Whatever "socialism" the African socialists are advocating, it is abundantly clear that the analytical and theoretical unit of inquiry is the nation and its people rather than a class or classes, however defined. Both Ghana and Senegal possess reasonably well-articulated classes that either have special entrepreneurial functions in the economy or enjoy special status or income, but both reject the Marxist concept of class struggle and emphatically advocate class collaboration in the service of national well-being. The clear intention of the doctrinal injunctions of African socialism is to create an atmosphere of dedication on the part of all elements in the population for the larger collectivity, the nation.[5] This emphasis was already implicit when Padmore identified the three fundamental principles of Pan-Africanism as *nationalism*, political democracy, and socialism.[6]

The recurrent theme of uniting the entire community to further national ends receives various expressions in the statements of the theoreticians and practitioners of African socialism. At the Dakar Colloquium on African Socialism, Mali Minister of Development, Seydou Kouyate, expressed himself in the following fashion: "We can say that the socialist path that we have adopted is based on two fundamental notions: (1) a socialism set up by a movement led by elements not essentially proletarian;

and (2) a socialism recognizing spirituality as an integral part of man. . . . [We] believe that the political organization of the people, considered as the driving force of the people, can lead the country in setting up socialism. . . ."[7] Mamadou Dia, a former prime minister of Senegal, has maintained that ". . . development requires a complete and conscious association of the entire people. It is, before anything else, a collective will for development. . . ."[8]

The entire people is identified with the *national will*; this will finds concrete expression in the state. "If the nation is a conscious determination to reconstruct, the state is its major means. . . . It fulfills the nation's will and ensures its permanence. . . . [The] state is the expression of the nation; it is primarily a means to achieve the nation."[9] Since this is the case, the theoreticians of African socialism have been indisposed to suggest any "withering away" of the state. All have advocated a strong, centralized state authority: The state is conceived as the immediate means of effecting the nation's will. But that will articulates itself only in an explicit ideology. Cheikh Amidou Kane, the commissioner-general of the Senegal Development Plan, has indicated that "the socialist revolution is above all structural change animated by ideology. . . ."[10] An ideology is a set of propositions that includes "fundamental principles, . . . beliefs about the nature of man and the type of society which must be created for man. . . . [It] does not seek merely to unite a section of the people; it seeks to unite the whole of the society in which it finds itself."[11] Society, it is pointed out, represents a dynamic unity, a unity sustained by a "theoretical basis for the cohesion." Ideology constitutes that theoretical basis. It is composed of immutable components and constantly changing programmatic applications determined by regional differences and prevailing local circumstances.[12]

Such an ideology cannot be the product of an unstructured aggregate of people; it must be the organic and integral product of a political party. And this is why the political party looms large in the theoretical works of African socialists. If "the socialist objective implies the universal good of the nation, and in the interests of that socialist objective it will be necessary for all . . . to forgo some immediate personal desire for a greater benefit a bit later on,"[13] it becomes essential that an agency exist that can foster a self-sacrificing, disciplined national consciousness.

Thus Nyerere enjoins "all" to make sure that the "socialist attitude of mind is not lost through the temptations to personal gain . . . or through the temptation to look on the good of the whole community as . . . secondary . . . to the interests of our own particular group."[14] Nkrumah maintains that "the spirit of service to the nation must permeate throughout our society."[15] What is required is "discipline, authority . . . a spirit of devotion and of sacrifice, and organization."[16] An agency is necessary, therefore, to restrain social groups from embarking upon class warfare inimical to the future of the nation. That agency is the mass party of solidarity equipped with the political formulas for fostering and maintaining the sense of common purpose, dedication, and sacrifice essential to the realization of a national consciousness. "Just as political independence could not have been attained without the leadership of a strong, disciplined party, so . . . economic independence and the objective of socialism cannot be achieved without decisive party leadership." This decisive party leadership welds the "amorphous collection of people into an organic and dedicated body of men and women sharing an identical view of human society. To achieve this objective, party education is conducted at all levels. . . ."[17] The party serves to articulate and inculcate an ideology that

> . . . seeks to bring a specific order into the total life of its society. . . . The ideology of a society is total. It embraces the whole life of a people, and manifests itself in their class-structure, history, literature, art, religion. . . . [If it] seeks to introduce a certain order which will unite the actions of millions towards specific and definite goals, then its instruments can also be seen as instruments of social control. It is even possible to look upon "coercion" as a fundamental idea in society.[18]

Since the party is so conceived, the single-party system has become the most characteristic feature of the contemporary African political scene. The mass-based one-party system under which national conformity is essential constitutes the foundation of African socialist political doctrine. In Ghana and Guinea the party exemplifies the model of Leninist political organization in which all levels of the party organization must follow the directives of the Central Committee. "All this," Nkrumah has indicated, "will lead to one useful result—discipline. The whole nation from the President downwards will form one regiment of disciplined citizens."[19] In Senegal one political party, the Union Progressiste Sénégalaise, controls the government, and the party is directly under the control of its Executive Bureau, a self-perpetuating body that coopts into its membership those it deems qualified to serve its integralist and totalitarian functions.[20]

Because the function of the political party is so conceived, African socialist states tend to be uniformly totalitarian in tendency, in that no aspect of public or private life is understood to be, in principle, intrinsically self-regarding. Such parties develop a multiplicity of activities that involve the party in everything from baby clinics, trade union activities, youth organizations, farmers' councils and women's federations to marketing cooperatives and cultural associations. In effect, what they implicitly and explicitly reject is the Western liberal conception that man inherently possesses privacy in some area of activity (however vaguely defined). There is, in fact, less concern with civil liberties and the protection of the individual under the law than the West is accustomed to.[25] Nyerere has expressed this thesis by maintaining that

. . . our problem is just this: how to get the benefits of European society—benefits which have been brought about by an organization of society based on an exaggerated ideal of the rights of the individual—and yet retain the African's own structure of society in which the individual is a member of a kind of fellowship. . . .[21]

African socialism conceives the individual only as a member of a community in which he sees "no struggle between his own interests and those of the community. . . . he is 'communitary' in thinking and in his way of living. . . . [He] is a member of a genuine community or a brotherhood."[22] This is the conception of man advanced by Dia at the Dakar Colloquium. "African development," he maintained, "is characterized by an underlying conception of man. Not individualistic man, but *l'homme personnaliste*, who finds his full blossoming in the coherence of a living society, of an organic community."[23] Thus Senghor insists that "Negro-African society is collectivist or, more exactly, communal, because it is rather a communion of souls than an aggregate of individuals." In that communion of souls "man is defined, or better still, fulfilled by his practical activity as a producer-consumer." It is in the "passage from individual to the collective" that the individual is fully personalized, that he becomes a truly human being.[24] This is the animating conception of man and society common to all doctrinal and philosophical expressions of African socialism. It is the philosophical and doctrinal basis for the mass movements of solidarity that direct the life and fortunes of African socialist states. It is identified as "communitary" by Nyerere, "*communaucratique*" by Touré, "*communautaire*" by Senghor, and "communalist" by Nkrumah.

The most significant instance of this focus on the national community has been the domestication of labor organizations. The nature and function of these organizations have been radically reconceived; labor unions are no longer tolerated as organizations whose essential function is to protect the interests of labor. The interests of labor are protected by the organic community and more specifically by the African socialist state. There is, in fact, an identity of ultimate interest between the labor unions and the state as the express will of the national community. Nkrumah has maintained:

> The workers understand that they are working for a state which is directed by a government of their own choosing, whose programme they have helped to formulate through party membership, and which they actively endorse and support. Hence the aspirations of the people and the economic and social objectives of the government are synonymous. The role of the trade unions, therefore, in our circumstances, is entirely different from that in a capitalist society where the motivating force is the accumulation of private profit. The aims of our trade unions, being identified with those of the government, weds them to active participation in the carrying out of the government's programme.[25]

Thus, "nobody has the right to call himself a true labor fighter if he is not also an honest and loyal member of the . . . Party. . . ."[26]

As a consequence of this reinterpretation of the nature and function of trade union organizations, labor unions in Ghana are permitted to strike only with the permission of the state. They are united into the state-organized Ghana Trade Union Congress through a forced process of deregistration for those who balk at merger, and their membership is incorporated into the party by making the party membership card the only qualification for membership within these organizations.

A similar process, following a similar justificatory rationale, has been pursued in the remaining African socialist states. Thus, Senghor insists that labor unions in "struggling" against the government stand in "unnatural contradiction" with their own ultimate interests, while Nyerere maintains that trade union leaders and their followers "as long as they are true socialists, will not need to be coerced by the government into keeping their demands within the limits imposed by the needs of society as a whole. Only if there are potential capitalists among them will the socialist government have to step in and prevent them from putting their capitalist ideas into practice!"[27] What this has meant in practice is the breaking of the independent trade union movement by imposing "preventive detention" upon labor leaders such as Victor Mkello and Christopher Tumbo and incorporating the entire trade union movement into a government-sponsored National Union of Tanzanian Workers. Strikes are virtually outlawed, and all collective bargaining takes place within limits established by the state. Fixed wage scales are being gradually replaced by a scale of wages geared to productivity.

In effect, the interests of the trade union organizations are made subordinate to those of the nation as interpreted by the unitary party. Nyerere describes the trade unions as "prongs" or "legs" of the nationalist movement that consequently *must* cooperate in the furtherance of national interests.[28] In Ghana the labor unions are enjoined to "make sure that national economic output is increased because such increased production is a condition precedent to a fuller life for the entire people."[29] Labor unions are conceived as essentially concerned with implementing, in the national interest, the productionist and developmental programs of the party. They have no separatist interests, no class or sectional interests antagonistic to those of the nation in its entirety. This follows from conceiving the individual and the national community as sharing a substantial identity. Such a conviction fosters a now familiar set of substitutions. The labor unions, the farmer organizations, the cooperatives, the youth organizations, and subsidiary adjuncts equal the people; the people equals the nation; the nation finds expression in the ideology of the party; and the ideology of the party is articulated by the leadership, most characteristically one leader, of the party.[30] This series of substitutions is expressed elliptically by Senghor in the epigram "We and you are the state" and by Nyerere's admonition to the Presidential Commission on the Establishment of a Democratic One-Party State to remember that "the state . . . is the people. . . ."[31]

It is evident that African socialism tends to produce a rationale for what has been called a "focal institutional" society, a society in which a single institution penetrates every sphere of private or public activity. That institution becomes, in reality, the foundation upon whose sufferance the activities and continued existence of all other institutions depend. In other words, that society tends to become totalitarian, and the focal institution is the political party. To effect its totalitarianism, the party must seek to inculcate a belief system that fosters infrangible solidarity. Nkrumah characterizes such a belief system when he speaks of the ideology of "the dominant segment of society," which in "communalistic societies . . . coincides with the whole," and goes on to indicate that "there can be no such thing as peaceful coexistence between opposing ideologies."[32] Given this conviction, any individual or group of individuals who does not identify with the ideology of the party of solidarity is adjudged a traitor to the community. Wherever nonconformist political expression is permitted at all, it is permitted only as long as its activities are understood by the dominant mass party to be "constructive."

In Tanzania, where the one-party state has been fully established, the members of the National Assembly are subject to the party's "right to insist on adherence to its basic principles and policy."[33] Since the dominant or unitary party reserves for itself the prerogative of deciding whether criticism is constructive, in the general and not factional interests, and in conformity with the basic principles and policy of the party, it is evident that all the institutional prerequisites for a totalitarian state obtain. That such is the case is indicated by the fact that in African socialist states, political liberalism with its advocacy of multiparty

representation is considered either a counterrevolutionary force
or a doctrine wholly inappropriate to the African situation. The
arrangements between "rulers and ruled have tended to take on
a monolithic quality in which society is perceived as an organic
whole, rather than a series of contractual relations between the
parts."[34]

The tendency to identify the party, its ideology, and its
leaders with the corporate will of the people, an undifferentiated
and organically conceived community, has provided the rationale
for deportation acts, preventive detention acts (through which
the government has the power, in some cases, to detain persons
for up to five years without trial), disqualification acts, the ban-
ishment of political opponents, and the suppression of opposition
newspapers. Within the compass of such a rationale the equation
of dictatorship and democracy becomes facile, and Touré can
sincerely maintain that it is his party's will to "affirm, with no
misunderstanding, that [it] wanted to apply dictatorship which is
by its nature the logical consequence of a democracy established
at the level of [the] people and by the people, and which finds
expression in the application of democratic centralization."[35]
Whatever distinction once obtained between dictatorship and
democracy has been lost. In orthodox Marxism as long as the
dictatorship of the proletariat meant the exercise of force against
the class enemy, a meaningful distinction could be made between
dictatorship and the democracy that would prevail after the
withering away of the state and the suppression of classes. In the
context of African socialism, where there is no class enemy and
dictatorship is understood to be the state-embodied expression of
the will of the entire people, no meaningful distinction can be
made.

Kwame Nkrumah as an Ideologist of African Socialism

·   Francis Nwia Kofie Kwame Nkrumah was certainly among
the best educated of the leaders of African socialism. He gradu-
ated from Lincoln University in Pennsylvania, where his majors
were economics and sociology. He then undertook postgraduate
work in education, philosophy, and theology at the University
of Pennsylvania. During these years of intellectual maturation

in the United States, Nkrumah came under the influence of Hegel, Mazzini, Engels, and particularly Marx and Lenin. There was one other source that contributed to the complex of ideas that were to constitute Nkrumah's African socialism, a book that did more than any other to fire his enthusiasm, a book containing the thought of Marcus Garvey.[36] In the nineteen-twenties Garvey was the leader of the most spectacular Negro mass movement in the Western Hemisphere, the Universal Negro Improvement Association. It was a movement of Negro solidarity directed by a highly centralized elite and animated by a fierce and unremitting nationalism. It was in the intensity of the thought of Marcus Garvey that Nkrumah found inspiration rather than in the urbane democratic socialism of W. E. B. Du Bois. Even the democratic socialism of George Padmore, which influenced Nkrumah after his active involvement in revolutionary politics, retained all the elitist and vanguardist characteristics common to Garveyism and Leninism. African socialism, for all Nkrumah's protests, had no popular roots in Ghanaian society. Its manifestation in Ghana was the result of the deliberate imposition of a doctrine by the elite of the Convention Peoples party under the charismatic leadership of Nkrumah.[37]

For Nkrumah, as for Lenin and Mussolini, it is the politically organized elite that exercises the decisive influence, and it is this elite alone who can impose a revolutionary consciousness on the masses. This was the thesis with which Lenin began his massive revision of classical Marxism and the thesis that made Mussolini a revolutionary syndicalist. The ideology around which an organizational elite collects is important. This is particularly true where the vanguard party is composed of heterogeneous elements recruited during periods of political and economic crisis. Commitment to an explicit ideology provides the cohesiveness and solidarity necessary among the revolutionary cadre. All such vanguard organizations tend to produce a fairly elaborate doctrinal and philosophical statement.

The system, however, is rarely complete during revolutionary crisis, and such mass movements of solidarity tend to take on pragmatic postures while consolidating their position and effecting initial revolutionary legislation. The legislation effected and the original doctrinal statements that carry the movement to power are later finally synthesized into an ideological system.

Leninism, for example, was only completed after the death of Lenin. Fascism produced its mature ideology only after ten years of political power. Nkrumah's African socialism attempted such a synthesis only after about five years of undisputed power.

Nkrumah's early doctrinal statements were often at odds with each other. Originally, in his autobiography, Nkrumah mildly suggested that capitalism might prove too complicated a system for newly independent Ghana. In 1964 this had hardened to a conviction that "the presuppositions and purposes of capitalism are contrary to those of African society" and that "capitalism would be a betrayal of the personality and conscience of Africa."[38] While he early identified himself as a Christian Marxist, in 1964 he espoused an explicit materialism. Often his conception of socialism was blandly pragmatic; it was not socialism for socialism's sake, but a concern for full employment, good housing, and equal opportunity for education and cultural advancement. Still later socialism meant the control of the nation's economy under a strong, highly centralized state, in which "the party is the state and the state is the party"[39] and in which power is concentrated in the office of the executive.

Doctrinal statements are loosely articulated propositions more calculated to inspire sentiment than to inform. Not fully coherent and consistent, their implications are not immediately evident. It is always possible for one or another component faction of a revolutionary movement to interpret doctrine in such a way as to engender serious structural and organizational tensions. This is illustrated by the periodic "purging" of the Communist Party of the Soviet Union, particularly during the Stalinist period. At that time, almost the entire original leadership of the Bolshevik party was eliminated. It was equally evident in Mussolini's periodic "changing of the guard," particularly during the early years of the regime, and it was as true in National Socialist Germany with the Röhm executions of 1934 and the ultimate suppression of volkish and nationalist elements in the party.

In Nkrumah's Ghana the Convention People's party (CPP) began to show increasing signs of dissidence within the party hierarchy after 1961. Several distinct groups began to crystallize. Middle-class supporters of the CPP began to object to Nkrumah's increasing emphasis on "socialism," and the more orthodox

Marxists emphasized the importance of the class struggle in the socialist transformation of Ghana. This latter group insisted that without the concept of class struggle, scientific socialism would, in fact, be abandoned. Evidently a fuller statement of the ideals, nature, and purpose of the revolution was required. Nkrumah's *Consciencism*, published in 1965, was a volume explicitly devoted to providing that statement. *Consciencism*, coupled with his *Neo-Colonialism: The Last Stage of Capitalism*, also published in 1965, comprise the finished system of Nkrumah's African socialism.

Consciencism was apparently Nkrumah's own work, but passages, even entire sections, are literally borrowed from the work of W. E. Abraham, *The Mind of Africa*. Abraham, a professor of philosophy at the University of Ghana, was the main theoretician of the Philosophy Club, which Nkrumah organized to assist in the formulation of CPP ideology.[40] It was, in fact, to this club that Nkrumah dedicated the volume. *Consciencism* was written to answer the "abstract, 'liberal'" arguments advanced by middle-class intellectuals whose impaired "national consciousness" had led them to "accept some theory of universalism . . . expressed in vague, mellifluous terms."[41] More than that, it was to dispel the conviction, entertained by "scientific" socialists, that the class struggle was an intrinsic part of the theoretical machinery of a serious African socialism. That Nkrumah should be antiliberal is not surprising, but that he should invoke national sentiment and explicitly reject the class struggle marks a radical departure from the doctrinal postures of orthodox Leninism. Although most Leninist parties have effectively abandoned class concepts as serious theoretical and political concepts, they have almost uniformly retained the familiar Marxist terminology. Nkrumah, on the other hand, insists that classes as the orthodox Marxists have sought to define them have never existed, and do not now exist, in Africa. In traditional Africa the state serves no factional, private, or class interest. It is the welfare of the people that is all important. Based upon this conception of traditional African practice, Nkrumah identified "philosophical consciencism" with a political theory and a social-political practice that together seek to ensure that the fundamental principles of *ethics* are effective. Consciencism, in other words, is a "philosophical materialism shot through and through with ethical principles that . . . govern social practice. . . ."[42]

The emphasis on ethical principles governing the vanguard party of solidarity characterizes only latter-day Leninists. Coupled with the identification of the state and the party, it generates a conception of the state as an ethical entity mediating factional conflict, obligated to fulfill essentially pedagogical functions, to introduce an "ideology [that] seeks to bring a specific order into the total life of its society."[43] It is not economic forces that will make men socialists, as classical Marxism contended; it is the mass party "armed with an ideology" that will fashion them, and they will, in turn, create a socialist economy. In such a system socialism can hardly be conceived, as it was in classical Marxism, as "nothing but the reflex, in thought," of the conflict between the productive forces and the modes of production—a conception whereby economics absorbs politics. For Nkrumah the revolution cannot fulfill itself "without a strong and well-organized political party . . . and decisive leadership . . . to guide and lead it."[44] This constitutes Nkrumah's conception of an ideologically elite party—a party whose main function is to serve as an educative and disciplinary vehicle for government policy.

Since ideology functions in so critical a capacity in Nkrumah's philosophy, a brief synopsis of its normic model of man and society is imperative. The model it displayed had all the distinguishing traits of radical collectivism. Basic to its exposition is the recognition that Nkrumah's system rejects the conception of the individual as an "anarchic unit" (an expression he borrows from Abraham).[45] The African socialist conception of man is identified by Nkrumah as "communalistic" and is developed in considerable detail in Abraham's *The Mind of Africa*. It is a conception fundamentally opposed to any that would "emphasize individualism," for

. . . society implies a degree of organization, and the atomistic view of it is contradictory in terms. A collection of unbounded men living poor, nasty, brutish, short, and fearful lives, collected in the mere sense of a plurality, do not form a society. . . . The Western view of society . . . makes certain specified rights antecedent to the organization of society . . . [but] where duty is not explainable in terms of keeping peace between rights, that is, where the *raison d'être* of duties is not the safeguarding of rights, being in a society becomes recognized as essential to the human condition. Society becomes antecedent to rights, not rights to society.[46]

Abraham feels this conception is compatible with what he calls "paradigmatic African tradition," a notion of a

> . . . perfectly integrated and cohesive society in which men have a place somewhat comparable to the parts of a machine. . . . [for] a nation has no personality unless it is highly systematized in its attitudes and in its responses. . . . This community personality is the crux of the [paradigmatic] Akan theory of the state. The state is almost personified and takes precedence over every individual. . . . This is how the [paradigmatic] Akan society comes to be founded on duties rather than rights. . . . The absoluteness of the state's claim on the individual's obedience was . . . endorsed. The state's call on the individual was, however, not arbitrary and gratuitous but based on reflection and decision of a public kind, and tending towards the public good. . . . To go against the consensus of the people even in expression of opinion, let alone action, was a piece of rashness looked upon with scant favor. The time to express one's eccentricity was in the period of deliberation. To persist in one's individual opinion, when this deviated from the public opinion deliberately arrived at and publicized, was a piece of malice. The unity principle was very strongly cherished. . . . [The] appearance of unanimity must be preserved at the time of action. . . . The persistent expression of divergent views when a decision had been reached, was seen by the Akans, not unreasonably, as disruptive and divisive, and so weakening. It was therefore proscribed. This kind of proscription, in emphasizing collective responsibility, strengthened unity, for public decisions were equally binding on all, irrespective of positions and views antecedent to their arrival.[47]

This is the paradigm of "traditional" African political theory, which Abraham calls the basis of African socialism, the cultural elements of the African Personality that are to provide unity for African nationalism. "Africa," he insisted, "needs a constant reminder of its massively traditional nature. And its best prospects lie in utilizing this tradition and heritage."[48] Nkrumah himself defines the concept African Personality, which subtends his social and political philosophy, as that cluster of principles underlying the traditional African society. Abraham's book is devoted to an exposition of those principles. Abraham informs us that Nkrumah read the typescript of *The Mind of Africa* before its publication and apparently approved it.[49] Even if we did not know that Abraham served as Nkrumah's chief theoretician, a comparison of the texts of *Consciencism* and *The Mind of Africa* would indicate an intimate collaboration and agreement between the authors. Abraham insists that classes in African society are "cooperative, not antagonistic as in the Marxian account," while Nkrumah maintains that in African circumstances "it was impossible for classes of a Marxian kind to arise" and that "communalism in contemporary idiom" is African socialism, a "new harmony" in which "both workers and employers must pull their weight."[50] Abraham maintains that "One must admit that every society has its own forms of terrorism," and Nkrumah reveals that "it is even possible to look upon 'coercion' as a fundamental idea in society."[51] Both reject the contractualist theory of society. According to Abraham, "even a social contract cannot be agreed without some common language . . . ," and Nkrumah maintains that to argue that such a contract is the origin of society is contradictory since the contract itself is predicated on a "common language [as] . . . a social fact. . . ."[52]

The parallels are manifest throughout the texts. What is significant is that Abraham provides some operational meaning for Nkrumah's vague but constantly reiterated appeal to the African personality as the basis of his political program for Ghana and for Pan-Africa as well. It is Abraham's paradigmatic traditional African political theory that reveals the implications of Quaison-Sackey's contention that "the proponents of the African Personality are conscious of their ancient roots, and from this sense of tradition they gain their strength. . . ."[53] The criticism that the notion of African personality constitutes a "glorious myth" that does not "mean anything in practical terms"[54] fails to consider the implications of the appeal to ancient roots and tradition contained in accounts like that of Abraham. It is difficult to understand what Nkrumah means when he refers to the "egalitarianism" essential to the African personality, and the "projection of the African Personality upon international politics" seems to mean little more than the actions of the various statesmen who represent the independent states of contemporary Africa. But what the African personalty means for the internal organization of Ghana is obvious: It means the transposition of relations understood to obtain between members of the traditional family, clan, and tribe in the African past to the contemporary *nation*. It means that "the welfare of the *people* is supreme," that the objective of the Convention People's party is "the universal good of the *nation*," that "the spirit of service to the *nation* must permeate throughout our society," that an opposition will be permitted only insofar as it is "constructively critical" and does not "jeopardize the state."[55] It means that "the party and the nation are one and the same, namely: the Convention People's Party is Ghana and Ghana is the Convention People's Party."[56] It means that the party, state, and society are merged into a single, totalistic community, organically related in the service of the nation under the "power . . . concentrated in the country's leadership" and the focus of that leadership at the time was the officially proclaimed *Osagyefo*, the Redeemer, the Messiah, President of the Republic, Life Chairman and General Secretary of the Party, Chairman and Secretary of the Party's inner Central Committee, and Supreme Commander of the armed forces, Dr. Francis Nwia Kofie Kwame Nkrumah.

The projection of the African personality on Ghanaian society involved a transformation of hitherto existing individual and corporate functions. Labor unions became integral parts of the party and no longer served the factional interests of their members. Rather, they became instruments of state policy. They were no longer conceived as having evolved out of conflict between employer and employee. Their role was to work in collaboration with employers to increase the overall productivity of Ghana. The roles of farmers' councils, womens' organizations, cultural associations, and youth groups were conceived in a similar fashion. The cry was "Serve Ghana." Since the Convention People's party *was* Ghana, what was required was collective and individual service to the party. Since the party was disciplined to the obedience of the party leadership, the party leader spoke for Ghana, representing its national will. This was, of course, the language and mystique of nationalism. It represented the unifying and energizing appeal to sentiment via political formulas that gird men and factions to national purpose. Its appeal was based on myth. The myths were, in turn, supplemented by ritual. When Nkrumah appeared, the drums were beaten and libation was poured. He was the physical embodiment of the nation.

Léopold Senghor as an Ideologist of African Socialism

• Perhaps the most interesting and original of the thinkers who have contributed to the development of African socialism is Léopold Sédar Senghor, born in October, 1906, to a prosperous Serer family in what was at that time French West Africa. An intellectual and a practicing Roman Catholic, Senghor is at once an internationally recognized poet and Africanist, president of Senegal and principal theoretician of the Union Progressiste Sénégalaise (UPS). He was educated at the Catholic school at N'Gasobil and the Lycée in Dakar, and completed his education in Paris. In 1935 he joined the faculty of a *lycée* in Tours and then transferred to another in Paris. With the outbreak of World War II, he enrolled in the French Army and was captured by the Germans. At the end of the war Senghor returned to West Africa as an active politician. In 1947, together with Alioune Diop, he founded the *Présence Africaine*, a journal that was to be one of the principal vehicles for the development of his doctrinal and philosophical ideas. In 1960, when Senegal became an independent republic, Senghor was elected its first president.

In July, 1959, Senghor delivered his "Report on the Doctrine and Program of the Party," in which he provided the doctrinal outline of what was to be his version of African socialism. The Report included doctrinal elements that had appeared in his published works as early as the nineteen-thirties. But it was only with the publication of "The Theory and Practice of Senegalese Socialism" in 1962 [57] that the intellectual rationale for the belief system that characterizes contemporary Senegal was complete. This body of literature and the legislative enactments and social policies of the regime constitute the ideology of the UPS.

Although the political ideology of Senegal shares common traits with all African socialism, Senghor's views are sufficiently unique to warrant special exposition. Their uniqueness emphasizes certain implicit tendencies to be found in less explicit form among the collection of philosophical and doctrinal arguments iterated and reiterated on the African continent. For example, Senghor's explicit "revisionism" of classical Marxism and Leninism serves to document what has, in fact, transpired among the ideologues of African socialism in Ghana, Guinea, Mali, Tanzania, and the Ivory Coast.

Senghor is careful to document the sources of his revisionist tendencies. His pages are dotted with the names of standard critics of classical Marxism and Leninism. Foremost among these are Catholic critics, primarily Pierre Teilhard de Chardin and luminaries such as Pierre Bigo and Maurice Merleau-Ponty. Among the non-Catholic critics, Max Adler, Fritz Sternberg, and Lucien Goldmann receive prominent mention. Even Georg Lukacs' early work, *Geschichte und Klassenbewusstsein*, long since repudiated by Lukacs as revisionist, augments Senghor's critical apparatus.

Senghor frankly advocates a searching revision of "scientific socialism" in its classical or Leninist forms. Classical Marxism and Leninism are to be scrutinized against the background of contemporary science and African realities, and their infirm elements are to be abandoned in the service of a Senegalese socialism dedicated to the new nation.

The principal and immediate focus of Senghor's criticism of classical Marxism turns on its scientific pretentions and the determinism that it entails. Senghor maintains that "the major contradiction of Marxism is that it presents itself as a *science*, whereas, despite its denials, it is based on an ethic." As an ethic it is essentially nonscientific. "Science notes facts and their relations; it explains, it does not demand. It cannot pass from a factual to a value judgment." Marxism, on the other hand, seeks to implement values, to level normative judgments, and to advocate specific courses of action. Senghor conceives a radical tension between Marxism's scientific determinism and its ethical advocacy. A strict determinism would leave no foothold for moral injunctions; it would sacrifice mind to matter, freedom to determinism, and man to things. A consistent revolutionary policy, Senghor insists, requires that men be "animated by a *conscious and practical revolutionary will*. . . . [which is] above all . . . the elaboration of a morality, of a new *ethic*." Such a revolutionary ethic is an ideology, and "ideologies are crystallized spiritual products." On the basis of this reasoning, Senghor can maintain that "it is spirit, in the final analysis, that judges and transcends the material determinants that have formed it. *Priority* of matter, if you will, but *primacy* of Spirit."[58]

The revolutionary will finds expression in an ethic, a social and political *myth*, around which men and women organize their lives. Free enterprise, democracy, and communism are just such political myths. They permit the orientation necessary for the fulfillment of moral ends. It is the fulfillment of these ends that make life *human* life, for "man . . . lives truly and solely on the myths that are his spiritual nourishment."[59] Senghor's distrust of scientific socialism is not so much a consequence of his reservations concerning its truth claims as it is a fear that such an account will engender a doctrine of resignation. The rigid determinism of classical Marxism, he maintains, threatens human freedom. Only the political and ethical myth restores that freedom, for it alone is the stimulant to action, allowing the assumption of revolutionary responsibility and the discharge of duty.

Senghor's revision of classical Marxism is surprisingly similar to that of the revolutionary syndicalism of Sorel, who saw in the political myth the necessary organizational and ethical adjunct of the socialist program. Senghor's critique of classical Marxism parallels that of Sorel, Pareto, Mosca, and Michels, who conceived social dynamics in terms of a complex interrelationship of variables among which economic or material factors influence but do not determine the course of development. All these men considered the political or ethical consciousness of human agents a dynamic determinant that could not be reduced to strictly economic forces. Such a consciousness is animated by a functional myth, a political or ethical formula that sustains and directs collective effort. The parallelism is not restricted to the functional role of political or ethical myths. For Pareto, Mosca, and Michels, as well as Sorel, the animating myth was the product of a strategic elite who bring to the elemental energy of the masses a consciousness of purpose.

This conception of political elitism is specifically espoused by Senghor.

The problem . . . is to awaken "dormant energies." . . . In a word, we must awaken the national conscience. . . . Understanding this, the

Senegalese Government decided to awaken the consciousness of the masses. . . . But the Government cannot and must not do it all. It must be guided and helped by the party. . . . Our party must be the consciousness of the masses. . . . It must guide the masses. The consciousness of the masses, who lack education and culture, still remains confused, lost in the fog of animal needs. It does not rise to the level of "political consciousness, a superior form of consciousness." This can only reach the masses from the outside, from the intellectuals.[60]

The conception of the vanguard party is, of course, common to both Leninism and Fascism, but the employment of political mythology relates Senghor's formulations more intimately to those of Mussolini rather than to those of Lenin. The emphatic espousal of ethical purpose, the explicit rejection of materialism, and the adherence to an epistemological and ethical idealism make Senghor's socialism far more akin to philosophical and doctrinal Fascism than Leninism. Gentile insisted that Fascism acquired from revolutionary syndicalism "a faith in a moral reality, purely ideal (or mythical, as was said), for which one lived and died and sacrificed. . . ."[61]

The political or ethical myth for Sorel was that of the "general strike" and the proletarian revolution. It was only the advent of World War I that precipitated the crisis in syndicalism that transformed revolutionary proletarian syndicalism into the national syndicalism that became one of the principal doctrinal components of Fascism. It was, as we have seen, the circumstances surrounding that war that forced Mussolini to recognize the insistent sentiment of nationality against all the established prejudices of international Marxism. Thereafter the concept of the nation took theoretical and analytic precedence over the concept of class. For Senghor the process has been surprisingly similar. The struggle for Senegalese independence made him acutely aware of the theoretical and practical importance of the concept and sentiment of nationality.

Nation is the first reality of the twentieth century. . . . Marx did not pay sufficient attention to . . . the *Nation*, which is not effaced by class. . . . If the creator of scientific socialism returned to this earth, he would perceive with amazement that . . . the concept of *Nation* [is a living reality] in the twentieth century.[62]

The concept of the nation has become so prominent in Senghor's political thought that the existence of classes and the class struggle is specifically denied. What exists is the nation. Within this society, it is the group that is stressed, and the emphasis is on community effort and solidarity rather than on the autonomy of the individual. Senegalese socialism is, in fact, "built on national values. . . . [The] nation must inspire all its members, all individuals, with faith in nationhood. . . ." This faith is the "national spirit," the sentiment of nationality that suppresses parochial or class divisions and finds expression in the state. "[The state] fulfills the nation's will and ensures its permanence. In domestic affairs, it . . . shapes the individuals into the mold of the archetype. . . . For only this action can make of our various populations a *People,* that is to say, a *Community* ("*Communauté*"), where each individual will identify himself with the collective whole and vice versa."[63]

This conception of the relationship between the people, the nation, and the state permits not only the familiar substitutions that identify the individual and the community with the state, but also conduces to an assessment of social change that makes politics a prime, if not the sole, determinant. Senghor can then argue that "socialism is essentially politics, that is, an art of governing men. . . ."[64] How far removed this is from the socialism of classical Marxism is indicated by comparing it to Engels' conviction that socialism obtains when the government of persons is replaced by the administration of things. Senghor's insistence on the primacy of politics follows from his assessment of the role and function of nationality in the organization of society. He maintains that a strong party is the best vehicle to arouse nationalist sentiment. This sentiment is the prime requisite to animate and sustain a "truly national revolution" that would unite all elements of the population in the effort to bridge the gap between proletarian and capitalist nations.[65] For Senghor, the historical protagonists of the twentieth century are not classes, but nations.

Senghor's entire rationale literally follows that of Italian Fascism's national syndicalism. In 1927 the prime characteristic of Fascist syndicalism was described as its nationalist character. Fascist syndicalism abjured the class struggle and advocated a collaboration of productive categories in the service of national interest.[66] The distinction Fascists drew between themselves and socialism of whatever sort turned chiefly on their substitution of the formula "interclass solidarity and national struggle" for the Marxist "international solidarity and class struggle," for chief among the elements of Fascist social theory was the conviction that the struggle between nations is more serious and critical than the class struggle. These are convictions central to African socialism in its various forms and specific to Senghor's social and political philosophy.

Fascist syndicalists argued that Italy needed industrialization in order to reduce the gap between itself and the favored nations of Europe. They maintained that the doctrine of class struggle served only to impair Italy's position in the contemporary world and impoverish still further its laboring classes. They demanded abandonment of the doctrine of class struggle and disciplined collaboration of the productive categories in a concerted effort to augment the gross national product. Trade unions were therefore to be incorporated into the state; they were no longer to serve as instruments of self-defense in the fratricidal struggle between capital and labor but were to implement state policy.[67] A similar process and a similar supporting rationale developed in Senegal. The UPS began its program of domesticating the labor movement immediately after the 1958 referendum on national independence. The dominant party in Senegal demanded that labor's loyalty be shifted from a class to a national plane and that the role of the union be changed to educating and rallying the workers behind a given governmental policy rather than defending their particular interests. This is a position commonly held in African socialist states. Labor unions, in effect, cannot operate in contradiction to the interests of the majority of the people.

It is the task of the party to instill in the various productive categories the consciousness of national responsibility and discipline. In order to effect its purpose, the party requires a strong state apparatus, for the state "is primarily a means to achieve the nation. Political history teaches that the lack of state organization is a weakness that brings on the fatal distintegration of the nation."[68] It was by just such conceptions that Fascism sought to distinguish itself from Marxist socialism in whatever guise. Fascists regarded their conceptions of people, nation, and state and their interrelationships as a unique contribution to contemporary social and political philosophy.

For Marxists, whose theoretical machinery was economic interpretation and whose unit of analysis was class, the talk of mobilizing the energies of the people in the service of the nation under the direction of a political elite armed with myths could only represent a complete betrayal of socialism. One would expect this sort of judgment to be tendered particularly in a country such as Senegal, whose population is riven by strong quasi-caste systems that have produced a government composed almost exclusively of members of the noble castes. In 1963 all but three of the seventy-nine UPS deputies were of noble origin. Irrespective of the fact that over 80 percent of the Senegalese are peasants, there are few farmers among the leadership of the dominant party. This suggests that the hierarchy of the party and public office are at least partially closed to members of the lower castes and to peasants. Criticism of the dominant party (which for some time now has been the *sole* party) is permitted only within the limits of what that party itself considers to be "constructive." The dominant party has used emergency powers and special courts to outlaw political opposition and has maintained an effective program of press censorship. All this, coupled with the fact that there is literally no nationalization in Senegal, suggests that its "socialism" is of a singular sort: a nationalist, idealist, elitist, and statist socialism that explicitly rejects the economic interpretation of history, renounces the class struggle, and insists that national faith and social myths are more necessary for man than food.

More interesting, and perhaps more ominous, is Senghor's conception of the central myth of Senegalese socialism: Negritude. It is one of the earliest component elements of Senghor's socialism, having been formulated at least as early as the mid-thirties. With the publication of his "Ce que l'homme noir apporte" in 1939, Senghor laid down the outline of this conception. For him culture is the product of the "reciprocal interaction of race, tradition and environment," with African culture conditioned by a specific "Negro style," the manifest expression of the "Negro soul."[69] Senghor speaks regularly of a Negro soul, of its requirements and its achievements. For him culture is that which is "rooted in native soil and expressed by a race."[70] Senghor provides a partial account of the manifestations of the Negro race soul. The Negro is, according to him, emotional, as the Hellenes were rational. The European possesses a "reasoning eye" while the Negro is given to "the reason of touch," for the "Negro African is . . . a pure field of sensations. . . . European reasoning is analytical, discursive by utilization [while] Negro African reasoning is intuitive by participation." Thus the foundation of Negro African epistemology is "mystic emotion" that rejects "the abstract analysis on the European pattern" and employs "analogous imagery, the metaphor. . . . [the] symbolic short cut in its sensitive, sensual qualities. . . ."[71] For this reason the Negro is fundamentally religious, given to what Senghor calls the mystic "reasoning embrace," which infuses the individual in an ascending series of concentric circles of being. The foundation of the ethnic personality of the Negro African is a religious feeling of participation, of communion, in which all members of the community fuse in a "single soul," in a "high ideal of solidarity in which all commune."[72] The individual works for his community and finds in that labor the fulfillment of himself, a self that transcends the restrictions of time and place, fusing itself with the hosts of his ancestors and leading to ultimate union with God.[73] Only through such a process can the individual become a person, the corporate personality that is the product of his family, his corporation, his fatherland, and his nation. Outside such a communion the individual is not a person. Senghor maintains that man cannot live or realize himself except in and through society. Thus,

Negro African society puts more stress on the group than on the individual, more on *solidarity* than on the activity and needs of the individual, more on the *communion* of persons than on their autonomy. . . . The member of the community society . . . feels . . . thinks . . . can develop his potential, his originality, only in and by society, in union with all other men. . . .[74]

Senghor recognizes the affinities this conception of man as a communal being shares with the social and political philosophy of the early Marx. But Marx failed to appreciate the significance of nationality, and Senghor, as a consequence, musters Hegel, the philosopher of the nation-state, to supplement his exposition. Senghor's account is, in fact, Hegelian, neo-Hegelian, almost Gentilean—with one major difference. Senghor *insists* on the importance of race in his account. He chides Marx for having failed to assess the importance of race as a historical and cultural determinant. Because of this shortcoming, Senghor maintained, classical Marxism developed all the characteristics of a monocausal theory of historical development that fails to accord itself to Negro African reality. That reality is a spiritual patrimony, a world view rooted in the character of the ethnic personality of the race. Senghor is quite specific in stating that the disposition to construe the world in this way is more than induced. It is at least in part hereditary. He talks of the constancy of Negro psychic characteristics, a permanence of Negro African characteristics, not only physical but also psychical, that persist irrespective of miscegenation and varied environment.[75] He then provides a list of Negro psychic traits, which includes reflex spontaneity, intuitive rather than analytic thinking, a sense of rhythm, and an insistent empathic sense that characterizes him as a communal being, and he contends that these traits are substantially hereditary. As a consequence, Senghor maintains, races are not equal but complementary.[76] Negroes have a "different temperament, a different soul." He argues that Negro Africans have something to contribute in the "interfecundation" of peoples that constitutes universal history—a contribution that is unique and that is the consequence of the integration of European socialism, Negro African nationalism, and "the values of Negritude, defined as the common denominator of all Negro Africans. . . ."[77] With Chardin, Senghor insists that "fully conscious nations are needed for a total earth," and he adds that "a nation that refuses to keep its rendezvous with history, that does not believe that it bears a unique message— that nation is finished, ready to be placed in a museum."[78]

There is no way to draw out the full implications of Senghor's "antiracist" racism. At one point he speaks of Negritude as a "totality of civilizing values. . . . It is not racism, but culture" and at another of culture as being "rooted in a native soil and expressed by a race." Elsewhere he objects to the Negro

African adopting political, economic, social, or cultural institutions "that are the natural fruits of the geography and history of another race," and then he suggests that the values of Negritude are the common denominator of all Negro Africans "whatever their race. . . ."![79] In what sense a race comes to express itself in a culture, and why one should abjure institutions produced by another race, and how one can be a Negro African of *whatever* race, are problems difficult to resolve. But since Senghor maintains that one of the values of Negritude is a special method of cognition that is intuitive and mystic and that "transcends the principles of identity, noncontradiction and the 'excluded middle,'" rejecting "abstract analysis on the European pattern," couching itself in "analogous imagery" and "metaphor," these apparent obscurities may exemplify his epistemological method.[80] Be that as it may, it is, as a consequence, difficult to divine the implications of Senghor's qualified racism. Certainly, there is no evidence yet that it is malevolent. It seems to be employed as a political formula, a unifying myth. It has the virtue of possessing high emotional salience but is impaired, as all myths are impaired, by a studied imprecision, a lack of specificity, a tendency to overgeneralization. Thus, the myth of Negritude can be employed in a variety of tasks. It would seem that the task in the service of which it is employed determines the character of the myth. When Senghor was attempting to realize the Mali Federation, he spoke of the "mystique of the Federation" that was to animate the people. On other occasions he has spoken of the myth of nationhood and on still other occasions of Negritude as providing the foundation for Pan-Africanism.

Apparently, only Senghor is capable of explicating the tactical and strategic implications of the myth of Negritude. Since whatever claims Senghor makes for such applications can only be licensed by an appeal to "Negro African cognition," unembarrassed by contradiction and rooted in metaphor, it seems that he is forever insulated against telling criticism. What all this will bring to Senegal in the future is, of course, impossible to predict. But whatever it is, it will certainly not be any form of socialism that would be recognizable to Marx or even to Lenin. Mussolini, on the other hand, might find it a bad copy of the Fascist state.

Conclusions

• It seems obvious that African socialism, as exemplified in nationalist mass movements of solidarity, elitism, and statism, is a contemporary variant of Mussolini's Fascism. That this has not been generally appreciated is the result of several considerations. First, and perhaps foremost, is the fact that classical Marxism, Leninism, and Fascism all share a common normic model of man, a collectivist or communitarian conception of man that conceives the fulfillment of human personality as a function of social interaction. Man outside society is nothing. What Tom Mboya describes as the basic tenets of socialism—the "dictum that man is a social (political) animal which has no potency and no life outside the society," that "society is an organic thing with individuals playing the role of cells in the organism"[81] —are the basic tenets of Italian Fascism as well. African socialists refer to these theses as "traditional" in Africa and well they may be, but they are also at least as old as Plato and receive their full modern expression in the philosophy of Hegel. In Hegel, Marx, and Gentile these theses are elaborately developed. In African socialism they are conceived as essential traits of the African Personality or Negritude. These "socialist" tenets are in fact common to all contemporary radical social and political ideologies. They are fundamental to National Socialism and apartheid as well as to Leninism and fascism.

That African socialism is not a variant of classical Marxism is obvious. By the turn of the century, classical Marxism had ceased to be a viable social and political ideology. Its major thesis, historical materialism, underwent massive revision at the hands of both Lenin and Mussolini. Lenin insisted that the revolutionary consciousness could only be introduced by a self-selected and self-perpetuating elite of declassed intellectuals. Mussolini introduced a similar conception of the vanguard party; but, under the influence of Pareto, Mosca, and Sorel, characterized this elite as infused with a moral or ethical voluntarism that found expression in the form of political myths calculated to energize the masses. It was Mussolini who insisted that "mankind has need of a creed," for a "faith that moves mountains." Senghor advances the same contention—and Quaison-Sackey of

Ghana contends that it is faith that moves people and nations. It is evident that the form of vanguardism African socialism has made its own was first expressly formulated by Mussolini prior to World War I. Even contemporary Leninism, which has increasingly taken on the attributes of fascism, has not been able to bring itself to explicitly adopt such conceptions. Leninism remains an inconsistent and half-articulated fascism, a fascism whose practical measures are clearly at fisticuffs with its doctrinal and theoretical rationale. African socialism has, on the other hand, simply adopted with little qualification the vanguardism of Mussolini's Fascism. The prominence given to ethics as an independent determinant, so much at variance with classical Marxism and Lenin's Leninism, is ample evidence of this. The fact that African socialism denies that it is "proletarian" in any sense of the term is further confirmation. The vanguard elite simply informs the elemental consciousness of the masses. Thus, in Mali the unitary party seeks to "create a national consciousness within the . . . masses. . . . Subsequently [it] must use this national sentiment, to extract from it its constructive content and orient it toward collective tasks. . . . [It] must progressively inculcate the sense of collective responsibility demanded by our new objectives. . . ."[82] The recurrent and systematic appeals to political myths and faith, to national sentiment, national values, and national solidarity, to discipline, sacrifice, and responsibility, coupled with the rejection of class as a theoretical unit of analysis, all characterize African socialism as fascist rather than Leninist.

Even Margaret Roberts' suggestion that African socialism is socialist because Africa's "claims of the have-nots in relation to the haves" appeals to the "emotional heart of socialism" does not constitute a serious objection to identifying African socialism as a variant of Italian Fascism.[83] Fascism conceived Italy to be a proletarian nation struggling against the have nations of the world for a place in the sun. That African socialists make nations historical protagonists bespeaks a greater kinship to fascism than it does to any form of socialism. Such a conception was central to Fascist syndicalism and only began to manifest itself as a feature of Leninism after 1924 when Stalin began to advance the thesis of socialism in one country. But even today orthodox Leninism does not accept the doctrinal and theoretical legitimacy of the doctrine of class and productive category (occupation) collaboration in the service of national interests. The rejection of the necessity of class struggle and the advocacy of class collaboration was long identified by Marxists of all and sundry sorts as the species traits of Mussolini's Fascism and an explicit betrayal of socialism. Yet just these features characterize the social and political doctrine of African socialism.

The identification of the nation with the people, an identification that effaces class distinctions, was yet another feature of fascist syndicalism now characterizing African socialism. This identification permits the vanguard party—the unitary, elitist national party first fully articulated in fascist doctrine—to identify itself with the nation and the people. Latter-day Leninism only grudgingly advances such a thesis. It is a posture forced upon it by events and not a derivative of any doctrinal or theoretical assumptions. African socialism, on the other hand, freely and openly advances and defends such a conception. Unencumbered by the necessity of making constant and fruitless references to class, class interest, and class priorities, the African socialist, like the fascist, can identify his party with the nation, the state, and the people. The *parti unique* of Mali, the Union Soudanaise, describes the relationship thusly:

> People in Africa and in the world know that when the Party and the Government take a position, when Modibo Keita speaks, all the Malian people are unanimously behind them. The deep harmony which reigns between the People and the Party, between the People and the Government, between the Party and the Government, finally between the People and the Chief of State, are the elements which give to all our national and international positions their true weight.[84]

At one time its conception of the state was sufficient to distinguish fascism from any form of socialism. The thesis that the state would wither away under socialism was conceived as central to the Marxist world view. Fascists conceived the state as "integral," as "total," the concrete expression of a people's will against which no private, parochial, or economic interest could prevail. It was the whole that gave substance to its component parts. As a consequence it was Fascist syndicalism that transformed the Italian trade union movement into an agency for the imple-

mentation of state economic and productionist policy, a transformation that occurred in the Soviet Union only with the
Congress of 1921, when labor unions were no longer conceived
as defense organs of proletarian interest but as agencies of state
policy. African socialists have simply opted for the fascist position. The rejection of the legitimacy of proletarian interests as
distinct from national interest and proletarian leadership as distinct from the leadership of a national and nationalist elite—
the insistence upon a strong, highly centralized, hierarchically
organized, and omnicompetent one-party state charged with the
obligation of creating a sense of national community—is doc-
trinally indistinguishable from fascism.

Because many of its ideologists employ Leninist vocabulary,
African socialism is sometimes conceived as a variant of Leninism. That there are, in fact, substantive similarities is only the
consequence of the rapid disintegration of Leninism as a coherent ideology. By 1933 Mussolini suggested, with considerable
justification, that Leninism in the Soviet Union had abandoned
Marx and was applying the principles of fascism. Contemporary
Leninism has, for all intents and purposes, adopted the most
essential doctrinal postures of fascism. This has been done, of
course, at the cost of considerable ideological tension. African
socialism, on the other hand, has simply rejected those philosophical and doctrinal encumbrances that embarrass Leninism
and has espoused a frank, if ideologically primitive, fascism.
That its ideology is primitive results from African socialism's
dependence upon notions like the "African personality," the
sum of "traditional values," to support its rationale. Abraham
argues as though his description of "paradigmatic Akan society"
provides an ideological foundation for Pan-Africanism. Joseph
Ki-Zerbo refers to African personality as the "cultural or emotional base of Pan-Africanism" and charges the state with the
responsibility of "recapturing" the "traditional forms."[85]

This appeal to the values of traditional African society has
much to recommend it as a political myth, but little merit as a
justificatory argument for contemporary political practice. Igor
Kopytoff has considered these attempts on the part of African
Socialists and Pan-Africanists to define the African personality,
upon which their political conceptions rest, in terms of the study
of local groups, either the Akan by Abraham or the Baluba by

Tempels (to whom Senghor regularly refers). Kopytoff's qualified judgment is that these efforts constitute little more than confusion. To attempt to project the findings established among the Baluba or the Akan upon the entire subcontinent is to court error.[86] To suggest that "solidarity" is intrinsic to the ostensible "personality" of a people is so rank a simplification as not to merit serious assessment. Even if solidarity tended to characterize familial, clan, or tribal relationships in agrarian communities, there is no evidence that the Negro African can extend this sense of solidarity to include an industrially emergent and correspondingly complex nation unless African socialists are seriously convinced that the people of tropical Africa possess a hereditary collectivist or communitarian disposition. Whatever community solidarity exists among tribes of pastoralists cannot be predicted to obtain among detribalized and urbanized individuals. African socialist ideologists seem at least intuitively aware of such problems. They entertain a revealing variation in the verbs they employ in referring to the African personality with which they are preoccupied. Some insist that it must be "projected," others that it be "asserted," while still others intend to "establish" or "promote" it. For Senghor, Negritude is to be projected and asserted, for as Ezekial Mphahlele indicates, it is "something biological." For Nkrumah, African personality was something to be established, fostered, or promoted. In either case, it is a slender thread on which to hang an ideological system.

Only Senghor, with his recourse to the personalism of Catholic philosophers, has sought to produce a mature ideology. In its kinship with the "positive existentialism" of Gentile, Senghor's social philosophy, of all the forms of African socialism, manifests the greatest affinities to paradigmatic fascist ideology.

The one principal programmatic commitment that would seem to draw a *prima facie* distinction between fascism and African socialism is the latter's commitment to continental unity. African socialism is committed to Pan-Africanism, the political and economic unification of the African continent. But the conception of continental unity was not, in principle, alien to fascism. As early as 1930, fascist theoreticians had begun to speak of an *Internazionale fascista*, a Pan-Fascism, a union of kindred European states. The theme was reiterated by Fascists in various parts of Europe. By 1935 Italian Fascists maintained that Fascism recognized that the ravages of war and depression in Europe could only be undone by *international* reconstruction, and they argued as a consequence that Fascism was both patriotic and international at the same time. By 1940 such conceptions were incorporated in authoritative doctrinal expositions of Fascist "imperialism." Imperialism was understood to imply the expansion of a moral doctrine or culture beyond the nation that was its source until it came to animate a collection of racially and culturally related (and geographically contiguous) nations. Thus there were at least two conceptions of Fascist imperialism: one was a "moral" or "cultural" Pan-Europeanism originally conceived as a consequence of treaty agreement, and the second, a more familiar "colonial" imperialism, which was justified in terms of a "civilizing mission" on the African continent.

Of particular interest in the present context is the moral, or cultural, Pan-Europeanism, because it is the analogue of Pan-Africanism. It found ultimate expression in the doctrine of an ethnarchic imperialism *("l'etnarchia imperiale")* that included a federation of European nations retaining, in principle, adequate room for their individual "identities" or "personalities." Such a Pan-European federation could include a polyarchic directorate that would provide Europe with the minimum political unity that Mussolini insisted, as early as 1933, was necessary for its contemporary viability.[87] By 1942 Fascist political and cultural journals referred constantly to a European consortium of nations sharing national, cultural, and ethnic affinities, dedicated to the furtherance of continental regional interests in what was called a "European regime of federal union." One of the principal doctrinal planks of the Fascist Republican party founded in November, 1943, was "the realization of a European community, with a federation of all nations" dedicated to "the abolition of the capitalist system; the struggle against the world plutocracies and the development, for the benefit of European peoples and of the natives, of Africa's natural resources, with absolute respect for those peoples . . . who . . . have already achieved civil and national organization."[88]

Pan-Africanism harbors all the paradoxes and complexity of Fascist ethnarchic imperialism—Pan-Europeanism. It harbors an intercontinental ideal based on passionate nationalism. The founders of Pan-Africanism dedicated themselves to an ideology of continental unity, nationalism (orientated toward political independence but with racialist overtones), and socialism that has greater intellectual affinities to mature fascism than to any variant of Marxist socialism. For the Monrovian group of African states, the political unity of Africa must respect "the legal equality" and the "self-determination" of the several component states, states that "can be as separate as the fingers in their domestic affairs, but . . . united as the fist in matters of external and general concern" in an association in which national sovereignty and continental federation were to be reconciled.[89] The Brazzaville group has advocated a union "within the framework of national diversity and of the personalities of each state."[90] Senghor has called for a federation of states sharing ethnic and cultural affinities ("uniting populations whose natural characteristics—climate, soil, blood, language and customs, art, and literature—are similar") in an echo of "ethnarchic imperialism."[91] Even for Nyerere Pan-Africanism can only be expressed through national sovereignty. Nkrumah's advocacy of continental suprastate political unification found little response in Africa and still less practical implementation. The failure of the Mali Federation and the efforts at East African integration are object lessons in the difficulties attending any attempt at supranationalism. But the purpose here is not to assess the prospects of Pan-Africanism nor to analyze the tensions involved in Pan-African nationalism; it is only necessary to indicate that they reflect the same difficulties and tensions harbored by the ethnarchic imperialism of Pan-European Fascism.

Even granting the vast differences in historical, economic, and political circumstances in Africa, the ideology of African socialism seems to display all the vices and virtues, all the potential dangers and dynamic qualities of Italian Fascism. Fascists sought, through a revolutionary mass movement of solidarity, to make of a "geographic expression" a united and integrated nation-state. To effect this end, a unitary party, armed with a unitarist ideology, identified itself with the state and with the nation, permitting opposition only when it was in the national interest. Fascist racism as an adjunct to its general ideology of national solidarity was originally benign and only developed its malevolent features under the political pressure of association with National Socialist Germany. Fascism's Pan-Europeanism, in turn, ultimately sought to effect its purpose through force. All these elements obtain within the complex ideology of African socialism and Pan-Africanism. Under present historical and political circumstances its racism and supranational or federationist aspirations are essentially benign, but they do remain a potential source of continental if not worldwide threat. The presence in Africa of large non-Negroid populations, occupying as they do privileged status, is a real source of prospective violence. That the racial mythology of African socialism, with its exalted sense of racial achievement, should become a racial chauvinism under special circumstances is a prospect that cannot be lightly dismissed. That the search for African unity may ultimately seek recourse to a military solution is a real possibility.[92]

African socialist states evidence all the doctrinal and programmatic features of paradigmatic fascism. As they mature economically they will, in all probability, assume its more specific features. In this respect it is instructive that Ghana's parliament, immediately prior to Nkrumah's ouster, organized itself along "corporative" lines with its membership tending to represent productive categories rather than geographic areas. This course seems predictable in the context of a national and totalitarian state structure.

That Marx and Lenin are frequently referred to in its doctrinal literature should not obscure the fact that African socialism is an ideological variant of fascism. Significant in this regard is the increasing emphasis given to Hegel and even to Mazzini; nor should the influence of Marcus Garvey be overlooked. Garvey was among the first to influence Pan-Africanism and African socialism, and it was Garvey who proclaimed, "We were the first Fascists. We had disciplined men, women, and children in training for the liberation of Africa. The black masses saw that in this extreme nationalism lay their only hope, and readily supported it."[93]

Notes

1. See *Ghana: Second Development Plan, 1959–1964* (Accra: Government Printer, n.d.), p. 18; "Economic Notes: Guinea Government Relaxes Code for Foreign Investors," *Africa Report,* VII (April, 1962), 17; "Economic Notes: United States and Guinea Sign Investment and Aid Agreements," *Africa Report,* VII (June, 1962), 9; C. Morse, "The Economics of African Socialism," in W. H. Friedland and C. G. Rosberg, Jr. (eds.), *African Socialism [AFS]* (Stanford: Stanford University, 1964), pp. 35–37.

2. G. Padmore, "A Guide to Pan-African Socialism," *AFS,* p. 224; L. S. Senghor, *On African Socialism [AS]* (London: Pall Mall, 1964), pp. 9f.

3. *AS,* pp. 3, 25. Italics supplied.

4. K. Nkrumah, *I Speak of Freedom: A Statement of African Ideology* (New York: Praeger, 1961), p. 169.

5. W. H. Friedland and C. G. Rosberg, Jr., "The Anatomy of African Socialism," *AFS,* p. 8.

6. G. Padmore, *Pan-Africanism or Communism?* (London: Dobson, 1956), p. 181; see also K. Nkrumah, *Africa Must Unite* (New York: Praeger, 1964), p. 53.

7. S. Kouyate as cited in "Dakar Colloquium: Search for a Definition," *Africa Report,* VIII (May, 1963), 16, 17.

8. *Ibid.,* p. 17.

9. *AS,* pp. 12, 25.

10. C. A. Kane, "First Steps Toward a Planned Economy," *Europe Outremer* (Paris), September, 1962.

11. K. Nkrumah, *Consciencism: Philosophy and Ideology for De-Colonization and Development with Particular Reference to the African Revolution* (New York: Monthly Review, 1965), p. 57. Reprinted by permission of Heinemann Educational Books Ltd.

12. *Some Essential Features of Nkrumaism* (New York: International, 1965), pp. 92, 105.

13. Nkrumah, *Africa Must Unite,* p. 123; Padmore, "Guide . . . ," *AFS,* pp. 233f.

14. J. Nyerere, "Ujamaa: The Basis of African Socialism," *AFS,* p. 243.

15. Nkrumah, *Africa Must Unite,* p. 124.

16. *Chabi Mama* (Dahomey), Mimeographed Colloquium Paper, pp. 12f., cited in A. Zolberg, "The Dakar Colloquium: The Search for a Doctrine," *AFS,* p. 125.

17. Nkrumah, *Africa Must Unite,* p. 128; *Some Essential Features,* p. 93.

18. Nkrumah, *Consciencism,* pp. 59f.

19. K. Nkrumah, *Guide to Party Action* (Accra: Central Committee of the CPP, 1962) , p. 8.

20. See W. J. Foltz, "Senegal," in J. S. Coleman and C. G. Rosberg, Jr. (eds.) , *Political Parties and National Integration in Tropical Africa* (Berkeley: University of California, 1964) , p. 38.

21. J. Nyerere, "Africa's Place in the World," an address at Wellesley College, February 17, 1960. See J. Nyerere, "Will Democracy Work in Africa?" *Africa Report,* V (February, 1960) , 4.

22. Nyerere, "Africa's Place. . . ."

23. M. Dia as cited in "Dakar Colloquium . . . ," [*AFS*], p. 18.

24. *AS,* pp. 49, 109, 147.

25. Nkrumah, *Africa Must Unite,* pp. 126f.

26. Nkrumah, *I Speak of Freedom,* p. 188.

27. *AS,* p. 56; Nyerere, "Ujamaa," *AFS,* p. 245. See also R. Schachter, "Single-Party Systems in West Africa," *American Political Science Review,* LV (1961) , 294–307.

28. J. Nyerere, "The Task Ahead of Our African Trade Unions," as cited by W. H. Friedland, "Basic Social Trends," *AFS,* p. 28; see also A. Segal, "Where is Tanzania Heading?" *Africa Report,* X (October, 1965) , 15.

29. "Socialist Parties in Africa," *The Spark* (Accra) , March 8, 1963.

30. W. H. Friedland, "Four Sociological Trends in African Socialism," *Africa Report,* VIII (May, 1963) , 10; see also G. W. Shepherd, *The Politics of African Nationalism* (New York: Praeger, 1962) , p. 92.

31. *AS,* p. 56; J. Nyerere, "The National Ethic," *African Report,* X (October, 1965) , 25.

32. Nkrumah, *Consciencism,* p. 57.

33. *AS,* p. 53. See also "Blueprint for a One Party Democracy," *Africa Report,* X (October, 1965) , 23f.; G. Carter, *Independence for Africa* (New York: Praeger, 1960) , p. 131; Nkrumah, *Africa Must Unite,* p. 73.

34. D. E. Apter, *Ghana in Transition* (New York: Atheneum, 1963) , p. xiv.

35. S. Touré, "The Role of the Party," in R. Emerson and M. Kilson (eds.) , *Awakening of Africa* (Engelwood Cliffs, N. J.: Prentice-Hall, 1965) , p. 132.

36. A. J. Garvey, *Garvey and Garveyism* (Kingston: Garvey, 1963) , p. 159.

37. C. Legum, "Socialism in Ghana: A Political Interpretation," *AFS*, pp. 133f.

38. Nkrumah, *Consciencism*, p. 74.

39. *The Party*, July, 1959, as cited in Legum, "Socialism in Ghana . . . , " *AFS*, p. 140.

40. Legum, "Socialism in Ghana . . . ," *AFS*, p. 155. See W. E. Abraham, *The Mind of Africa* (Chicago: University of Chicago, 1962).

41. Nkrumah, *Consciencism*, p. 3.

42. Nkrumah, *Some Essential Features*, p. 116; see also K. Nkrumah, *The Old and the New: Law in Africa* (Accra: Ministry of Information and Broadcasting, January 4, 1962) and *Consciencism*, pp. 69, 97f.

43. Nkrumah, *Consciencism*, p. 59.

44. *Some Essential Features*, p. 87; Nkrumah, *Africa Must Unite*, pp. 50, 128.

45. Nkrumah, *Consciencism*, p. 62. Compare with Abraham, *op. cit.*, p. 183. Nkrumah states this: "The individual is not an anarchic unit. He lives in orderly surroundings, and the achieving of these orderly surroundings calls for methods both explicit and subtle." Abraham makes this: "The individual is not an anarchic unit. He lives in orderly surroundings, and the effecting of the orderliness of his surroundings calls for a degree of subjection and regimentation, where education has not inculcated the desired responses."

46. Abraham, *op. cit.*, pp. 21, 24f., 26.

47. *Ibid.*, pp. 52, 64, 65, 75f., 153, 194f.

48. *Ibid.*, p. 188.

49. *Ibid.*, p. 10.

50. *Ibid.*, p. 134; Nkrumah, *Consciencism*, pp. 69f., *I Speak of Freedom*, p. 171.

51. Abraham, *op. cit.*, p. 182; Nkrumah, *Consciencism*, p. 60.

52. Abraham, *op. cit.*, p. 25; Nkrumah, *Consciencism*, p. 60.

53. A. Quaison-Sackey, *Africa Unbound: Reflections of an African Statesman* (London: Deutsch, 1963), p. 49.

54. E. Mphahlele, *The African Image* (New York: Praeger, 1962), pp. 19f.

55. Nkrumah, *Africa Must Unite*, pp. 123, 124, 68, 66.

56. Nkrumah, *I Speak of Freedom*, p. 209.

57. Contained in *AS*, pp. 105–65.

58. *AS*, pp. 83, 36, 130, 117, 84; see also pp. 26, 32f., 43–45, 47, 55, 76, 83f.

59. *Ibid.*, p. 52. See also L. Senghor, "Eléménts constitutifs d'une civilisation d'inspiration Négro-Africaine," *Liberté I: Négritude et Humanisme* (Paris: Editions du Seuil, 1964), p. 284.

60. *AS*, p. 159.

61. G. Gentile, *Origini e dottrina del fascismo* (Rome: Littorio, 1929), p. 22.

62. *AS*, pp. 63, 47.

63. *Ibid.*, pp. 3, 11, 12, 25; see also pp. 47, 55, 84, 93f.

64. *Ibid.*, p. 108.

65. *Ibid.*, pp. 51, 145, 97, 142–44.

66. See R. Melis (ed.), *Sindacalisti Italiani* (Rome: Volpe, 1964), particularly S. Panunzio, "Sindacalismo integrale e nazionale," pp. 272–81.

67. *Che cosa è il sindacalismo fascista?* (Rome: Durare, 1927), p. 16.

68. *AS*, p. 25.

69. Senghor, "Ce que l'homme noir apporte," *Liberté*, p. 23.

70. *AS*, pp. 46, 11.

71. Senghor, "Ce que l'homme . . . ," *Liberté*, p. 24; see also *AS*, pp. 72–74.

72. *AS*, p. 59.

73. Senghor, "Ce que l'homme . . . ," *Liberté*, p. 26.

74. *Ibid.*, p. 30; Senghor, "Sorbonne et Négritude," *Liberté*, p. 317; "Eléménts constitutifs . . . ," *Liberté*, p. 268; *AS*, p. 94. See also *AS*, p. 11.

75. Senghor, "Eléménts constitutifs . . . ," *Liberté*, pp. 253, 254.

76. *AS*, p. 13.

77. *AS*, p. 133.

78. *Ibid.*, pp. 140, 65.

79. Senghor, *Pierre Teilhard de Chardin et la politique africaine* (Paris: Editions du Seuil, 1962), p. 20; *AS*, pp. 11, 8, 133.

80. *AS*, pp. 75, 74.

81. T. Mboya, "African Socialism," *AFS*, p. 252.

82. *L'Essor Hebdomadaire*, May 22, 1959, as cited in F. Snyder, *One Party Government in Mali* (New Haven: Yale, 1965), pp. 94f.

83. M. Roberts, "A Socialist Looks at African Socialism," *AFS*, p. 82.

84. *L'Essor Hebdomadaire*, December 26, 1961, as cited in Snyder, *op. cit.*, pp. 92f.

85. J. Ki-Zerbo, "African Personality and the New African Society," *Pan-Africanism Reconsidered*, ed. by the American Society of African Culture (Berkeley: University of California, 1962), pp. 267–82; see also p. 289.

86. I. Kopytoff, "Socialism and Traditional African Societies," *AFS*, Chap. iii. See also P. Tempels, *Bantu Philosophy* (Paris: Presence Africaine, 1959).

87. B. Mussolini, "Discorso per lo stato corporativo," *Opera Omnia*

(Florence: Fenice, 1951–1963), XXVI, p. 91; see also C. Costamagna, *Dottrina del fascismo* (Turin: UTET, 1940), pp. 236–41.

88. E. Cione, *Storia della repubblica sociale italiana* (Caserta: Cenacola, 1948), p. 175.

89. D. Nelkin, "Socialist Sources of Pan-African Ideology," *AFS*, p. 72. See also J. L. Sterne, "The Lagos Conference," *Africa Report*, VII (November, 1962), 4–6.

90. Houphouët-Boigny as quoted in G. Carter (ed.), *African One-Party States* (Ithaca: Cornell, 1962), p. 311.

91. *AS*, p. 14.

92. See also J. S. Nye, *Pan-Africanism and East African Integration* (Cambridge: Harvard, 1965), pp. 248f.

93. J. A. Rogers, *The World's Great Men of Color* (New York: Rogers, 1946), II, p. 602.

This will be the century of authority, a century of
the Right, a century of Fascism. For if the nineteenth
century was a century of Individualism (liberalism
always signifying individualism), it may be expected that
this will be the century of collectivism, and
hence the century of the state.

It was not bluster when I affirmed that Fascism would be
the idea of the twentieth century. The failure of
an accomplishment, even of a number of them, has no
absolute significance. Circumstances in part, and the
weaknesses of men in part, provoke such an eclipse. But
one cannot turn back. History will vindicate me.[1]

MUSSOLINI

VIII · *POLITICAL THOUGHT IN THE TWENTIETH CENTURY*

That the twentieth century is a century of collectivism is a judgment that does not require Mussolini's confirmation. It has become increasingly evident that the age of philosophical and theoretical individualism as it had hitherto been understood came to an end approximately at the close of the last century. It is not our purpose to either lament or applaud its passing, but to provide some descriptive detail for its obituary. Still more relevant to the purposes of our exposition is the attempt to specify in what sense the collectivism of the twentieth century can be understood to be intellectually responsible for the fascism of our time.

To maintain that the nineteenth century was the century of classical liberalism is not to contend that a strong undercurrent of collectivism is not to be traced in the work of some of the most celebrated minds of the period. The German idealist, nationalist, and volkish literature as well as its by-products in classical Marxism are sufficient evidence of that. To say that the nineteenth century was the century of classical liberalism is to say that the prevailing philosophical, social, and political thought of the time was dominated by Jeremy Bentham, John Stuart Mill, and Herbert Spencer. Among them they produced what might be legitimately called the ideology of classical liberalism, a relatively coherent and consistent body of thought that provided a belief system that animated an age and legitimized a specific type of political system. Fundamental to that belief system was a normic model of man. Man was conceived as an empirical and individual self, the root of all affections and relations, and society was viewed as a complex entity entirely derivative. The independent, homogeneous, and unitary selves who were antecedent to society were conceived to be endowed by nature and nature's God with imprescriptible rights and values insulated from the incursions of society and the state. Social life was compartmentalized with the governmental function of the state restricted to agential police duties. The remaining "nonpolitical" compartments were nonpublic or private. Society and the state were suspect. They were understood to constitute a continual threat to the liberties of the individual self—liberties that only the dispersal of state powers into many compartments, each designed to check and restrain the other, could ensure.

These views held almost undisputed sway over at least the Anglo-Saxon countries during much of the nineteenth century. Outside those countries they had pervasive influence. But alternate and counter influences existed throughout this period, and toward the end of the nineteenth century the normic model of man that sustained the complex of conceptions supporting classical liberalism became subject to increasing criticism. This criticism mounted with particular insistence in the nascent social sciences. As early as the Saint-Simonians an alternate conception of man and society had begun to be formulated. In France, from Auguste Comte, a student and intimate of Saint-Simon, to Emile Durkheim, French sociology fell under the increasing influence of a conception of society that saw it as an organic, developing entity subject to dynamic but determinate laws of growth and change. The Saint-Simonians, who were to have both direct and indirect influence on the development of classical Marxism, committed themselves to a conception that they described as organistic. They construed the state, society, and the people as substitution instances of each other. Man was by nature a social being who, withdrawn from an organically and hierarchically organized society, failed to attain fulfillment in the three principal modes of his existence—the physical, the intellectual, and the moral. That such a society, the ground of human fulfillment, was governed by determinate, descriptive laws made governing the responsibility of an informed elite—a hierarchy composed of those naturally gifted or specially trained—rather than of the members of the conventional or traditional elite. Such men, equipped with a science of society, were the natural rulers of society. Their rule was facilitated by the fostering, maintenance, and inculcation of a regulative belief system calculated to produce an orderly, stable, and unanimous society. In such a society true freedom reigned, for the interests of one were the interests of all.[2]

It is not our intention to forge the links in the chain of thought that stretches from the Saint-Simonians or Rousseau to the various forms of authoritarian collectivism that are our concerns. It is only necessary to indicate the presence of a complex of ideas, found early in the nineteenth century, that indicate that the collectivism of our own time shares essential features with a tradition often identified with the "left" and with socialism, if not classical Marxism itself. The fact is that the labored distinction between "right" and "left" has little conceptual significance. What is more significant for an assessment of the justificatory arguments supporting the radical collectivism of our time is the recognition that they are all rooted in a normic conception of man and society in which individual men are conceived as natural and integral parts of an organic and indivisible whole as opposed to a view of man that saw each man an isolated unit who sought society only to regulate the ravages of unbridled competition. Saint-Simon and his followers advanced a "positive" conception of the state to counter the "negative" or strictly regulative state of the classical liberals. Such an advocacy was a consequence of an organismic conception of society that synthesized the interests of the individual, the faction, the society, and the state. Its echoes are found in classical Marxism and are

damped only by the arguments of the anarchists of the nineteenth century, with which Marx himself had to contend. That
such a conception of the state is the natural consequence of the
organic model of man and society seems evident. It made its
reappearance in Leninism as soon as a Marxist party found itself
the heir of an entire society. Anarchism conceived society to be
the product of the interaction of discrete and substantial selves,
while "Marxism conceived the individual only as a member of
a social order. . . ."³ The state had to be a threat to the anarchist's conception of man but might well be a fulfillment of the
social and political conceptions of the Marxist. This has proved
to be the case for contemporary Leninism just as it was for
paradigmatic Fascism. The conception of the positive, unitary
state is implicit in the organismic conception of man and society
whether that conception be characterized as of the right or the
left.

The increasing influence of the organismic model can be
traced throughout the nineteenth century. In Germany it rapidly
expanded beyond the confines of philosophy and became a sug-
gestive and instrumental concept in the developing social sciences. The "organism" to which the individual is integrally
related, the "organism" that enjoys logical and theoretical priority over the individual, was diversely characterized as "social
elements, swarms, hordes, groups" with "man [as] their product,
both in body and mind. . . . The social phenomenon is always
primary; the thought of the individual and the ethico-social
products, such as religion, rights, morals, etc., are derived."⁴ By
the end of the century Ludwig Gumplowicz could contend that

Herbert Spencer errs when he maintains that with respect to
"human society" that the "characteristics of the units (understood as
individuals) determine the characteristics of the aggregate that they
constitute." The relationship is precisely the opposite. The characteristics of the group, its strivings and its perspectives determine the
characteristics of the individual. . . . [The] individual is not prior to
his group, rather the group is prior to the individual. We are born in
a group and we die in it—the group preceded us and will survive
us. . . . Aristotle more correctly conceived the relationship when he
maintained: "the whole is necessarily prior to its parts."⁵

Much of the impetus behind this development can be traced directly or indirectly to Hegel.[6] But such determination is not significant for our purposes here. Whether or not Hegel is directly or mediately responsible for the collectivist model of man that developed throughout the nineteenth century as a challenge to the classical liberal model is not of real concern. The significant fact is that such a model was formulated and that it gradually came to displace the classical liberal model throughout Europe and even extended its influence to the United States. The increasing employment of this model was positively correlated with an increasing emphasis upon the theoretical priority of social entities of whatever sort vis-à-vis the individual and the increasingly positive role accorded the state. For a variety of reasons, which need not detain us, the state gradually began to transform itself from a relatively modest instrument of negative restraint into an imposing agency of positive social control. Contemporaneous with this impressive change in the objective character and function of the state was a searching criticism of the rationale that had supported the negative state of classical liberalism. The criticisms leveled against the negative state were provided by the newly developed social sciences armed with an organismic and functionalist conception of society in which the distinctions that classical liberalism sought to draw between the individual and his society were explicitly renounced. This is no more evident than in the United States and England.

By the turn of the century Charles Horton Cooley, whose work marked a major turning point in American social thought, could write: "Most people not only think of individuals and society as more or less separate and antithetical, but they look upon the former as antecedent to the latter. That persons make society would be generally admitted as a matter of course; but that society makes persons would strike many as a startling notion. . . ."[7] The entire first part of Cooley's *Social Organization*, published in 1909, was devoted to "demonstrating the classical proposition that man is a social animal, against the profound American sentiment that opposes self and society. . . . Man owes the form of his individuality not to his own creative ego but to the creative collectivity." These contentions were conjoined with the conviction that "one is never more human, and as a rule never happier than when he is sacrificing his narrow and merely private interest to the higher call of the congenial group."[8] Cooley spoke of the individual "disciplined" by group membership, a benign discipline born of the sentiment of membership that would produce the enlarged self. He spoke of community responsibility and obligation to the historical and traditional collectivity. Cooley, leagued with notables of the stature of Albion Small and Lester Ward, advanced the case against the prevailing individualism that characterized the nineteenth century. They made common cause against what Small once called "the preposterous initial fact of the individual"—in effect, they argued against the essentials of the belief system generated by the model of man entertained by classical liberalism.

The complex of arguments advanced against classical liberalism were drawn from a multitude of sources. Not only were Hegel and the various exponents of German collectivism prominent influences, but the names of Emile Durkheim, Gabriel Tarde, and Gustav Le Bon also dot the pages of American journals and texts. Concepts like the "group mind" and "consciousness of kind" became increasingly commonplace, concepts whose theoretical explanations involve references to "bonds of sentiment" and "induced imitation." Arguments became increasingly anti-intellectualist and methodologically collectivist. Man was a social animal, the natural denizen of a structured and organic community, bound to his fellows in sentiment and reflecting their values, attitudes, and norms in imitation. Within such a context the conception of the state underwent significant changes. If it is tradition and stable social structure that lend substance to the life of the individual, the role of the state as a pedagogical and control agency becomes increasingly positive. Against the residual and negative conception of the state natural to the atomistic and mechanistic model of classical liberalism a positive conception of the state appeared, a state that increasingly "interfered" in the lives and activities of its citizens. Edward A. Ross, an associate of Small and Ward, concluded that in order to effect a truly social life, a life in which the individual would achieve fulfillment, it would be necessary to develop the state.[9]

It becomes increasingly evident that the organic model of man and society provides the foundation for justificatory arguments supporting the integralist state. The nature of the relationship is illustrated in the work of Spencer. Spencer, who all but dominated Anglo-American social thought at the close of the nineteenth century, attempted to provide a consistent and coherent defense of the contractualist and atomistic society of classical liberalism. His *Man versus the State* is still considered in some quarters to be the model statement of the individualist position. But Spencer himself was under the insistent influence of the organismic conception of society, and as a consequence his work is a confusion of organismic and atomistic models. Society is at one and the same time an "organism" and the product of a "contract." On the one hand he speaks of man prior to society, when man disported himself in the world free and unrestrained. Society was simply the mechanical aggregation of such men who were forced to a sacrifice of freedom. If society is the consequence of aggregation or contract, it seems to follow that rights are antecedent to society and are somehow inherent in the individual. But elsewhere Spencer speaks of society as an organism, characterized by the essential traits of organicity. If so, it would seem that the rights of component elements of such an organism would be relative and contigent upon the general welfare. Spencer never succeeded in resolving these contradictions. He argued that land belongs to society since it is essential to general well-being; yet he maintained that private property cannot be violated. He maintained that the individual had contracted with his peers and created the state to provide police protection for himself and could therefore not legitimately be restrained in his purely economic activity. But can such a state, discharging its obligations, avoid restraining the evident rapacity of individuals so often prejudicial to the common good when they function as employers or landlords?[10]

What is today called "welfare" or "positive" liberalism has resolved these problems by opting for a relatively consistent organicism that understands the individual to be an element in a structured and integral whole of one or another order. Men such as John Dewey and Thorstein Veblen were in the organicist and historicist tradition of Hegel and Marx. That Dewey sought to support his earlier Hegelian convictions with Darwinian arguments is not relevant here. What is interesting, and perhaps significant, is that Dewey advocated social reconstruction through education. He conceived education as the public regulation of the process of coming to share in the social consciousness. On the basis of the adjustment of individual activity to a general social consciousness, he sought the attainment of the good life for both individual and society. Such an account provides for increasing public supervision and direction in matters hitherto conceived as "private." The goal was a working compromise between what was sometimes referred to as "socialism" or "collectivism" and the *laissez-faire* individualism of the preceding decades.

Similar trends were evident in England. The most interesting development in social and political thought was the direct consequence of Hegel's influence.

From T. H. Green to Bernard Bosanquet the crescendo of emphasis fell increasingly upon the independent principle of the state. . . . The social interests of free individuals, on which the liberalist tradition had relied for its construction of the state, were disregarded. The state, according to Green, is based on an "ideal principle of its own, and the common good, which the state embodies and guards, cannot result from the free play of individual interests. There are no individual rights separate from the universal right represented by the state. To ask why I am to submit to the power of the state, is to ask why I am to allow my life to be regulated by that complex of institutions without which I literally should not have a life to call my own, nor should be able to ask for a justification of what I am called to do."[11]

But it was in the social and political philosophy of Bosanquet rather than Green that the full implications of the organismic conception were provided in specific detail.

In *The Philosophical Theory of the State* Bernard Bosanquet committed himself to what he called the "fundamental idea of Greek political philosophy," an idea to which Hegel was equally committed. Bosanquet contends

. . . that the human mind can only attain its full and proper life in a community of minds, or more strictly in a community pervaded by a single mind, uttering itself consistently though differently in the life and action of every member of the community. This conception is otherwise expressed by such phrases as "the state is natural," i.e., is a growth or evolution, apart from which the end implied in man's origin cannot be attained; "the state is prior to the individual," i.e., there is a principle or condition underlying the life of the human individual, which will not admit of that life becoming what it has in it to be, unless the full sphere or arena which is constituted by the life of the state is realized in fact. . . . We are reminded that [with the state], after all, we are dealing with a self-conscious purposive organism, which is aware of a better and a worse, and has members bound together by conscious intelligence, though it may be not by conscious intelligence alone. . . . Our theory insists on the will and personality of the state, and with them on its moral responsibility. . . . [The] state [is] the main organ and condition of the fuller liberty. . . . [Our theory conceives of an] identification of the state with the Real Will of the Individual in which he wills his own nature as a rational being. . . . [The] state as such is a necessary factor in civilized life; and . . . no true ideal lies in the direction of minimizing its individuality or restricting its absolute power. By the state, then, we mean society as a unit, recognized as rightly exercising control over its members through absolute physical power.[12]

Bosanquet's neo-Hegelian treatise on the "new state," written in 1899, constitutes the first protofascist rationale of the twentieth century. It is a rationale for the integralist, organic, or totalitarian state. It is a radical expression of the collectivism that had been maturing, as a minoritarian intellectual movement, since the French Revolution. Its sustaining basis was the organismic model of man and society, a basis on which, as Jay Rumney indicated, "it was easy . . . to justify state sovereignty and omnicompetence, a corporate society, a totalitarian state and every other kind of social absolutism."[13] In this regard Corrado Gini argued, "The normal condition of an organism is characterized by a *consensus* governing its organs by virtue of which the advantage of each is compatible with and based upon the common advantage of the whole. . . . In the individual organism such a *consensus* is achieved only through the action of central regulating forces. . . . a *consensus* which cannot be obtained without the regulatory action of a central force."[14] That central force is the state.

Organismic analogies typify collectivist arguments, and they regularly recur in the justificatory arguments advanced to support fascism, National Socialism,[15] and apartheid. They are no less essential to classical Marxism, Leninism, and African socialism.

Each ideology differentiates itself only when the collectivity to which the analogies are applied is identified. For classical Marxism and Leninism (at least in its theoretical language) that organic collectivity is *class*, for National Socialism *race*, for apartheid *volk*, and for fascism and African socialism the *nation* and the *"ethnarchic" community*.

It is at this point that the arguments advanced to support welfare or contemporary liberalism can be distinguished from those that attend radical ideologies. Contemporary liberalism does not generally accord priority to any *one* specific community; it tends to conceive society as a complex of interacting communities, reference or interest groups, with government policy the consequence of a series of compromises between them. There is no privileged community to which component communities must be subordinated or synthesized. In a complex and obscure fashion political parties and religious, social, and economic interest groups seek to influence government. What results is a government of compromise with political parties representing local, regional, and special interests at different times and in different places. In the theoretical literature these conceptions are expressed in the description of society as a "web of group affiliations." Government is described as "pluralistic" with a multiplicity of political parties prepared to compete for and represent the real or imagined interest of any demographic, economic, or social community. Thus the same political party may represent the interests of labor unions or entrepreneurs in one section of the country, those of a racial minority in another, and those of the racial or ethnic majority in still another. The same political party may be "conservative" in one part of the nation and "liberal" in yet another. Candidates for national office will tend to be all things to all groups and once in office will attempt to compromise the multiplicity of often conflicting interests, all of which they have pledged themselves to defend. As needs and interests change, party posture tends to reflect those changes, and the same political party finds itself defending divergent and sometimes contradictory positions at different times in its history.

It is only when collectivism fixes upon a unique community as the ultimate and fundamental source of values that pluralism gives way to totalitarianism. When class membership is the ultimate determinant of human personality and all other associations are conceived derivative, the unitary party makes its appearance. The theoretical account that subtends totalitarian ideologies is monofactorial. The theoretical literature of Marxism explains political, religious, and philosophical association on the basis of class membership. All other associations represent derivative associations, ultimately explicable on the basis of class. For National Socialists art movements, religious affiliation, class, and party membership are ultimately explicable on the basis of race. Thus, for Marxists of whatever variety there is a class art, a class philosophy, and a class science. For National Socialists there is a racial art, a racial philosophy, and a racial science.

The most consistent totalitarian ideologies have the most consistently monofactorial account of collective phenomena. There is one ultimate community of which the individual is an organic member. The individual, beset by confusing and conflicting stimuli, may fail to appreciate his organic relationship to such an ultimate community, and then it becomes the responsibility of a specially equipped elite to restore the lost consciousness of his real interests. The unitary party makes its appearance as an ethical or pedagogical necessity. It brings to individuals that absent consciousness. It is the agency that fosters or restores the missing class, racial, volkish, or national consciousness. Possessed of the wisdom that will restore or promote the fullness of self that attends the identification with the ultimate collectivity, the unitary party demands political monopoly and arrogates to itself the right to interfere at its own discretion in all spheres of public and private life. Society ceases to be distinguished from the state; it is totally permeated by the political prerogatives of the unitary party. Since the party is understood to represent the ultimate interests of all members of the essential community, its interests and those of the society it governs are identical. Because it speaks in the name of those ultimate interests, the party is the ultimate authority. The political structure of society becomes totalitarian and authoritarian. The manifest traits of such a society are unanimity and consensus, the artifact of a communications and a police monopoly.

The entire system is predicated upon the conviction that a minority of men possesses a body of inviolable truth. This constitutes a further critical and still more essential difference between the collectivism of welfare liberalism and totalitarianism. Contemporary liberals tend to entertain a pragmatic theory of knowledge. They tend to admit human fallibility and conceive values and interests to be but little amenable to cognitive control. They tend, as a consequence, to advocate tolerance and compromise, to be relativistic in a broad and not necessarily pejorative sense. Fundamental to radical social and political ideologies, at least on the doctrinal level, is an epistemology that precludes any substantial fallibility. It is in this sense that totalitarian ideologies can be characterized as "transrational," but this characterization must be qualified in something like the following fashion: Absolute rule tends to require an absolute justification. It tends to require that the elite burdened with the totalitarian governance of the modern state license its rule by claims to substantial infallibility.

Claims to infallibility should not be confused with the effects of totalitarian rule—with the homogeneity of opinion produced by the quasi-religious character of modern totalitarian ideologies that requires doctrinal orthodoxy coupled with a communications monopoly. The unanimity of opinion that results can be correctly described as "nonrational," but the movements that effect such results can hardly be deemed "irrational" because of it. The employment of myths or political formulas calculated to engender what Plato called the "temperance" of the masses, that is, the acquiescence to rule, is not irrational or transrational in and of itself. The recognition that the psychologically homeless, the anomic masses so prevalent in our time, the semieducated, the disgruntled, and the economically insecure can be, and perhaps must be, led through the manipulation of sentiment does not characterize a political strategy or the movement that employs it as irrational. The issuance of slogans, the use of elaborate ritual and ceremony, the appeals to sentiment may, in fact, constitute eminently rational organizational devices for the mobilization of masses of men behind a collective enterprise. (One need but consider advertising techniques or the systematic and directed cultivation of popular sentiment employed in nontotalitarian states during a war to appreciate the calculated rationality of such programs.)

The significant elements of irrationality or transrationality of totalitarian ideologies collect around the peculiar knowledge claims made by some of them. The pressure to adopt transrational justification is strong. For National Socialism it seems to have been central to the ideological system. Senghor's African socialism with its "intuitive" Negro African "mystic emotion" seems wedded to a similar transrationality. Leninism's doctrine of "partisan truth" became, at least after 1929, a permanent feature of the doctrine. By 1932 the party issued dicta governing the "truth" in areas as divergent as engineering and ichthyology, insisting that all knowledge was subject to what David Joravsky termed "caesaropapist dogmatism," dictates of orthodoxy that became a ritualistic incantation of the one true *Weltanschauung* inspired by the one true party.[16] Leninists consider themselves possessed of the only certain and scientific solution to all contemporary problems. An elite, under the guidance of a specific man of "genius," licenses its absolute rule by an appeal to its monopoly of truth. Only within such a system is it comprehensible that a man like Stalin could be called upon to resolve disputes in disciplines as varied as psychology, linguistics, biology, and philosophy.

Fascism made recourse to a similar rationale. F. T. Marinetti spoke of Mussolini's "lightning intuitions," and even as sober an ideologue as Alfredo Rocco insisted upon Mussolini's "infallible intuitions."[17] The unfortunate slogan *"Mussolini ha sempre ragione"* ("Mussolini is always right") has now become part of the history of Italian Fascism and exemplifies the endemic necessity of radical collectivism to legitimize, at least on the doctrinal level, its monopoly of power with an absolutistic epistemology.

At this point a further qualification must be made on the transrational character of contemporary ideologies. Some contemporary ideologies do use claims to mystic infallibility or privileged truth to win the confidence of the masses, employing essentially normal procedures for the confirmation and disconfirmation of theoretical and descriptive propositions in the formulation of policy and principles of consistency in the articulation and modification of the ideological system. These rational and critical activities are reserved, however, for the elite, with the fiction of special truth being maintained before the general population as a control expedient. This seems to have been the case with Italian Fascism and also seems to be true in some

Leninist parties. Fascist "myths" were articles for popular consumption. "If by mysticism one intends the recognition of truth without the employment of reason," Mussolini insisted, "I would be the first to declare myself opposed to every mysticism."[18] The School of Fascist Mysticism and Fascist mysticism itself were doctrinal adjuncts to the ideological system. The hierarchs of the system, with Mussolini at their head, employed pragmatic tests of truth, most of them having been directly or indirectly influenced by pragmatism of one or another sort. Sorel had advanced pragmatism as an essential component of revolutionary syndicalism at a time when Mussolini was most directly under its influence, and on several occasions Mussolini alluded to his intellectual debt to William James.[19] Giuseppe Prezzolini's volume dedicated to syndicalist theory, written in the first decade of the twentieth century, devoted considerable space to the discussion of Sorel's and James' pragmatism and exercised a decided influence on the maturation of Mussolini's thought.[20] This kind of social pragmatism was not incompatible with Gentile's actualism, and the result was a confluence of elements producing an "ethical pragmatism." In what sense and how far such a synthesis was successfully and convincingly achieved by Fascism in Italy is impossible to say. All that is necessary to indicate is that Mussolini's Fascism, at the level of social and political philosophy, made an effort to distinguish itself from mysticism and irrationality.

An even stronger case can be made for various forms of Leninism. Whatever claims are made at the doctrinal level, there is a serious effort to formulate a convincing epistemology at a more systematic and demanding level. At the doctrinal level Soviet Leninism, for example, has an image of unyielding and dogmatic finality, and yet there is evidence that elaborate and perhaps far-reaching criticism has been undertaken by Russia's intellectual elite. By way of illustration, Arnost Kolman in the nineteen-sixties has written that "philosophy . . . must be daring and combative, and not limit itself to the automatic interpretation of each new physical discovery from the old viewpoint of Engels."[21] Criticism of this type takes place publicly or privately, but it takes place nonetheless. How such discussions come to influence public policy or doctrinal expression is difficult to specify, but that they do is obvious in the very fact that Soviet Leninism has gradually transformed itself in the years since the October Revolution.

Elitist systems tend to take on the character briefly outlined above. There are doctrinal "truths" advanced to win the acquiescence of the ruled majority. Such truths are advanced with a pretense of finality, for as Mussolini expressed it, "Dictatorial regimes need, more than praetorians, a coterie of fanatic believers. Criticism is to be left to those competent to undertake it. . . . The masses should obey: one cannot afford them the luxury of wasting time in the search for truth."[22] The critical search for truth is the privilege of the elite. Only they can maintain that no man, or group of men, has uniquely privileged insight into the ideally rational life. Gentile, for example, throughout his life insisted that he never "believed in the infallibility of any man. . . ."[23] Soviet philosophers abjure dogmatism as inimical to science; yet the elite is not expected to embark on criticism outside the confines of the unitary party and is, in fact, constrained from doing so. Criticism must be "self-criticism"; it must be conducted within the confines of the party. What this means in actual practice is difficult to objectively assess. Whether the range of permissible criticism is too narrow or whether the rigidities of the system suppress searching and significant criticism are considerations of critical importance. There is good *prima facie* evidence that the system malfunctions.

National Socialism, on the other hand, seems to have been unique insofar as it was apparently seriously committed to an intuitionistic and mystical epistemology. Hitler appealed to intuition to provide both the issuance and the confirmation of descriptive and theoretical propositions. But this kind of trans-rationality does not seem to characterize totalitarian ideologies as such. How far it characterizes African socialism is, as yet, impossible to determine.

In this respect the ideology of apartheid is unique among contemporary radical ideologies. It does not make special knowledge claims nor has South Africa developed a specifically political or party elite. This is probably because apartheid is essentially conservative. It does not seek to generate, restore, or maintain a factitious consensus. It is the expression of a traditional volkish sentiment. Apartheid is attempting to maintain, in the face of rapid and threatening change, the traditional volkish integrity of Afrikanerdom. Among Afrikaners there has long existed a diffused, decentralized, or popular totalitarianism that generates consensus through spontaneous mutual repression rather than through centrally organized repression or propaganda.[24] There is, and has been, substantial unanimity among Afrikaners with respect to the problems to which apartheid addresses itself. In South Africa volkish unanimity and sentiment *preceded* the advent of the National party to power, and the forces aligned against it, the white English-speaking minority and the nonwhite majority, were and are politically ineffectual because they either failed to advance a real alternative or were disenfranchised entirely. Since virtual unanimity obtains among the Afrikaner volk on the issue of apartheid, there is no real necessity to make special claims to privileged knowledge in order to buttress the program of the National party or foster consensus. English-speaking whites cannot mount effective opposition, and the nonwhite majority, inept and badly organized, was never a political threat even before the advent of Malan.

In general it can be said that unitary parties, as a consequence of their radical collectivist bias, seek to foster consensus among members of the primary collectivity, be it a class, a race, a volk, or a nationality. They seek to identify that collectivity and its constituent members with the party and the party with the state in a series of now familiar substitutions. Where consensus is not traditional, a systematic and concerted effort is undertaken to produce it. The party takes on an apocalyptic, chiliastic, and missionary character. It assumes the attributes of a religious order, enjoining obedience, discipline, and strict adherence to revolutionary doctrine. It constitutes the secular surrogate for religious organization in our postreligious era. Mussolini quite frankly identified the Fascist movement as religious in character. National Socialist Germany characterized itself as an *Ordenstaat*. Leninist parties have produced moral codes, hagiographies, ritual language, and ceremony that cultivate genuine religious fervor. African socialism, in its turn, has been described as a "political religion." Nkrumah, for example, was identified as the Messiah.

This tendency was, of course, most manifest in Alfred Rosenberg's suggestion that a National Socialist religion based on the "myth of blood" be imposed upon Germany. Nonetheless, it is a characteristic shared by all totalitarian systems. The exception again is apartheid, which is traditionalist and identifies itself with the traditional religious forms of the volk community, the Dutch Reformed churches, whose peculiar interpretation of Scripture constitutes one major *source* of apartheid ideology.

Revolutionary totalitarian parties seek to generate a sense of community with which the individual can identify himself. The single party possesses the insights necessary to bring about that identification, the state represents the concrete will of that community, and the leader is its voice. To this end all the means of communication and the instruments of instruction are employed. This requires that the party exercise a communications and pedagogical monopoly. What totalitarian parties seek to produce is the "New Man," possessed of a generalized belief system that produces the behavior patterns leading to the attainment of those values central to the system.

In our own time it has become increasingly evident that fascism typifies the form that totalitarianism has taken and in all probability will continue to take during the twentieth century. Collectivist ideologies focus on an essential community, volk, race, class, or nation with which the individual must identify if he is to attain fulfillment. That volkish ideologies are not adequate to our time need hardly be argued. Traditional or historic volk constitute communities that are too restricted in size to be viable in the highly industrialized and highly competitive twentieth century. A volkish ideology, to be consistent, must seek to dismember highly evolved industrial communities into homogeneous volkish enclaves or stratify society into closed castes in which a superior caste dominates an inferior one. In our own time these societies tend to be highly unstable and require the continual and increasing employment of violence to suppress passive resistance and rebellion. They tend to become increasingly dysfunctional.

Modern industry requires that workers receive minimal education to function optimally. It requires that workers learn to obey orders and work in concert. It further requires large concentrations of men at critical and centrally located areas. All these circumstances, however, are conducive to effective political organization. In order to meet the requirements of large-scale industry, contemporary society renders the persistence of a caste system all but impossible. Under the conditions of modern industry a disadvantaged caste finds itself so circumstanced that political organization is eminently possible and resistance has every promise of success. A caste system is suitable for an agrarian age, where caste members are so deployed that their organization and political mobilization is significantly hampered. These are the considerations that face apartheid, as they would face any volkish ideology in the twentieth century.

Similar objections militate against race serving as the essential community fundamental to an ideology of solidarity. Such an ideology aspires either to a dysfunctional separation of races —to the exclusion, expulsion, or extermination of unwanted racial communities or to a stratified society composed of distinct racial castes. Certainly the crabbed and restricted Nordicism of National Socialism was dysfunctional and the prospects of its resurgence are extremely remote. The vitality of National Socialism was derived essentially from its nationalism, its populism, its promise to unite the national community and breach the traditional and invidious distinctions of class, region, and confession. In effect, the vital elements of National Socialism were consciously or unconsciously borrowed from Mussolini's Fascism. Its morbid elements were congenital, the confused and simplistic racial doctrine it had inherited from a Romantic and quasi-scientific tradition. National Socialism was ultimately revealed as fundamentally antinationalist and threatened to divide Germany along racial lines, segregating its population into permanent racial castes. In the service of "Nordic solidarity" the unity of the historic national community was to be sacrificed. But to talk of Nordic solidarity is to neglect the enormous and resistant differences that distinguish Icelanders from Danes and Danes from Nordic North Italians and Brahman Indians. To generate the requisite sense of solidarity that would be the necessary condition for viability in the twentieth century would require effacing historical, cultural, political, and religious differences of such magnitude as to make the entire enterprise unrealistic. Even to entertain a notion of a more inclusive "white solidarity" one would have to prescind from differences so compelling that they have inhibited even regional solidarity in Europe. To aspire to unite all "whites"—Russians, Germans, Frenchmen,

Spaniards, Italians, Egyptians, Syrians, Norwegians, among a host of others—is obviously utopian.

To conceive class as the essential community is to assume a position similarly fraught with difficulties. That the German worker has something substantial in common with a Congolese or a Chinese worker, something sufficiently compelling to permit the organization of an international class party of solidarity, is a conception manifestly unrealistic, a fact to which all contemporary socialist and Leninist parties can attest.

The nation has become the focal community of contemporary movements of solidarity, and in this sense Italian Fascism is paradigmatic of twentieth-century totalitarianism. Nations have developed as a response to historic and economic needs. With the maturation of industrial techniques, local or volkish communities have had to expand into economically viable units. These units, when viable, have typically displayed a collection of ethnic and sociocultural affinities that have permitted them to develop the minimal sense of community requisite to the operation of a complex industrial society. In general, this is as true of the development of nations in Europe as it is of the newly emergent nations of Asia and Africa.

The sense of community, the foundation of any community life, is conditioned by a variety of factors, not the least of which is economic exigency. A food-gathering community or a hunting band will be only as large as its means of subsistence and its productive techniques permit. Whatever affinities it shares with allopatric groups, these will not conduce to a political life in common unless the expanded life can rest on an adequate economic base. Contemporary communities, industrialized or aspiring toward industrialization, require access to adequate raw materials, a consumer market of suitable size, and geographic circumstances that permit the development of an infrastructure that unites the area into an operationally effective unit. But the presence of such a unit does not necessarily mean that it will constitute itself a nation. Sociocultural and ethnic distinctions constitute serious deterrents to the formation of communities animated by a pervasive sense of unity. Religious and linguistic differences and racial traits of high visibility can engender among different population groups an emphatic sense of distance prejudicial to the development of a unified nation-state.

The national idea preserves no negligent element of attachment to the historic past, to a common soil, and to ethnic affinity. When these are combined in a unit enjoying economic viability and an alluring program of community purpose, we have a remarkably stable national entity. To share common glories in the past, evident affinities, and a common purpose in the present (conjoined with the means to the accomplishment of that purpose), to have done notable things in communion, to share overt similarities, and to wish to accomplish great things in the present and in the future—all these are the necessary conditions for stable nationhood in the twentieth century. One of the most imposing political features of the twentieth century is the existence of national movements of solidarity devoted to the realization of the nation. However they begin, or however they perish, they function most effectively as nationalist movements. The various national forms of Leninism are cases in point. The political effectiveness of National Socialism was greatest when it indulged itself as a radical nationalism. Since World War II nationalism has provided the dynamic power of anticolonialism.[25]

In this sense, once again, Italian Fascism provides the paradigm for contemporary totalitarianism. It represents the first mature national totalitarianism. Its identification of people, party, and state; its subordination of all regional and special interests to the real or fancied interests of the nation; its appeal to national sentiment and national tradition; its conception of the unitary party and its leader as the concrete will of the nation; all these exemplify its paradigmatic character. That Leninist parties have gradually assumed these features under the pressure of circumstances serves to support the contention.[26] That African socialism has manifested all the species traits of Italian Fascism is its confirmation.

All totalitarian or protototalitarian collectivisms share a constellation of diagnostic traits that makes them more nearly like each other than like any other system of government, including the autocracies and tyrannies of the past. The attempts to distinguish between radical ideologies on the basis of their "reactionary" or "progressive" character produce more confusion than classificatory distinction. Nor is the effort to distinguish the "class" character of the varieties of totalitarianism any more instructive. Radical value-orientated movements of solidarity are characteristically led by declassed intellectuals or autodidacts who commit themselves to a particular collection of doctrinal values or a social and political philosophy that provides the sustaining emotional force for their enterprise. While the normative values they have made their own undergo significant, sometimes startling, change under the impact of time and circumstance, only the presence of a relatively stable constellation of ideas makes the behavior of such men comprehensible. That the original constellation of ideas is vague, even when the ideas are as elaborate as those of Marx, permits far-reaching modifications. These modifications can be understood by attempting to understand the influences operative in each historical and intellectual environment.

That class relationships, understood in any consistent Marxist sense, fail to operate as determinant variables in the organization of the mass party and the state it produces is obvious. Leninist parties, for example, have never succeeded in winning the allegiance of the proletarian class wherever there was a proletarian class to be won. Wherever Leninists have succeeded to power, it has always been where a declassed intellectual elite has been able to direct the elemental energies of petty bourgeois or peasant masses. In China the urban working class played only a peripheral role in the long struggle for Communist domination. In Cuba the urban working classes were effectively excluded from participation in the revolutionary struggle. In African socialist states the proletarian classes are not only excluded, in fact, from participation in the revolution, but are even denied, in theory, an effective and determining role. In Argentina, in contradistinction, the urban working classes provided the principal support for Peronist fascism and the middle and upper classes constituted its principal opponents.[27] Italian Fascism as a national socialism was essentially a populist movement, and at its inception and during the final years of the Social Republic appealed to the petty bourgeoisie and the working class. Getulio Vargas' neofascist appeals in prewar Brazil were made to the working classes; as a consequence, his was a mass movement of solidarity that was working-class based and yet anti-Marxist and nationalistic. What all such movements have in common is their ability to win support in situations of acute crisis. Any attempt, of course, to provide a convincing definition of crisis is extremely difficult. Such attempts generally degenerate into tautologies that make acute crisis to be that crisis which permits a totalitarian movement to win support. Even if some useful index to crisis were forthcoming, local conditions, historical antecedents, the personal character of the leader of the potential mass movement, and the intensity and skill of the organizational drive of the party are all factors that influence each specific case.

More significant for our analysis is the fact that all radical collectivist movements represent a manifest radicalization of trends already evident at the commencement of the twentieth century and increasingly apparent even in the nontotalitarian states. There has been an increased tendency toward centralization in the economy, increasing centralization of power in the executive branch of government, a proliferation of state agencies, and an increasingly refined and centralized network of communication. In fact, some of the principal species traits of totalitarianism are already common to all industrially advanced countries. Police, communications and weapons monopoly, as well as increasing centralization of the economy, are the necessary consequences of technological development. Without the rapid technological advance that has characterized the twentieth century, totalitarianism would be impossible. This trend, coupled with recurrent crises that threaten large segments of the population with downward mobility and dislocation, foster the development of mass movements of solidarity as a defense. Totalitarian appeals are made to those segments of the population most directly threatened by the impending or prevailing crisis. Thus, "working class" parties will appeal to the peasants where the peasantry are most numerous and restive; "nationalist" parties will appeal to petty bourgeois or working class strata where they display most revolutionary potential.

Totalitarian ideologies are, in fact, radicalizations of some of the collectivist features evident in the social and political thought of welfare liberals. Totalitarian movements would be inconceivable outside the context of mass democracy and modern technology (for this reason African socialism might better be characterized as protototalitarian). Classical liberalism disintegrated under the impact of criticism, and by the turn of the century the advent of mass democracy had made some form of collectivism all but an organizational necessity. For a variety of reasons, the ideology of classical liberalism could satisfy the aspirations of only the entrepreneurial middle class. The shortcomings of the economy and social system it supported had become so obvious by the end of the nineteenth century that collectivism in its various guises had all but won the field. Today classical liberalism has few defenders. Welfare liberalism has by and large preempted its place as the rationale for social democracy. In our secular age, in situations of protracted and profound crisis, value-oriented parties mobilize masses of men in apochryphal and chiliastic movements of solidarity that are radicalizations of welfare liberalism. "Creeping socialism" becomes a frank and explicit collectivism in which the people telescope into the party and the party finds expression in the voice of an inspired leader.

The increasing sophistication of our time has led, therefore, to the abandonment of what had hitherto been a commonplace distinction between fascism and the various forms of socialism that turned on the right/left dichotomy. Collectivist totalitarianisms are members of the same species. The emphasis given to their subspecific differences will depend on a variety of considerations, prejudice being not one of the least important. Marxists of every stripe, for example, have insisted that a species difference distinguishes the left from the right, and that distinction turns on the issue of private property. The right defends private property. Should this be so, African socialism would be *ipso facto* a movement of the right. The African socialist states have displayed little interest in nationalizing private property. A more significant question would be: What is the real significance of private property in a system committed to state control of the economy? Fascists early insisted that private property, in and of itself, was a matter of little consequence if, once property became of social consequence, it was subject to social control. It is conceivable that the fundamental issue of our century is not the *ownership* of property but its *management*. In this respect the corporativism of fascism would be no less radical, in principle if not in effect, than the state socialism of the Soviet Union. An integralist movement that approaches the economy with the conviction that the general interest, as interpreted by the unitary party, has precedence over private interest can and has as effectively dominated the productive and distributive processes of the nation irrespective of whether an enterprise and private property in general is or is not in private hands. This belated recognition is the hub of Milovan Djilas' criticism of the socialism of the Soviet Union.[28]

The distinction between right and left totalitarianism has been fostered by an interpretation that makes "right-wing" totalitarianism the "creation of monopoly capitalism." Tracts arguing this thesis are legion.[29] They are almost all the products of orthodox Marxists—and they are almost all equally mistaken. There is scant data that could be convincingly employed to support the thesis that the totalitarianism of the right, Italian Fascism, or German National Socialism, is the "creation" of large-scale capitalist interests. Both movements received the support of large segments of the working class, particularly the unemployed, and found their most extensive support among the petty bourgeoisie, primarily the self-employed urban elements who traditionally support the liberal center. The National Socialist movement in Germany received no support from the conservative large-scale business interests until the party had achieved the status of a serious contender for power in 1932. On the whole, the National Socialist movement was anticapitalist and was recognized as such by those interests.[30] Both Fascism and National Socialism were essentially "populist" movements, as anticapitalist as they were antilabor where either capital or labor sought to function independently and in its own interests within the national economy. Both Fascism and National Socialism domesticated capital and labor in the interests of what they understood to be the national interest. The compelling fact of the National Socialist and Fascist dictatorships is not that Hitler and Mussolini answered to the dictates of monopoly capitalism but that they had to answer to no one. All the documentary evidence indicates that Hitler and Mussolini were the all but absolute rulers of their respective countries. Their decisions were final, and the power they exercised was as absolute as that wielded by any man in history.[31] In this sense they can be compared to Stalin and Mao Tse-tung. To equate right-wing radical collectivists with the exacerbated radicals of classical liberalism who have collected in the John Birch Society and the conservative wing of the United States Republican party is a manifest absurdity.[32]

There is little merit in attempting to distinguish totalitarianisms on the basis of some constellation of values—for example—"freedom, equality, and peace" versus "subordination, inequality, and war." "Freedom" and "equality" are dynamic terms employed systematically by social and political philosophers to negotiate a licit transit from descriptive propositions to normative conclusions. All ideologies employ these highly emotional terms to effect this transition. The dynamic term appears in the premises of the argument, and its emotional force provides the necessary impetus for the normative conclusion; but the dynamic term retains its emotive and changes its conceptual meaning. Thus, as we have seen, classical liberals, Leninists, Fascists, and National Socialists alike proclaim themselves defenders of "freedom" because the term has strong commendatory force. The term freedom appeared, in fact, on the masthead of every issue of the *Nationalsozialistische Monatshefte.*

A similar account could be forthcoming for the dynamic term "equality." Fascist ideologues, for example, insisted that each man was understood to be an end in himself.[33] "Human life," Gentile maintained in outlining the philosophy of Fascism, "is sacred. . . . Things are instruments, men are ends."[34] In his last apologetic for Fascism, Gentile argued that since all men are members of the kingdom of ends, they are, in the final analysis, "identical" and "love" is the "crowning perfection of knowledge."[35] The "immutable, beneficial, and fruitful inequality of mankind," which Mussolini proclaimed, was the evident inequality in the distribution of natural gifts that neither Leninists nor democratic socialists deny. The point being labored is that any attempt to classify ideological systems by simply identifying a syndrome of values that purportedly characterizes them is to mistake semblance for substance. The question is not whether terms like freedom or equality appear in the doctrinal literature of a political movement. The issues turn on the cognitive or conceptual contents of such persuasive terms, and this can be determined most effectively by inspecting the normic model of man and society advanced by the ideologists of the movement. All political movements, operating as they must within the confines of a given historic era, use similar emotive vocabulary. All advance, in some sense, "equality," "freedom," "democracy." That each alters their conceptual meaning is shown by the fact that each appends adjectival qualifiers, such as "true," "real," or "effective." The cognitive meanings of such expressions differ in accordance with the normic model from which they are derived. Insofar as the normic models approximate each other, the cognitive meanings of such terms have similar meaning. In some cases—Leninisms constituting the principal example—where doctrinal changes of compelling magnitude have created tensions within the ideological system, it is difficult to determine *what* such persuasive terms can mean.

Contrary to much current opinion, fascism has the advantage of a relatively consistent ideology. It is collectivist, nationalist, elitist, and statist. The fulfillment of man, his "freedom," is realized only in a law-governed association of equals who, in principle, prescind from traditional, confessional, regional, and class interests. The governance of law and the spiritual heritage it transmits are assured only in the sovereignty of a strong centralized state, a state led by an elite of natural competence under the direction of a leader gifted with the faculty of speaking in the ultimate interests of the association. The law-governed association is the historic nation and its colonies or the ethnarchic empire. Peace between nations is assured only by the perpetual preparation for war. This is an ideological system remarkably Hegelian in character and content. As an ideology it represents in theory what the most significant radical systems do in fact. Its social and political philosophy could quite effectively provide the justificatory arguments for contemporary Leninisms and African socialisms as well as for the varieties of fascism.

It appears that in the tension of the protracted conflicts which will continue throughout the remainder of this century, the several totalitarian states will probably take on more and more of the features of Mussolini's Fascism. Such a system seems eminently suited to underdeveloped economies. The advanced economies have, in general, developed a variety of well-organized and articulate interest groups that would resist radical collectivization and would be disposed to deploy effective arguments against any rationale that would advance the thesis that all individual, class and strata interests were, in some speculative sense, ultimately identical.

No contemporary contending or established political system can base itself on simple coercion. Arguments must be forthcoming to justify revolution or legitimize rule. The led and the governed must be prepared to see authority behind power and legitimacy or right behind authority. Contemporary radical ideologies provide either the revolutionary rationale or the charter myth for totalitarian or potentially totalitarian systems. They are predicated on a singular logic of substitutions that makes private and public, individual and collective, interests ultimately one. They all exemplify forms of secular humanism and appeal to some ultimate self-interest on the part of the led or the governed even if the led or the governed are too intellectually or morally obtuse to recognize it.

Since all ideologies couch themselves in the language of advocacy, having specific normative intention, such ideologies are never true in the literal sense of true. They are neither the strictly deductive conclusions to formal arguments nor the highly confirmed probability statements of science as we understand science. In this sense they are myths, neither literally true nor false. They can be plausible or implausible, functional or dysfunctional, relevant or irrelevant, appropriate or inappropriate or all or any of these together when considered from diverse points of view. Every commitment to them involves a moral choice. Ideological arguments are characteristically a subclass of moral arguments. The advocacy of change, reform or revolution, constitutes itself a programmatic, functional or revolutionary myth. Arguments that ground *de jure* government on some principle of legitimacy or right are charter myths. Essentially the same rationale can act in both capacities with a change of emphasis and the mustering of a special class of factual considerations. Thus Hegel's social and political thought has been employed both to legitimize established government and as the "algebra of revolution." Hegelian formulations have been employed to support the conservative Prussian government of the last century and have been used by Marxists, fascists, and African socialists to support revolution in the present.

Our concern has been largely with recurrent argument forms. To serve in the explanatory and predictive enterprise of science, the concern with thought itself must be restored to the living context in which thought originates and has effect. The similarity of justificatory arguments in a variety of political environments suggests *something* about contemporary politics. Precisely what it suggests can only be the consequence of restoring all the historical, cultural, and economic details that make an abstract schema more faithful to empirical reality.

Their use of Hegelian and quasi-Hegelian arguments suggests *something* about radical ideologies and ideologists. It suggests that they are disposed to treat individuals, and what the West calls individual rights, in a certain manner. Assigning dispositions is, of course, always undertaken at considerable risk. Before such dispositions can be confirmed, we require a significant amount of empirical evidence concerning overt behavior. Some totalitarian or protototalitarian systems can be, in practice, relatively benign. Mussolini's Fascism, which has been cited as paradigmatic of totalitarian regimes, was, in fact, relatively restrained (when compared to Stalin's Russia and Hitler's Germany) in its use of violence as a tool of public policy. Some political analysts have, as a consequence, refused to identify Fascist Italy as a totalitarian state.[36] There seems to be no real cognitive merit to such reservations. Soviet rule, for example, has become less and less characterized by overt coercion and violence. Is the Soviet Union therefore no longer totalitarian?

Allen Kassof has suggested that totalitarian regimes be spoken of as "administered societies" to better represent the tutelary, pedagogical, and sociocentric character of such governments.[37] What is typical of totalitarian systems is not the coercion and violence they harbor as a real potential, but the socially sanctioned conformity and institutionalized anxiety that always accompany them. Because no distinction is permitted between private and public interests, the individual is forever obliged to move in lock-step with his community. Since the unitary party may, without warning, alter public policy, the individual must be always prepared to anticipate unforeseen changes. What is right and proper today may be "counterrevolutionary" tomorrow. Individuals are in a perpetual state of anxiety.

All of this rests on the kinds of arguments we have here considered. These arguments are productive of what can be called a collectivistic or totalitarian ethic. Kassof cites a speech of Khrushchev that exemplifies some of its implications:

> Each person must, like a bee in the hive, make his own contribution to increasing the material and spiritual wealth of society. People may be found who say that they do not agree with this, that it is coercion of the individual, a return to the past. To this my answer is: We are living in an organized socialist society where the interests of the individual conform to the interests of society and are not at variance with them.[38]

Gentile drew similar conclusions from essentially the same arguments:

> In the way of conclusion, then, it may be said that I, as a citizen, have indeed a will of my own; but that upon further investigation my will is found to coincide exactly with the will of the state, and I want anything only insofar as the state wants me to want it. . . . Since the nation, as the state, is of the essence and nature of our very being, it is evident that the universal will of the state is identical ["*tutt 'uno*"] with our concrete and actual ethical personality.[39]

Similar justificatory arguments could be culled from the speeches of Mussolini, Hitler, Verwoerd, Nkrumah or Senghor. Such sentiments express the operational meaning of collectivist arguments. They justify the pedagogical and punitive role assumed by the ethical totalitarian state. This role need not be discharged with terror and violence. Under certain conditions, however, it seems clear that such arguments would vindicate their use.

If the assessment offered in this work is at least partly correct, it would suggest that the long shadow of Hegel is cast across our century. Those radical movements that have proved most vital, those that have been and will be of historic significance in our time, have been directly influenced by Hegelian social and political thought. Leninism, Mussolini's Fascism, and at least Senghor's African socialism trace their lines of descent directly to Hegel. In Leninism the features of Hegelianism have all but obscured the traces of the original classical Marxism from which it sprang. It is the collectivist normic model of Hegel, generating the authoritarian, integralist state charged with the pedagogical responsibility of creating a totalitarian national sentiment, a new ethics, that is characteristic of contemporary radical ideologies. It is the ethical state that is central to those ideologies, and it is historic personalities, chosen by history itself and conscious of the developments of our time, who dominate men. The unique contribution of the twentieth century is the unitary party.

Radical social and political thinkers have provided justificatory arguments in support of an alternate vision of social order that has challenged most of our conventionally accepted political and social conceptions. Each such radical challenge has, in the past, been attended by the mass immolation of our young and ultimately the decimation of whole populations. That continued recourse to violence can be the only response to any such future challenge is a possibility. But it is the threat of violence that exercises the real and ultimate tyranny over men—and it is that tyranny that men of whatever conviction must abjure.

Notes

1. B. Mussolini, "Dottrina del fascismo," *Opera Omnia* [*Opera*] (Florence: Fenice, 1951–1963), XXXIV, p. 128; "Colloquio con il giornalista Cabella," *Opera*, XXXII, p. 195.

2. An interesting and authoritative exposition of the Saint-Simonian conception of man and society can be found in G. Iggers, *The Cult of Authority: The Political Philosophy of the Saint-Simonians* (The Hague: Nijhoff, 1958).

3. M. Adler, *Die Staatsauffassung des Marxismus* (Darmstadt: Wissenschaftliche Buchgesellschaft, 1964), p. 243.

4. L. Gumplowicz, *The Outlines of Sociology* (Philadelphia: American Academy of Political and Social Science, 1899), p. 39.

5. L. Gumplowicz, *Die sociologische Staatsidee* (Innsbruck: Wagner'schen Universitäts, 1902), p. 211. Compare H. Spencer, *The Study of Sociology* (Ann Arbor: University of Michigan, 1961), p. 44f.

6. There are many treatments of Hegel's influence in social and political thought, and no attempt will be made here to indicate any more than a few representative and interesting instances. For example, H. Marcuse, *Reason and Revolution: Hegel and the Rise of Social Theory* (New York: Humanities, 1954); C. Antoni, *Dallo storicismo alla sociologia* (Florence: Sansoni, 1951); P. Barth, *Die Geschichtsphilosophie Hegel's und der Hegelianer bis auf Marx und Hartmann* (Leipzig: Reisland, 1890).

7. C. H. Cooley, *Human Nature and the Social Order* (New York: Schocken, 1964), p. 42.

8. P. Rieff's introduction to C. H. Cooley, *Social Organization* (New York: Schocken, 1962), pp. xv, xix.

9. S. Fine, *Laissez Faire and the General Welfare State* (Ann Arbor: University of Michigan, 1964), p. 267. See also H. Girvetz' *The Evolution of Liberalism* (New York: Collier, 1963) for an exhaustive discussion of these developments.

10. For a good discussion of Spencer's thesis, see J. Rumney, *Herbert Spencer's Sociology* (New York: Atherton Press, 1966), pp. 159f.

11. Marcuse, *op. cit.*, p. 391.

12. B. Bosanquet, *The Philosophical Theory of the State*, 4th ed. (London: Macmillan, 1951), pp. 6, 34, xlix, 127, 144, 172.

13. Rumney, *op. cit.*, p. 63.

14. C. Gini, *Il neo-organicismo* (Catania: Moderno, 1927), p. 43.

15. See M. Marotta, *Organicismo e neo-organicismo* (Milan:

Giuffre, 1959), p. 71; G. Sabine, *A History of Political Theory*, 3rd ed. (New York: Holt, Rinehart & Winston, 1961), p. 901.

16. D. Joravsky, *Soviet Marxism and Natural Science, 1917–1932* (New York: Columbia, 1961), pp. 246, 256f., 311.

17. F. T. Marinetti, Introduction to Y. de Begnac, *Trent'anni di Mussolini* (Rome: Menaglia, 1934), p. vii; A. Rocco, *La trasformazione dello stato* (Rome: La Voce, 1927), p. 9.

18. Mussolini as cited in Y. de Begnac, *Palazzo Venezia: storia di un regime* (Rome: La Rocca, 1950), p. 186.

19. "The pragmatism of James was of great value to me because it taught me to measure actions more by their results than by their doctrinal bases." (Mussolini as cited in De Begnac, *Palazzo Venezia*, p. 118. See also "Intervista con la 'United Press,'" *Opera*, XXII, p. 41; "Secondo messaggio al popolo Americano," *Opera*, XXIV, p. 329; and M. Howard, *Fascism: A Challenge to Democracy* [London: Revell, 1928], Chap. i.)

20. G. Prezzolini, *La teoria sindacalista* (Naples: Ferrella, 1909), pp. 247–53; see also Mussolini's review of Prezzolini's volume in *Opera*, II, pp. 123–28.

21. A. Kolman, *Considerations about the Certainty of Knowledge*, Occasional Papers: No. 2 (New York: AIMS, 1965), p. 12.

22. Mussolini as cited in De Begnac, *Palazzo Venezia*, p. 652.

23. G. Gentile, *Che cosa è il fascismo* (Florence: Vallechi, 1925), p. 138.

24. See B. Moore, *Political Power and Social Theory* (New York: Harper & Row, 1962), Chap. ii.

25. There are a number of good books devoted to nationalism as a political phenomenon. The material in this section has been culled largely from works such as E. Kedourie, *Nationalism* (New York: Praeger, 1960); B. Shafter, *Nationalism: Myth and Reality* (New York: Harcourt, Brace & World, 1955); H. Kohn, *The Idea of Nationalism* (New York: Macmillan, 1944); E. Lemberg, *Nationalismus* (Munich: Rowohlt, 1964), 2 vols.; R. Michels, *First Lectures in Political Sociology* (New York: Harper & Row, 1949), Chap. viii.

26. See F. Borkenau, *World Communism* (Ann Arbor: University of Michigan, 1962), p. 423.

27. S. Lipset, *Political Man: The Social Bases of Politics* (Garden City, N. Y.: Anchor, 1963), p. 174.

28. M. Djilas, *The New Class: An Analysis of the Communist System* (New York: Praeger, 1962).

29. Typical examples of this kind of argument are found in R. Brady, *The Spirit and Structure of German Fascism* (New York: Viking, 1937); J. Strachey, *The Menace of Fascism* (New York: Covici

Friede, 1933); R. Palme Dutt, *Fascism and Social Revolution* (New York: International, 1934).

30. See Lipset, *op. cit.*, Chap. v; E. Weber, *Varieties of Fascism* (New York: Van Nostrand, 1964), Chap. iv; D. Schoenbaum, *Hitler's Social Revolution: Class and Status in Nazi Germany 1933–1939* (New York: Doubleday, 1966), Chap. iv.

31. C. J. Friedrich and Z. K. Brzezinski, *Totalitarian Dictatorship and Autocracy* (New York: Praeger, 1962), pp. 17f.

32. See *The New Fascist Danger* (New York: New Century, 1962).

33. Gentile maintained this as early as 1914, see P. Siena (ed.), *Gentile* (Rome: Volpe, 1966), p. 53.

34. Gentile, *op. cit.*, p. 35.

35. G. Gentile, *Genesi e struttura della società* (Florence: Sansoni, 1946), pp. 46f.

36. H. Arendt refuses to identify Mussolini's Fascism as a "true totalitarianism" because of "the surprisingly small number and the comparatively mild sentences meted out to political offenders." (*The Origins of Totalitarianism* [New York: Harcourt, Brace & World, 1951], p. 303, *n.* 8.) Arendt has made the exercise of violence, by definition, diagnostic of totalitarianism. The present work would emphasize the rationale supporting such violence—that is, the potential for intra-societal violence—as diagnostic, and not its exercise. For a discussion of these issues, see D. L. Germino, *The Italian Fascist Party in Power* (Minneapolis: University of Minnesota, 1959), pp. 141f.

37. A. Kassof, "The Administered Society: Totalitarianism Without Terror," *World Politics*, XVI (July, 1964), 558–75.

38. *Ibid.*, p. 558.

39. G. Gentile, *La riforma dell'educazione* (Florence: Sansoni, 1955), pp. 25, 14.

Suggestions for Further Reading

This bibliography is provided in order to suggest books that will supplement the survey contained in this volume. No attempt has been made to provide an exhaustive bibliography. The books suggested are those that are in English and are, in general, easily obtainable. For the more advanced student, or colleagues, a perusal of the notes will provide further bibliographic references and an indication of the foreign language literature found to be most substantial. Where appropriate, the works have been annotated with a brief description of contents and orientation.

Chapter I: Introduction

APTER, DAVID E. (ed.) : *Ideology and Discontent*. New York: Free Press, 1964.

BENN, S. I., and R. S. PETERS: *The Principles of Political Thought: Social Foundations of the Democratic State*. New York: Collier, 1964. Among the best books devoted to the analysis of political theory.

DAHL, ROBERT A.: *Modern Political Analysis*. Englewood Cliffs, N. J.: Prentice-Hall, 1964.

DEININGER, W. T.: *Problems in Social and Political Thought: A Philosophical Introduction*. New York: Macmillan, 1965. An elementary introduction to social and political philosophy.

GEWIRTH, A.: *Political Philosophy*. New York: Macmillan, 1965. A collection of essays by representative philosophers preceded by a good, elementary introduction to social and political philosophy.

JENKIN, T. P.: *The Study of Political Theory*. New York: Random House, 1955. An excellent introduction to social and political analysis.

LASLETT, P. (ed.) : *Philosophy, Politics and Society*. New York: Macmillan, 1956. A collection of essays by contemporary thinkers devoted to the conceptual and descriptive analysis of social and political problems.

———, and W. G. RUNCIMAN (eds.): *Philosophy, Politics and Society: Second Series*. Oxford: Blackwell, 1964.

RUNCIMAN, W. G.: *Social Science and Political Theory*. London: Cambridge, 1965. A careful and insightful treatment of empirical science and normative evaluation.

VAN DYKE, V.: *Political Science: A Philosophical Analysis*. Stanford: Stanford University Press, 1960. A substantial treatment of the analytic tools of contemporary political science.

WELDON, T. D.: *The Vocabulary of Politics*. Baltimore: Penguin, 1953. An excellent analytic treatment of the language of politics.

Chapter II: The Foundations in Hegel and Marx

A. *PRIMARY SOURCES*

HEGEL, G. W. F.: *Early Theological Writings*. Translated by T. M. Knox. Chicago: University of Chicago Press, 1948. An excellent introduction to Hegel's social and political thought.

————: *The Phenomenology of Mind*. Translated by J. B. Baillie. New York: Macmillan, 1949.

————: *The Philosophy of History*. Translated by J. Sibree. New York: Dover, 1956.

————: *The Philosophy of Right*. Translated by T. M. Knox. Oxford: Clarendon, 1942. The full statement of Hegel's social and political philosophy.

————: *Reason in History: A General Introduction to the Philosophy of History*. Translated by R. S. Hartman. New York: Bobbs-Merrill, 1953. A new translation of the Introduction to the *Philosophy of History* and considerably superior to that found in the standard version.

MARX, K.: *Capital*. 3 vols. Moscow: Foreign Languages Publishing House, 1954–1962.

————: *Early Writings*. Edited by T. Bottomore. New York: McGraw-Hill, 1964. A collection of Marx's early works in excellent translation. These writings provide the essentials of Marx's normic model of man and society.

————: *The Poverty of Philosophy*. Moscow: Foreign Languages Publishing House, n.d.

————, and F. ENGELS: *The German Ideology*. Parts 1 and 3. Edited by R. Pascal. New York: International, 1947. The first full statement of the materialist conception of history.

————, and ————: *Selected Works in Two Volumes*. Moscow: Foreign Languages Publishing House; several editions. This anthology includes a substantial part of the mature works of Marx and Engels. Some works are presented in their entirety; others are given in selection.

B. *SECONDARY SOURCES*

BOBER, M. M.: *Karl Marx's Interpretation of History*. New York: Norton, 1965. An excellent standard introduction to Marx's theory of history.

FEDERN, K.: *The Materialist Conception of History*. New York: Macmillan, 1939.

FINDLAY, J. N.: *Hegel: A Re-examination*. New York: Collier, 1962. One of the best contemporary introductions to Hegel's thought.

LABRIOLA, A.: *Essays on the Materialistic Conception of History*. Translated by C. H. Kerr. Chicago: Charles Kerr, 1904. An authoritative introduction to Marx's conception of history by an orthodox classical Marxist.

LICHTHEIM, G.: *Marxism: An Historical and Critical Study.* New York: Praeger, 1962.

MARCUSE, H.: *Reason and Revolution: Hegel and the Rise of Social Theory.* New York: Humanities, 1954.

MEYER, A. G.: *Marxism: The Unity of Theory and Practice.* Ann Arbor: University of Michigan Press, 1964.

REYBURN, H. A.: *The Ethical Theory of Hegel: A Study of the Philosophy of Right.* Oxford: Clarendon, 1921.

ROTENSTREICH, N.: *Basic Problems of Marx's Philosophy.* New York: Bobbs-Merrill, 1965.

SELIGMAN, E. R. A.: *The Economic Interpretation of History.* New York: Columbia University Press, 1961.

VENABLE, V.: *Human Nature: The Marxian View.* New York: Knopf, 1945. One of the best general introductions to Marx's views on man and society.

Chapter III: Leninism and Leninisms

A. *PRIMARY SOURCES*

GUEVARA, CHE: *Guerrilla Warfare.* New York: Monthly Review Press, 1961.

LENIN, V. I.: *Collected Works.* Moscow: Foreign Languages Publishing House, 1960–. To date Volumes 1–38 have been published.

——: *Selected Works in Two Volumes.* Moscow: Foreign Languages Publishing House, 1950–1951. A good collection of Lenin's mature works, published in four parts.

MAO TSE-TUNG: *Selected Works.* 5 vols. New York: International, 1954–1956.

STALIN, J.: *Problems of Leninism.* Moscow: Foreign Languages Publishing House, 1953.

——: *Works.* Moscow. Foreign Languages Publishing House, 1952–1955. Thirteen volumes published. There were to have been at least sixteen volumes, but since the denunciation of Stalin, the translations have ceased.

B. *SECONDARY SOURCES*

COHEN, A. A.: *The Communism of Mao Tse-tung.* Chicago: University of Chicago Press, 1964.

DENNO, T.: *The Communist Millennium: The Soviet View.* The Hague: Nijhoff, 1964. An interesting exposition of Leninist conceptions of the future society.

DRACHKOVITCH, M. M. (ed.): *Marxism in the Modern World.* Stanford: Stanford University Press, 1965. A collection of essays devoted to contemporary Leninisms.

DRAPER, T.: *Castroism: Theory and Practice.* New York: Praeger, 1965. Perhaps the best single volume of Castroism as an ideology.

GREGOR, A. J.: *A Survey of Marxism: Problems in Philosophy and the Theory of History.* New York: Random House, 1965.

LAPENNA, I.: *State and Law: Soviet and Yugoslav Theory.* New Haven: Yale University Press, 1965.

LEWIS, J. W.: *Major Doctrines of Communist China.* New York: Norton, 1964.

McNEAL, R. H.: *The Bolshevik Tradition: Lenin, Stalin, Khrushchev.* Englewood Cliffs, N. J.: Prentice-Hall, 1963.

MEYER, A. G.: *Communism.* New York: Random House, 1963.

———: *Leninism.* New York: Praeger, 1957. Among the best books devoted to an exposition of Leninism.

MOORE, B., JR.: *Soviet Politics—The Dilemma of Power.* New York: Harper & Row, 1965.

PLAMENATZ, J.: *German Marxism and Russian Communism.* New York: Harper & Row, 1965. A competent and interesting comparison between classical Marxism and Leninism.

SCHRAM, S. R.: *The Political Thought of Mao Tse-tung.* New York: Praeger, 1963. Contains a good introduction to Maoism as a political ideology as well as important selections from Mao's writings.

WOLFE, B. D.: *Marxism: 100 Years in the Life of a Doctrine.* New York: Dial, 1965.

Chapter IV: Fascism and Fascisms

A. *PRIMARY SOURCES*

GENTILE, G.: *The Genesis and Structure of Society.* Translated by H. S. Harris. Urbana: University of Illinois Press, 1960. Contains all the essentials of the Fascist rationale. Its arguments, when not elliptical, are stenographic, but they constitute the most authoritative statement of Fascism as social and political thought.

———: "The Philosophic Basis of Fascism," in *Readings on Fascism and National Socialism.* Selected by the Members of the Department of Philosophy, University of Colorado. Denver: Swallow, n.d.

———: *The Reform of Education.* Translated by D. Bigongiari. New York: Harcourt, Brace & World, 1922.

MUSSOLINI, B.: *The Corporate State.* Florence: Vallecchi, 1938. A collection of speeches on the corporate state with appendices devoted to the Labor Chapter and a variety of legislative enactments characteristic of applied Fascism.

———: "The Doctrine of Fascism," in *Social and Political Philosophy.* Edited by J. Somerville and R. E. Santon. Garden City, N. Y.: Doubleday, 1963.

———: *My Autobiography.* Translated by R. W. Child. London: Paternoster, 1936. This volume, based upon documents and materials provided by Mussolini, was actually written by Mussolini's brother Arnaldo. Chapter X, "The Fascist State and the

Future," is a good doctrinal statement of the Fascist conception of the state.

B. *SECONDARY SOURCES*

FINER, H.: *Mussolini's Italy.* New York: Grosset & Dunlap, 1965.

GERMINO, D. L.: *The Italian Fascist Party in Power.* Minneapolis: University of Minnesota Press, 1959.

HARRIS, H. S.: *The Social Philosophy of Giovanni Gentile.* Urbana: University of Illinois Press, 1960. The best volume in English on the social and political thought of Gentile.

NOLTE, E.: *Three Faces of Fascism.* Translated by L. Vennewitz. New York: Holt, Rinehart & Winston, 1965.

SCHNEIDER, H. W.: *Making the Fascist State.* New York: Oxford University Press, 1928. Although difficult to obtain, this volume is among the best works devoted to the philosophical and doctrinal influences that matured into Fascism.

STEINER, H. A.: *Government in Fascist Italy.* New York: McGraw-Hill, 1938. This good, objective study is not limited to government, as such; includes several authoritative chapters on ideology.

WEBER, E.: *Varieties of Fascism.* Princeton, N. J.: Van Nostrand, 1964. A brief volume with representative selections from various Fascist and National Socialist sources. Among the very best expositions of Fascist doctrine.

Chapter V: National Socialism

A. *PRIMARY SOURCES*

GÜNTHER, H. F. K.: *Racial Elements of European History.* Translated by G. C. Wheeler. London: Methuen, 1927.

HITLER, A.: *Hitler's Secret Book.* Translated by S. Attanasio. New York: Grove, 1962.

———: *Hitler's Secret Conversations: 1941–1944.* Translated by N. Cameron and R. H. Stevens. New York: Signet, 1961.

———: *Hitler's Speeches, 1922–1939.* 2 vols. Edited by N. H. Baynes. New York: Oxford University Press, 1942.

———: *Mein Kampf.* Translated by R. Manheim. Boston: Houghton Mifflin, 1943.

———: *My New Order.* Edited by R. De Roussy De Sales. London: Angus and Robertson, 1942.

ROSENBERG, A.: *Memoirs.* Translated by E. Posselt. Chicago: Ziff-Davis, 1949.

B. *SECONDARY SOURCES*

ABEL, T.: *The Nazi Movement: Why Hitler Came to Power.* New York: Atherton, 1966. A reissue of an early analysis of National Socialism. The author's interpretations are based on data collected from National Socialist party members and sympathizers.

BAUMONT, J. H., E. FRIED, and E. VERMEIL (eds.): *The Third Reich.*
New York: Praeger, 1955. A collection of articles on various
aspects of National Socialism. Part One is devoted almost ex-
clusively to National Socialist ideology.
CHANDLER, A. R.: *Rosenberg's Nazi Myth.* Ithaca, N. Y.: Cornell Uni-
versity Press, 1945. A brief account of Rosenberg's racial phi-
losophy.
MOSSE, G. L.: *The Crisis of German Ideology: Intellectual Origins of
the Third Reich.* New York: Grosset & Dunlap, 1964.
STERN, F.: *The Politics of Cultural Despair: A Study in the Rise of the
Germanic Ideology.* Garden City, N. Y.: Doubleday, 1965.
VIERECK, P.: *Metapolitics: The Roots of the Nazi Mind.* New York:
Capricorn, 1961.

Chapter VI: Apartheid

A. *PRIMARY SOURCES*

*Counter-memorial Filed by the Government of the Republic of South
Africa.* 10 vols. International Court of Justice: South West Africa
Cases (Ethiopia and Liberia v. The Republic of South Africa),
1963.
Rejoinder Filed by the Government of the Republic of South Africa.
2 vols. International Court of Justice: South West Africa Cases
(Ethiopia and Liberia v. The Republic of South Africa), 1964.

B. *SECONDARY SOURCES*

BUNTING, B.: *The Rise of the South African Reich.* Baltimore: Penguin,
1964. The author's polemics often obscure the interesting and
valuable account of apartheid ideology.
GINIEWSKI, P.: *The Two Faces of Apartheid.* Chicago: Regnery, 1965.
An apologetic account but with valuable and interesting insights
into doctrinal and ideological considerations.
NEAME, L. E.: *The History of Apartheid: The Story of the Colour War
in South Africa.* London: Pall Mall, 1962.
RHOODIE, N. J., and H. J. VENTER: *Apartheid: A Socio-historical Expo-
sition of the Origin and Development of the Apartheid Idea.*
Cape Town: HAUM, n.d. An expository volume written by
Afrikaner academicians.
VAN DEN BERGHE, P. L.: "Apartheid, Fascism and the Golden Age," in
Africa: Social Problems of Change and Conflict. Edited by P. L.
van den Berghe. San Francisco: Chandler, 1965. An insightful
and analytic essay devoted to apartheid and its relationship to
Fascism.

Chapter VII: African Socialism

A. *PRIMARY SOURCES*

ABRAHAM, W. E.: *The Mind of Africa.* Chicago: University of Chicago

Press, 1962. A volume by one of Nkrumah's chief ideologues. A descriptive account of the "African Personality."

FRIEDLAND, W. H., and C. G. ROSBERG, JR. (eds.): *African Socialism*. Stanford: Stanford University Press, 1964. Among the best volumes devoted to an exposition and analysis of African socialism. Includes a collection of excellent original essays by African leaders setting forth the doctrinal basis of African political theory. See in particular M. Dia: "African Socialism"; T. Mboya: "African Socialism"; G. Padmore: "A Guide to Pan-African Socialism."

NKRUMAH, K.: *Africa Must Unite*. New York: Praeger, 1964.

————: *Consciencism: Philosophy and Ideology for Decolonization and Development with Particular Reference to the African Revolution*. New York: Monthly Review Press, 1965.

————: *Ghana: The Autobiography of Kwame Nkrumah*. New York: Nelson, 1957.

————: *I Speak of Freedom: A Statement of African Ideology*. New York: Praeger, 1962.

————: *Neo-colonialism: The Last Stage of Imperialism*. New York: International, 1965.

PADMORE, G.: *Pan-Africanism or Communism: The Coming Struggle for Africa*. London: Dobson, 1956.

SENGHOR, L. S.: *On African Socialism*. Translated by M. Cook. London: Pall Mall, 1964.

B. *SECONDARY SOURCES*

BRETTON, H.: *The Rise and Fall of Kwame Kkrumah*. New York: Praeger, 1966.

COLEMAN, J., and C. G. ROSBERG, JR. (eds.): *Political Parties and National Integration in Tropical Africa*. Berkeley: University of California, 1964. An excellent treatment of various African socialist states.

KOHN, H., and W. SOKOLSKY: *African Nationalism in the Twentieth Century*. Princeton, N. J.: Van Nostrand, 1965.

SNYDER, F. G.: *One-Party Government in Mali*. New Haven: Yale University Press, 1965.

Some Essential Features of Nkrumaism. The Editors of the *Spark* (Accra). New York: International, 1964. A doctrinal outline of Nkrumah's African socialism written by the editorial staff of the party's theoretical paper.

TEMPELS, P.: *Bantu Philosophy*. Paris: Presence Africaine 1959. An exposition of the philosophy of the Baluba tribe of central Africa. Its account provides much of the substance of Negritude and the African Personality.

Chapter VIII: Political Thought in the Twentieth Century

ARENDT, H.: *The Origins of Totalitarianism.* New York: Harcourt, Brace & World, 1951.

BARBU, Z.: *Democracy and Dictatorship.* New York: Grove, 1956.

FRIEDRICH, C. J. (ed.): *Totalitarianism.* New York: Grosset & Dunlap, 1964.

————, and Z. K. BRZEZINSKI: *Totalitarian Dictatorship and Autocracy.* New York: Praeger, 1962.

GIRVETZ, H. K.: *The Evolution of Liberalism.* New York: Collier, 1963.

NEUMANN, F.: *The Democratic and the Authoritarian State.* New York: Free Press, 1964.

Index